THE
CERTIFIED DIVER'S
HANDBOOK

THE
CERTIFIED DIVER'S
HANDBOOK

The Complete Guide to Your Own Underwater Adventures

CLAY COLEMAN

INTERNATIONAL MARINE / McGRAW-HILL

Camden, Maine • New York • Chicago • San Francisco • Lisbon
London • Madrid • Mexico City • Milan • New Delhi
San Juan • Seoul • Singapore • Sydney • Toronto

The McGraw·Hill Companies

4 5 6 7 8 9 DOC DOC 0 9 8 7 6

Library of Congress Cataloging-in-Publication Data

Coleman, Clay, 1953–
  The certified diver's handbook : the complete guide to your own underwater adventures / Clay Coleman.
    p.   cm.
  Includes bibliographical references and index.
  ISBN 0-07-141460-6 (pbk. : alk. paper)
  1. Deep diving—Handbooks, manuals, etc. I. Title.
  GV838.672.C65 2004
  797.2´3—dc22   2004006424

Questions regarding the content of this book should be addressed to
International Marine
P.O. Box 220
Camden, ME 04843
www.internationalmarine.com

Questions regarding the ordering of this book should be addressed to
The McGraw-Hill Companies
Customer Service Department
P.O. Box 547
Blacklick, OH 43004
Retail customers: 1-800-262-4729
Bookstores: 1-800-722-4726

Photographs by the author unless otherwise noted.
Illustrations by Jim Sollers unless otherwise noted.

Warning: Scuba diving can take divers into harm's way, exposing them to risks of injury, cold-water exposure and hypothermia, drowning, and other hazards that can lead to serious injury or death.

  This book is not intended to replace instruction by a qualified teacher or to substitute for good personal judgment. In using this book, the reader releases the author, publisher, and distributor from liability for any injury, including death, that might result. It is understood that you scuba dive at your own risk.

CONTENTS

ACKNOWLEDGMENTS

AS MUCH FUN AS IT'S BEEN TO WRITE THIS BOOK, it would have been impossible without the help of special friends and talented associates. A million thanks go to Bob O'Daniels—friend, frequent dive buddy, master dive instructor, and marine biologist—who read every word, corrected mistakes, and wrote funny stories in the margins. Therefore, if you find any serious errors in the book, all lawsuits should be sent directly to Bob.

More thanks go to my girlfriend, life buddy, mom to the two boys, dive buddy, photo model, and wife of twenty-some years, Sharon Uhl Coleman. This project could not have been undertaken without her unflagging affection, support, and encouragement.

Special thanks to Bonnie Cardone, Barry Lipman, Sharon Elkins, David Breidenbach, Art Malone, Rick Allen and Cindy Burnham of Nautilus Productions, and Tom Wilson for their excellent photography that appears throughout the book.

Thanks also to Christine O'Daniels and Ted Elkins for their friendship, advice, and support; Brad Barousse; Ken Berthelot and the staff of LA Scuba in Baton Rouge; Mark Smith and the staff of Underwater Adventures in Baton Rouge; Nancy Cohagen and the staff of Seven Seas Diving in Baton Rouge; Danny Bourque, Alicia Hale, and the staff of Kadair's Photography in Baton Rouge; and Don Denova for their help. Also thanks to Deb Fugitt, Ken Knezick, and Katrina Kruse for their knowledge and participation.

Finally, thanks, Mom and Dad. Your contribution was the greatest of all.

INTRODUCTION

CONGRATULATIONS, YOU'VE DONE IT. You've actually spent the time and effort necessary to become a certified scuba diver—an accomplishment that says quite a bit about you. You've gotten out of bed and bellied up to the table to take a bigger bite out of life's cookie; you've acted on a decision that could change your life and your lifestyle. I'm proud of you.

At the same time, I'm a little worried about you. Now that you've dried off from your certification dives, bolted an (unofficial) license plate displaying the "diver down" flag to the front of your car, and folded that shiny, new diver's license (C-card) into your wallet, I'm afraid of what you might do next. Or more accurately, I'm afraid of what you might not do.

According to various studies, 60 to 80 percent of new divers drop out of our sport, and it's a sad fact that many would-be divers end their diving careers with their certification dives. By any measure, you, as a newly certified diver, are a high-risk water baby.

How could this happen? The dropout scenario seems to follow a general pattern. After attaining certification, the new diver decides to take a break from the hectic schedule of dive training and makes vague plans to dive the destinations celebrated in the dive magazines. Months go by, then a year. When the new diver finally gets around to seriously considering an expensive dive vacation sponsored by the local scuba shop, the skills he or she learned in scuba class seem hazy and distant. A refresher course seems to be in order. Refresher course? The diver whose last dive was for certification now needs a refresher course? Good grief, let's just forget the whole thing . . .

I want to talk to you about that. As an avid and active diver for the past thirty years, I want to assure you that you can achieve a lifestyle that includes active diving. I want to provide you with the practical information you need to enable the adventure and intrigue of flying unfettered within the liquid domain to become your reality.

This book is a tool meant to salt the slippery slope between your initial dive training and a lifetime of active diving. Within its pages I hope to give you a solid idea of what the real world of independent diving is like. You already know the techniques and physics involved to allow you to live for a few minutes beneath the surface of the water; I will not bore you with that. Rather, I will expose you to the things you need to consider as you start your adventure as an independent scuba diver—a diver who has discarded the training wheels of your instructor, a diver prepared to pursue your own interests and agenda on your own terms.

Even if you've been diving for a while, this book will help you get more out of your diving dollar and may present ideas to which you have not been exposed. Things as simple as the recipe for homemade ear flush will likely save you the price of this book in a short period of time (but remember, if you're browsing this introduction in a bookstore, no peeking).

Many of the recommendations contained in this book, things like what equipment to buy or how best to use it, are my own opinions based on my own experiences. As such, they are subject to challenge and debate. That's a good thing. Challenge and debate require thought, and thoughtful people make the best divers.

This book also discusses well-accepted procedures that you are likely to encounter if you decide to pursue advanced dive training. They are subject to challenge and debate as well. Just because something has been said before does not make it sacrosanct.

I assure you that I have never been wealthy, nor do I possess an extraordinary measure of courage or physical prowess. I simply like to dive, and active, independent diving has rewarded me with rich experiences and has taken me to places that I might have otherwise missed. I have come face-to-face with magnificent marine creatures large and small, potentially dangerous and beautifully benign. I have witnessed the drama of life and death on grand stages and small. I have gained insight into the large picture of life by my exposure to the underwater ecosystem. I have experienced the thrill of discovery on the bottoms of murky rivers. I've even found treasure, genuine pieces of eight on the Spanish Main, only to have lost them to pirates posing as divemasters long ago in the Florida Keys.

Maybe it's better that way. Maybe the story is more interesting than those blackened bits of metal would be today. It's a story that is clearly beyond the scope of this book.

On the other hand, if we ever find ourselves together on the sundeck of a comfortable boat anchored at night in calm water, gazing lazily at the dome of the universe (which is always there, if only the lights of civilization allowed us to see it or the travails of daily existence gave us the time to consider it), and if our quiet conversation about what we saw that day and what we hope to see tomorrow lags, remind me of the pieces of eight that got away. I'll be glad to tell you all about it.

CHAPTER I

SWITCHING ATTITUDE GEARS

A S THE SAYING GOES, there are old divers and there are bold divers, but there are no old, bold divers. I have no idea where the saying came from. It could have originated from a wise old diver who wanted to make a point about the foolishness of youth, but I think it was more likely first proclaimed by a young person as a way of thumping the chest and announcing to the world, "Look at me, I'm young and bold." I think this because the corollary, "Look at me, I'm old and cowardly," just doesn't sound right. Whatever the case, now that I'm what must be considered an old diver, the saying doesn't seem quite as pithy to me as it once did.

Of course, being old does not necessarily mean being smart, but it does give me a perspective on the evolution of the sport of scuba diving that younger divers might not have.

Don't panic! I'm not about to start waxing nostalgic about the "good old days" of scuba. The fact is, there has never been a better time to be a scuba diver than right now. Scuba divers today have the benefit of options that simply did not exist in the past—options ranging from interesting and accessible destinations to a veritable plethora of training opportunities.

PADI (Professional Association of Diving Instructors) was a young certifying agency when I got my Basic certification in 1973. The class was made up entirely of young men, and it was conducted in a pseudomilitary fashion. We swam laps and treaded water; we swam with blackened masks in a pool while our instructor harassed us. When it was all over, we took a written test and made a single dive in the ocean. Surviving that, we were certified scuba divers—as qualified on paper as Jacques Cousteau himself.

Our visits to the local scuba shop after initial certification were solely for the purposes of filling tanks or replacing gear. Advanced training was available, but it was not promoted and was primarily for those wishing to become instructors. Nobody logged dives (something I regret today), and divers were known locally only by reputation. Scuba certification was an either-or proposition. Either you were certified or you were not. Degrees or classifications of certification simply did not exist as a practical matter.

Equipment was basic in those days. We had hard backpacks onto which steel 72-cubic-foot tanks were strapped. The negative buoyancy of the tanks pretty much negated the need for weight belts. We had uncomfortable safety vests that could be inflated on the surface by means of a small CO_2 cartridge, but we seldom wore them. Submersible pressure gauges to keep track of our air were newfangled gadgets that were actually condemned by some hard-core divers of the day. Choices regarding gear were limited, and our rubber masks and fins rotted quickly.

Much of our gear was manufactured by the AMF/Voit/Swimaster Company and was comparable in fit and quality to the packaged snorkel gear that can be found in drugstores today. We typically dove in nothing but a bathing suit or a pair of shorts. Those who chose to dive in an "exposure suit" wore jeans and a long-sleeved shirt. The really fancy guys wore coveralls.

The lack of an established dive infrastructure limited our dive opportunities. Charter boats that catered to divers were virtually nonexistent in most areas of the country. Dive travel to the Caribbean was exotic and dicey. The islands were difficult to reach and provided little, if any, support to recreational diving. Pacific destinations were worse.

Yet, we dove. We drove to the Florida Keys and other isolated pockets with dive infrastructures. We weaseled our way on board local fishing boats, and we made trips on independently owned boats. We dove off beaches and jetties. We dove any way and anywhere we could.

Dive techniques in those days differed significantly from techniques used today. We made no safety stops, and our ascent rate was determined by the smallest bubbles of our exhalations. Of course, there were no dive computers, and our use of the dive tables was sporadic and undisciplined. Sometimes we dove with common sense, but sometimes we dove with the common nonsense of youth. The fact that nobody in my personal dive fraternity of friends ever suffered a serious dive injury is a testament to the inherent safety of the sport of scuba diving.

Recreational scuba diving has certainly come a long way since then. In the past thirty years, scuba has evolved into a mainstream activity enjoyed equally by men and women. Manufacturers now offer a baffling array of high-quality equipment, and most scuba shops offer an entire curriculum of training options. The sport is far safer and more convenient than it has ever been.

At the same time, something seems to have been lost. Despite an exponential explosion in the number of certified divers, relatively few divers are actually striking out by themselves and going diving. A whole new genre of "classroom divers" has emerged as divers continue to pursue dive training but never seem to get around to using it.

I can think of more than one explanation for this. As scuba became more available to those with only a casual interest, it stands to reason that more casual divers would be produced. There's nothing wrong with that. Many resorts cater to the casual diver, and the diving is supervised, fun, and safe.

There's another possible explanation that bothers me a little. As advanced-training options became commonplace, many divers began to get the idea that their Open Water I certification was somehow inadequate. If you enjoy diving and if you are reasonably confident and comfortable in the water, this idea is simply false. Your Open Water I certification is not merely a prerequisite for more-advanced training. It is your ticket to real diving adventure, and it is proof that you are a "real" diver, albeit possibly an inexperienced one.

Let's make this analogy: Scuba diving is like driving a car. Both activities require special training and the development of skills, and both can take you to places that you might otherwise not be able to reach. Once training is complete, both require a written test and a transitional period before you become licensed. For driving a car, this transitional period consists of behind-the-wheel practice with a learner's permit; for diving, it is your open-water training (checkout) dives made under the supervision of your instructor for your diver's license (C-card).

You weren't ready for Daytona on the day you received your driver's license. On the other hand, you probably didn't feel the need to get a chauffeur's license before you actually started driving a car. You probably began your driving with short excursions at times of light traffic until your skills and confidence grew.

Likewise, Open Water I divers are not ready for a dive to the *Andrea Doria*. However, they are certainly qualified to dive most sites. By limiting their dives to areas and conditions with which they feel comfortable, Open Water I divers gain experience, skill, and confidence—attributes that are essential to diver development and cannot be learned in a classroom.

I certainly do not mean to disparage training beyond Open Water I. Quite the contrary, I wholeheartedly recommend that you continue your formal training in all areas that interest you. Later in the book I recommend some of the advanced training that I think is most worthwhile. The point is that advanced classroom training cannot take the place of actual dive experience.

A relatively new phenomenon has developed in this age of advanced and specialty training. Some divers seem to be engaged in "card competition"—a game in which the diver with the most impressive array of certification and specialty cards is considered the "best" diver. While this kind of game might be more suitably addressed in a book on ego management, it can present a real danger to the players. Far too many divers mistake classroom training for actual competence.

The key to becoming an independent diver is a marriage between formal training and actual dive experience. Even though formal training beyond your initial Open Water I course is necessary for some types of diving, your Open Water I training is enough to get you into the water to start building the experience that is crucial to independent diving. Only through actual dive experience can you realistically develop water skills and risk assessment skills, and only by the development of those skills can you become a diver capable of planning and making safe dives in a variety of conditions or situations.

Independent divers are those divers who have developed confidence in their capabilities to the point that they assume sole responsibility for their dives. Of course, they will adhere to the buddy system, and they will seek the advice of those with local knowledge and experience or of those with greater general knowledge and experience, but independent divers do not defer to anyone on matters of their personal safety or well-being. Becoming an independent diver is an act of personal responsibility as much as it is a declaration of freedom.

If you are a newly certified diver whose only dives have been under the supervision of your instructor or a divemaster, it's time to change attitude gears. You are a trained diver, and, as such, your safety underwater is no longer the responsibility of your instructor or of your dive buddy. It's yours.

As an example of independent decision making, I was recently on a live-aboard dive boat a hundred miles out in the Gulf of Mexico for two days of diving. (*Note:* Miles are statute miles unless otherwise indicated.) The weather was marginal, and the diving was marred by a hellacious surface current, poor visibility, and high seas. After a full day of diving in those conditions, the boat's divemaster made an announcement that a night dive would be available but that it was not for the squeamish.

I knew about half of the divers on the boat, having dived with them many times before. I knew them to be more than capable of making the night dive. The other divers on the boat were newer divers, and some had struggled to overcome problems during the day with the diving conditions. After assessing the effort of the night dive against the probable reward, I told the divemaster that I would not make the dive and retired to my bunk for a bit of reading.

I returned to the dive deck some time later to see how the dive was progressing. Joining me on deck were most of the divers I knew. They had each decided to pass on making the dive. All of the newer divers were paired with each other in the black water.

The newer divers made it back on board without incident. Many exchanged stories of problems encountered and overcome. The whistling wind and heaving sea made a dramatic setting for their tales of adventure. Those of us who had passed on the dive smiled and nodded at the stories.

We smiled because we had eaten all of the brownies and ice cream normally provided by the boat for returning night divers.

All the divers on that boat could be considered independent divers. The newer divers who had made the dive knew full well the conditions they would face and decided that stretching their experience envelope was worth the effort. The more experienced divers who had passed on the dive felt no need to make a dive that would not be much fun.

Or maybe we were just a bunch of old, un-bold ice cream bandits.

DIVING AS A LIFESTYLE

I wish scuba diving was more like the game of golf. I don't mean that I wish scuba diving was more like a long walk interrupted by whacking a little ball with a stick and cursing, but I do wish it was something that could be easily done for a few hours on a Sunday afternoon.

Scuba requires travel and expense for the vast majority of us, and the planning and commitment involved tends to limit our time in the water. However, with proper commitment, scuba is an activity that can be enjoyed for most of the year.

A common trap into which many divers fall is the tendency to plan only for the annual Big Dive Trip. These trips are typically to popular destinations, and they are typically time-consuming and expensive. Don't get me wrong; they're great. However, by putting all of their proverbial dive eggs into one basket, these divers generally limit their diving to one week out of the entire year.

Wherever you live, there is probably a body of water suitable for diving within a day's drive of your home. It may not be the warm and beautiful blue-water diving advertised by the most popular sites, but the diving may well be interesting and worthwhile. A summer of short dive trips to nearby destinations rounded out by the Big Dive Trip in winter will provide you with more diving for your investment in time and equipment than will a single annual trip. Local trips are usually worth the small expense, and the dive experience gained will always serve you as an independent diver. In fact, some divers become so intrigued by local diving that they dispense with the Big Dive Trip altogether. We explore the possibilities of local diving in more detail in chapter 13.

Active diving is a lifestyle. Whether actually in the water or not, the active diver stays interested and committed by keeping current on destinations, equipment, dive fitness, and dive skills. Always have a trip planned.

PURSUING YOUR OWN INTERESTS

As an admitted tunnel-visioned fanatic, I'm always curious about why anyone would give up scuba diving. Some of the reasons are understandable. Some people simply don't like the water. Some people feel claustrophobic in scuba gear.

There is another reason that I hear too often, and it pains me each time I do. The reason is, "Scuba wasn't what I thought it would be." This is clearly a statement that requires further investigation. To return to our "driving-a-car" analogy, making this statement is like saying, "I quit driving because the car didn't take me anywhere I wanted to go."

Like most people taking up adventure sports, prospective divers tend to romanticize the activity. They envision themselves as explorers of the liquid domain, going where no one has gone before on quests of discovery. Unfortunately, many experience something quite different. Here's an example:

I was recently engaged in a conversation with a casual friend at a social gathering. As in most of my conversations, the topic turned to diving. He told me that he did not care for diving—he enjoyed more adventurous and less crowded activities. Needless to say, my curiosity was piqued.

My friend told me that he had always enjoyed the water and that he had always wanted to learn to dive. He made a point of watching TV shows about the underwater world. He did well in his certification class and he enjoyed all the pool sessions. His open-water training (checkout) dives were made in poor weather, but he got through them with flying colors. He was so excited to be a certified diver after his checkout dives that he immediately signed up for an exotic trip that was being promoted by the shop that had certified him. He had been assured that the destination had some of the best diving in the world and that the shop personnel accompanying the trip would provide for his every need.

I recognized the destination as an excellent choice. It does, indeed, have world-class diving off its shores. I wondered what could have gone wrong.

My friend said that he began to have misgivings about the trip at the airport. The group with which he was traveling was large and boisterous, and its members seemed more excited by the prospect of visiting a famous bar on the island than they were about the diving.

Things got worse when the group arrived at their destination. The local dive operator was not prepared for such a large group. Rental equipment was quickly exhausted, and gear was borrowed from other operators to make up the difference. My friend ended up with a tattered buoyancy compensator that was too large for him and a regulator that he did not trust, even though it performed well when he dove with it.

The group had a big first night at the bar and arrived generally unfit for diving the following morning. The boat was crowded and chaotic. My newly certified friend was surprised to notice that several divers in the group acted as if they had never seen dive equipment before and had trouble with their simple setups. The divemaster gave strict instructions that the group was to dive together and follow her. As few of the divers had computers, the divemaster planned the dive for the entire group, and she expected strict adherence to the plan.

Perhaps the biggest disappointment for my friend was the diving itself. The dive site chosen was a shallow patch reef in a sandy area. Most of the coral was dead or damaged, and the large group kicked up enough sand to spoil visibility. All there was to see were the fins of the diver in front of him. A lone stingray was the highlight of the day.

The second day of diving was more of the same.

My friend declined to dive on the third and last day of planned diving. He instead rented a jeep and explored the island on his own. It turned out to be his most enjoyable day of the trip. He finished his story wondering why anyone would spend a month's salary to travel so far only to be stuck on a crowded boat, then to follow a jaded divemaster for an uneventful swim over a dead reef.

I had to admit to my friend that his experience was not uncommon. In fact, many people seem to actually enjoy it. However, it's a sad fact that many would-be divers who have had this type of experience mistakenly believe that this scenario is what diving is all about.

I explained to my friend that one of the most spectacular sights on the planet was only a few miles from where he dove. While he was dutifully following his divemaster like a cod on a conveyor belt, other divers nearby were safely soaring along a fantastic underwater cliff festooned with outrageous corals and teeming with fish. He had come within a hairsbreadth of the diving experience that had been his lifelong dream, yet he had missed it. Worse still, since he had missed it, he had assumed that it was unattainable.

My friend had been what I call a dependent diver. He depended upon others to fulfill his wishes. He even depended upon others to provide him with the equipment he needed. He assumed that everyone wanted to do what he wanted to do, so he was willing to go along for the ride.

Diving is a vehicle. It is up to you to decide where it will take you. Whatever your vision of diving was when you first decided to get certified, no matter how romantic or exotic, that vision is attainable. It is up to you to decide what you want to do and to research the best way to get there.

If the vision is deep diving on difficult wrecks or cave diving into the bowels of the earth, your Open Water I training is only a good introduction to what you need to know. However, if your vision of diving is exploring the beautiful coral reefs celebrated in most dive magazines, you are ready to go. If your vision is to enter the underwater world as a hunter of game or treasure, your Open Water I training is enough to get you started. If you are fascinated by the otherworldly diversity of the creatures of the sea, you are prepared to go visit most of them firsthand.

Your mission as an independent diver is to build upon your dive training and experience to the point that you're diving where you want to dive and doing what you want to do.

A REALISTIC ASSESSMENT OF RISK

Every now and then I watch extreme sports on TV. You know, the skateboarders who fly off those half-pipes, the motorcyclists who jump their bikes and do all sorts of crazy things while the bike is in the air—X Games stuff. It's fun to watch and it looks like even more fun to do.

That is, it looks like fun if you have the skills to do it without killing yourself. Every time I watch it, I can't help but wonder how any of those people tried those stunts for the first time.

It's easy to get the same feeling upon seeing pictures of divers at the extreme end of the sport of scuba diving. Prepared to dive to great depths in frigid water, they have tanks containing different gas mixtures hanging all over them. The slightest mistake or distraction, such as breathing from the wrong tank at the wrong depth, could have fatal consequences. Are they crazy? How did they get to that level of competence?

The answer is that they progressed slowly. For most of us, the simple act of breathing underwater for the first time was an alien experience. In time, it became second nature, and this allowed us to concentrate on other matters to the point that we became fully certified divers in a matter of just a few weeks. As you gain experience in real-world diving, your progression as a diver will be a natural one. As you become comfortable diving to shallow, then moderate depths, you will eventually become comfortable diving anywhere within the limits of recreational diving.

But is comfort derived from positive experiences always a good thing? To revisit the driving-a-car analogy yet again, I mentioned earlier that you were not ready for Daytona when you first got your driver's license. However, there's a good chance that at some point during your early driving years you imagined your driving talents to be second to none. Your initial trepidation about driving a car seemed foolish; you imagined that your control of the car was perfect and that you were infallible behind the wheel.

It was probably sometime during this period of initial confidence that your first accident or close call occurred.

Terms like "sophomore slump" are given to this natural phenomenon. As you get a few (or many) safe dives under your belt, it becomes hard to imagine that something could go wrong. This is when the unexpected becomes most dangerous; novices generally dive with a greater safety margin.

Using your checkout dives as an experience base, you must gain a certain amount of additional dive experience to enable you to develop the ability to assess additional risk. At the same time, dives without negative consequences make it easy to underestimate risk until you obtain an even greater amount of experience. The key is to stretch the limits of your experience slowly and to be fully aware of increased dangers.

It is clear that scuba diving is a reasonably safe activity. It is also clear that entering an environment that is hostile to human life involves risk. As your experience, confidence, and competence grow, only you will know when it's time to take the next step. It is your personal responsibility as an independent diver to accomplish your diving goals as safely as possible. Likewise, it is your personal responsibility to stretch your experience envelope until you are comfortable making the types of dives you want to make.

As you build on the experience of your checkout dives, it is important that you obtain new experience in a planned and controlled manner. Unexpected temptations are not uncommon during dives. What is that down there, deeper than you've ever been? Can we safely navigate to the other side of that reef?

Resist the impulse to deviate dramatically from your planned dive, especially if the deviation involves breaking new ground in your diving career. However, the temptation may be worth discussing with your buddy once the dive has ended. If the object of interest is within accepted recreational-dive limits or the limits of your training and equipment, perhaps you should plan to explore it on your next dive. It's your decision. Make it thoughtfully.

TAKE YOUR BEST SHOT

There are good reasons why photography and videography are the most popular underwater activities worldwide:

- It's a great way to share your underwater experiences with nondiving friends.
- It provides a means of artistic expression based on the unique palette of the underwater world.
- It adds a sense of mission or purpose to any dive.
- It provides a nondestructive way of hunting and collecting.
- It provides an opportunity to present your vision of the underwater world to the nondiving public as a means of education and conservation.
- It provides a great way to relive past dive experiences.
- It provides a way to study details of undersea life that are hard to see in "real time."

These are exciting times for imaging, as digital photography and videography are rapidly replacing traditional film and videotape as recording mediums (see the appendix for more information on underwater photography). However, regardless of the medium you use to record images, the fundamental techniques of photography and videography remain unchanged. The best first step toward becoming involved with underwater photography or videography is to gain a good understanding of general photography and videography. Even if your camera is a "point and shoot" with few controls, a basic knowledge of how images are captured on film, tape, or digital chip will enable you to better understand what your camera is trying to do so that you can use it to its full capability.

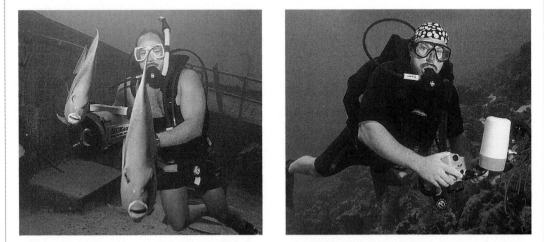

Underwater photography and videography are some of the most popular activities of recreational divers worldwide. Your Open Water I certification is enough to get you started. Photography is a great way to add a sense of mission to your dives and to share your underwater experiences with friends.

The unique photographic environment of the underwater world will affect your imaging even after you understand the basics of photography or videography. Here are some tips to make your underwater images better:

- Get as close to your subject as possible. This means using lenses with the widest possible angle of view to frame your subjects. The object is to shoot through as little water as possible, as even the clearest water will diminish the color and contrast of images.
- Use artificial light to bring out the color of your subjects. This means using a strobe for still cameras or video lights for video. If you are not using video lights, you can obtain good color in video by using a red or orange filter over the video camera lens in shallow water.
- Attempt to aim your artificial light so that it illuminates your subject but not the water between the camera and the subject. Even the clearest water has particles suspended within it, and your artificial light will cause these suspended particles to appear as "snow" in your images. Photographers and videographers refer to this snow effect as backscatter. Backscatter is the bane of underwater photography. Move the artificial light source away from the camera lens if possible to minimize backscatter. Use artificial light only if you are within 5 feet of your subject; otherwise, turn off your artificial light source, as even the most powerful light or strobe won't be able to effectively light the subject and will only create backscatter.
- Try to balance the intensity of the artificial light with natural light so that the resulting image is seamlessly lit.
- Make an attempt to separate your subject from distracting background clutter. You can often accomplish this by shooting upward toward the surface instead of horizontally toward the reef or downward toward the bottom.
- Maintain your camera meticulously. Sensitive optics and electronics don't mix very well with salt water. Consider purchasing flood insurance for expensive gear. Camera equipment is far less hardy than regular dive equipment.
- Become familiar with a dive site. Photographers often dive the same site over a period of several days. Once you learn where the residents live, you'll be better prepared to capture them on film, tape, or digital chip.
- Spend some quality time with your subjects. If you find something of interest, cover all the angles before moving on.

Still photography and videography are task-loading activities, and all divers should have confidence in their diving and buoyancy skills before adding a camera. Here are some important safety factors to consider when taking pictures:

- Be conscious of your breathing. It's a natural tendency to hold your breath when looking through a viewfinder. Of course, you should never hold your breath when diving with scuba.

continued on next page

- Be conscious of the environment. It's easy to lose track of where your fins are when you are concentrating on a subject. Taking pictures is no excuse for damaging the reef.
- Following a subject while looking through a viewfinder can be very disorienting. Reestablish your position for navigation after each shooting episode.
- Don't let your camera distract you to the point that you lose track of your dive. Regardless of what may swim in front of your lens, your air management, bottom-time management, navigation, and contact with your dive buddy are more important.

Risk assessment skills are crucial to independent diving, and they are a two-part process. Not only must you be able to reasonably predict the challenges presented by a dive, but you must also be able to balance those challenges against your personal capabilities to deal with them. It's always a good idea to seek information from others about challenges that a specific dive site may present. It's not so easy to get the same sort of information about your own capabilities. Only you know, and you must be sure.

You did not learn to dive in order to avoid risk. Part of the thrill and excitement of diving is the knowledge that you are invading an alien environment. The dive/no dive decision for the vast majority of your dives will be a no-brainer. You will be excited by the opportunity, you'll jump in, and you'll have fun. Even so, it is important that you, as an independent diver, make a personal and conscious decision each time you dive—even if the decision is an easy one to make. It's your dive; it's your life. You decide.

A REALISTIC ASSESSMENT OF COST

I'm going to go out on a limb and make a guess about you. When you first approached a dive shop to see about getting certified to dive, your first two questions were these: how much does it cost, and how long does it take?

While I'm at it, I'll make a guess about the dive shop's response: the cost is low, and you could actually learn to dive over a single weekend.

Now that you've gone through the process of certification, you've come to realize that neither response is totally factual. Even if the initial cost of certification was low, by the time you purchased your basic equipment (mask, fins, and snorkel) and paid for your checkout dives, you probably put at least a dent in your bank account. If you were one of the few students to actually get certified from a weekend course, your checkout dives did not occur over the same weekend. Plus, if you did get certified over a weekend, the cost was not cheap. It's time to face the music—scuba diving requires a commitment in both time and money. Divers have come up with their own colloquialism for the money that can be spent on diving. If you hear someone referring to a "scuba buck," they're talking about $100.

That doesn't mean that scuba is beyond the means of most of us or that diving will necessarily be a bank-busting experience. The point of becoming an independent diver is to maximize the safety and rewards of diving while minimizing the investment in time and money. However, the idea that scuba can be regularly enjoyed without a significant outlay is one that usually leads to frustration and disappointment. You will need to buy equipment, you will generally need to travel to dive sites, and you will generally need to pay for your actual diving.

You can figure to pay at least twice the money to be outfitted for scuba than you'd pay to be outfitted for golf (not counting the plaid pants). If you charter a boat for diving, the cost will generally be comparable to the greens fee at a resort golf course. Of course, the cost of getting to the boat depends upon how far you must go and how long you intend to stay.

Every now and then a nondiver will ask me why I spend so much of my time and money diving. This is what I tell them:

Imagine that you are standing outside in front of your house or apartment building looking up at the roof. Now imagine that you can rise from the ground, fly effortlessly and with no fear of falling, and slowly gain altitude until you are looking down at the roof. Hundreds of birdlike and insectlike animals accompany you in your flight—creatures with fantastic shapes and colors. You soar over the roof to the chimney and hang without effort there, attached to nothing.

Imagine further that something is looking back at you from within the chimney. It is an alien creature, a creature so totally unlike you that it seems impossible that it could inhabit the same planet. It is a creature with green, copper-based blood, no bones, eight arms, and the ability to change its shape and color at will. But this creature has intelligence. It is curious about you. It stares with its large eyes and extends an arm to touch you, to greet you, to find out more about you.

If this experience was actually possible, what would you pay to do it?

CHAPTER 2

EQUIPMENT

HAVING GOOD EQUIPMENT is fundamental to the enjoyment of most outdoor activities. For adventure sports such as rock climbing, skydiving, and scuba diving, having good equipment can mean the difference between routine enjoyment and a life-threatening experience. Indeed, one of the great risks of scuba is the risk of equipment failure.

As divers who assume total responsibility for their dives, independent divers must be able to exercise control over risk. Of course, this means that independent divers must have control over the quality and maintenance of their equipment.

Am I beating around the bush? Am I acting like a car salesman who won't tell you what the ride really costs? The fact is, in addition to the mask, fins, and snorkel that you bought for your certification class, you must dive with a minimum of life-support equipment that includes a regulator with an alternate air source and a submersible pressure gauge, a buoyancy compensator, and a dive computer/depth gauge. To be a truly independent diver, you must own and maintain that equipment. Additional equipment includes tanks, a good compass, and an exposure suit that fits well enough to be comfortable and effective. The purchase of all of this stuff at one time requires a significant outlay.

As an intermediate step (assuming the equipment you used during your certification and checkout dives was of good quality and was well maintained), you may decide that you want to get a few more dives under your belt before you invest in your own equipment. By renting from the local dive shop that certified you, you will be using equipment you are familiar with and that is supplied by someone you know and trust. This gives you far more control over the quality of your gear than simply showing up at a dive operator that touts equipment rental and having to settle for whatever they have.

But even renting equipment is not cheap. As you become an active diver, it will soon become apparent to you that owning your own gear is far more cost-effective than renting. This is in addition to the obvious safety benefits of owning your own equipment. You will become intimately familiar with your own gear, and your maintenance of it will give you confidence when you use it. Simply put, you'll have more fun and have safer dives if you own your own gear.

Buying life-support equipment can be a tricky thing. Obviously, you want to buy gear that will work properly to keep you alive and healthy. On the other hand, you want to be efficient with your budget. It's a salesman's dream. "*Cheap?!*" they'll say. "You want gear that will keep you alive in a hostile environment, and all you want is *cheap*? How much is your *life* worth?"

If you want to get high-quality gear at a reasonable price, it's best to know something about what you're buying.

MASKS, FINS, AND SNORKELS

This is stuff you probably already have, and I hope it fits and works well for you. Since active diving requires more from this gear than the pool sessions of your class and your certification dives, it might be helpful to mention a few things about these items.

Masks ($40–$150)

All masks on the market today are fit for diving if they fit you well. They all provide a reasonable view and a means by which the nose can be pinched to clear the ears via the Valsalva maneuver.

Fancy lens configurations, prisms, and gadgetry aside, the biggest concern in buying a mask is that it fit you as perfectly as possible. A mask that fits well will be comfortable and will have a minimum of leakage. To test the fit of a mask, place it on your face without the strap and stop breathing. The mask should stay securely in place without you having to suck through your nose to keep it there. Try the cheap ones first. The mask that fits you best is the one you should buy.

Most masks sold today have the traditional rubber-band-type mask strap. These straps are notorious for pulling hair. The kind of strap that most active divers use is a wide neoprene strap. They come in two types—one that fits over the traditional strap and one that replaces the traditional strap altogether. These straps were popularized by Innovative Scuba Concepts under the trademarked name Slap Strap.

Neoprene mask straps were first marketed by Innovative Scuba Concepts under the trademarked name Slap Strap. These mask straps are far more comfortable and less likely to pull hair than the straps that come with most masks.

The neoprene strap that fits over the traditional mask strap will require you to remove one side of the traditional strap. The neoprene strap slides over the traditional strap to create a more comfortable one that is less prone to pull hair.

The neoprene strap that replaces the traditional mask strap will typically have Velcro strips on each end. The Velcro strips loop through the strap holders on the mask and connect back to more Velcro on the strap. This type of strap is very easy to adjust even when the mask is in place and the diver is in the water. They are sometimes disparaged for wearing out

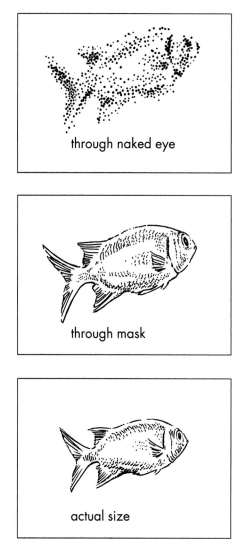

through naked eye

through mask

actual size

Here's an example of "seeing" a squirrelfish underwater. The top illustration is as seen with the naked eye. It's blurred because the speed of light in water is too slow to be refracted (focused) correctly by the human eye lens. The middle illustration is as seen through a mask, and is clear, but it is magnified by 25 percent due to the refractive effect of water. The bottom illustration shows the actual size of the fish.

quickly, but my experience with them has been that they last for many years. (Not many $20 investments will enhance your diving comfort as much as a neoprene mask strap.)

The only other modification you can make to a mask that fits well is to change the lens. If you wear prescription glasses, it is possible to have a mask lens made in your prescription for any mask you buy. There are several providers of these lenses—ask your dive shop about them.

If you wear bifocals or reading glasses to read, you might want to outfit your mask with an insert for presbyopia. Keep in mind, though, that the magnification caused by using the mask in the water may mitigate your need for correction. If the water magnification is not enough, inexpensive inserts are available for all popular reading-glasses magnifications. These inserts are made of soft plastic and stick to the inside of the mask lens like a suction cup. If you don't like them, you can remove them without damaging the mask lens.

One last word about the need for reading glasses underwater: It would seem to make sense that bringing a small magnifying glass underwater would solve all of the problems. The glass would be out of the way until needed, and no modification to the mask would be necessary. Unfortunately, a magnifying glass that has water on both sides does not work very well. The magnifying effect of the lens is caused by the difference in the densities of the lens and air. (This is why mask inserts must be placed on the inside of the mask lens, where the air is, rather than on the outside of the mask, where the water is.) The difference in density between the lens and water will be less, altering the optics of the lens. Simply put, a traditional magnifying glass will not produce nearly the effect underwater that it will in air. Try some experiments in the bathtub. (But remember, it's always a good idea to have an excuse ready in case your spouse asks what you're doing in the tub with a magnifying glass.)

Finally, a lens choice that has become popular in recent years is the tinted lens. Water absorbs the spectrum of sunlight starting with colors on the low end of the spectrum. This means that reds disappear underwater at shallow depths. Some divers wear lenses that are tinted pink or red to restore as much color as they can. Of course, this color correction comes at the cost of light reduction. For more on seeing underwater, see chapter 7.

Fins ($40–$250)

Fin technology has been a hot topic in recent years. Radical designs abound, with the split blade (with a V-shape like a fish's tail) being the current rage. However, since fins are such a personal item, it is best to choose the ones that work best for you. This is gear that you definitely want to try in a pool before you buy.

There are two traditional types of fins: full-foot and pocket. Your entire foot goes into full-foot fins, and they are worn like slippers. Pocket fins are designed to accept the front two-thirds of your foot and are held in place by a strap over the heel. Neoprene dive booties are almost universally used with pocket fins to secure a snug fit and to prevent chafing.

A third general type of fin pocket is a more recent introduction—the open-toe pocket. This design was popularized by Bob Evans's Force Fins in the early 1990s. The foot goes beneath a hard top strap and is secured at the heel by an adjustable strap. The toes remain uncovered. The point of this configuration is to reduce pressure on the ankles and prevent blisters that can form on the tops of toes with traditional pocket fins or full-foot fins.

Fins of the pocket variety are the most popular and offer the largest selection. This may be because it was thought in the past that full-foot fins did not provide enough propulsion for scuba purposes—an idea that has been seriously challenged by recent objective tests.

Any attempt to recommend a specific fin for you would be like telling you what kind of shoe to wear. However, I can say

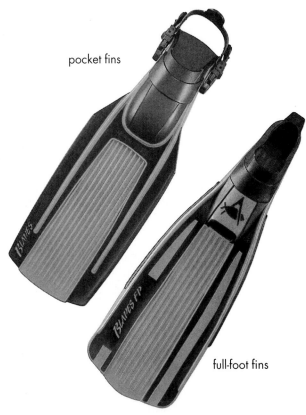

pocket fins

full-foot fins

Full-foot fins are worn like slippers, while pocket fins are held in place with a heel strap.

that a common mistake made by inexperienced divers is to buy fins that are too large for them. By that I mean that the blade of the fin is too stiff or too large for the diver and causes undue fatigue, cramping, or blistering. Look for a fin that propels you efficiently in the water and that you can kick comfortably for an extended period of time. If the fins cause stress that would lead to cramping anywhere in your legs or if they rub in a blistering way, try another type.

Snorkels ($12–$100)

The necessity of carrying a snorkel while scuba diving has come into question in recent years. I enjoy using a snorkel for surface sightseeing and free diving. However, snorkels create drag, are a snag hazard, and can be a general nuisance when used while diving on scuba.

I recommend that you dive in the way you were trained until you have attained the experience necessary to deviate from your training. However, I admit that I do not scuba dive with a snorkel attached to my mask unless I've planned for a long surface swim and I want to keep my head in the water for some sightseeing or navigation without using any of my compressed-air supply.

Manufacturers have been falling over each other in recent years to devise improvements to the snorkel. To hear (or read) the advertising, you'd think that snorkel research and development was a matter of national security.

Improvements have, indeed, been made. Modern snorkels clear easily and are convenient to use. Some have evolved to the point that intake air is separated from exhaled air to prevent rebreathing of stale air in the tube. Some offer completely dry operation even if the snorkel tube is temporarily submerged. It is now possible to pay $100 for a snorkel.

On the other hand, it's still possible to pay $15 for the same old tube that divers used thirty years ago. They are also easy to clear and convenient to use.

Perhaps the greatest improvement to the snorkel has been the simple clip device that replaced the old two-ring "snorkel keeper" for attaching the snorkel to the mask strap. Another useful innovation has been the development of the folding snorkel. These snorkels fold up to fit into a small pocket, which is where I think they belong for most scuba applications.

Dive Knife ($30–$150)

For some reason, a dive knife seems to be a high-priority purchase for some new divers. Knives have a sort of primitive coolness that appeals to the Crocodile Dundee or James Bond mentality in all of us. It is not uncommon to see divers at dive resorts with knives that are only a bit smaller than samurai swords strapped to their legs. In fact, some divers wear dive knives as a fashion accessory. You'll see them sitting at the lunch bar in their bathing suits and T-shirts with large, dangerous-looking knives strapped to their calves. I guess some people just like to be prepared in case the burger tries to bite back.

Dive knives are tools, not weapons. Their primary use should be to cut divers free in the unlikely event that they become entangled in kelp or fishing line underwater. I carry a small dive knife as a piece of emergency gear, but as with most emergency gear, I seldom actually use it.

Dive knives should be short, sharp, and out of the way, but accessible if needed. A buoyancy compensator shoulder strap is a good place to carry one.

Regulators ($250–$1,500)

I was fascinated as a child by a common scene in action movies of the time. The good guy would be fleeing from the bad guys, with no good place to hide. He'd stumble into a stream, notice some hollow reeds growing in the water, and have an inspiration. He'd splash into the water, break off a hollow reed, put it in his mouth, and sink beneath the surface. And there he'd stay, breathing air through the reed while underwater, totally invisible to his pursuers. It worked every time.

My own childhood experiments with this idea began soon after I recovered from my experiments involving "parachuting" off the roof of my home with a bedsheet. I cut a 10-foot length of garden hose and headed for the neighborhood swimming pool, convinced that I could spend the day underwater in the deep end breathing from the hose. It was such an obvious thing to do; I wondered why nobody (except Roy Rogers and Tarzan, who were admittedly exceptional) had thought of it before.

I tested my underwater breathing device when I arrived at the pool. It worked fine on land. I waded into the shallow end of the pool and breathed through the hose. It was a cinch, despite the fact that I was blithely rebreathing my own exhalations that were being trapped in the hose. I pinched my nose and walked toward the deep end.

I stood upright, and my head was not yet fully submerged when I found that I couldn't breathe through the hose anymore. I spent the rest of the day accusing my friends of plugging the hose as soon as my eyes went underwater. Of course, that wasn't the problem.

Water is heavy. At a depth of only a few inches, the weight of the water on my chest was more than my young diaphragm could lift. Nobody can breathe surface air through a snorkel tube at depths of more than a few feet—not even Tarzan.

What I needed was a regulator to provide pressurized air to my lungs that exactly offset the weight of the water. Too much pressure, and air would be wasted or my lungs might overexpand; too little, and I wouldn't be able to breathe at all.

That's what regulators do. Their function is to take air being stored at very high pressure and reduce it to the point that it can be breathed effortlessly on demand. Considering the fact that the ambient water pressure changes constantly as a diver changes depth, this is a pretty neat trick.

The regulator is the center of your life-support system for scuba diving. Air delivery is life. No air, no life. Life support can't be more direct than that.

Fortunately, regulators are rather simple devices renowned for their dependability and durability. Even better news is that every regulator marketed today by the established manufacturers is of sufficient quality in design and workmanship to adequately perform its task for recreational diving. That is, every well-maintained regulator on the shelf of your local dive shop will provide air for casual diving to depths of 130 feet.

So buying a regulator should be a piece of cake, right? They all work, so just get one you can afford, right? Well, sort of. Manufacturers have taken different approaches to a few themes to provide regulators that can vary in price from $250 to $1,500. What's the difference?

Modern regulators perform their function in a two-part process and are known as two-stage regulators. Each stage is a point at which pressure reduction takes place.

Regulators deal with pressure in three stages:

1. High pressure—the pressure of air in the scuba tank, which is usually a maximum of 3,000 pounds per square inch (3,000 psi) and, of course, decreases as the air is used.
2. Intermediate or low pressure—a moderate pressure that can be easily controlled for breathing. This pressure is maintained constantly between the first and second stages of the regulator regardless of the diver's depth.
3. Ambient pressure—the pressure surrounding a diver at any given time.

The whole point of a regulator is to enable a diver to breathe effortlessly regardless of his or her depth by delivering air at a pressure that matches the surrounding water pressure. This pressure changes as the diver ascends or descends.

The First Stage

The regulator's first stage is the part that attaches directly to the tank. This first stage is a valve mechanism that receives the high-pressure air of the tank and delivers the air at intermediate pressure to a low-pressure hose that is attached to the regulator's second stage (the part that goes in your mouth). The sole function of the first stage is to maintain this intermediate pressure within the system. Intermediate pressure in scuba jargon is considered to be within the range of 90 to 150 psi, with 140 psi being the most common. This pressure remains at a constant level that is above ambient pressure regardless of a diver's depth.

Modern regulators use one of two types of valves to accomplish this: the piston valve or the diaphragm valve. This is where the fun and the debates begin.

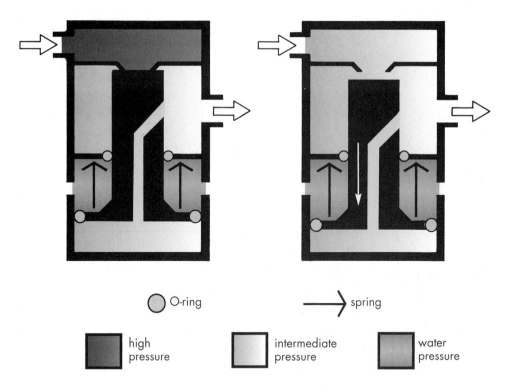

 O-ring   ⟶ spring

high pressure   intermediate pressure   water pressure

In a standard downstream piston regulator, the valve seats directly against the high-pressure air in the scuba tank. This regulator has few parts and is easy to maintain and service. JIM SOLLERS BASED ON AN ILLUSTRATION FROM NAUI MASTER SCUBA DIVER

Piston Valve Regulators

The piston valve first stage is the simpler of the two types. The valve comprises only two parts: a large piston and a spring. This valve measures ambient water pressure by allowing water to enter the mechanism and press against one side of the piston. The other end of the piston is seated against the high-pressure air in the scuba tank. As the diver inhales and reduces the intermediate pressure, the piston moves to allow more air into the system to maintain constant intermediate pressure. The advantages of piston regulators are their dependability and simplicity. The disadvantage is that the inner workings are exposed to the harsh environment of seawater or sediment-rich water.

It should be noted that piston valves can be "environmentalized" to prevent water from entering the valve. Silicone grease is contained within a cap over the valve, and the grease transfers the ambient water pressure to the valve without letting the water in. This is usually not necessary for a properly maintained regulator, as the materials used in these valves are chosen for their ability to withstand exposure to water.

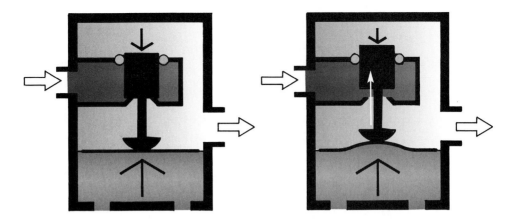

Diaphragm regulators prevent water from entering the valve. When a diver inhales, the diaphragm is bowed. The bowed diaphragm pushes a poppet, and the poppet opens the valve. All modern diaphragm regulators are "balanced," which means that the valve does not seat directly against the high pressure of the scuba tank. JIM SOLLERS BASED ON AN ILLUSTRATION FROM NAUI MASTER SCUBA DIVER

Diaphragm Valve Regulators

Diaphragm valve first stages also measure the ambient water pressure, but they seal the mechanism from contact with the water through the use of a diaphragm. These valves can have up to ten moving parts. As the diver inhales and intermediate pressure is reduced, the diaphragm is bowed and pushes a poppet, which allows more air into the system to maintain constant intermediate pressure. The advantage of diaphragm regulators is their integrity against the harsh environment. The disadvantage is their complexity.

Balanced vs. Unbalanced

First, a word about the nature of pressure valves. A balanced valve is not one that's easy to spin around on your finger, and an unbalanced valve is not one prone to wobble off a tabletop.

Valves that deal with pressure come in three types: upstream, downstream, and balanced. Upstream and downstream valves seat directly against pressure, such as the high pressure in a scuba tank. Downstream valves operate by opening with the flow of the high pressure, or "downstream" of the airflow. Upstream valves open against the pressure, or "upstream" of the airflow. Balanced valves are not directly seated against disparate pressures, and their operation is not affected by pressure.

In the extremely unlikely event of a valve failure in the first stage of a scuba regulator, a downstream valve will be forced open, which will deliver air to the diver in a free flow until all the air in the tank is gone. Balanced valves may or may not continue to deliver air in the event of failure, depending on the nature of the failure. Upstream valves will be forced closed by the pressure in the tank and will cease air delivery.

Standard piston valves are downstream valves that depend to some degree on air pressure in the scuba tank to perform their function, as one end of the piston is seated directly against the high pressure in the tank. This means that as the air in the tank is depleted and the pressure is reduced, the valve's ability to maintain a constant intermediate pressure above the ambient pressure will be diminished. Naturally, as a diver goes deeper and ambient pressure increases, it will become increasingly difficult for the valve to maintain a constant intermediate pressure above ambient. Low tank pressure and deep diving can combine to affect the regulator's ability to maintain the intermediate pressure, and if the intermediate pressure is reduced, it will be harder to breathe. Regulator first stages that seat directly against tank pressure are called unbalanced regulators.

It wasn't long before the regulator manufacturers began to devise valves that circumvent tank air pressure and perform their function of delivering air at intermediate pressure by purely mechanical means. By routing high-pressure tank air around both valve ends, these devices negate the influence of air pressure in the tank. This results in a valve that performs the same regardless of the air pressure in the tank. Regulators that contain a first-stage valve that is configured in this way are called balanced regulators.

There is considerable confusion regarding balanced and unbalanced diaphragm regulators. The unbalanced diaphragm was one of the first regulator designs and was in use for a number of years. However, standard diaphragm valves are upstream valves,

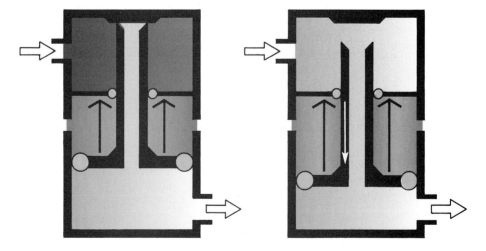

With a balanced piston regulator, the valve does not seat directly against the high pressure of the scuba tank. This improves performance of the valve when the pressure in the scuba tank is low.
JIM SOLLERS BASED ON AN ILLUSTRATION FROM NAUI MASTER SCUBA DIVER

meaning that the valve opens against the force of the air pressure in the tank (it must work "upstream" of the airflow). The problem with this kind of valve for scuba diving is that a malfunction would cause the valve to be forced closed by the tank air pressure, which would suddenly stop all airflow—not a very good thing for a diver at depth. For this reason, upstream, or unbalanced, diaphragm regulators are no longer marketed. Due to the design of diaphragm valves that are not upstream valves, all modern diaphragm regulators are balanced.

So far, we've come up with three different kinds of regulators and we haven't even gotten past the first stage. The three types of first stages are 1) unbalanced piston (which could also be called a downstream piston), 2) balanced piston, and 3) balanced diaphragm. Fortunately, second stages are not as diverse or as complicated.

The Second Stage

The second stage of a regulator is the part that goes into your mouth. It is at the end of the low-pressure hose that contains the air at intermediate pressure delivered by the first stage. It's a simple device. As the diver inhales, a diaphragm is bowed, which presses a lever connected to a valve. The harder the diver inhales, the more the lever is depressed, with the resultant increase in air. As long as the diver inhales, air is delivered.

The diver's exhalation is pushed through a simple one-way flap valve that allows the exhaled air to escape without allowing water to enter. The exhaled air is funneled through a tee beneath the mouthpiece to disperse the bubbles.

That's all there is to it. The purge button on your regulator simply pushes the lever that allows air to flow—the same lever that is pushed by the diaphragm when you inhale.

Variations on this simple device are in workmanship, engineering, and materials used. Also, manufacturers have come up with a multitude of diver-controlled means by which divers can fine-tune the flow of air. The mechanisms vary, but they include names like *air assist*, *vanes*, and *venturi effect* devices. The object is to deliver air as easily as possible without having the regulator deliver more air

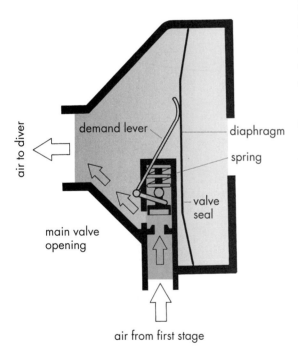

The second stage of a regulator goes into your mouth. As the diver inhales, a diaphragm is bowed, which presses a lever connected to a valve. Manufacturers of high-quality regulators balance this second-stage valve. JIM SOLLERS BASED ON AN ILLUSTRATION FROM NAUI MASTER SCUBA DIVER

than is demanded by the diver—a fault called positive-pressure breathing that can be more than an annoyance. Positive-pressure breathing may cause a regulator to be less stable or lead to free flows.

Most high-quality modern regulators will have a tendency to free-flow at the surface if the second stage is in the water and if the mouthpiece is not in a diver's mouth and is higher than the purge button. This happens because the second stage is so finely tuned that the difference in pressure of only a few centimeters of water is enough to start the delivery of air. To stop the free flow, simply turn the second stage over so that the mouthpiece is pointed downward.

So now we know what a salesman is talking about when he mentions pistons, diaphragms, balanced this, and unbalanced that. The salesman will tout pistons for their simplicity, diaphragms for their integrity, balanced valves for their efficiency, and unbalanced valves for their economy. We know that if he mentions things like air assist, vanes, or venturi effect, he's talking about bells and whistles on the second stage that allow a diver to fine-tune the delivery of air from the second stage into his or her mouth. The salesman can't go wrong selling you his most expensive stuff. It's good business for him, and he is confident that he has provided you with safe equipment.

The most expensive (and most complicated) regulators on the market are typically diaphragm regulators. The least expensive (and most simple) regulators on the market are typically unbalanced piston regulators. Various diaphragm, unbalanced piston, and balanced piston regulators fill the middle of the market. For many years, there was very little to go on other than theoretical and subjective opinion about which one was best, which one was good enough, which was a good buy, which was a waste of money, or which was a death trap.

Scuba Lab

One objective test is worth a thousand opinions. Conscientious consumers in the past tried to get objective information from navy tests. However, those tests were hard to find, hard to understand, and even harder to apply to recreational scuba equipment.

Fortunately, objective tests regarding work of breathing and stability of breathing at different depths are now available for virtually every recreational regulator on the market. The results of these tests are somewhat surprising, and the tests themselves are published by an unlikely source.

Scuba-diving magazines have been around since the early 1950s, and they have for the most part been a valuable resource for divers. Many destinations became popular by taking advantage of mass exposure to the diving public. And, of course, equipment manufacturers had a perfect opportunity to introduce their new gear to the market. New gear received glowing reviews, and the magazines raked in the advertising dollars. The diving public realized that reviews of gear that was being advertised in the magazines would naturally have a positive skew, but the reviews were a great way to see what was on the cutting edge of recreational-diving technology. It was a comfortable truce between the magazines, the manufacturers, and the public. That alliance came under direct fire in the early 1990s.

In 1992, the managing editor of a popular scuba magazine based in Savannah, Georgia, met with the founder of a testing laboratory in Catalina, California, and an unusual collaboration was formed. The testing laboratory agreed to objectively test recreational scuba gear, and the magazine agreed to publish the results. For the first time, advertisers be damned, the diving public would have an impartial resource to enable a real comparison of the performance of the gear being advertised.

The magazine was Rodale's *Scuba Diving*, the testing laboratory was Scuba Lab, and the collaboration continues to the present as the only objective resource readily available to recreational scuba divers regarding the performance of consumer gear. Test results are published periodically in the magazine, and interested divers can receive mailed reports on request or access reports online at www.scubadiving.com/gear.

Perhaps the most studied of these tests are the Rodale's Scuba Lab reports on regulators. The tests include an objective evaluation of how well regulators perform against navy standards on a breathing machine. No hype, no tricks, no brand loyalty—just a determination once and for all of how well these gadgets work.

The first part of the test is to determine work of breathing (WOB) at a simulated depth of 99 feet. With a tank pressure of 1,500 psi, a breathing rate of 25 breaths per minute, and a volume of each breath of 2.5 liters (otherwise known as "sucking air like a racehorse"), WOB expressed in joules per liter can be calculated. The navy maximum allowable WOB ratio is 1.4 joules per liter (otherwise known as "like breathing on the boat"). This first test is to establish a baseline for performance.

The second step of the testing is to determine WOB at a simulated depth of 198 feet. The same tank pressure and breathing criteria are used. This is the standard navy test.

The third step is to determine the stability of the regulator by comparing loss of WOB performance from 99 to 198 feet. Obviously, the less a regulator drops in performance, the more stable it is and the easier it is to use.

The last objective test is for positive-pressure breathing at a simulated depth of 165 feet.

Scuba Lab reports test results by ranges of WOB required. In the past, the lowest number meant the lowest (best) range of WOB. Tests are currently reported in ascending numbers, with performances falling within the lowest (best) WOB ranges receiving the highest score.

Scuba Lab typically reports tests of regulators grouped within price categories. However, it is important to note that WOB and stability results are reported in hard numbers. That is, the WOB and stability numbers reported for budget regulators can be directly compared to the same numbers reported for high-priced or premium regulators.

And what do you know? Although the very best WOB and stability test results come from the most expensive regulators, and although the more expensive regulators perform better as a group, some well-designed and well-engineered budget regulators perform at unexpected levels. In fact, some modestly priced unbalanced piston regulators and diaphragm regulators perform nearly as well as the best of the best.

So much for theories and subjectivity—if you want a regulator that delivers air, you can get one for $300 if you do your homework. I certainly hope that you will never be at a depth of 198 feet sucking air like a racehorse with 1,500 psi in your tank. But if you ever are and if you are equipped with a high-performance regulator, it won't be the regulator that kills you.

So that's that, right? Why would anybody pay more than $300 for a regulator? There are lots of reasons, the most obvious being that all divers are different and none of them are machines. While many active and independent divers use high-performance budget regulators (including yours truly—an unbalanced piston), they are not for every application. The higher-priced regulators not only deliver performance, but they also pay more attention to ergonomics and ease of use than do the budget regulators.

Scuba Lab also tests regulators for their ergonomics. While any such test ultimately boils down to a subjective opinion, the opinions of the Scuba Lab testers are more objective than the opinions of friends who have already bought (and feel the need to defend) equipment or of salespeople who are trying to sell equipment to you. Strict procedures are used by the testers to rate regulators on such things as ease of breathing, ease of clearing, bubble interference, comfortable performance in different swimming positions, how "wet" or "dry" the regulator breathes (i.e., how much water, if any, gets into your mouth when breathing), general comfort, and the convenience and performance of diver-controlled adjustment devices on the second stage.

In addition to comfort considerations, premium-priced regulators do deliver premium performance. Some regulators actually exceed Scuba Lab's ability to test them. These are clearly the choice for divers in extremely demanding situations, such as deep technical divers or ice divers.

A good way to think about high-performance budget regulators versus premium regulators is to refer back to our handy driving-a-car analogy. The Ford Mustang and the Lotus Esprit are both considered high-performance cars despite a huge difference in price and sophistication. The Lotus has more panache and features details and refinements beyond those of the Mustang, but for normal driving both will perform pretty much the same and both are more than capable of exceeding the speed limit. However, for high-speed driving on a narrow mountainside road, the Lotus would be the clear choice.

Likewise, high-performance budget regulators and premium regulators will perform pretty much the same under normal recreational-diving situations. The premium regulator may have details and refinements that the budget regulator doesn't, but either will perform well beyond what is normally required of them. However, for deep and/or strenuous diving in subfreezing water, the premium regulator would be the clear choice.

Of course, there are plenty of high-quality regulators to choose from. If you do the research, you will find one that matches your needs and budget. I mentioned that I personally use a budget regulator. I'll add that I also drive a 1989 Mustang. I'll add further that if my childhood hose idea had worked in the swimming pool, I'd probably still be using that. If one regulator was perfect for everybody, there wouldn't be so many from which to choose.

Shop at a reputable store, decide on a budget, do your research, and try to test as many of your possible choices as you can in the water. You'll have to take the word of the Scuba Lab tests regarding performance limits, but you'll be able to personally experience the feel of the regulator in actual use. Once you do that, it will be easy to make your decision based on price, performance, comfort, your personal diving needs, and your personal budget concerns.

Ports

Regulators do more than deliver air to your mouth. They also deliver air to other devices, such as the inflator for a buoyancy compensator, an alternate air source, or a dry suit. Additionally, the regulator must provide a means by which tank pressure can be monitored. The regulator must have ports to which devices can be connected via hoses to perform these tasks.

Ports are fittings in the first stage of the regulator through which air can pass. All regulators provide two different kinds of ports—high-pressure (HP) and low-pressure (LP) ports. The full force of the tank pressure moves through the HP port, which is typically used to measure the pressure in the tank. LP ports are used to deliver intermediate-pressure air to inflation devices or to divers through second stages.

Regulators typically have one or two HP ports and three or four LP ports. Only

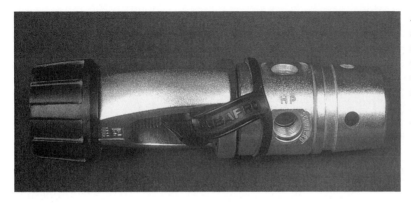

A piston regulator with all hoses removed. The large, threaded holes are ports, and the appropriate hoses are simply screwed into them. The high-pressure port is clearly marked "HP"; unmarked ports are LP ports.

high-pressure hoses may be connected to HP ports. The ports are clearly marked and the fittings are of different sizes to prevent hose mistakes. Some models may mark only HP ports; unmarked ports are LP ports.

Your submersible pressure gauge is connected to the HP port via a high-pressure hose. The three LP ports are typically used with low-pressure hoses for the primary second stage of your regulator (the one you breathe through), the secondary or alternate (octopus) second stage, and the BC inflator. So far, so good.

But what if you need to dive with a dry suit? Dry suits need a source of intermediate-pressure air for their inflation, and all of the LP ports have been used up. There are only two solutions for this. You must either find a way to share intermediate-pressure air between two devices, such as combining the alternate air source with the BC inflator (we'll cover this in detail in the buoyancy compensator section), or you need more LP ports on your regulator. This is another distinction between budget and higher-priced regulators. The more expensive regulators typically provide more ports, both HP and LP, allowing you to more easily configure your gear.

Alternate Air Source ($80–$250)

Your regulator will need the capacity to provide air to another diver in an emergency situation. The most common configuration for this is to attach a secondary second stage to one of the LP ports of the first stage. This secondary second stage is commonly called an octopus. While the octopus is typically for the benefit of your dive buddy in a share-air situation, it can also be of use to you in the event that your primary second stage malfunctions or your mouthpiece becomes unattached.

The octopus second stage is the same kind of gadget as the primary second stage that goes in your mouth. However, octopus second stages are not typically as finely tuned as the primary second stages that divers use for their own air delivery. This is not merely a matter of selfishness or antisocial behavior. Finely tuned second stages have a tendency to free-flow to some degree when not in a diver's mouth near the surface. A leaking or free-flowing octopus second stage is a pure waste of air.

So if you're not worried about how finely tuned an octopus second stage is, just buy a cheap one that works, right? Almost. It is true that an octopus second stage will not cost as much as a finely tuned primary second stage. However, you must put some thought into buying one.

We explained earlier that the function of the first stage of a regulator is to convert high tank pressure into intermediate pressure within the range of 90 to 150 psi. Each individual regulator is designed to deliver a specific intermediate pressure within that range. An intermediate pressure of 140 psi is most common, but regulators may differ. It is important that whatever octopus second stage you buy be matched and tuned to the intermediate pressure being delivered by your first stage.

An additional concern regarding an octopus second stage is the drag it causes. Not only does undue drag waste air due to the effort required to move through the water, but it also robs a diver of energy. Air and energy are the two most precious commodities a diver has. Therefore, small size is a virtue in octopus second stages. The more expensive rigs will be smaller and thinner and produce less drag.

Submersible Pressure Gauge ($90–$150)

The submersible pressure gauge (SPG) is the device that monitors your tank's air supply expressed in psi. The SPG is attached to a high-pressure port on the first stage of the regulator by means of a high-pressure hose. The high-pressure port on the regulator's first stage will be clearly marked "HP" and the fitting will be larger than those of the low-pressure ports (marked "LP") to prevent the use of a low-pressure hose on the high-pressure port. Obviously, a low-pressure hose connected to an HP port is a disastrous combination (the low-pressure hose would rupture if subjected to the pressurized air from an HP port).

All analog (as opposed to digital, which we'll cover in the section on dive computers later in the chapter) SPGs are based on what is known as a Bourdon movement, which is simply a helical tube that unwinds as internal pressure is applied—just like those paper party favors that uncurl when you blow into them.

Analog SPGs are hardy, simple devices, and they are reasonably accurate. It is important to know, though, that most analog SPGs are designed with an accuracy range of 35 to 100 psi with a pressure of 500 psi in the tank. This means that if your gauge reads 500 psi, it is entirely possible that you really only have 400 psi. At full pressure (normally 3,000 psi), the gauge will be accurate to within plus or minus 5 percent. As I'm sure you learned in your certification class, no dive should end with an SPG reading of less than 500 psi.

The last thing I need to mention about analog SPGs is their potential to blow up in your face. Maybe that should have been the first thing I mentioned. Anyway, if a leak occurs in the Bourdon tube inside the gauge, high-pressure air will quickly fill the casing of the gauge and cause it to burst. If this occurs, it will happen as soon as the tank valve is opened to allow the high-pressure air into the gauge. Avoid the temptation to stare at the SPG as you open the tank valve to see how much air is in the tank. Many experienced divers turn the SPG over, or away from themselves, when they initially open the tank valve to avoid this unlikely but possible accident.

Buoyancy Compensators ($250–$1,000)

The buoyancy compensator, often referred to as the BC or the BCD (buoyancy compensating device), is perhaps the most complicated piece of life-support equipment that you will own. I say "life-support equipment" because BCs are considered to be so,

JACKET vs. BACK-INFLATION BCs

Back-inflation BCs have been around for quite a long time. The Watergill At-Pac was the first back-inflation BC, introduced in 1972. The At-Pac was a revolutionary design that incorporated many of the features of modern BCs, including weight integration and power inflation, but the design was resisted by divers of the day. Most BCs have been jacket-style garments since the DEMA introduction of the Stabilizing Jacket in 1977.

Jacket BCs contain an air cell that encompasses a diver's rib cage. This type of configuration is still the most popular, but back-inflation BCs have reemerged from the cave-diving sector to achieve a new popularity among recreational divers. Back-inflation BCs are popularly known as "wings."

Back-inflation BCs have some real advantages over the traditional jacket, the principal ones being significantly less drag and increased stability when the wearer is swimming horizontally underwater. Also, since the air cell is behind the diver, the cell does not squeeze the diver's rib cage when inflated. A diver's chest remains comfortably unencumbered when he or she is using a back-inflation BC.

The back-inflation BC comprises three main components: the front harness, the back plate that holds the tank(s), and the air cell. In some models, these components can be mixed and matched to create a custom-made BC oriented to a specific use.

The back-inflation BC, sometimes referred to as wings, has earned a loyal following among many technical and recreational divers due to its comfort and stability underwater.

On the other hand (there's always the other hand), back-inflation BCs are generally more expensive than traditional jacket-style BCs. Also, since all of the flotation is behind the diver, they have a tendency to float a diver on the surface facedown. Manufacturers may offer different kinds of trimming weights to counteract this tendency, but none of them really work. Your dive instructor was probably equipped with some of the best gear money can buy, but he or she probably didn't wear a back-inflation BC on your checkout dives. Instructors spend a lot of time floating on the surface

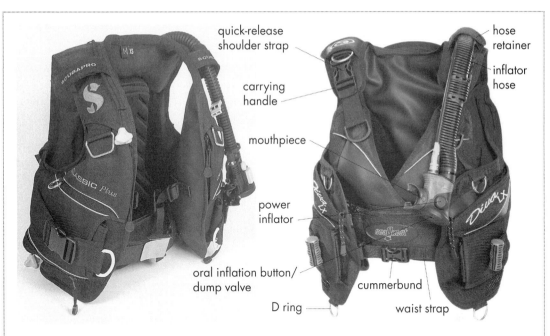

quick-release
shoulder strap

carrying
handle

mouthpiece

power
inflator

oral inflation button/
dump valve

D ring

hose
retainer

inflator
hose

cummerbund

waist strap

The full-jacket BC is a direct descendant of the original Stabilization Jacket first marketed by ScubaPro in 1977. Full-jacket BCs offer great stability with lots of lift.

The contour-jacket BC is the most popular among recreational divers. These jackets offer good stability, comfort, and less bulk with plenty of lift.

during instruction, and floating on the surface is definitely not the forte of the back-inflation BC.

Jacket-style BCs are still the most common and offer the best selection. They are cost-effective and they work. Jacket styles come in two general types—the traditional full jacket and what is known as the contour jacket. The contour jacket is basically a cut-down jacket with a smaller air cell, which leaves more of the chest area unencumbered.

While back-inflation BCs offer more stability, that doesn't mean that jacket-style BCs are unstable in the water—they're not. Once again, divers are faced with a decision between cost-effective gear that works and more-expensive gear that works a little better.

As you might have guessed from my Mustang mentality, I use a jacket-style BC, and a fairly inexpensive one at that. It doesn't turn any heads on the dive boat, but it works well enough. Come to think of it, high-priced BCs don't turn heads on dive boats, either, even though they may work better than well enough.

notwithstanding the fact that I dove and stayed alive for ten years without the benefit of one.

The granddaddy of all modern BCs was the Stabilization Jacket, informally called the "stab jacket," and it was marketed by ScubaPro. I remained unaware of its existence until it became popular after the first DEMA (Diving Equipment and Marketing Association) show in 1977. The first time I saw one, it appeared to me to be an ungainly and cumbersome thing.

Divers until that time used hard backpacks onto which a tank was attached. The only type of buoyancy device normally worn was an inflatable horse-collar life jacket. The jacket could be inflated at the surface either orally or with the aid of a small CO_2 canister—much like the life jackets displayed today on airplanes during those flight attendant demonstrations that everybody ignores. They could not be used to aid in achieving neutral buoyancy while underwater. My cadre of friends and I didn't like them and seldom wore them.

When we started our dives, we were a bit negatively buoyant due to the weight of the air in our tanks, and we were a bit positive by the time we surfaced with tanks that were nearly empty. We regulated our buoyancy during the dive simply by the way we breathed. We used our own lungs (glottis always open, never holding our breath) as underwater buoyancy compensating devices—a skill upon which I still rely today.

I don't mention this to belittle the importance of the BC for modern recreational scuba. It's interesting, however, that a piece of equipment that did not exist for the first twenty years of recreational scuba has become the foundation for the entire modern scuba kit. It is a tank holder, an adjustable swim bladder for achieving neutral buoyancy underwater at any depth, a flotation device on the surface, and a sort of commando vest for attaching all sorts of incidental gizmos. While I realize that diving can be done without one, I'd sure miss my BC if I had to dive without it today.

All BCs share some common features: a harness, which is a means by which the BC can be attached to the diver's body, usually with a Velcro cummerbund plus adjustable straps; an air cell that can be inflated either orally or via a power inflator that uses intermediate-pressure (LP) air from the diver's regulator; an overpressure relief valve to prevent the air cell from bursting due to overinflation; a means by which air can be dumped from the air cell, either through the oral inflator or through dump valves positioned at various places on the air cell; and a back plate to which a scuba tank can be attached. Most BCs also contain D rings on the front harness to which things can be clipped or attached.

Weight Integration

Despite initial resistance to the weight-integrated At-Pac BC in the early 1970s, weight integration has become a popular feature of modern BCs. Weight-integrated BCs negate the need for a weight belt by offering the option of carrying dive weights in specially designed pockets. Not only does this mean that you'll never forget your weights when you jump into the water, but diving without a weight belt that must be supported by the small of the back is also an important comfort consideration.

Weight-integrated BCs also allow a diver to ditch weights selectively. That is, a diver can ditch some weight without having to ditch all of it the way a diver wearing a weight belt would have to do. Weight-integrated BCs also float divers more comfortably on the surface, as they are less likely to "ride up" when inflated.

Weight-integrated BCs were a bit problematic when they were first introduced. The weight retaining mechanisms were finicky. Weights either had a tendency to fall out unexpectedly or they were difficult to remove in an emergency. These problems have, for the most part, been resolved. However, there is still no universal mechanism for holding weights in a BC.

Divers who use weight-integrated BCs have a neat, complete, and comfortable package for their entire scuba kit, and many divers swear by them. But, as always, there's that other hand.

As you might guess, a weight integration feature on a BC does not come for free. Also, while the weight retaining mechanisms have been improved, many systems remain imperfect and seem to cause owners some frustration.

Another disadvantage of a weight-integrated BC is the weight of the system. Divers who dive off small boats in the open ocean may want to hand their tank and BC up to someone on the boat before boarding. Handing up a weight-integrated BC will not make you any friends on the boat.

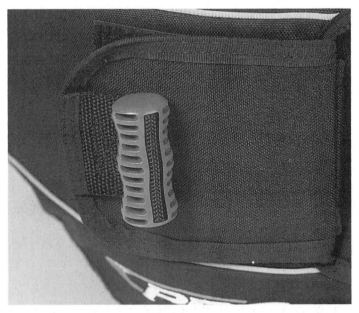

Weight-integrated BCs typically carry soft weights in specially designed pockets that are secured by Velcro. The weights can be quickly released by pulling the handle. Some manufacturers use a Fastex clip to further secure the weights in the pocket.

The weight of a weight-integrated BC will also complicate the task of changing tanks. Most divers on a multitank day change tanks by disconnecting the regulator from the tank, removing the BC from the tank, and transferring the whole rig to a fresh tank. It's not very convenient to fool with weights when doing this, and the BC with regulator attached to the BC's power inflator and weights in the weight pockets will result in quite a load. The effect of this weight is magnified when you are trying to change tanks on a small boat rocking in the open ocean—especially if three other people are trying to do the same thing at the same time in a cramped space.

One last consideration in deciding whether to use a weight-integrated BC is a safety factor. As its owner, you will be very familiar with how the weight retaining system works and how to quickly dump weights if the need arises. However, other people are not likely to be familiar with it at all.

As we'll cover in chapter 12, a primary rule in assisting another diver in the water is to get him or her positively buoyant at the surface. This sometimes requires the dropping of weights, and divers in distress are often too distracted to do it themselves. A weight-integrated BC might frustrate an attempt by a potential rescuer to help you in a time of need.

Some BCs offer the option of carrying weights that are not releasable. This is a good way to take some of the weight off the weight belt (your lower back) and reposition it in the BC, where it can be supported by your upper back and shoulders. The weight is limited, as it cannot be dropped in an emergency, but taking 5 pounds off the belt can make a serious difference in comfort for multiday, multitank diving. The lift capacity of the BC more than compensates for the nonreleasable weight to assure positive buoyancy at the surface. Non-releasable-weight BCs are a good compromise between the fully weight-integrated BC and the BC that does not accommodate any weights at all. Additionally, some weight-integrated BCs also offer non-releasable-weight pockets that enable a diver to spread the weights around for better comfort, balance, and stability.

I don't use a weight-integrated BC. Do I sometimes forget to put my weight belt on? Not very often. Does my back get tired from holding a weight belt during long dive trips? Yeah, it sometimes does. Cheapness comes with a price. I would certainly consider a weight-integrated BC if I could get my old BC to break or wear out. You should buy the BC that bests suits your needs and budget.

Lift Capacity

Lift capacity is the weight the air cell of the BC will float when fully inflated. Generally speaking, lift capacities of BCs vary depending on the size of the BC. Many XS (extra-small) BCs only have a lift capacity of 15 to 20 pounds, while some XL (extra-large) BCs can lift up to 70 pounds or more. This is mostly a matter of convenience for the manufacturers, as it is obviously easier to put a bigger air cell on a bigger garment. However, it's a convenience that works out. Larger people generally need more lift capacity than small folks for a reason that is not immediately apparent (I'll tell you in a minute—no peeking). Most BCs have a lift capacity of somewhere near 40 pounds.

Why would the average Joe or Jane need 40 pounds of lift? Well, they normally don't for recreational diving, but they need more than you might think. It's not just a matter of their physical fitness or water skills. To a large extent it's a matter of what kind of exposure suit they're wearing.

Neoprene is the material used for the most common types of exposure suits (wet suits), and neoprene floats at the surface. The larger the suit and the thicker the suit, the more it floats (that is, larger suits—for larger divers—have more lift). Divers must wear weights to overcome this buoyancy in order to submerge.

But neoprene is also compressible, and the material will compress as a diver goes deeper. Neoprene loses its buoyancy when compressed. A diver weighted to submerge comfortably at the surface wearing a neoprene suit will begin to sink like a stone at a depth of only 30 feet or so. The buoyancy compensator must be inflated to counteract the compressed and sinking neoprene. The deeper the diver goes, the more the neoprene will compress and the more it will sink. The BC must be continually inflated to compensate for this. Divers who make deep dives in thick neoprene wet suits need plenty of lift from their BCs.

As a side note, you may see advertisements from BC manufacturers that make reference to "travel" or "warm-water" BCs. This is another way of saying that the BC in question has limited lift. BCs with small air cells will be smaller and easier to pack. They are fine for warm water because, of course, less neoprene is needed in warm water.

Neoprene compression compensation is the primary concern of lift capacity in a BC for normal recreational diving. Technical divers who carry large loads of equipment, including several negatively buoyant steel tanks, will require additional lift.

Generally speaking, full-jacket BCs offer the most lift, contour-jacket BCs offer medium lift, and back-inflation BCs offer the least lift. However, back-inflation BCs can be custom-ordered with large air cells from some manufacturers.

Unless your dive plans include carrying an abundance of heavy equipment for deep dives while wearing a heavy neoprene wet suit, you'll find that maximum lift capacity is seldom a limiting factor in any modern BC marketed by the major manufacturers. As a general rule, lift capacity should be 5 or 10 more pounds than the maximum weight worn on any given dive.

BC Valves

Modern BCs have three different kinds of valves—the power inflation/oral inflation valve, exhaust or dump valves, and an overpressure relief valve.

The power inflation valve is the most complicated valve on the BC. It is a valve type known as a Schrader valve—an enlarged version of the air inflation valve on the tires of your car. Most BC power inflation valves are balanced to allow efficient inflation even if there is little air pressure in the tank. As might be imagined, since it is the most complicated, it is also the most prone to malfunction. We'll cover the care and maintenance of these valves in chapter 3.

Dump valves are, perhaps, the least-used convenience in recreational diving. They are valves placed strategically around the BC air cell that allow you to dump air by pulling a lanyard connected to the valve. They work very well, but few divers seem to use them. This is not a dive manual, and you should dive the way you were taught until you've reached a level of comfort to allow for experimentation, but if you're not using the dump valves on your BC, you should consider giving them a try. Almost all BCs have a shoulder dump with a valve-release lanyard over the right shoulder. A quick tug on the release lanyard of this valve is a much easier way to descend from the surface than the more traditional way of dumping air to descend—the tried, true, and clumsy technique of holding the oral inflation valve over your head and dumping air from it.

One of my more memorable dives occurred in the Florida Keys in the mid-1970s. My buddy and I got lost, he ran out of air, and we surfaced a considerable distance from the boat. He was getting panicky on the surface, so I pulled the lanyard to inflate the old horse-collar-type vest he was wearing by means of a CO_2 cartridge.

The CO_2 cartridge was apparently too large for the vest. The vest inflated until it blew out the seams on the collar—an event that scared the hell out of both me and my suddenly sinking buddy. It was one of those moments you tend to remember.

Of course, modern BCs are inflated either orally or by the low-pressure hose from the regulator, and such mismatches are no longer possible. However, even the low pressure from the regulator is enough to explode an air cell in a modern BC. For that reason, all modern BCs are equipped with an overpressure relief valve. The valve is usually positioned high on the air cell and is often combined with the right-shoulder dump valve. The valve is designed to dump air in the event that air pressure inside the air cell exceeds 2 psi. This valve is an important safety device, and you should know where it is on your BC and make sure that it is functioning properly.

Alternate Air Source Integration

Some manufacturers offer the option of combining an alternate air source with the power inflator of their BCs. This is a clever idea. The combination negates the need for the traditional octopus second stage alternate air source, which frees an LP port on the regulator for another use. It results in a neat, streamlined rig and keeps the alternate air source handy and easy to find.

The downside of an alternate air source on the BC is the cost. Such an arrangement will generally cost about double what a traditional octopus alternate air source costs.

Another disadvantage of the arrangement is the relatively fragile nature of power inflation valves. As we discuss further in the next chapter, power inflation valves on BCs have a tendency to wear out quickly unless they are meticulously cared for, and they are difficult to repair. Most divers simply replace the valve when problems

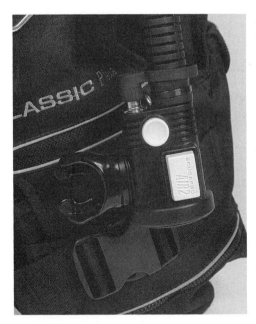

Some BCs offer the option of incorporating a second-stage regulator with the power inflator. This alternate air source takes the place of the octopus second stage, which means that one fewer low-pressure hose must be connected to the regulator's first stage and the cumbersome octopus does not need to be retained.

arise—an easy fix that costs around $50. A similar replacement of an alternate air source combination valve will cost more like $200, so repairing these valves is more cost-efficient.

While I recognize the advantages of alternate air source/power inflation combination valves (reduced drag and greater convenience), I don't use one. Why? Do I have to admit it again? I'm too damned cheap. However, you should buy the BC that best fits your needs and budget.

Cams

Tanks are attached to BCs by means of one or two tank bands that are tightened around the tank by a cam device. Most cams are threaded buckles that are easy to adjust to different-sized tanks. However, these cams must be tightened regularly to prevent tank slippage.

Some BC tank cams are adjustable from the inside of the tank band—a consider-

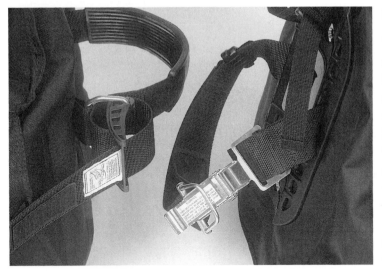

Two BCs back to back. Tank bands with threaded-buckle cams (left) are very easy to adjust to tanks with different circumferences, but they must be tightened before the cam is closed every time they're used. They do not disconnect during normal use, and the tank band remains a loop at all times (the loop is loosened and slipped over a tank when the cam is open). Tank bands that disconnect into two parts (right) are associated with ScubaPro BCs. The two parts connect via a hook-and-loop mechanism before the cam is closed, and the band is loosened or tightened by adjusting the length of the band connected to the loop. Adjusting this kind of tank band is more difficult than the threaded-buckle version, but once the band is set to fit a specific tank, it seldom needs further adjustment. These details shouldn't play a large role in which BC you purchase, but—depending on the type of diving you do—it may affect how convenient the BC is to use.

The same two BCs with the cams closed and the tank bands secured to the tanks. Once the tank bands are adjusted and the cams are closed, each works as well as the other.

ably more troublesome adjustment than the traditional threaded cam. However, once the tank band is set up for a particular size of tank, the cam is maintenance free and easy to use. Just whang the thing shut and you're done.

I don't recommend buying a BC based solely on a detail like a tank band cam, but details do make a difference. If you dive with the same-sized tank for virtually all of your dives and if you dive from small boats that are cramped for space, the convenience of a fixed cam rather than a threaded cam can make a real difference when setting up your rig or changing tanks.

As with many of the decisions you'll make when considering equipment, it's best to have a good idea of intended use and conditions of use before you buy. Once the intended use is known, details like tank band cams may very well influence your decision.

D Rings

D rings are attachment points placed on the harness of a BC to which all sorts of things can be clipped. They are a detail that can affect how convenient a BC is to use.

The call for more and sturdier D rings originally came from technical divers to help them manage all the extra stuff they carry on their dives. Manufacturers of more-recreational gear quickly followed suit. The addition of extra D rings did more than make relatively conservative gear look like expensive technical gear. The extra D rings made it easier for divers to personalize their rigs by providing convenient ways to clip hoses and gauges close to their bodies. In a real sense, additional D rings on BCs have helped divers of all skill levels protect the diving environment, as a hose or gauge clipped to the BC is a hose or gauge that is not inadvertently dragging across a reef. Gauges that are clipped to a fixed point on a BC are also easier for divers to find when they need them.

Most modern BCs have at least four D rings—one on each side of the chest and one on each side below the chest. However, it is not unusual to see BCs with six or more large D rings hanging from the harness. There is no harm in this, but divers have a tendency to use as many D rings as are available. It's sort of like shelf space—the more you have, the more you need. If the kitchen sink could be clipped on, some divers would carry one.

Four D rings will provide enough clip space for almost every recreational use, but there's never any disadvantage in having extra D rings. D-ring configuration is a detail that should not be an overriding factor in a decision to buy a BC, but it's something to consider.

Scuba Lab

Now that you are familiar with the common features of and distinctions between BCs, it's useful to know that Scuba Lab regularly tests these features. Go to www.scuba diving.com/gear and click on the BC icon to access the tests.

Much of the testing involves ergonomics, which are tests you can easily perform yourself in the dive shop. However, Scuba Lab also tests for mechanical operations that won't be apparent in the dive shop. The most important tests are for inherent buoyancy, air trapping, and exhaust rate.

Inherent buoyancy is exactly what it sounds like. A BC that floats excessively is something to watch for and avoid. An inherently buoyant BC is a buoyancy problem rather than a solution.

Air trapping is a measure of how much air remains in the BC after the air has been dumped in a normal swimming position. Air dumping should be efficient to avoid potentially dangerous buoyancy problems. Once again, air trapping is a buoyancy problem rather than a solution.

Exhaust rate is a measure of how fast air can be dumped from the air cell. The exhaust rate should exceed the power inflator's ability to inflate the vest in the event that the power inflator malfunctions and continuously inflates the air cell. Of course, should this occur, the first fix should be to disconnect the power inflator from the valve, but it is helpful if the exhaust system of the BC can dump air quickly and efficiently.

Scuba Lab test results are interesting reading. Most of the reports include suggested manufacturer's retail price along with the test results. It's a great way to get an idea of which BCs may suit your individual needs and budget.

Fit and Comfort

Once you have narrowed your choices based on features and cost, the most important consideration of buying a BC can be addressed. Simply put, a BC that does not fit well is a bad buy regardless of cost and features.

A BC should fit snugly without binding with the harness adjustments near their medium settings. It's best to try on BCs while wearing the thickest exposure suit you plan to wear while diving. Inflate the BC to see if it squeezes your rib cage too much when fully inflated. Your arms should fit comfortably in the armholes with no binding. If the armholes are too loose, the BC will tend to rise when you are floating on the surface—especially if the BC is not weight integrated. This is easy to imagine. If the weights are on your body and sinking while the BC is inflated and floating, the combination will tend to make you sink beneath the BC.

BC manufacturers ignored the special requirements of female divers for too many years. However, the major manufacturers now offer a nice selection of BCs specifically designed to accommodate the female form. Many women find back-inflation BCs to be very comfortable.

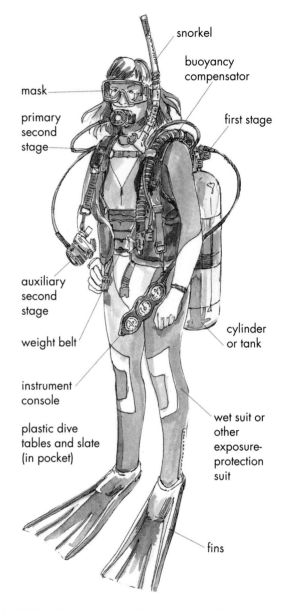

The full kit of a recreational diver has a lot of parts and pieces. Divers should think about how they will all work as a unit when purchasing each piece. ELAYNE SEARS

I don't need to tell you what something feels like when it fits right. In addition to having the features you want at a price you can afford, the BC you buy should fit like a comfortable garment. Controls and pockets should be convenient to find and use. If at all possible, make a pool dive in the BC before you buy it. Test it for stability when swimming, for smooth inflation and deflation, for convenient and efficient air dumping in various swimming positions, and for the way it floats you on the surface.

Speaking of floating on the surface, let me make one last point about BCs. You may hear accounts of how a particular BC will float a diver on the surface. I've mentioned this a few times in this review. However, some sales pitches may go beyond endorsements of comfort and convenience and claim that this or that BC will float a diver faceup in a survivable position even if the diver is unconscious. Take this assertion with a large grain of salt. Most BCs will not float an unconscious diver faceup on a consistent basis. Even if the diver is floating faceup, there is no assurance that his or her nose and mouth will be out of the water. BCs are dive gear, not life vests. I would not take a claim to the contrary into account when buying a BC.

DEPTH GAUGES ($70–$200)

There are lots of different methods of measuring depth. The simplest are devices that use a capillary tube that relies on compression of air in the tube caused by water pressure. Others use Bourdon tubes similar to the ones used in submersible pressure gauges. However, most depth gauges used today are incorporated into dive computers and measure pressure electronically.

DIVE COMPUTERS ($200–$1,500)

Dive computers are another component of the modern scuba rig that did not exist when I began my diving career. Now I consider them to be mandatory equipment. While it is true that dives can be safely made using tables, my experience has been that precise monitoring of time and depth is the exception among table divers, and tables are useless without precise monitoring. Many table divers use the tables conservatively to compensate for their lack of diligence in monitoring time and depth. This results in even shorter dive times for subsequent dives. Bottom line: If you are not using a computer, you are subjecting yourself to unnecessary risk and you are probably cheating yourself out of valuable bottom time.

So it's clear that you need a computer. Computer manufacturers, though, seem to have adopted a strategy of confuse and conquer in the marketing of their products. You'll hear about the modified Haldane ratio, half-times, tissue compartments, Workman M-values, Buhlmann M-values, and algorithms in most of the computer literature, but it seems as if few retailers really know what all the hype is about. Before we tackle computers, we need to go over some basic decompression theory to learn something about what the computer guys are talking about. This is the kind of thing that tech divers argue about with each other. It can be deadly boring, but you need at least a general understanding of the theories in order to understand what dive computers do.

Decompression Theory

As you'll remember from your certification class, decompression sickness (DCS, or the bends) is caused by the body tissues' absorption of inert gases (nitrogen in air) when under pressure. If the pressure is reduced too quickly as a diver ascends, the inert gas comes out of solution within the tissue, forms bubbles, and causes problems.

The British Theory (Haldane's Model)

In 1908, the British Royal Navy contracted a man named John S. Haldane to solve the problem of DCS. Haldane is considered to be the father of decompression theory, and his studies produced several breakthrough ideas that are still in use today.

Haldane theorized that different tissues in the body absorb and release nitrogen at different rates. He came up with five hypothetical tissue types, which he called compartments, and he calculated how long it took each compartment to absorb or release one-half of its maximum saturation. This time came to be known as the compartment's half-time. Haldane's five-compartment model of the human body consisted of compartments labeled T5, T10, T20, T40, and T75. Each number refers to a half-time of a tissue expressed in minutes. For example, a T5 tissue would absorb half its maximum saturation in the first 5 minutes, half of its remaining maximum saturation in the next 5 minutes, etc. It takes about six half-times for a compartment to absorb or release its capacity of inert gas. So far, so good.

Haldane then discovered that goats showed no signs of DCS when they returned to 1 atmosphere from a simulated depth of 30 feet, no matter how long they had been subjected to the pressure of that depth. This depth should ring a bell, as it happens to be the depth in seawater at which pressure is doubled from the surface pressure of 1 atmosphere. Haldane reasonably came up with a ratio of 2:1 to define how quickly a diver could ascend without having to worry about DCS, which was that the diver could reduce pressure by one-half without suffering ill effects. For example, if a diver could safely ascend from 2 atmospheres to 1 atmosphere, then the diver could also safely ascend from 4 atmospheres to 2 atmospheres. Haldane went on to compute the first decompression tables for the Royal Navy based on the Haldane ratio of 2:1 and the half-times of his five tissue compartments.

The U.S. Theory (Workman's Model)

The British Royal Navy tables were used by the U.S. Navy until the latter developed its own tables in 1937. Ascent rates and half-times were modified and the tables were expanded to account for repetitive dives, but the theory remained constant until a man named Robert Workman began a systematic review of the decompression model in the mid-1960s.

One of Workman's first observations was that the old Haldane ratio of 2:1 was expressed in atmospheres of air, while the culprit of DCS is actually nitrogen. Since nitrogen comprises 79 percent of air, the new ratio became 1.58:1 (79 percent of 2 is 1.58). You may hear this ratio called the modified Haldane ratio, but this is a misnomer. The new ratio is simply an expression of the same thing in terms of nitrogen rather than air. Workman also found that the ratios for tolerated overpressure (the maximum inert gas pressure that a tissue can tolerate without showing overt signs of DCS) varied by tissue compartment half-time and by depth. The compartments with faster half-times tolerated greater overpressure than did those with slower ones, and the ratios became smaller in all compartments as depth increased.

Sometime during the review, Workman made a profound switch in the way he thought about tissue compartment saturation. Instead of thinking in terms of ratios as Haldane had done, he began to think in terms of mathematical values. He described the maximum saturation of each compartment at any given depth or pressure as its M-value, for maximum value. He went on to make a linear projection algorithm of these M-values as a function of depth and found that the mathematical model closely approximated the empirical data that had been gathered through years of table use.

For those of you who are totally confused, I'll point out here that we are really getting somewhere with the idea of a decompression model expressed in terms of a linear mathematical equation. Computers are good at math, and a linear equation is one that can be computed on the fly as the variables of depth and time change. Workman's M-value model is the genesis of all decompression computer programs.

The Swiss Theory (Buhlmann's Model)

The Swiss professor Albert A. Buhlmann began his decompression research in 1959 in Zurich. He published a book of his studies in 1983, and an English translation of the book was published in 1984. Buhlmann's book was the first comprehensive reference on making decompression calculations that was available to the general public. The significance of this was that, for the first time, computer programmers had a reference from which to start writing programs for dive computers. The Buhlmann algorithm became the basis for do-it-yourself and consumer computer programs.

Buhlmann's method of computing decompression was very similar to Workman's. It included M-values and a linear relationship between the M-values and tolerated gas pressure in various tissue compartments. The major difference is that the Workman model uses 1 atmosphere (sea level) as its base, while Buhlmann's model uses 0 atmospheres as its base. As such, the Buhlmann algorithm can calculate decompression for dives at high altitudes—a nice consideration for diving in the mountain lakes of Switzerland.

Although the Buhlmann model is a derivative of the early Haldane theories, things have come a long way since Haldane. The Buhlmann model includes sixteen tissue compartments with half-times ranging from 2.65 to 635 minutes, can determine no-decompression limits for single dives and repetitive dives, can calculate decompression requirements for longer and deeper dives, and can accommodate diving at different altitudes.

The Canadian Theory (DCIEM Model)

The Canadian theory, sometimes known as the DCIEM model (for Defense and Civil Institute of Environmental Medicine), is different from all the others in that it did not evolve from the work of John Haldane. Rather than using a variety of hypothetical tissue compartments, the DCIEM model uses a set of serial tissues. After the first tissue absorbs and releases inert gas, successive tissues absorb and release from the preceding tissue. However, like the models derived from Haldane's, the DCIEM model can be expressed in a linear mathematical equation. Tables and programs produced from the DCIEM model give more conservative bottom times as compared to the U.S. Navy model.

DSAT and DCAP

The last terms that you might hear bandied about at your neighborhood dive counter are DSAT and DCAP. Neither of these are real decompression models. Rather, they refer to sets of M-values that can be plugged into established algorithms.

DSAT (Diving Science and Technology) is a corporate affiliate of the popular certifying agency PADI. Most PADI divers are familiar with their Recreational Dive Planner. The M-values used for this dive planner were developed and tested by two doctors and colleagues with DSAT.

DCAP (Decompression Computation and Analysis Program) refers to a set of M-values that resulted from the development of new air decompression tables for the Swedish navy.

You now know more about decompression theory and modeling than you probably need to, but I think it's important for independent divers to understand the rationale behind the equipment they buy. Plus, you never know when decompression theory might pop up as a category on *Jeopardy!* Anyway, let's finally take a look at what is available today in dive computers.

All modern dive computers perform the minimum functions of keeping track of depth, time, nitrogen loading, decompression status, and surface time and providing a means by which future no-decompression dives can be planned. Nearly all of them also incorporate ascent-rate warnings to keep ascent rates within acceptable limits or within the limits of the programmed decompression model being used in the computer. Nearly all computers retain information from previous dives for reference and logging, although some lose these data when the computer is turned off. Most also calculate a safe time to fly on a commercial plane with cabin pressurization. However, many time-to-fly calculations are simple timed countdowns from the last dive and are not true indicators of nitrogen remaining in a diver's tissues.

As you might imagine from the evolution of computers in modern society, the sky is the limit on the other end of the spectrum. Some computers seem to be capable not only of keeping track of your dive in a million different ways but also of finding your car keys when you get off the boat. The following are some of the basic distinctions between computer types.

Computer Types

Stand-Alone

When a dive computer is referred to as a stand-alone, it simply means that the computer is independent of all other dive gear. Specifically, it means that the computer cannot measure the diver's air supply and is not hooked to the diver's regulator.

Because stand-alone computers limit their monitoring to a diver's depths and times, they are generally the most simple of dive computers and also the least expensive. Stand-alone computers are usually small and can be carried either on the diver's wrist or in a console. Stand-alones are convenient should a diver need to change regulators for any reason, as the computer can be easily removed from any console and carried by the diver independently of all other gear.

Since stand-alone computers are generally at the lower end of any given manufacturer's computer line, they usually don't have the fancier applications of more expensive computers. However, the fancy applications have no bearing on the computer's primary function of keeping track of decompression status. The value of any computer is its ability to perform this function, and by that measure stand-alone computers work as well as any.

Given my established cheapness and the fact that stand-alone computers work, do I have to tell you that I personally use a stand-alone computer?

Gas-Integrated

Gas-integrated computers, often called air-integrated computers, are connected to a diver's regulator via a high-pressure hose, and they replace the SPG in addition to computing decompression status. There are several advantages to this. Computers are far more accurate in their measurement of tank pressure than the traditional Bourdon movement of analog SPGs. Also, since the computer is performing more than one function, there is less for the diver to carry.

One disadvantage of having a digital SPG combined with a computer is the need for batteries to monitor air supply and the relative delicacy of electronic devices as compared to analog ones. Plus, if a diver needs to use a different regulator, he or she must disconnect the high-pressure hose that feeds the SPG function of the computer in order to continue to use the computer with the different regulator.

By providing computer programmers with the additional information of tank pressure, gas-integrated computers can offer far more information than stand-alone computers. I'll leave it to you to decide if this is an advantage or a disadvantage. Since time and tank pressure change are known, many of these computers can calculate how long your air supply will last at different depths. Some computers will compare this time to your decompression status and let you know if you'll run out of air or out of bottom time first.

I mentioned that I personally use a stand-alone computer. If I had a reason to buy a new computer, I would certainly consider a gas-integrated model.

Nitrox-Compatible

Nitrox diving utilizes a gas mixture that contains more oxygen and less nitrogen than air. We'll cover the details later in the section on continuing training in chapter 6, but the primary reason for using nitrox is to increase no-decompression dive times. The drawbacks of nitrox include strict depth limits and a strict limit on a diver's exposure to oxygen-enriched gas over time—the so-called oxygen clock with which certified nitrox divers are familiar.

As nitrox has become increasingly popular, many dive computers have added the feature of allowing the gas mixture to be entered into the computer for decompression-status computation. The gas mixture can usually be entered on a dive-by-dive basis, with different mixtures used for different dives.

Nitrox-compatible computers are more complicated than traditional air computers, as they must perform more functions. Not only must they compute decompression status based on whatever gas mixture is being used, but they must also keep track of how long a diver has been breathing oxygen-enriched gas and the depth limit for each gas mixture. This information must be conveniently displayed on each dive.

In my opinion, there is no reason to use nitrox unless you have a nitrox-compatible dive computer. Without one, the principal advantage of using nitrox (longer bottom times) is lost. Likewise, there is no reason to use a nitrox-compatible computer unless you are diving on nitrox.

Nitrox-compatible computers are available either as stand-alones or as gas-integrated computers. If you plan to dive on nitrox, get one.

Hoseless Computers

Some gas-integrated computers can measure tank pressure without having to be attached to the regulator via a high-pressure hose. This is done by means of a radio transmitter attached to the HP port of the regulator that communicates with a receiver on the computer. Cool.

The advantages of this are the elimination of drag caused by the hose, the fact that no high-pressure hose must be maintained, and the convenience of carrying the computer on the wrist or in a console without regard to a hose connection. Not to mention the "neato" factor of having such an arrangement.

The disadvantages of hoseless computers are the complexity of the technology and design, the cost, the batteries necessary to make them work, and the potential for interruptions of the radio signal caused by camera strobes or other electronic devices being used in close proximity to the transmitter or receiver.

My opinion is that the disadvantages far outweigh any practical benefit of hoseless computers. I offer this opinion with a full disclaimer of my pragmatism and the fact that I'm a dinosaur diver. I appreciate the gizmo wizardry required to make a thing like a hoseless computer, but tank pressure information is too important to trust to such a gadget for the limited rewards. My normal diving includes some banging around on boats, and the delicacy of a hoseless computer is simply not up to my standards of robustness, simplicity, and dependability.

Dive Logging and PC Interface

All modern dive computers offer some means by which dives can be reviewed and logged. Computers on the bottom end of the scale typically keep the last ten dives in memory. These dives can be scrolled to show maximum depth, time, decompression status at the end of each dive, and ascent information. This is useful for logging dives, but the information is often lost when the computer is turned off.

Some computers take logging dive information more seriously and can hold many more dives in memory.

Some computers, though, take dive logging to the ultimate step. They provide an interface to personal computers (PCs) so that all dive information can be downloaded for study. Once this is done, dives can be reviewed in great detail. Depth graphs can be called up to show a diver the exact depth profile and time of any given dive. Divers can review which of their theoretical tissue compartments were on-gassing (absorbing nitrogen) or off-gassing (releasing nitrogen) at any point during the dive. Divers can virtually re-create the dive from a physiological standpoint.

Of course, this feature does not come cheaply. If you are interested in examining your dives in great detail, high-end dive computers certainly give you the opportunity to do so. However, this feature has no bearing on the primary function of a dive computer: managing your dives safely in the water.

Computer Lockout

Some computer manufacturers get pretty upset if the parameters of their computers are violated. Of course, you should never violate the parameters, but accidents happen. Many computers will respond to a violation, such as a missed required decompression stop, by "locking out" the computer. That is, the computer will stop providing decompression information to the offending diver. Some will revert to a "gauge

CONSERVATIVE vs. LIBERAL

We're not talking politics here. We're talking about M-values and models that will allow more or less dive time for any given dive without violating the dive computer. Liberal computers allow more dive time; conservative computers allow less.

I feel that divers should avoid computers on either extreme end of the scale. I get suspicious whenever I hear one computer touted above all others based on its conservatism or liberalism, as such claims are more suited to advertising than for actual diver use. Liberal computers are claimed to "allow more diving freedom," while conservative computers are hyped as being "safe."

This is nonsense. The purpose of a dive computer is to provide a reliable estimate of what is really happening to a diver's body at depth.

The best way to deal with the conservative/liberal debate in dive computers is to use reliable information either liberally or conservatively as you see fit. My preferred nitrogen-load display on a dive computer is a graph that moves from green to yellow to red. Green is conservative, yellow is liberal, and red is required decompression.

I ascend to a shallower depth whenever my computer hits the yellow area, and I don't surface until my computer is in the green.

This conservatism is a personal decision. As an independent diver, you should make a similar decision. It's your health. You decide. However, it's important that you base your decision on the best information available, and information tainted by an advertising gimmick is not the best place to start.

Of course, each computer will compute decompression status a little differently, and there will be some variance in the dive times allowed. However, I think it's best to stick with computers provided by established manufacturers that do not stretch the conservative/liberal envelope in either direction.

mode" and continue to provide depth and time, but others will go into a full pout and revert to "black box mode" or "bracelet mode," which provides no information whatsoever to the offending diver.

Manufacturers who program lockouts in their computers are depriving divers of crucial information at the very time that they need it most. Computer lockout is sort of like a car disconnecting the seat belt if it goes into a skid.

Providing information for a dive-profile violation requires more-complex programming than monitoring a dive that is within a model's accepted parameters. However, this is information that may become critical during a dive. I would personally rather spend money on this kind of programming than on a feature that lets me see my past dives in graph form on a PC.

I have never come remotely close to violating a computer, and I consider any such violation as an inexcusable offense. However, if I ever do, I expect my dive computer to help me overcome my blunder. Avoid computers that lock divers out for violations.

Computer Miscellany

The technology related to dive computers is evolving faster than that for any other type of dive equipment. Now that we've provided a general overview on the subject, here are some other points to keep in mind when shopping for a dive computer.

Batteries could not be changed by the user in many early computers, which meant that the computers had to be shipped back to the manufacturer for a simple change of batteries. Thankfully, most modern computers offer user-changeable batteries. The current trend is toward more-commonplace batteries. Look for a computer that uses a common type of battery, such as AA or AAA, as opposed to exotic button-type batteries. The more commonplace the power source, the easier and more convenient the computer will be to maintain.

If your dive plans include diving in bodies of water other than the ocean, make sure your computer is compatible with those environments. For example, if you plan to dive at high altitudes, get a computer that can easily accommodate this. Some computers calculate altitude diving automatically. Similarly, some computers automatically detect whether they are being used in salt or fresh water.

Make sure you understand how any computer operates. If a salesman can't show you how a unit works in a matter of a minute or two, look for a computer that is more intuitive and easier to use.

Some computers are activated by buttons or by contact points. Think about how convenient those buttons or points will be to operate in your intended diving environment. For example, if you expect to be diving in cold climates, the gloves you are likely to be wearing might not work very well if the buttons are small. A current trend is for gas-integrated computers to activate themselves as soon as the tank valve is opened.

You should also be aware of other ergonomic considerations: the computer should be easy for you to see and include a backlight for low-light situations, it should display information that is intuitive to you, and it shouldn't arbitrarily change to alternate screens that confuse you. Naturally, you won't be able to determine these things unless you can hold the computer in your hand, push the buttons, and generally fool around with it.

Scuba Lab

As with virtually every other type of dive equipment available, the folks at Scuba Lab have tested just about every dive computer on the market. To access the information, go to www.scubadiving.com/gear and click on the computer icon.

Much of the Scuba Lab information pertains to ergonomics and subjective opinion—things that you can determine yourself by actually looking at computers at your local dive shop. The Scuba Lab reports do sometimes include information regarding decompression models used by particular computers, and they include the computer's features. Most of the reviews also include the manufacturer's suggested retail price, which provides a good window-shopping opportunity to see what kinds of features are available in different price ranges. The Scuba Lab reports usually include an opinion about the clarity of the owner's manual, which is an important consideration for gear as complex as dive computers.

Exposure Suits ($35–$2,000)

An exposure suit is often the first item of equipment divers on the road to independence buy. This is because the fit of most types of exposure suits is crucial to the effectiveness of the suit, and many equipment renters lack the size selection necessary to ensure a good fit.

There are two general types of exposure suits—those designed to physically protect divers from stings and scrapes and those designed to keep divers warm in the water. Of course, suits primarily designed to keep divers warm in the water also serve to protect divers from stings and scrapes.

The Coonass Wet Suit

For those of you who may be culturally challenged due to living outside the great state of Louisiana, *coonass* is the proudly accepted designation of a person descended from the Acadians who settled in Louisiana after their expulsion from Nova Scotia in 1755. You may be more familiar with the corruption of the word *Acadian*, which is *Cajun*. Cajuns do more than cook spicy foods and sing waltzes in French. They also dive beneath the thousands of oil rigs off the Louisiana coast—structures that are typically encrusted with sharp barnacles and covered by a fine coat of stinging hydroids.

You already have a coonass wet suit hanging somewhere in your clothes closet. It's nothing more than an old pair of jeans and a shirt or an expendable pair of coveralls. This type of exposure protection works well enough for avoiding minor bumps and scrapes and for protection against stings, and it is still very popular with southern divers in general and with Louisiana oil rig divers in particular.

Coonass wet suits have some admitted shortcomings. They create drag in the water and offer no insulation for warmth. Because water flows freely down the shirt collar, any stinging organism suspended in the water may become trapped beneath the shirt. Also, because they become totally saturated with seawater and are slow to dry, most coonass wet suits quickly lose any other use as clothing, as they have a tendency to "go to permanent stinking" after the first use.

Still, the idea has merit. For cheap protection against bumps and stings in warm water, consider a look into your clothes closet. A recent innovation has been the use of polyester from the disco era. The stuff sheds water, dries quickly on the boat, and provides some of the panache for which the Cajun culture is famous.

Dive Skins

Lycra dive skins serve the same function as the coonass wet suit. They protect divers from the sun, scrapes, and stings without providing any insulation against cold water. They also provide a cushion against heavy dive equipment, which makes diving more comfortable, and Lycra material against the skin is certainly more comfortable than a wet pair of jeans.

Dive skins are the most popular exposure protection for diving in warm water, and they are usually the first exposure suits that divers buy. They are an improvement over the coonass wet suit in that they create virtually no drag and their snug fit offers much better protection from stings by organisms suspended in the water. They also dry quickly and are easy to pack. However, a wet Lycra dive skin may chill a diver on the boat, so it should be removed upon surfacing.

Dive skins also provide divers with a means to make a fashion statement. I don't see how any of them could make more of a statement than paisley angel-wing collars and flared pants from the disco era, but maybe that's just me.

Wet Suits

In addition to protecting divers from scrapes and stings, neoprene wet suits also provide insulation against cold. The way this is actually done may be different than what you were taught in your certification class.

There is considerable confusion regarding how wet suits work, and since some wet-suit manufacturers contribute to this confusion with their advertising, I think we'd better go over some cold facts about why people get cold in the water. Divers lose heat in the water through two processes: conduction and convection.

Heat is energy, and water is a tremendous conductor of heat. How well does water conduct heat? The answer is nearly *twenty-five times* as well as gases such as air. That's why your car's radiator is filled with water.

Gases, on the other hand, are very poor conductors of heat. That's why garments made of fleece or down are so warm—those are materials that trap air, and since air is such a poor conductor of heat, the trapped air provides an insulating barrier of poor conductivity between your warm body and the cold outside the garment.

The conduction difference between water and air is the reason you can walk into a deep freezer at 0°F and stay there for a few minutes before you feel cold, but a dip into 70°F water will cause instant goose bumps.

Since wet suits are made of neoprene, you might logically conclude that neoprene is a good insulator against cold. You'd be wrong. Wet suits are made of neoprene because neoprene contains pockets that hold air (OK, it's usually nitrogen, but I'm on a roll), and it's the air that provides the insulation.

So, the first way that divers lose heat in water is through conduction. That is, the water provides a very efficient means by which the heat from your body can be channeled away. The way to prevent conductive heat loss is to insulate the body with a poor conductor of heat, and that poor conductor of heat is air. Therefore, the first functions of an effective wet suit are to keep the "wet" to a minimum and to maintain a barrier of air between the diver and the cold water. This is accomplished through the use of the air pockets in neoprene and by a snug enough fit to minimize the entrance of cold water into the suit.

A good way to envision heat loss by convection is to imagine that you're driving in a car with the heater on. Even if it's cold outside, you remain comfortable in the heated bubble of air inside the car. But what happens if you roll the windows down? Of course, the cold air rushes in, the warm air flies out the window, you feel the cold, and your heater must start all over again to warm up the air in the car. You've experienced a heat loss due to convection. Think of convective heat loss in a wet suit as a sort of underwater wind chill factor.

By their nature, wet suits allow some water to enter the suit and conduct heat away from your skin. If the water is kept to a minimum, the amount of heat that it will conduct from your body will be manageable. However, if a flow of new water is added to the suit, the energy expended to warm the water already in the suit will be flushed into the sea. That is how divers lose heat by convection when wearing a wet suit. Therefore, the second function of an effective wet suit is to keep water flow to a minimum. This is accomplished by a snug fit, especially around the wrists and neck where water can enter, with a minimum of bulges and folds in which water can accumulate.

We are now ready to dispel the most popular myth about how wet suits keep divers warm. Wet suits do not work by keeping an "insulating layer of warm water" against a diver's body, as many ads and dive instructors suggest. Water does not insulate against cold, and any water inside an exposure suit will contribute to heat loss. However, if a small amount of water can be held in place, a diver's body can expend enough energy to keep it warm for a while and further heat loss will be mostly by convection.

That's simple enough. All you need in a wet suit is a barrier of air contained in neoprene and a good, tight, supple fit to keep the water entering and accumulating in the suit to a minimum. Although this seems to be a simple objective, it is practically impossible to attain. The difference between a good wet suit and a bad one is how close the suit comes to this ideal.

We discussed earlier (in the buoyancy compensator lift capacity section) how neoprene floats on the surface but loses much of its buoyancy when submerged. This happens because the air pockets in the neoprene compress with depth. Since it's the air in the neoprene that insulates the diver, and since the air space is reduced by compression as the diver descends, guess what? Neoprene wet suits lose a high percentage of their capacity to insulate against conductive heat loss at a depth of only 30 feet. Repetitive compression of neoprene will eventually break down the air pockets permanently, the suit will lose its insulating capability, and it will no longer keep you warm.

The solution to neoprene compression is to use a higher-quality neoprene—one that has air pockets with sides rigid enough to resist compression. The problem with this is that such a material will also resist bending and will result in a very stiff suit. Stiff suits are more than uncomfortable. They lack the suppleness for a snug fit and are more prone to allow water to flow and accumulate inside the suit. The diver will have more air insulation against conductive heat loss but will now flush away heat due to convection. Uh-oh. We seem to be on the horns of a conduction/convection dilemma.

All neoprene wet suits are a compromise between neoprene compression and stiffness, and, as such, all suffer to some degree from compression. Wet suits from the established manufacturers use a neoprene of medium quality in an attempt to find the optimum balance between flexibility and compression, but some manufacturers use neoprene that is of such low quality that the resulting suits have practically no insulating properties at normal diving depths, although they fit and feel great when you try them on in a store. In fact, if a wet suit goes on easily, and has a comfortable stretchiness when you try it on dry in a store, then it probably lacks insulation. This is a counterintuitive test. If a wet suit is too comfortable when you try it on in a store, it probably won't keep you very warm in the water.

Wet suits come in three general configurations to optimize comfort and insulation. The three configurations are shorties, full suits, and farmer john/jane types.

Shorty suits are normally 2 to 3 millimeters thick and are designed for warm water (high 70s Fahrenheit and warmer). They cover only the torso of the diver and have short sleeves and legs. They are very easy to put on and take off, and they provide some insulation against the cold. Because so little neoprene is used, a minimum of extra dive weight is necessary to counteract buoyancy. The principal disadvantages are exposed arms and legs and minimal insulation.

A shorty wet suit is my habitual dress in warm water. It is warmer than a dive skin and easier to put on and take off. The exposed skin of the arms and legs (which could mean bumps and scrapes) is not a problem if good buoyancy is maintained, and I enjoy the total freedom of movement that shorties allow.

Full wet suits (sometimes called "jump suits") vary in thickness from 3 to 7 millimeters or thicker. They are appropriate for colder water (to the mid-50s Fahrenheit, depending on their thickness). Naturally, thicker suits provide more insulation, but they are more difficult to get on and take off and they restrict movement.

Farmer john/jane wet suits come in two pieces—a piece that covers the legs and torso with shoulder straps and a jacket that adds an additional layer over the torso. A common thickness is 3 millimeters for each piece, which results in 6 millimeters of neoprene over the torso.

Farmer john/jane wet suits lack insulation in the arms and legs, but the thinner layer of neoprene on these areas allows more comfort and freedom of movement. The two pieces are more trouble to keep up with, but I like the fact that I can more easily put these suits on all by myself like a big boy.

Scuba Lab tests wet suits and offers information on neoprene quality and construction plus the opinions of testers. To access this information, go to www.scubadiving.com/gear and click on the exposure suit icon.

Regardless of the type of wet suit you buy, here are some things to look for:

- A quality of neoprene that resists compression.
- A snug fit that touches as much of your skin as possible with reasonable comfort and freedom of movement.
- A realization that the first two qualities are countervailing and will require a compromise.
- A reasonably tight fit around the neck, wrists, and any other place where water can enter. Pay close attention to zippers to make sure that a minimum of water entry is allowed.
- A suit that has been favorably reviewed by Scuba Lab with a price tag that you can afford.

Likewise, now that you understand wet suits, here are some things that should raise suspicions about their ability to keep you warm in the water:

- "One size fits all" or few size selections. If a suit is stretchy enough for this, the neoprene is of poor quality and will not be effective for insulation against cold.
- Things that work in air but not in water. This includes fuzzy linings and reflective linings that are claimed to reflect body heat back toward the diver. This doesn't happen in water. Fuzzy linings might work a little bit to inhibit water flow inside the suit, but they lose all insulating capabilities when wet. Many divers find them comfortable to wear in warm water, and they work well when used as a dry-suit undergarment. A reflective lining will not hurt a suit's warming capability, and the smoothness of this lining may cause the suit to fit better against the skin, but the lining will not really reflect heat back through the water to your skin. Some high-quality suits incorporate this feature, and the feature should not disqualify a suit if its other characteristics are good.
- Claims that a suit will keep you warm without affecting buoyancy. Remember, it's the air (or gas) in the suit that provides the insulation, and air floats. Ergo, warmth floats.

Hoods and Vests

If you need a wet suit for cold water, you will also need protection for your head. Since the head receives such a copious blood supply, the heat loss potential is great, although not as enormous as once believed. A neoprene hood is the most common type of head protection against cold.

Neoprene hoods come in three basic types: beanie hoods, bibbed hoods, and hoods that are incorporated into vests.

Beanie hoods keep the head warmer in the same way that wet suits keep the body warmer. The air-filled neoprene inhibits conduction and the tight fit inhibits convection around the head. These hoods do not cover the neck.

Bibbed hoods are the more traditional type. The hood is connected to a bib that covers the neck and throat. These hoods not only work to keep the head warmer in the same ways that beanie hoods work, but they also inhibit convection in the wet suit by inhibiting the flow of water into the neck seal. Many divers wear the bib inside the wet-suit neck seal—a strategy that looks good but usually backfires. When the bib is worn inside, the neck seal cannot work as it was designed and more water actually enters the suit. However, if the bib is worn outside the wet suit, it will work to shed water away from the neck seal.

Hooded vests carry the bib idea to its natural extreme. The hood is attached to a vest that covers the torso. This arrangement layers more neoprene over the diver's torso and inhibits water flow into the wet suit. Most of these vests seem to have been designed to be worn inside the suit, but a diver might achieve a better watershed around the neck seal by wearing the hooded vest outside the wet suit.

Dry Suits

Dry suits offer the ultimate protection against cold because they eliminate water inside the suit altogether. Since no water is directly against the diver's skin, heat loss by conduction is greatly reduced. Also, since no water can enter the suit, heat loss by convection is eliminated completely. However, divers who take advantage of this ultimate protection must pay a price in terms of both money and convenience. In fact, it is usually necessary for a diver to modify other gear in order to use a dry suit.

Most dry suits either incorporate boots built into the suit or are designed to be worn with sturdy boots. Divers who use these suits must also use fins with foot pockets large enough to accommodate the boots.

All dry suits must be somewhat inflated with air to counteract uncomfortable compression at depth. This is accomplished via a low-pressure inflator that is attached to a low-pressure port on the regulator—just like the inflation mechanism on the buoyancy compensator. Divers who use dry suits must have an extra LP port on their regulator or must find a way to share an LP port in order to inflate their suits.

Dry suits are more buoyant than wet suits, so a diver must wear more weight to counteract the extra buoyancy. It is not unusual for a diver to carry more than twice the weight when diving with a dry suit as he or she would carry when diving in a dive skin, and the extra weight on a weight belt can be very hard on the diver's back. Divers who often dive in a dry suit should consider using a weight-integrated BC to better distribute the extra weight. Some manufacturers offer shoulder harnesses to more comfortably carry weights. Also, since the diver wears more weight, the BC should have sufficient lift capacity to deal with the extra weight.

Diving in a dry suit feels weird at first. The air bubble inside the suit moves around depending upon your posture in the water. If you position yourself upright in the water, the bubble will move toward your chest and your feet and legs will be squeezed. If you position yourself head down in the water, the bubble will move to your feet above your head and make it tricky for you to right yourself again. Should you inadvertently ascend a bit while your feet are above your head, the bubble of air near your feet will expand, you will begin to ascend at an increasing rate, and it will become more difficult to right yourself. Rapid feetfirst ascents are a danger of dry-suit diving.

A dry suit will broaden your dive opportunities perhaps more than any other piece of gear. However, dry suits are task-loading devices that require training and practice to use safely. This diver is practicing with her dry suit in the controlled environment of a freshwater spring.

Dry suits are more than exposure protection. The air inside the suit will affect buoyancy, and the air will contract and expand as you move about in the water column. You should minimize the amount of air inside the suit to prevent uncomfortable pinching and squeezing (dry suits should not be used as buoyancy compensators), but you must manage the air when ascending to avoid rapid ascents. I recommend that you acquire specific training in the use of dry suits before you make any serious dives in one, as a dry suit is a task-loading device.

That said, no piece of equipment can expand your dive season more than a dry suit can, and many fascinating cold-water sites cannot be explored without one. Here's the skinny on them:

Dry suits come in three general styles—foam neoprene suits, shells, and crushed neoprene suits.

Foam neoprene dry suits are made out of the same stuff as wet suits and provide the same insulation against conduction. They are also subject to the same compression and subsequent loss of insulation at depth. Foam neoprene dry suits are very buoyant and must be used with a substantial amount of dive weights. However, this inherent buoyancy may become an advantage should the suit flood with water. Foam neoprene suits are subject to cuts and abrasions, and they are typically at the lower end of the cost scale of dry suits. Because of their inherent insulation, they may be used without insulating undergarments. Foam neoprene stretches, so the dry suit may be somewhat form-fitted to the user. However, the material is thick and bulky and may restrict movement.

Shell-style dry suits are thin, waterproof coverings. They are usually made of vulcanized rubber or of a sandwich of butyl rubber between layers of nylon—a material commonly known as trilaminate. Shells have no inherent insulation, so all insulation against conductive heat loss must come from warm undergarments worn beneath them. The materials used for shells do not stretch, and the resulting suits are somewhat baggy, which creates drag in the water. However, since the warmth of the suit depends upon the undergarments worn beneath, these suits can be comfortable in water temperatures ranging from 75°F to the freezing point of water, depending on the undergarments used. Shells are tough, dry quickly, and are easy to pack for traveling.

Crushed neoprene suits, sometimes called small-cell neoprene suits, combine the advantages of foam neoprene and shells. Crushed neoprene is tough, provides some inherent insulation, and stretches to some degree. Although insulating undergarments are usually worn beneath them, these suits are more form-fitting than shell suits. Crushed neoprene suits dry quickly and pack easily for traveling.

Beyond these general distinctions, dry suits also vary in the types of seals, valves, and zippers used, as well as in zipper placement. Seals are typically made of latex, but some suits use neoprene seals. Neoprene seals are more durable but are harder to replace. Latex seals are easy to replace but are subject to tears and deterioration. It should be noted that no seal is perfect and a small amount of water can be expected to enter a dry suit. Wrist seals are the most prone to leakage.

One of the most common complaints of divers using dry suits is the comfort of the neck seal. The seal must be tight enough to keep water out, but it should not choke or restrict breathing. Seals are custom-cut to fit the wearer's neck. Personally speaking, neck seals are the most uncomfortable when the suit is first donned. The seal becomes more comfortable after the suit has been on for a while, and it is not noticeable once the dive begins. However, a neck seal that is too tight may be more than uncomfortable. The seal might trick your body into decreasing your heart rate and may cause dizziness or fainting. Here's what happens:

The major blood vessels that carry blood from your heart to your brain are called your carotid arteries, and they go up each side of your neck. The arteries fork before they reach your head, and there are small bulges at these junctions. These bulges are called your carotid sinuses, and they contain receptors that sense changes in your blood pressure. If these sensors sense that your blood pressure is too high, they will cause your heart to slow down to reduce the pressure. This phenomenon is called the carotid sinus reflex.

A tight neck seal that presses against your carotid sinus may trigger this reflex by restricting blood flow and causing higher blood pressure at the restriction. The reflex causes your heart to slow down and results in an insufficient blood supply to your brain. A neck seal that causes dizziness or light-headedness can result in unconsciousness, and unconsciousness underwater often means death by drowning. You'll learn more about this in your formal dry-suit instruction, but it's too important to completely omit here.

The air intake valve is typically placed near the center of the chest, and the outlet valve is usually positioned on the upper left arm. However, these placements may vary. Some suits feature an adjustable outlet valve to enable a diver to regulate how fast air can escape the suit. Some feature a small orifice in the air intake valve as a precaution against valve malfunctions that might overinflate the suit.

All dry-suit zippers are, of course, waterproof. The integrity of the zipper seal, as with all dry-suit seals, must be carefully maintained. Zipper placements vary to allow easier donning of the suit, but getting into most dry suits will require assistance from another person.

So a dry suit is an expensive, bulky, high-maintenance piece of dive gear that requires specialty training to use. However, as with most new things, diving in one becomes second nature with practice and experience, and a dry suit will enable you to go where few go and to see what few see. After all, isn't that what got you interested in diving in the first place?

TANKS ($125–$160)

Scuba tanks are usually the last piece of dive gear bought by independent divers. This is due to the simple fact that tanks are often available on charter dive boats as part of the dive package, and tanks can usually be rented from the local dive shop whenever they are not provided by the boat or dive operator.

On the other hand, divers who own their own tanks enjoy the ultimate in independence, as they can pack up and go at any time without reliance on anybody for equipment. It is also important for independent divers to understand something about scuba tanks in order to protect themselves against obsolete or poorly maintained rental gear.

Air Capacity

Air is good; more air is better. However, more air requires a larger and heavier tank, and there is certainly a point at which excess air becomes an unnecessary burden. Nitrogen loading is often the limiting factor on the time and depth of dives regardless of the air supply.

STEEL vs. ALUMINUM

Scuba tanks are made from either steel or aluminum. Steel tanks were the norm when I began diving in the early 1970s, and they still have a staunch following.

Steel tanks have less inherent buoyancy than aluminum tanks, which means that divers using steel tanks can dive with less weight on their belts. The weight-belt reduction is usually around 3 pounds, but for larger tanks the weight reduction is greater. Steel tanks are also more compact than their aluminum counterparts.

The pressure capacity (working pressure) of steel tanks is somewhat less than for aluminum tanks. Most steel tanks are filled to a pressure of around 2,400 psi, whereas most aluminum tanks are filled to 3,000 psi.

Both steel and aluminum tanks are subject to oxidation if water gets inside them. However, oxidation in steel tanks results in rust, which is somewhat more serious than the oxidation in aluminum tanks.

The reason that aluminum tanks have become far more common than steel tanks among recreational divers is the cost of steel tanks. Figure to pay about twice the money for a steel tank as you'd pay for a comparable aluminum tank.

The capacity of a scuba tank is described by the number of cubic feet of gas at 1 atmosphere that can be compressed into the tank at the tank's working pressure. This capacity is combined with the material from which the tank is made to describe the tank. For example, a steel-72 is a tank made of steel that can contain a maximum of approximately 72 cubic feet of gas compressed inside.

Tanks come in a wide variety of capacities, but the most common are tanks that hold between 63 and 120 cubic feet of gas.

The Aluminum-80

There seems to be some mysterious force that causes one option out of many to become the accepted standard. VHS won out over Betamax in the early days of videotapes; Windows became more common than Macintosh in personal computers. It's not that one is clearly superior to the other, but once one option gains an edge, it becomes more practical to choose that option in order to be compatible with everybody else.

The tank that has become the clear standard among recreational divers is the aluminum-80—a tank made from aluminum that has a maximum capacity of approximately 80 cubic feet of gas.

The aluminum-80 is as good a choice as any. It's an inexpensive tank that holds a substantial amount of air, and it is a manageable size for most divers. Smaller divers

Aluminum-80 tanks are staged prior to loading them onto a boat. The aluminum-80 has emerged as the standard scuba tank, and most commercial dive boats are configured to carry them.

may be more comfortable with an aluminum-63; larger divers who use lots of air may find a larger-capacity tank more convenient. However, if you plan to rent tanks or use tanks provided by dive operators, expect to be using an aluminum-80.

Since the aluminum-80 has become the standard tank, most tank accessories such as tank carriers and tank retainers on boats have been configured to the size and shape of the aluminum-80. Divers who decide to buy and use larger tanks may be discouraged from bringing them aboard some charter boats, as the boats may not have any convenient means to stow or retain the larger tanks. Likewise, steel tanks usually have a larger diameter than aluminum tanks, and boats may not be able to accommodate their girth. However, divers who bring their own smaller tanks can usually be accommodated, and many charters and operators carry a few aluminum-63s for their smaller guests.

Most aluminum-80 tanks are manufactured either by Catalina or Luxfer, and some nitpickers will argue that one is better than the other. There is no practical difference between the two. However, aluminum-80s that were manufactured by Luxfer before 1988, which used a particular aluminum alloy, have been implicated in more than their statistical share of tank failures and have been recalled by Luxfer.

Tank Valves

The standard valve on tanks is the so-called K valve. Don't bend your mind trying to make the valve look like the letter *K*—the letter was a designation from a valve catalog of many years ago.

The same catalog offered another valve under the designation *J*, which was a valve that provided a lever to access a "reserve" of air in a scuba tank. This reserve was not actually extra air in the tank. The valve simply stopped delivering air once the pressure of the tank was reduced to about 300 to 500 psi, and the remaining air could be accessed only by pulling the lever to allow the remaining air to flow. So-called J valves are obsolete and are not used on tanks today.

Standard K valves have a few important safety features. They have a snorkel device designed to lower the air intake of the valve. This is done to prevent any water or debris inside the tank from clogging the valve. Of course, there should never be any water or debris inside the tank.

The most important safety device on a tank valve is the burst disk, a weak spot built into the valve that is designed to fail if pressure inside the tank gets too high due to overfilling or heat. A blown burst disk is a noisy, chaotic affair and will render a tank unusable until repaired. On the other hand, an exploding scuba tank may render anyone standing close by not only unusable but also irreparable.

There is a relative newcomer to tank valves in the United States that is gaining favor. As divers look for more air in smaller tanks, tanks with greater working pressures are becoming more popular. Instead of the K valve and regulator yoke that is most familiar to American divers, the increased tank pressure calls for the use of a DIN valve. DIN valves offer a more secure connection between the tank and the regulator, as the regulator is threaded onto the valve rather than simply yoked on. DIN valves have been the valves of choice in Europe for many years, and it is yet to be seen if they will supplant the yoked K valve in the United States. American regulators must be modified with an adaptor before DIN valves can be used. The fact that many American regulator manufacturers now offer DIN adaptors with their regulators may be a harbinger of things to come.

Hydrostatic Testing and VIP

Hydrostatic testing and VIP testing are maintenance requirements for tanks. I'm mentioning them here as well as in the maintenance chapter (chapter 3) because it's important for divers renting tanks to understand the maintenance procedures and to check to see that the procedures have been performed for any tank they use.

Hydrostatic testing, commonly known as a hydro, is a procedure that actually puts the physical integrity of a tank to the test. The tank is filled with water and placed into a container that is also filled with water. The water inside the tank is then pressurized to five-thirds of the tank's working pressure, and the expansion of the tank is measured by how much additional water it displaces in the water-filled container. Assuming the tank does not burst due to the pressure inside, the pressure is gradually reduced. The tank must then return to within 10 percent of its original volume. If the tank is permanently expanded by more than 10 percent, it must be discarded. In the United States, hydrostatic tests are required every five years throughout a tank's life, and the test dates are stamped onto the tank's shoulder (the area below the valve).

Both aluminum and steel tanks are put to the same test. Some testers will renew the 10 percent overfill allowance for steel tanks and will signify this with a plus sign next to the hydro date.

VIP tests are visual inspections by qualified personnel. The tank valve is removed, and the interior of the tank is scrutinized for faults or oxidation. The neck of the tank is also carefully examined. If the tank passes this visual inspection, a dated VIP sticker is affixed to the outside of the tank. VIP tests must be performed annually throughout the life of a tank.

Scuba tanks are most dangerous to the people who fill them. However, a tank that has not been properly maintained and doesn't have a current hydro stamp and a current VIP sticker can also pose a danger to the user. An out-of-date hydro stamp may indicate a tank prone to explode, and a scuba tank explosion is a catastrophic event that will not only affect you but will probably also bring bad news to your next of kin. A tank that does not contain a current VIP sticker may be corroding inside. Corrosion and oxidation impair the tank's ability to deliver air through the valve and may also adversely affect the quality of the air inside the tank—the air that you will be breathing. It's always a good idea to make a simple check whenever using a rented tank.

Tank Markings

All scuba tanks have information stamped onto them. The information appears in two rows of markings on the tank's shoulder and includes the tank's manufacturer (Catalina or Luxfer in most cases), the regulatory agency (usually the Department of Transportation, or DOT), and the material from which the tank was made (3AA steel or 3AL aluminum). The most important markings are the tank's working pressure and the hydro date, which appear in the second line of information. Obviously, the tank's working pressure must be compatible with the regulator you are using (most regulators are rated to a working pressure of at least 3,000 psi) and the hydro date should be current. If the tank is more than five years older than the stamp on the second row, look around the shoulder of the tank for a current hydrostatic test date. VIP stickers may be placed anywhere on the tank, and an older tank will have several stickers. Look for a current one.

WEIGHTS AND WEIGHT BELTS ($10–$75)

We're not talking about rocket science here, but there are some differences in the types of weights divers carry and there are significant differences in the ways divers carry them.

Nylon-Web Belts

The nylon-web weight belt is the traditional belt onto which traditional molded lead weights are threaded. They're cheap and they work. However, they are not very comfortable unless they're worn over a thick exposure suit, and wearing them over a neoprene suit can actually damage the suit.

Some of the discomfort of wearing a nylon-web belt can be mitigated by using

EUROPEAN MARKINGS

1. gas type
2. owner
3. scuba equipment
4. service pressure
5. EWG design permit
6. country of manufacture
7. manufacturer symbol
8. serial number
9. standard
10. test pressure
11. EWG trademark
12. repeat test
13. empty weight
14. minimum volume
15. galvanized

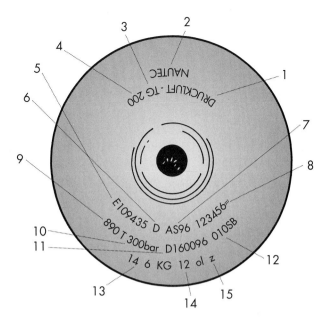

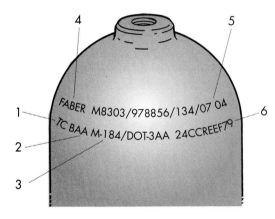

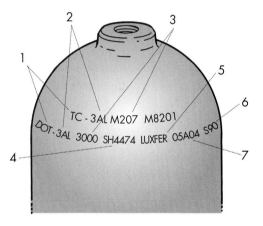

U.S. MARKINGS
Steel Cylinder (3AA=Steel)

1. regulatory agency
2. type
3. working pressure (bar)
4. manufacturer
5. test date
6. serial number

U.S. MARKINGS
Aluminum Cylinder (3AL=Aluminum)

1. regulatory agency
2. type
3. working pressure
4. serial number
5. manufacturer
6. size
7. test date

Scuba cylinder markings. JIM SOLLERS BASED ON AN ILLUSTRATION FROM NAUI MASTER SCUBA DIVER

weights with rounded shapes that are sheathed in rubber. That's not to say that wearing these types of weights on a nylon-web belt is really comfortable on the hips after you've made repetitive dives over several days in a thin suit. It's more like saying that being hit on the hips with a rubber mallet is more comfortable than being hit with a ball-peen hammer.

However, the discomfort of wearing a nylon-web belt pales in comparison to the discomfort of picking up the belt and having a molded weight slip off and land on your foot. A way to avoid this is to use a technique called a lock thread on the last weight before the end of the belt. To do this, thread the belt through the first slot of the weight, then twist the belt one half-turn before threading it back through the second slot of the weight. This "lock thread" will inhibit the movement of the last weight and make it less likely to slip off.

The lock-thread technique will also shorten the belt. Divers not blessed with an abundant girth may lock-thread all their weights onto a belt in order to avoid having a great length of the belt dangling after it has been tightened around the waist and buckled. It should be noted that lock threads have a tendency to work themselves out after a few days of diving, which may leave some weights on the belt inside out. Of course, the weights must be removed and rethreaded when this happens.

You may have surmised by now that my cheapness does not extend to nylon-web weight belts, although I do carry one as a spare.

Neoprene Pocket Belts

The neoprene pocket belt is a tremendous improvement over the nylon-web belt. The belt contains several pockets that hold any type of weight put into them, and the weights are firmly secured by a top flap with a Velcro lining that runs the full length of the belt. Neoprene belts are comfortable even when loaded with hard molded weights, and loading them is a cinch. Because the length of the belt is not really affected by the number of weights used, you can trim the dangling end for a custom fit.

You can increase the comfort of a neoprene belt by using soft weight bags that contain lead shot. My experience has been that this is not necessary as a matter of comfort and that the lead shot has a way of finding its way out of these types of weights. However, soft weights in a neoprene pocket weight belt are the ultimate in comfort.

Neoprene pocket belts usually come complete with little D rings on them, which allow divers to carry more stuff. Remember, however, that anything you clip onto a weight belt will be lost in the event that you ditch the weight belt.

The neoprene pocket weight belt is my personal choice, and I use mine with traditional molded lead weights. These weights tend to fray the belt from the inside out, but a neoprene belt loaded with hard weights meets my needs of cheapness and practicality and will last for a number of years.

Ankle and Tank Weights

It is sometimes best to distribute some nonditchable weight on the ankles or on the tank. This can be done by using specially designed weight belts.

Tank weights are attached to the scuba tank and are a good way to take some of the strain off the lower back. They provide the buoyancy benefits of a steel tank with the economy of actually using an aluminum tank.

Ankle weights also take weight off the lower back. Divers wearing heavy, buoyant wet suits may find this helpful in keeping their legs from floating above their head. Ankle weights are also a good hedge against rapid, feetfirst ascents when wearing dry suits; they make it easier for upended divers to get their feet back beneath them.

Dive Bags ($50–$300)

After accumulating some or all of the equipment we've discussed, a diver needs a bag to carry it.

Your main dive bag should be large enough to comfortably contain all of your equipment and spares. Many bags have caster rollers to help you move them more easily. However, while the casters are convenient for rolling a bag through an airport, they add weight to the bag itself and don't work very well in gravel parking lots or over wood-slat piers, which are common wherever dive boats are moored.

Dive bags should contain shoulder straps so that they can be worn like backpacks for short distances over any terrain.

Some dive bags are large enough to carry the gear of more than one diver, and some couples opt for them. I find such bags to be too unwieldy to be of much use to either diver. It's better for each diver to have his or her own manageable bag.

Regardless of the type of bag it is, a main dive bag has no place on the deck of a dive boat. This may seem to defeat the purpose of the bag, but main dive bags take up too much valuable deck space, and anything on the deck of a dive boat will be soaked. Divers should use a smaller mesh bag to contain their essential gear on deck. Many of these mesh bags conveniently fold into a self-contained pack that can be neatly stowed inside the main dive bag until it is needed. If a main dive bag is taken aboard a boat, it should be stowed out of the way belowdecks, where it will remain dry.

In addition to being able to withstand repetitive soakings on dive decks, mesh bags can be used to dip dive gear in freshwater tanks after the diving is done. The gear remains contained so that it is less likely to be lost or left behind, and the gear can also dry somewhat while in the mesh bag.

Divers traveling to dive sites by car typically carry a waterproof plastic bin large enough to contain the wet-gear-filled mesh bag, so you can get wet equipment home without soaking the car's interior.

CHAPTER 3

GEAR MAINTENANCE

Your investment in dive gear mandates that you take good care of it. If you want to get a better understanding of how your equipment is made and how to best maintain it, you might consider taking a gear maintenance specialty course from your local dive shop. This handbook is a poor substitute for formal training, but we'll talk about some general things that will help keep your gear in proper working condition.

Before we start, let me make the point that your dive gear was designed and made to withstand diving and that it won't melt if it gets wet. Many active dive situations such as live-aboard diving require gear to be used constantly without the benefit of freshwater rinsing for a week or more. This is harder on equipment than a casual dive followed by immediate gear washing and maintenance, but your dive gear was made to be used. The colors may fade, material edges may fray, but high-quality dive gear is hardy enough to perform the functions for which it was designed for many years. In fact, it's not uncommon to hear veteran divers (OK, maybe it's just me) complain that they'd upgrade their gear if only they could get the stuff they already have to wear out.

That said, here are some ways to keep your gear performing at maximum efficiency for the long run.

Mask

A good mask is like a comfortable pair of shoes. But, like a good pair of shoes, masks need some "breaking in" before they perform at their best.

Initial Fogging

Fogging is the first problem you'll have with a new mask. Contrary to popular belief, the primary cause of mask fogging is not condensation inside the mask but rather water vapor inside the mask clinging to dirt or imperfections on the inside of the mask lens.

Modern silicone masks receive a coating during their manufacture that is designed to facilitate removing the mask from the mold. This coating remains on the lens after the manufacturing process, and the silicone skirt of the mask continues to secrete stuff onto the mask lens for the life of the mask. This coating is rough enough to hold tiny water vapor droplets and cause fogging. The coating and secreting process is at its worst when the mask is brand-new, which is the reason that new masks have a tendency to fog far more easily than older masks. No amount of defogger seems to work well on new silicone masks.

It is important to clean the lens of a new mask before using the mask for diving. The easiest way to do this is to finger-scrub the lens with a liberal glob of toothpaste. Toothpastes with mildly abrasive "whiteners" work best. Several scrubbings may be necessary before the fogging problem is brought under control.

If toothpaste doesn't do the trick, use a more abrasive cleaner like Soft Scrub to clean the lens. Don't use anything more abrasive than that, as scratches on the lens will compound the problem and may permanently ruin the mask. If you use a product like Soft Scrub, it's not a bad idea to follow that cleaning with a toothpaste scrubbing for a fresher smell.

Mask Box

So now that you've given your new mask a scrubbing with toothpaste and you're carrying shampoo to defog it before your dives (see sidebar, opposite), all that remains is for you to protect your mask from physical damage. Many divers carry their masks in a special mask box. Mask boxes are designed to provide physical protection for your mask while it's in your dive bag, and they may also keep the mask relatively clean to mitigate the fogging problem.

I have found mask boxes to be more of a nuisance than a benefit. They take up valuable room in the dive bag, and they seem to actually collect filth. I generally carry several masks in different compartments in my bag, and I just stuff them in among other soft gear such as booties or gloves. In more than thirty years of traveling, with my bag bouncing on boats, being thrown by airport luggage handlers, and being squashed at the bottom of airplane baggage bays, I have never had a mask break. Not once. Nor have I ever had a mask go out of shape due to being squashed. Masks are tough and don't really need a cumbersome box.

Postdive maintenance of a mask is a simple dip into fresh water and thorough drying to prevent mildew. If mildew develops, toothpaste will usually remove it.

Popular dive lore suggests that some crabs on tropical islands eat silicone. I've never experienced this myself, but it doesn't hurt to keep your mask and other gear in a locker or on a table off the ground between dives.

REGULATOR

Annual Professional Servicing

Proper maintenance of your regulator is more than a matter of preserving your investment; it could be a matter of life or death. All regulators must receive professional

HOME-BREW DEFOGGER

Once the silicone residue has been scrubbed from a mask, the lens must be cleaned before diving to prevent fogging. In the old days of rubber masks, the accepted procedure for cleaning a mask lens was a spit-shine with saliva. However, because modern masks continue to secrete silicone throughout their lives, most silicone masks will require a better cleaning than spit can provide. A wide variety of commercial mask-defogging agents is available.

Since the main cause of mask fogging is water vapor clinging to dirt on the lens, the object is to make the mask lens as smooth as possible so that water sheets instead of clings in droplets. Some defogging agents not only clean the lens but are also thick enough to coat the lens to fill any tiny imperfections to which water can cling. Commercial defogging agents work, but you can expect to pay several bucks for a tiny bottle from a dive shop.

Fortunately, you probably already have a perfectly serviceable mask-defogging agent in your home. It is readily available at your grocery store, drugstore, or convenience store, and you can get a great big bottle of it for the same price you'd pay for the tiny bottle of commercial defogger from the dive shop. It is a cleaner that was made to be easy on your eyes. It's shampoo. If you'd rather not carry a big bottle in your dive bag, you can buy a small plastic dispensing bottle from a drugstore or refill a commercial defogger bottle with the shampoo. Some divers dilute the shampoo with water and dispense it from a spray bottle. Baby shampoo is easiest on the eyes and is the choice of many experienced divers.

maintenance at least annually. This applies to a regulator that has had five dives during the year as well as to one that has had one hundred dives. In fact, even if you have not dived with your regulator for a year, you should have it professionally inspected before using it. Many regulators carry a lifetime warranty only if a regimen of annual authorized professional servicing is maintained.

Professional regulator servicing includes the replacement of all wearable parts. Replacement parts are provided by the manufacturer in the form of service part kits, and only authorized dealers or authorized service technicians can receive the kits from the manufacturers. Aside from warranty implications, it is therefore imperative that your regulator be serviced by a technician authorized to service your particular brand of regulator. It doesn't matter if you are a mechanical genius or if you fully understand the regulator and how it should be serviced. If you can't get the parts, you can't do the service.

Annual professional regulator maintenance involves more than changing parts. The regulator is tested to make sure that the intermediate pressure maintained by the first stage is within the manufacturer's specifications. The intermediate pressure can be adjusted by the use of shims in the first-stage valve of piston regulators or by a screw adjustment in diaphragm regulators. Most manufacturers will allow up to three shims to be used before a piston regulator is declared to be kaput and suitable for upgrading.

User Maintenance

One of the most important pieces of a regulator from a user maintenance perspective is the dust cap. The dust cap prevents water or dirt from entering the intake cone, where it can be blown into the valve by the high pressure of the scuba tank. Always keep the regulator covered by the dust cap whenever the regulator is not attached either to a tank or to a hanging device that contains a dust cap substitute. Dust caps should be replaced immediately after the regulator is removed from a tank—even if it's just for a few minutes while changing tanks.

You may have noticed some divers apparently blowing water from their regulators with noisy blasts of air from their scuba tanks after a dive. These divers are drying the dust cap and are not blasting air into the regulator. Never blast air into the uncovered intake cone of the regulator, as this will only force water inside.

Regulators should be soaked in fresh water after use in the ocean. Make sure that the dust cap is in place and that the purge button of the second stage is not pressed while the regulator is underwater or being rinsed. Pressing the purge button of a regulator will allow water to enter through the second stage unless the regulator is attached to a tank and the air is turned on.

Hoses

Regulator hoses should last a long time and are not replaced during routine servicing unless there is visible damage. Hoses usually wear out at the ends where they are attached to the first stage of the regulator. Be careful not to crimp the hose when storing the regulator or putting it into a dive bag, as such crimping will damage the hose.

Most divers use hose protectors to ward against crimping. A hose protector is nothing more than a somewhat rigid sleeve that covers the hose at the connection to the first stage, and its sole purpose is to keep the hose from bending too much at the connection. Hose protectors may trap salt water beneath them, so it's important to slide them down the hose when soaking the regulator to wash the salt water away. I often see hose protectors situated on hoses in a way that does not cover the connection to the first stage. These hose protectors do no harm, but they can't inhibit crimping unless they cover the connection.

I have damaged hoses to my regulator more than once by doing the same stupid thing. Here's what happens:

Most dive boats have aluminum benches for seats, and the tank rack is behind the bench. The tank rack consists of a recessed platform upon which the bottoms of the tanks rest, and the tanks are held upright in place by plastic fingers that wrap around the belly of the tank. Tanks are carried on the boat with regulators and BCs attached.

A natural way to replace a tank in the rack after a dive is to hold the tank somewhat horizontally and put the bottom of the tank on the platform. Once the bottom is resting on the platform, the top of the tank can be raised and pushed to clip the tank into the plastic fingers. This is an easy way to lever a tank back into the rack. However, when the bottom of the tank is put onto the platform, it's easy to lose track of how the hoses are hanging, and the hose to the second stage is usually hanging near the edge of the aluminum bench. If the mouthpiece hangs below the bench, it may hook the bench edge. The hooked hose can be damaged or torn loose from the connection to the first stage when the tank is shoved back into the plastic fingers. Always keep track of where your hoses are when carrying a tank with the regulator attached, and be especially careful of your hoses when putting a tank into an upright tank rack.

Damaged hoses must be replaced before a regulator is used.

In-Leaks

A regulator is said to have an in-leak whenever water is allowed to leak inside. Divers become aware of in-leaks when the regulator breathes "wet," which means that the diver receives not only air but also some water when breathing through the regulator underwater.

Any but the most expensive and well-made regulators will breathe wet in some dive conditions. A regulator that breathes a bit wet when the diver is hanging upside down in the water is fairly common and should not be cause for alarm.

In-leaks may emanate from the first stage due to the failure of an O-ring in a piston regulator or to a perforated diaphragm in a diaphragm regulator. These types of in-leaks require immediate attention from an authorized repair technician.

However, most in-leaks occur in the regulator's second stage, either in the mouthpiece, the air exhaust valve, or the second-stage diaphragm. The mouthpiece is the most common culprit, and it's the easiest to fix. If the mouthpiece is loose, try to seat it better by twisting it. If that doesn't do the trick, you can easily replace a mouthpiece on-site by simply cutting the plastic tie with diagonal wire cutters or toenail clippers, removing the old mouthpiece, and replacing it with a new one by means of a fresh plastic tie.

It's also common for the air exhaust valve to be held open by a bit of debris or a grain of sand. Water can enter if the valve is stuck open. Try to clear the valve by tapping the second stage on the palm of your hand and purging. Sand is the most common culprit for exhaust valve in-leaks, and divers should be careful to keep their second stages out of the sand between beach dives.

A hole in the second-stage diaphragm will also cause an in-leak. This can't be checked unless the second stage is opened and inspected. Many second stages simply screw together and are easy to disassemble. However, some second stages have locking devices, and no second stage should be disassembled by anyone who is not absolutely sure of what they're doing.

Regulators can be easily checked for second-stage in-leaks without their being attached to a tank. Simply put the second stage into your mouth and suck for air. If the regulator does not allow any air at all, it does not have an in-leak. If a tiny quantity of air can be sucked through the second stage, it is possible that it will breathe wet underwater. If a greater quantity of air can be sucked through, the second stage has an in-leak and should be repaired before diving.

Out-Leaks

A regulator is said to have an out-leak whenever air is allowed to leak from it. Divers become aware of out-leaks when they observe bubbles emanating from the first stage of the regulator underwater.

Out-leaks are usually caused by imperfectly sealed O-rings or valve seats in the first stage. A symptom of very small bubbles trickling from the first stage is not uncommon and is no reason to abort a dive trip.

The first order of business after detecting such a stream of bubbles is to determine the source. Bubbles may emanate from an imperfect seal between the tank and the regulator. Also, one respected regulator manufacturer (Sherwood) designs some of its first stages to be pressurized with air as a means to keep water from entering, and the pressurized air is allowed to escape by design. As such, these regulators have built-in out-leaks.

On the other hand, if your regulator is not designed to produce bubbles from the first stage and if it shows signs of an out-leak on a variety of tanks, it's time to have it serviced as soon as you return home. Of course, an out-leak serious enough to be heard in air or to cause bubbles to boil from the regulator underwater indicates a serious problem, and the regulator should not be used until serviced.

Packing and Storage

The main concern when packing a regulator is avoiding hose damage due to crimping. Many divers use a special regulator bag that holds a neatly coiled regulator and keeps the hoses from becoming entangled with other equipment. A regulator bag is a good way to carry a regulator in a dive bag, but the hoses will usually be coiled too tightly for long-term storage.

Several manufacturers make hangers designed to hold regulators, BCs, and other dive equipment. The regulator is yoked onto a fitting on the hanger in the same way that it would be attached to a scuba tank, and the hanger takes the place of the dust cap. These hangers are a secure way to hang a regulator in a closet, and hose protectors prevent hose crimping as the regulator hangs. Be sure to hang the regulator indoors instead of in a garage, as car exhaust is harmful to many of the materials used in your regulator.

A regulator in a regulator bag and packed within a dive bag should not have any problem surviving a trip in airplane baggage. However, peripheral equipment such as computers and submersible pressure gauges that is typically attached to regulators is more sensitive to the physical shocks and pressure changes to which airplane baggage may be subjected.

Most traveling divers carry their regulators in carry-on luggage to prevent damage or loss of use in case of lost luggage. X-rays will not damage your regulator or your computer, but you can expect a regulator in a carry-on bag to raise suspicions at each and every X-ray checkpoint. Airport security questions regarding a regulator in a carry-on bag are usually easily satisfied, and I always carry my regulator in a carry-on bag when traveling by air.

SUBMERSIBLE PRESSURE GAUGE

SPGs are hardy devices, but they are relatively sensitive to shock and abuse compared with other dive gear. Since the SPG is attached to a hose, it's easy to lose track of where it is. Be careful to protect your SPG by tucking it into your BC whenever your regulator is attached to a tank, as an SPG that is allowed to hang loosely is subject to being stepped on. Also, make sure the SPG is not hanging on the tank platform when your rig is sitting in a tank rack. Another tank placed in the rack on top of your SPG will almost certainly damage the gauge. Likewise, it is possible to put your own tank onto your SPG if the gauge happens to hang into the tank rack as you are replacing your tank in the rack.

Bursting

As we discussed in the previous chapter, the SPG is attached to a high-pressure hose. The high-pressure air is designed to fill the Bourdon tube inside the SPG, but if the tube is damaged by shock or abuse, the high-pressure air will leak into the casing. The casing will burst if this occurs. Some casings are equipped with a burst disk that is designed to pop out of the casing to allow the air to escape, but a popped burst disk may be as dangerous as a casing that randomly bursts.

Try to protect your SPG from shock. The best way to do this is to make sure that the SPG is snugly clipped to the BC so that it cannot swing and bang into things. Avoid looking at your SPG when opening the tank valve, as this is the time that an SPG will burst if it is damaged.

Casing Damage and Flooding

The casing of your SPG is the component most subject to wear and tear. No matter how diligent you may be in protecting it, the face of your SPG will eventually become scratched. Some divers protect the faces of their gauges by putting them in "jail," that is, covering them with a metal cage. This will help to protect the gauge face from scratches, but the cage itself will make the face harder to see and read.

Shock or abuse to an SPG may do more than scratch the casing. Hairline cracks that are impossible to see may develop in the casing. Divers with cracked SPG casings remain unaware of the problem until water invades the casing and condenses on the inside of the face. Such flooding immediately disqualifies the SPG from further use, and the condition is usually incurable.

A casing leak in an SPG may be so small and subtle that water is never visible inside. However, the leak can be detected when rust begins to form on metal parts inside the casing—usually on the small screws on the face card. Rust inside an SPG indicates a flood and immediately disqualifies the SPG from further use.

Out-Leaks

The point at which an SPG is attached to the high-pressure hose may develop an out-leak. This out-leak will manifest itself in the same way that regulator out-leaks become apparent—a stream of small bubbles will emanate from the connection of the SPG to the hose.

Your SPG is attached to the high-pressure hose by a swivel attachment that contains a fitting called an air spool. The air spool is a small fitting with a tiny orifice that allows high-pressure air to enter the gauge. The integrity of the air spool's connection is maintained by a tiny O-ring on each end of the spool. Virtually all SPG out-leaks are due to the failure of one of these tiny O-rings on the air spool.

A small out-leak from an SPG is no cause for panic. The high-pressure port of a regulator usually contains a very small orifice, and the orifice of the air spool is also very small. Thus, no great quantity of air should be lost by an SPG out-leak. However, the out-leak may affect the pressure of the air entering the gauge and may marginally affect the accuracy of the gauge. SPG out-leaks should be repaired as soon as possible. Replacement of the air spool can be quickly and inexpensively done by a qualified technician.

COMPUTER

Your dive computer is also subject to damage from shock or abuse. Since the computer is often encased in a console that also carries the SPG, measures taken to protect the SPG will also serve to protect the computer. It is important that the console containing these devices be clipped to the BC to avoid swinging and banging and to reduce the risk of the gauges being stepped on or damaged by tanks. Some divers protect the faces of their computers with metal cages to prevent scratching, but these cages also make the face harder to see and to read. Some computer faces are covered with clear plastic shields that take the brunt of the scratching. When the shield is scratched to the point that viewing is inhibited, the shield can simply be removed and replaced with a new one.

Batteries

Virtually all modern dive computers allow the user to change the batteries. This provides divers with the freedom to make sure that their computer batteries are fresh. But, like all freedoms, it places a responsibility on divers to do the work.

Computer batteries should be replaced annually or more often if recommended by the computer manufacturer. To replace the batteries, remove the computer from the console and remove the battery cover. The cover is usually made of soft plastic, so take care to avoid damaging it. Most covers are easily removed with a quarter coin. If the cover is tight, a quarter held by a pair of pliers will work to turn it. Avoid using a screwdriver, as screwdriver heads are usually too small and will damage the cover.

The waterproof integrity of the cover seal is maintained by an O-ring. This O-ring may not be contained in a retaining channel on some computers, and it may be possible for it to fall out and be lost. Remove the O-ring, make sure it is clean and supple, and make sure that any O-ring retaining channel is likewise clean. Do not use silicone grease on the O-ring unless recommended by the manufacturer, as some silicone greases may swell some O-rings. For example, the silicone grease used for Nikonos underwater camera O-rings may swell some O-rings not distributed by Nikon.

Once you have removed the cover and cleaned and replaced the O-ring, you can remove the batteries. Replace the batteries with fresh ones. Take care to avoid cross-threading the cover when you replace it. Screw the cover down finger tight, and you're done. If the computer can be activated, go ahead and activate it to make sure that the battery contacts are good and that the computer is working properly before putting the unit back into its console.

Heat

It is important to protect your computer from the heat of direct sunlight. Overheating will disrupt the computer's liquid crystal display and render it unreadable. If your computer's display becomes black from overheating, let it cool slowly. It is likely that the computer will not perform normally unless it is turned off and turned on again. Sometimes this is only possible by removing the batteries, waiting a minute, and then reinstalling the batteries. All data in the computer may be lost, and if your decompression-status data are lost, your diving for the day may be done. Keep your computer cool and out of direct sunlight to avoid this heavy penalty.

Out-Leaks

If your computer is air-integrated, it will contain the same kind of air spool contained in independent SPGs. As a result, it may develop the same kind of out-leak. These leaks are usually not serious, but the air spool should be replaced as soon as possible after an out-leak is detected.

Flooding

Damage to a computer's face or casing may produce cracks that lead to flooding. The first evidence of flooding is water condensing on the inside of the computer face. Due to the sensitive electronics inside, computer flooding is usually terminal. You can minimize the possibility of the computer case flooding by protecting the unit from shock.

Your computer's battery compartment may flood, which will cause the computer to suddenly cease to function. Unless the bulkhead separating the battery compartment from the rest of the computer is watertight, a battery compartment flood will usually result in a ruined computer. You can minimize the possibility of a battery compartment flood by careful maintenance and treatment of the battery compartment cap and O-ring.

BUOYANCY COMPENSATOR

As mentioned in the previous chapter, buoyancy compensators contain many parts that are subject to wear and failure. However, despite their complexity, my observation has been that most divers habitually neglect to properly maintain their BCs. Routine postdive rinsing or soaking of the outer shell is not enough. In addition to the user maintenance spelled out below, I recommend that your BC be checked out by a professional technician every time you send your regulator in for annual maintenance.

New buoyancy compensators come with maintenance instructions. If those instructions differ from the advice given below, of course, you should follow the manufacturer's instructions.

The Air Cell

It is normal for a small amount of water to enter the BC air cell during a dive. The salt and minerals in ocean water may damage the air cell by abrading or cutting its interior if the salt water is allowed to dry and crystallize inside.

If enough water gets into the air cell to add significant weight to the BC or to affect its function, you can easily dump the water after the dive by inflating the air cell and dumping the air and trapped water through a dump valve. The rear dump valve works best for this, as it is situated low on the BC, where the water will accumulate. It is important to remember, however, that simply dumping seawater from a BC will not prevent salt and mineral damage to the air cell. In fact, seawater will not be a problem for the cell until it evaporates and leaves its salt and mineral residue in the cell.

The only way to prevent salt and mineral damage to the air cell is to flush it with fresh water before the seawater dries inside. To do this, put a hose or faucet at the opening of the oral inflator, press the oral inflation button, and let the water flow inside. Fill the air cell about one-quarter full with water, then inflate the cell with air through the oral inflator. Slosh the water inside the air cell by inverting the BC several times before dumping the air and water from the BC via the oral inflation valve. This is a sloppy job that you should repeat a few times to ensure the removal of all salt water from the air cell.

The Power Inflation Valve

The power inflation valve (Schrader valve) is the part of the BC that usually causes the most trouble. The valve is complex, subject to clogging by sand or debris, and easily corroded by seawater.

Most divers put a short burst of air into their BC before entering the water. This serves the dual purposes of establishing positive buoyancy so that the diver can wait on the surface for a dive buddy, and also of testing the power inflator. A power inflator clogged with sand will sometimes stick in the open position and continue to inflate the BC even after the inflator button is released. This type of clogging is usually easy to remedy on the boat, but it can be a dangerous situation in the water.

Your first reaction to a clogged inflator valve that continues to inflate the BC should be to disconnect the power inflation hose from the valve. Once the hose has been disconnected, work the power inflation button until it is clear of clogging. Reconnect the hose and try the inflator again until it is working smoothly. Obviously, this is an exercise that cannot be done safely underwater.

Be careful to keep your power inflator out of the sand. This means making sure that the inflator does not drag on a sandy bottom during a dive as well as keeping the inflator out of the sand between beach dives.

A more common inflation valve problem is one caused by corrosion that results in a slow leak—a malady known as creeping. A creeping BC will gradually inflate and cause buoyancy problems. This kind of insidious inflation is seldom a danger to an attentive diver, but it is an inconvenient and frustrating problem that will only grow worse with time.

If you notice yourself becoming positively buoyant and if an unexpected amount of air is dumped from your BC when you trim for neutral buoyancy, it is likely that your BC is creeping and is in need of repair. I've seen some divers add as much as 5 pounds of extra lead during a day of diving and remain mystified as to why their buoyancy is so off. For some odd reason, the buoyancy compensator is the last thing many divers suspect when they're having buoyancy problems.

FIT TO DIVE

Divers are generally very good at maintaining their equipment. Most divers can tell you exactly when their regulator was last serviced or when their BC was last overhauled. However, many divers neglect the most important diving tool any diver possesses—their own bodies.

It's true that most diving situations don't require an extraordinary degree of physical prowess and that many types of diving can be enjoyed by young or old, fit or less than fit. However, a reasonable degree of physical fitness certainly adds to the enjoyment and safety of diving, and physical fitness directly affects the two most important commodities of every dive: air and energy. Physically fit divers are more aerobically efficient and have greater reserves of energy than unfit divers. Also, the physics of scuba diving put an unusual load on the heart, and aerobically fit divers are more likely to have healthy hearts. Furthermore, unexpected currents or slight errors of navigation that require reserves of air or energy might test a diver's stamina during any dive. So physical fitness has more relevance to diving than simply as a means to look good in a dive skin.

The actual act of diving is an aerobic activity, and aerobic exercises such as walking, jogging, bicycling, or stair climbing are excellent ways to maintain aerobic fitness for diving.

The total process of going diving, on the other hand, is more than an aerobic activity. Dive equipment is heavy, and carrying gear to and from dive sites and climbing boarding ladders while fully equipped involve a significant expenditure of muscle power. Active divers should also incorporate resistance or weight training (anaerobic exercises) in their fitness routines to get the most from their dive trips. Weight training increases lean muscle mass, which makes the body more efficient. Being stronger also makes divers more confident and less likely to injure themselves when handling dive gear or being tossed around on a rocking boat.

Snorkeling in a pool is the perfect exercise for diving. It works the exact muscles used in diving, keeps you comfortable in the water and familiar with basic equipment, and it's fun.

So, while it's not necessary that every scuba diver be trained like a triathlete, it is

It is possible to repair a corroded inflation valve seat in order to stop the slow, creeping leak. However, unless the damaged inflation valve is part of an integrated alternate air system, it is always easier and usually as cost-effective to simply replace the inflation valve rather than repair it. Air inflation valves are held in place by only one or two plastic ties, and on-site replacement is a matter of simply cutting the plastic tie

important that active divers be reasonably fit. Here are some exercises you should consider to make you a better and safer diver:

- Do aerobic exercises. Walk or jog on a treadmill or ride a stationary bike for twenty minutes three times a week. If weather permits, it's usually more fun to actually get outside and walk or ride a bike.
- Work those abs. Do sit-ups or crunches at least three times a week. Strong abdominal muscles greatly contribute to general body strength and help to prevent back injuries.
- Work the upper body with resistance training. Push-ups will work the chest; pull-ups (chin-ups) will work the upper back. Of course, if you're a member of a gym or fitness facility, there are many exercises for the upper body. Bench presses also work the chest, and rowing-type exercises work the back.
- Work the lower body with resistance training. Perhaps the best exercise for general strength with an emphasis on the back and legs is squatting with a straight weight bar across the shoulders. However, squatting with weights must be done correctly to avoid injury. If you're unfamiliar with this exercise, consult with a professional trainer at a gym to get you started. Squatting develops good balance and lower body strength, which is very useful on rocking boats. Also, squatters become accustomed to lifting heavy objects (like tanks or heavy dive bags) by using their legs rather than their bent backs, which greatly reduces the chance of injury.

If all of this is new to you, consult your physician and a professional trainer before you start an exercise program. I often hear people talking about taking a few weeks to "get into shape," but that's not what I'm talking about. General physical fitness is a lifestyle, not a sometime thing. You don't have to live like a monk to be fit to dive, nor do your workouts need to stretch your abilities to the limit. Develop an exercise regimen that you can comfortably and consistently perform three times a week. Consistency is the key.

While you can achieve general fitness for diving by a variety of means, there is one activity you can do year-round that works the exact muscles used in scuba diving. If you have access to an indoor swimming pool, the very best exercise specific to diving is snorkeling in the pool. Snorkeling keeps you comfortable in the water, maintains your familiarity with basic equipment, and is an excellent aerobic exercise. Remember to swim underwater at regular intervals during your snorkeling workouts. Adding some arm swimming to your snorkeling routine will round out the workout by exercising your upper body.

retainers, removing the damaged valve, inserting a new valve that is compatible with the BC, and replacing the plastic ties. Some models have a simple retaining pin as well. This takes about as long to do as it took for me to tell you about it.

A replacement power inflation valve is a good spare part to carry. Keep the leaking valve after replacement and have it professionally cleaned by your local dive shop. If the cleaning stops the leak, the old valve can become your new spare.

If you own a non-air-integrated BC that accepts an integrated alternate air source as an option, ask your local dealer if they have spare standard inflation valves. The BCs are usually shipped to retailers with a standard inflation valve, and the optional alternate air source valve is usually installed at the shop once a customer opts for it. The standard inflation valve is then set aside, so the dealer may have surplus standard inflation valves for sale at a reduced price if other customers have opted for the alternate air source valve.

Of course, if your BC is equipped with an integrated alternate air source, it is more cost-effective to repair a leaking valve than to replace it.

Controversy exists as to whether the power inflation (Schrader) valve should be flushed with fresh water as a matter of routine postdive maintenance. Some technicians discourage this; others say that it will cause no harm and may help to prevent corrosion. I recommend that the power inflation valve not be flushed unless you suspect contamination or clogging. If your power inflation valve is sticky or clogged and if the manufacturer does not specifically discourage flushing, you can flush it after you've flushed all the salt water out of the air cell by putting more fresh water into the BC, holding the BC upside down, and pushing the power inflation button. The fresh water should exit the valve in a two-pronged fountain. If you get tired of holding the BC after about thirty seconds of draining from the power inflation valve (the water will drain slowly), release the power inflation button and press the oral inflation button. The water will rush out of the oral inflation orifice.

Dump Valves

The dump valves on your BC are subject to the same clogging and corrosion as the inflator valve. Flushing the valves with fresh water is simply a matter of dumping a load of fresh water from each dump valve when flushing the air cell.

Storage

BCs should be stored hanging on a wide hanger designed for them. The hanging devices made for regulators often also have thick arms to hang a BC. Partially inflate the BC for storage to facilitate drying of the air cell and hang the BC indoors, away from sunlight and auto exhaust fumes. Agents that prevent bacterial growth inside the BC can be purchased from most dive shops.

TANKS

Tank ownership gives divers the ultimate in independence, as divers who own their own tanks are free to pick up and go diving at a moment's notice and are not bound to established dive areas where tank rental is available. Most divers who own a scuba tank own more than one; the amount of air typically needed for a full day of diving is considered to be three tanks.

Owning your own tank means that you can use whatever type and size of tank that is most convenient for you. However, as mentioned in the previous chapter, the aluminum-80 has become the standard size for boat racks and carrying racks, and the personal convenience of using tanks of another size may be outweighed by the inconvenience of trying to use different-sized tanks on commercial dive charter boats that are not configured to carry them.

VIP

VIP is the acronym for Visual Inspection Program, which originated as a voluntary annual internal inspection of scuba tanks. The procedure is now mandatory, and it is the responsibility of the owner to have all tanks VIP-inspected by a qualified technician annually. The VIP inspection is usually done on-site at the dive shop, and it is a relatively quick and inexpensive process. The tank valve is removed; the tank is visually examined for pitting, oxidation, or damage; and the tank valve is inspected for seat wear or bowing of the burst disk.

A dated VIP sticker is attached to the tank after the inspection. Reputable dive shops and fill stations will refuse to fill any tank that does not have a current VIP sticker.

Tumbling

It may happen that a VIP inspection does not end happily with a VIP sticker of approval. Sometimes oxidation or corrosion is found inside the tank. Fortunately, although internal oxidation is a serious problem, there is treatment.

Scuba tanks are cleaned of corrosion by a process known as tumbling. The affected tank is filled about half full with an abrasive material (carbide chips or aluminum oxide chips) and then rotated for a number of hours. The tumbling process removes corrosion and polishes the inside of the tank. Loose material is removed after tumbling by washing the interior of the tank with water, then the interior of the tank is dried thoroughly to remove any trace of moisture.

Tumbling is not normally done in dive shops, and the process will take some time and money (about $15 to $25). However, chances are very good that a tank with minimal corrosion can be saved.

Hydrostatic Testing

All scuba tanks must be hydrostatically tested ("hydroed") every five years by an approved tester. It is the responsibility of the tank owner to see that this testing is done.

To review what we covered in chapter 2, the test involves filling the tank with water and pressurizing it to five-thirds of its working pressure (5,000 psi for a tank with a working pressure of 3,000 psi), measuring its expansion, releasing the pressure, then making sure that the tank regains its original shape. If the tank fails to return to within 10 percent of its original volume, it is disqualified from further use as a scuba tank. A tank that fails cannot continue service with a reduced working pressure. The test date is stamped onto the shoulder of a tank that passes the test, and the tank is returned to service. Reputable dive shops and fill stations will refuse to fill any tank that does not contain a current hydro date.

Hydrostatic testing is not normally performed at dive shops, but your local dive shop will know a source (many testing facilities primarily work on fire extinguishers). The process usually costs $30 to $50 and may take weeks to complete.

User Maintenance

Any highly pressurized container should be handled carefully, and scuba tanks are no exception. The neck and valve are the most vulnerable points, and this should be taken into account whenever tanks are stored on rocking boats or in moving automobiles. Always make sure that tank valves cannot bang into things or that other heavy objects cannot fall on them.

Portable wire tank racks that hold tanks upright and close to each other like a six-pack of beer are commonly used on boats that are not specially configured to carry tanks. These racks work pretty well to keep tanks from rolling around on the boat, but they do not protect tanks well enough from banging into each other once the boat is at sea. Always cushion tanks in these racks with boat cushions, towels, or whatever else is handy to prevent the tanks from violently clanging into each other. You'll know if the tanks are colliding—they'll ring like bells. Take that bell sound as an appropriate warning and do something to prevent it.

In addition to handling tanks carefully to avoid physical damage, the most important preventive maintenance for scuba tanks is to make sure that water cannot get inside them. The way to keep water out of a scuba tank is to keep some pressurized air in the tank. Never completely empty your tank. If you have ever dived from a commercial dive boat, you were probably instructed to return to the boat with no less than 500 psi in your tank. If you assumed that this instruction was to encourage safe diving, you were only partly right. The ulterior motive was that the diving company wanted to ensure that enough air remained in their tanks to prevent water from entering.

Any tank that has been completely emptied of air should be VIP-inspected before further use.

Heat

It's a good idea to protect scuba tanks from the heat of direct sunlight whenever possible, as heat will cause the pressure in the tank to rise. However, the consequence of a tank heated by sunlight is probably not as catastrophic as you might have heard.

As you spend more time at the BS counter (see sidebar on page 119) of your local dive shop, you will eventually hear the story about the guy who put a scuba tank into the trunk of his black car and left it there in the broiling sun. In most versions of the story, the guy hears a loud explosion, rushes out to see what happened, and finds only the front portion of his car intact. Another version of the story is that the exploding scuba tank blows the gas tank into the pavement, the gas tank sparks, and the resultant fire burns down a city block.

It's a good story. I personally like the fire version—the more mayhem the better. However, like most good stories, it doesn't let fact get in the way of entertainment. Here are the facts:

Let's assume that an aluminum-80 tank is filled to 3,000 psi at a fill station and that the temperature in the fill station is 75°F. We know that the tank has been hydrostatically tested to withstand five-thirds of its working pressure, or 5,000 psi. We also know that the burst disk on the tank's valve is designed to blow at a pressure of less than 5,000 psi. Forgetting the fact that the burst disk should blow before the tank explodes (that's why the burst disk is there), how hot would the tank have to get before the pressure inside reaches 5,000 psi?

With a tip of the hat to Mr. Amonton and his law regarding heat and pressure given a fixed volume of gas, the answer is 430°F. At that temperature, not only has the ice in your cooler melted in the trunk, but the cooler itself has melted into a gooey, boiling mess. Likewise, all the beer cans in the cooler have exploded and the beer is also boiling. The air in the trunk has expanded to the point that either the trunk has flown open or the trunk lid has buckled. At that temperature . . . well, I think you get the idea. Tanks stored in car trunks are in no danger of exploding from the heat. However, if there's ever a fire in a place where scuba tanks are stored, my advice is to let somebody else put it out.

So why bother with keeping scuba tanks cool? As we've learned, the answer is not to prevent the tank from exploding. However, if a regulator is attached to a hot tank, the tank's pressure may exceed the regulator's maximum pressure. The regulator seal will break and the tank will hiss loudly and probably fall out of the tank rack. It's embarrassing.

The Tank Valve

Tank valves should be opened and closed gently to prolong the life of the valve seats. It seems that many divers open their tank valves as if they were revving a Harley at Sturgis. This will damage the valve over time.

I've mentioned several times that this is not a dive manual and that you should dive in the way you were taught until you have gained the experience to try something different based upon personal knowledge. I'm going to make an exception to that rule right now. Many divers are taught to open a tank valve completely and then close the valve by a quarter-turn to protect the valve seat. I don't know where or when the "close the valve a quarter-turn" dogma stared, but I'm convinced that it's a stupid thing to do. It's true that a true quarter-turn of the tank valve should not dangerously diminish a tank's ability to deliver air, but who can consistently estimate the quarter-turn? I have watched divers turn their tank valve to an open position and then turn it halfway back off—a dangerous mistake made while trying to follow a procedure that shouldn't have been taught in the first place.

Dive accident reports are full of accounts of divers suddenly being deprived of air from their tanks at depth, and almost all of the incidents are due to a partially closed tank valve. A partially closed valve will deliver plenty of air at the surface and at shallow depths, but as divers demand a greater volume of air as depth increases, the partially closed tank valve can't deliver it. The problem could be alleviated by ascending to a depth at which the partially closed valve can deliver a sufficient quantity of air, but divers deprived of air usually do not realize what has happened to them. A crisis ensues—one that is completely unnecessary and easily avoided.

Your tank valve should be gently and completely opened, and it should be left that way. If you want to take pressure off the tank valve seat, turn the valve just enough so that it is not jammed against the stop. Have the valve serviced if it becomes difficult to turn.

Boots and Accessories

Tank boots are plastic devices with flat bottoms that cover the bottoms of scuba tanks. They were originally meant to cap the rounded ends of old steel tanks to provide a flat platform upon which the tanks could be stood on end. That made lots of sense. However, all modern scuba tanks have flat bottoms, and tank boots no longer have relevance for their original purpose.

Chances are good that you learned to dive with a booted tank. This was because the relatively soft boot was less likely to damage the tile around the pool where you had your lessons.

Tank boots trap seawater, and tanks with boots don't fit into many tank racks. I do not recommend the use of tank boots unless a tank is relegated to pool use.

Some tanks are painted in a variety of colors. They look cool on the dive shop floor, but the paint is usually short-lived. As tanks are stacked and racked, the paint chips off. This not only affects the cosmetics of the tank and makes the tank appear damaged, but the paint chips are a nuisance and a potential hazard if they fall into the wrong places. I don't recommend painted tanks.

Some painted tanks are protected by webbing that covers the tank to prevent it from coming into direct contact with other tanks as a way of protecting the paint. The webbing will serve to prolong the life of the paint from short-lived to medium-lived. The paint will still eventually chip off, and the webbing makes the tank hard to put into a standard boat tank rack, as the plastic fingers of the rack don't fit well around the webbing. I don't recommend the use of protective webbing on scuba tanks.

Filling and Emptying

Tanks are quickly and inexpensively filled at your local dive shop or fill station. Rapid changes in pressure affect temperature, and filling should be performed slowly to avoid overheating the tank. Tanks that are filled too quickly become overheated, resulting in a "hot fill." A hot fill usually results in a "short fill." The compressor that fills the tank will shut off when the tank reaches its working pressure. However, if the tank has overheated due to a quick fill, the pressure will be less when the tank cools to a normal temperature. Even careful fills heat the tank to some degree (no pun intended), and you should expect a good fill to be within 10 percent of the tank's working pressure once the tank has cooled.

Temperature changes should also be taken into account should you ever bleed air directly from the tank. The tank will cool if the air is let out too quickly, and the tank may become so cold that water will condense inside.

Tank Storage

Most of the accepted procedures for storing scuba tanks for long periods of time are based on the possibility that water may be inside the tank. Of course, no water should ever be allowed to enter a scuba tank, and the procedures are based on an abundance of caution.

Tanks should be stored upright. This not only keeps the vulnerable valve and neck out of harm's way, but should water be inside the tank, it will collect at the tank's bottom, where the tank material is thickest. This is to prevent corrosion from weakening the walls of the tank to the bursting point.

Tanks should be stored with air compressed inside them to keep water or moisture out. It is usually recommended that the tank be stored half full. This obviously takes pressure off the tank's valve and walls, but it also serves another purpose that is not so obvious.

If water is inside the tank, the concentration of oxygen under high pressure will speed the oxidation process, and the oxidation will do more than damage the walls of the tank. Oxidation will remove oxygen from the air and leave a gas mixture with a higher percentage of nitrogen. Of course, a gas mixture low in oxygen and high in nitrogen is a bad mix for a scuba diver, predisposing the diver to DCS. In addition to physically protecting the tank, the half-full storage rule is also meant to discourage divers from using the air that has been stored for a long period in the tank. If you decide to bleed air from a tank to follow the half-full rule, be careful to bleed the air very slowly to prevent chilling that could lead to condensation inside.

CHAPTER 4

GADGETS THAT WORK, AND GOOD IDEAS

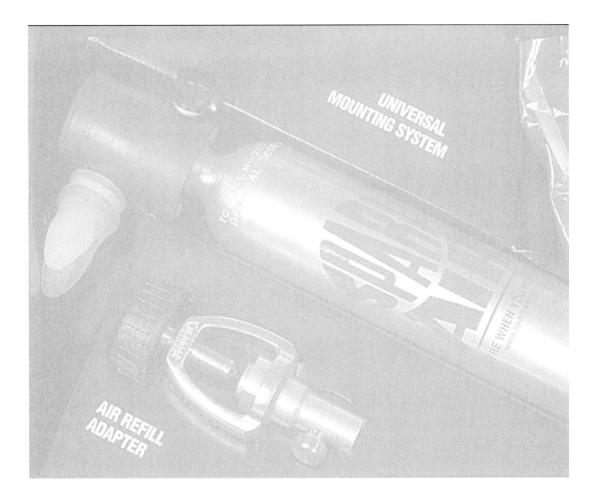

I F YOU TOOK A RANDOM SAMPLE of a hundred active scuba divers and closely examined their diving equipment and accessories, you'd discover close to a hundred different ways to configure gear and go diving. Gadgets abound, and a stroll through a well-stocked dive shop will leave the impression that a mad scientist might have had a hand in designing some of the "improvements" to standard dive gear that fill the shelves. The following is a discussion of accessory gear and gear configuration that I have found to be useful. The recommendations appear in no order of importance.

I will mention specific manufacturers of some of the gadgets that I personally use. Bear in mind that I have no affiliation with any of these companies and that I mention their products only because I have found them to be useful.

HOSE AND GAUGE RETAINERS

A diver typically has four regulator hoses to deal with during a dive. The first hose is connected to the primary second stage of the regulator, and the second stage goes into the diver's mouth. The second hose is connected to the power inflation valve on the diver's BC. These two hoses are naturally secured during diving.

The third hose is connected to the secondary second stage, or octopus. The fourth hose is connected to the SPG/computer console. These two hoses should be secured so that the instruments they carry can be quickly found when needed. Loosely hanging gear is also a snag hazard and a menace to reefs.

Octopus Retainers

Secondary second stages, or octopus rigs, are primarily emergency gear to be used in the event that another diver needs to share the air in your tank. The rig should be secured to the BC somewhere on your right side (within the "golden triangle," as you were taught in your certification class), where a diver in distress will expect to find it.

Octopus rigs are typically secured by soft plastic devices that are attached to a D ring on the BC. The mouthpiece of the octopus is inserted into the device and held in place. These devices come in two general shapes—a ball shape that holds both mouthpiece flanges collectively and a more molded shape that accepts the mouthpiece flanges individually. The molded shape holds the octopus more securely, but, of course, it's harder to get the mouthpiece properly inserted into it.

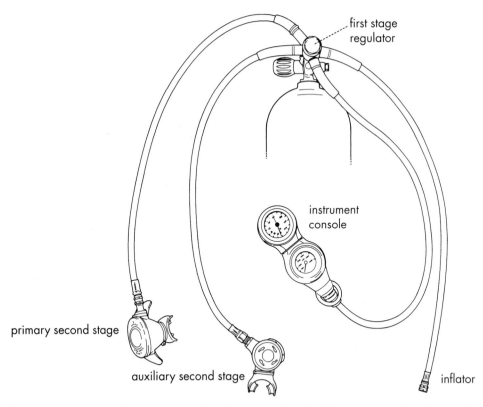

first stage
regulator

instrument
console

primary second stage

auxiliary second stage

inflator

The typical scuba regulator setup involves four hoses that should be secured when diving. The primary second-stage hose and the BC inflation hose are naturally secured, but divers should devise ways to secure their auxiliary second-stage and instrument-console hoses to prevent snags and to protect the diving environment.

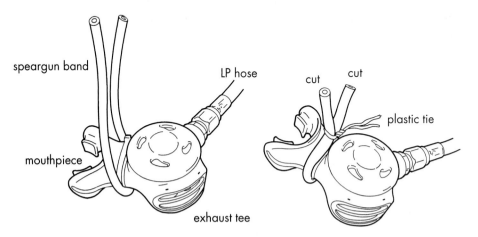

speargun band

LP hose

cut   cut

plastic tie

mouthpiece

exhaust tee

An octopus retainer can be easily made with some surgical tubing and a plastic tie. Speargun bands work perfectly as tubing. Simply place the octopus second-stage mouthpiece within the tubing, cinch the tubing tightly around the mouthpiece with a plastic tie, and then cut off the excess tubing. This leaves a circle of tubing into which the mouthpiece fits snugly. Attach the retainer to a D ring on the BC with another plastic tie.

My experience has been that these devices work well enough for most dives. The octopus will fall out sometimes, which means that you must resecure it while underwater. Reinserting an octopus mouthpiece into the device while you are underwater may take a few minutes, as it is hard to see the device when you are wearing your BC.

These standard octopus retainers do not work well for entries that require a long jump into the water or for entries that involve wading in surf. They are simply not secure enough to hold an octopus for rough entries. A solution that works for me is to use a retainer made by a company called Cetacea that contains an elastic loop that can be shortened by a slider. I put the loop over the entire mouthpiece of the octopus and tighten the loop with the slider. It works without being too difficult for another diver to remove.

Budget-conscious do-it-yourself types can easily make an octopus retainer from a short piece of surgical tubing. Form a loop in the tubing and fasten it with a plastic tie, then connect the loop to a D ring on the BC by means of another plastic tie. The octopus can be held by inserting the mouthpiece into the loop. You might be able to find free surgical tubing if you know any spearfishers. Worn speargun bands can be used to make the device.

One of the old-style snorkel keepers, the ones that look like a figure eight with an elongated waist, can be used as an octopus retainer in a pinch. Loop the snorkel keeper around a D ring and pass one snorkel-keeper ring through the other to lasso the D ring. Insert the octopus mouthpiece into the remaining, dangling snorkel-keeper loop.

Console Retainers

I hope your octopus was secured during your open-water (checkout) training dives, but it's possible that your gauge console was allowed to hang loosely from its hose. The reason for this was to allow your instructor to easily check your gauges. This was appropriate, as your instructor was the person primarily responsible for checking your gauges during your open-water certification dives.

Now, as a certified diver, you are the person primarily responsible for your dives, and your gauge console should be secured in a position that is convenient for you and that poses no snag hazard or threat to the reef. Some divers (my wife/dive buddy/photo model included) simply hold the console in their left hand for the duration of their dives. The console hose can be moved to the crook of the left arm in the event that both hands are needed for something. This works well for divers not encumbered by other equipment, such as a camera, that requires the use of both hands. However, most divers prefer to clip the gauge console to their BC in some way.

Hose clips are common accessories available at most dive shops. The hose clip is a short piece of plastic that attaches to a D ring on your BC at one end and has two clawlike plastic fingers at the other end into which a hose can be snapped—a miniature version of the fingers of common tank racks. They are cheap and easy to set up. Unfortunately, they don't work very well in any but the most benign diving conditions. Plastic hose clips simply do not hold hoses securely enough for most dives.

Many divers hold the gauge console on their chest or waist through the use of a large brass clip attached to a D ring on their BC. This is a good solution, as the console is held securely in a position that is easy for most divers to see and read. However, the type of brass clip used can make a big difference in the effectiveness of this arrangement.

Suicide Clips

Brass clips come in two common types: boat snap and bolt snap. The names sound so similar that it's often difficult to tell which kind of clip is being discussed. However, the boat snap has acquired a more descriptive name: it is commonly called a suicide clip or suicide hook.

The suicide clip is the familiar type that consists of a hook with a spring-loaded retaining gate that opens inward. Since the gate opens whenever anything is pressed against it and since the gate must be pressed inward to release anything hooked, suicide clips have three main shortcomings as retaining devices: they have a dangerous tendency to snag and clip onto things that were not intended to be hooked; they have a dangerous tendency to release things that were meant to be retained; and, when hooked onto large items, they are dangerously difficult to unhook.

Suicide clips should not be used as retaining devices by scuba divers.

Post Clips

The bolt snap is the equally familiar type of brass hook that employs a vertical spring-loaded retaining post that can be pulled downward to allow things to be hooked and

Many divers attach brass snap hooks to their BCs to retain various items. The boat snap hook (left) and the bolt snap hook (right) have similar names and are similar in appearance. However, the boat snap has earned the moniker suicide clip due to its tendency to snag on anything that happens to rub against it and for its tendency to "choke" on large objects. The bolt snap, more commonly referred to as a post clip, is more suitable for scuba-diving applications.

retained. These hooks are commonly called post clips or post hooks, and they don't have any of the shortcomings of suicide clips. Post clips are suitable retaining devices for scuba divers.

CLIP SYSTEMS

Most divers need some system of clips beyond those needed for retaining regulator hoses and gauges. Clip systems are used to hold extraneous equipment such as dive lights, dive slates, light meters, or any other small device or tool that a diver wants to carry.

Post Clips

Post clips work well for divers with BCs that feature several large D rings onto which things can be attached. The diver simply attaches a bolt snap hook, or post clip, to every device that might be needed for a dive. If the diver decides to carry a device on a specific dive, he or she simply clips the item onto an available D ring.

Fastex Clips

Fastex clips are a good solution for divers with BCs that do not feature many large D rings. Fastex clips (Cetacea sells them) are inexpensive two-part plastic clips that consist of a three-pronged component and a receptor that receives the prongs and locks them in place—the same type of connector that is commonly used for BC belts.

This diver is clipped, tucked, and ready to go. Starting with a back-inflation BC with plenty of D rings, he's carrying a knife and a safety sausage on his right shoulder, his gauges are neatly post-clipped to a D ring, and a compass and signaling whistle are attached to his left side. He's also attached strings to the pocket zippers on the left side of his BC that he can't easily see (bottom right). One string has a circular wind, and the other string has a flat wind, so he can feel which pocket he's opening. It's a good idea to personalize your gear in a way that makes sense to you.

By attaching any number of Fastex receptors to available D rings (more than one receptor can be attached to one ring) and attaching Fastex prongs to all devices and tools that might be carried, a diver can easily clip and carry whatever devices are needed on any given dive. I've found Fastex clips to be particularly useful for carrying dive lights. If you mount one receptor onto the dive light lanyard and another on the BC, you can easily move a light from the BC to the wrist lanyard and back again.

Retractable Lanyards

Some clip-on gadgets contain lanyards that you can extend to use or view the device and that retract back into a spring-loaded spool when released. This is a useful feature, as it allows you to use or view carried devices without first having to disconnect them from their retainers.

Regardless of the clip system you use, be careful to retain clipped-on devices so that they do not hang loosely. Try to tuck hanging devices into BC pockets so that they do not become snag hazards or a menace to the underwater environment.

DIVE LIGHTS

Dive lights aren't just for night diving. A small dive light attached to a retractable lanyard can be useful for looking into dark holes or crevices where critters may hide. A dive light also allows a diver to see color that is not visible underwater without artificial light. We will discuss dive lights in more detail in the section on night diving in chapter 10, but a dive light for daytime dives is a good idea.

DIVE SLATES

Dive slates have many uses. They provide a means to communicate with other divers and also serve as a personal notebook for navigational information. We will discuss the use of dive slates for navigation in chapter 11.

PLASTIC TIES

I don't know if a plastic tie (sometimes called a cable tie, wire tie, or Ty-wrap) should be called a gadget or a tool, but all independent divers should carry an assortment of plastic ties. Their uses are almost uncountable. A diver without plastic ties is like a rock-and-roll roadie without duct tape.

I just had a look at my BC and counted the plastic ties permanently attached to it.

There are six—two connecting the power inflation/oral inflation valve, one that is used to shorten the waist belt by folding the belt and tying it in place, one that is used to shorten the chest belt by folding it and tying it down (I shorten belts this way to avoid dangling straps), and two more to attach the holster for my Spare Air (a gadget we'll discuss shortly). That's not counting the plastic ties that hold the mouthpieces on both second stages of my regulator, nor does it count the plastic ties that hold post clips and Cetacea Fastex clips to a wide variety of gizmos that I regularly carry on my BC. I am using ten or so plastic ties by the time I am fully geared up for a normal dive.

Don't forget the plastic tie companion tool—straight-cut toenail clippers. These clippers will trim the excess tie flush with the tie retainer without leaving sharp edges.

CLIP-ON WEIGHTS

It sometimes happens that divers realize, when they first try to descend to start a dive, that their buoyancy is not quite right and that they need a bit more weight. This simple problem usually involves the time-consuming solution of reboarding the boat, removing the weight belt (which often means removing the BC and tank), adding more weight, putting the weight belt back on, and starting over. Trying to fix the problem while the diver is in the water usually takes as long and adds the risk of dropping and losing the weight belt. There's an easier way.

A clip-on weight is nothing more than a standard lead dive weight attached to a post clip with a couple of plastic ties. The clip-on weight can be simply handed to the buoyant diver while the diver is in the water and clipped onto one of the small D rings on the diver's weight belt. The weight will be securely attached, will not hinder the diver in any way, and will be released in the event that the weight belt is ditched.

A regular lead dive weight connected to a post clip with plastic ties is a convenient thing to keep handy on a dive boat. If you discover after you've entered the water that you need more weight to make a dive, you can easily attach the clip-on weight onto most weight belts without having to get back on the boat or remove the weight belt.

Make a few 2-pound clip-on weights and carry them whenever you go diving. Even if you get your buoyancy right, you will be hung up if your buddy needs buoyancy adjustment. Clip a deuce onto the belt, and you'll be on your way in no time.

Spare Air

I believe that every independent diver should be self-reliant. In fact, I believe that self-reliance is the core of independence. That doesn't mean that I don't believe in the buddy system—I do. It doesn't mean that I am unwilling or unavailable to help a buddy in need—I am. It doesn't mean that I mistrust my dive buddy's ability to assist me in the event that I run into trouble during a dive—well, sometimes I do. It does mean that I will always attempt to dive in such a way that maximizes my self-reliance and independence by minimizing my need for critical assistance from another diver.

The out-of-air emergency is the most buddy-dependent situation a diver can encounter underwater. The best way to mitigate that dependence is to carry an emergency air supply that is totally redundant to the primary air supply. I have found Submersible Systems's Spare Air to be the most practical redundant air source available for recreational divers.

The most commonly used Spare Air is a small, independent tank (often called a "pony bottle") that holds 3 cubic feet of air at a pressure of 3,000 psi and is equipped with an integrated regulator. The tank can be conveniently filled on-site from any full scuba tank with a working pressure of 3,000 psi, which includes the vast majority of scuba tanks used by recreational divers. The entire unit is small enough to be easily carried by any diver.

The Spare Air is far from perfect; 3 cubic feet of air is not very much. However, a reasonable ascent can be made from accepted recreational depths with a Spare Air, provided that the ascent is started immediately, the diver does not breathe at a panicked rate, and the diver has direct access to the surface with no decompression obligation. More air would be better, and some experienced divers disparage the traditional Spare Air's small air supply as a panacea that breeds a false sense of security. As if to answer the detractors, Submersible Systems recently introduced the Twin Spare Air, which consists of a pair of 3-cubic-foot tanks connected to a single integrated regulator and provides more-abundant emergency air.

The Spare Air by Submersible Systems is a completely redundant (sometimes called Type II), air supply that is popular with recreational divers. Its small tank holds about 3 cubic feet of air at 3,000 psi and can be filled from a regular scuba tank via the air refill adaptor. With its small air capacity, the Spare Air should be thought of as an underwater parachute to be used only to reach the surface in the event of an out-of-air emergency.

The Spare Air is usually carried by attaching the holster (supplied in the Spare Air kit) to the BC waist strap. A regular regulator mouthpiece retainer is attached to the BC chest strap. The Spare Air is held by the holster at the bottom and by the mouthpiece retainer at the top and is worn on the inside of the BC air cell. The Spare Air is conveniently out of the way but available if needed.

Of course, pony bottles are available in a wide variety of sizes. A redundant regulator can be attached to a pony bottle of any size, and the redundant setup can be carried on dives as a more abundant emergency air supply. These larger pony bottles are usually attached to the main scuba tank in some way. They create problems when changing tanks and when racking tanks on boats, and they are generally a pain to carry and use.

Most recreational divers will never experience an out-of-air emergency during a dive, and drastic measures taken to deal with such an unlikely event are out of place for purely recreational divers. The Spare Air is an expensive, imperfect, and sometimes finicky device. However, it is a good compromise of convenience and safety that could save your life in the unlikely event that your primary air supply becomes unavailable to you for any reason.

Spare Airs should be treated in the same manner as other scuba tanks. They should be stored upright, they should never be completely emptied unless they are used in an emergency, and they should be hydrostatically tested every five years. Most dive shops do not perform VIP inspections on Spare Air tanks.

MOLDABLE MOUTHPIECES

Personal comfort plays a large role in the enjoyment of scuba diving, and the comfort of a regulator mouthpiece plays a large role in personal comfort. In fact, mouthpiece comfort plays such a large role in enjoyment that many divers place an inordinate degree of importance on the mouthpiece when purchasing a regulator.

Regulator mouthpieces are easily and inexpensively changed. Buying a regulator based on mouthpiece comfort is like buying a new car based on the tires. Plus, the comfort of a regulator mouthpiece may not become apparent until the regulator is used over a period of time. If jaw fatigue or sore gums are part of your diving experience, it's time to look for a new mouthpiece.

Several manufacturers make mouthpieces designed to enhance comfort, but the mouthpiece that I've found to be best is made by a company called SeaCure.

The SeaCure mouthpiece has two important features that result in optimum comfort. It is very long—so long that it would surely gag most divers. The first customization of the mouthpiece is to cut it to the longest length that does not gag.

The second customization of the SeaCure mouthpiece is the ultimate one. The mouthpiece is heated in water and then placed into the mouth and bitten, whereupon it permanently conforms to the mouth in a matter of seconds. The resulting mouthpiece is completely customized to the diver's mouth and will fit snugly without requiring jaw pressure to hold it in place. As the mouthpiece will not move inside the mouth, it will not rub on gums.

SeaCure mouthpieces are available to fit all regulators, but they must be

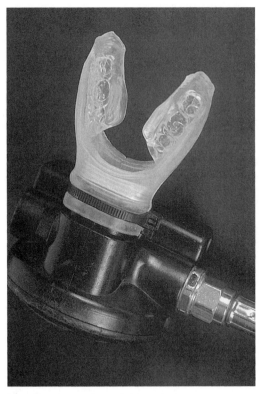

The moldable regulator mouthpiece marketed by SeaCure can be custom-formed to fit any diver's bite. It produces less jaw fatigue and gum soreness than a regular mouthpiece.

matched to specific regulators. As it is made from a relatively stiff material, installation may require a bit more effort than for a softer mouthpiece, and the SeaCure mouthpiece may be more prone to an in-leak that will lead to wet breathing. I've owned several SeaCure mouthpieces, and some of them have leaked a small amount of air when subjected to the in-leak test of sucking on the regulator while it is unattached to an air supply. However, they breathe reasonably dry, and any wet breathing is more than offset by their comfort.

Safety Sausages

Safety sausages are brightly colored inflatable tubes that are used to locate divers on the surface. I consider a safety sausage to be an integral part of every independent diver's equipment setup.

The surface is a dangerous place for a diver to be. Currents are often strongest near

Where's the diver? Even in clear, calm water, a diver at the surface can be difficult to see.

The use of a safety sausage clearly marks a surfaced diver's position in the water. This not only facilitates pickup, but it also alerts passing boaters.

the surface and may impede or prohibit a diver's progress back to the boat or shore. Boat traffic is an additional hazard, and divers on the surface are very difficult to see. High seas compound the problem, as divers are practically invisible in large waves and the waves complicate surface swimming. A safety sausage will more clearly mark a diver's position in the water so that he or she can be seen.

The safety sausage can be conveniently carried by curling it and clipping it to a shoulder D ring. It can be orally inflated and held upright whenever a diver surfaces far from the boat or shore, cannot easily swim to the boat or shore, or is faced with dangerous boat traffic.

Many safety sausages contain a pocket near the tip into which a Cyalume "glow stick" can be inserted. Some experienced divers carry a battery-powered strobe to insert into their safety sausage for better visibility in low light. The running safety sausage joke (no, it doesn't have anything to do with sausages) is that a $20 bill placed conspicuously into the sausage pocket will facilitate a pickup better than either a glow stick or a strobe.

Safety sausages are mandatory gear for some commercial scuba operators that offer offshore dive charters. Divers who do not own a safety sausage are required to rent one from the operator before they are allowed to dive from the boat.

Dry Boxes

Scuba diving is a wet sport. Boats and other areas in which scuba diving is done become very wet places. Anything and everything near scuba divers will become soaked. Divers need a dry space in which to store items not meant to be wet, and the only dry spaces on a dive deck are those that divers carry with them. Most experienced divers bring two waterproof boxes whenever they go diving—a small box for personal items and a larger box for larger items and tools.

Small Box

Small dry boxes are used to carry personal items. I usually leave my wallet locked in my room or car trunk when I go diving, but I carry my small dry box onto dive boats or to shore-diving staging areas; it contains car keys, room keys, C-card, and a bit more cash than I think I'll need, including tip money. The box must be small enough to conveniently carry and stow but large enough to hold the things I need. It must be crushproof and absolutely waterproof.

The Pelican Company makes watertight microcases that serve perfectly as small dry boxes for scuba divers. I prefer the model 1050—a box that measures about 7½ inches long, 5 inches wide, and 3 inches deep. This box is sturdily built, closes securely, is small enough to fit into a side pocket of my mesh dive bag, and is so waterproof that it is actually submersible. The box is also airtight and features a purge valve to let air into the box in the event that air pressure prevents the lid from opening. That's a seal tight enough to entrust with my personal things in an environment as wet as a dive-boat deck. The Pelican 1050 microcase can be locked by two small padlocks placed in convenient locking holes if desired. Many dive shops carry the Pelican 1050 as dive gear.

The small dry box serves double duty as an organizer and protector of small, fragile gear in the main dive bag when you travel.

Large Box

Large dry boxes are used to carry incidental dive gear, tools, and other things that make diving more convenient. The box should be crushproof, large enough to carry what you need, but small enough to stow conveniently on the dive deck or at the shore-diving area. The box should be waterproof, but it will be a wetter environment than the small dry box, as items within it are used for diving and then returned to the box.

The Pelican Company makes very sturdy and waterproof cases that are suitable as large dry boxes for scuba divers, but these can get expensive in the larger sizes. The box I use was made by MTM Molded Products of Dayton, Ohio. It measures about 14 inches long, 9 inches wide, and 8 inches deep. The box features a gasket that keeps the water out, and it closes securely with a cam latch. It was bought in the fishing department of a sporting goods store for far less than the cost of a comparably sized Pelican case. Many other fishing or general sportsman's boxes are suitable for use as large dry boxes by scuba divers.

WHAT'S INSIDE?

So what should you carry in your large dry box? Well, anything you want, including some of the smaller items recommended in this section.

- Two dive lights with Cetacea Fastex prongs attached
- Plastic dive table card
- Small dive slate with Cetacea Fastex prongs attached
- Small dispenser of shampoo for mask defogging
- Extra power inflation hose for use when I dive in my dry suit. The hose is in a quart-sized zipper-seal bag that also contains a $\frac{9}{16}$-inch crescent wrench and a 4 mm Allen wrench for removing the LP hose plug on my regulator and attaching the hose when needed.
- Quart-sized zipper-seal bag that contains spare computer batteries, a pair of pliers, and a quarter
- Quart-sized zipper-seal bag that contains acetaminophen, Dramamine, ChapStick, sunglasses, and reading glasses
- Quart-sized zipper-seal bag that contains my Spare Air filling device, which allows me to fill my Spare Air from a scuba tank
- Can of insect repellent
- Sunscreen
- Independent pressure gauge in a quart-sized zipper-seal bag that I sometimes use to check fills in tanks before attaching my regulator. It is especially useful for multitank boat dives, when it's easy to lose track of which tanks are full and which tanks have been used.
- Container of home-brew ear flush. I make my own with a 50/50 mixture of isopropyl alcohol and white vinegar. It's the same "swimmer's ear" stuff in the tiny bottles that sell for several bucks in drugstores.
- Combination padlock in a sandwich-sized zipper-seal bag. This lock can be used to lock any number of things, including the box itself. It is most commonly used to lock equipment lockers at dive staging areas.
- Spare regulator mouthpiece
- Spare BC power inflation valve
- Bag full of plastic ties that also contains straight-cut toenail clippers
- 2- and 4-pound clip-on weights
- Battery-powered underwater strobe and two battery-powered night-diving sticks
- Two wrist lanyards with Cetacea Fastex receptors attached
- Tube of neoprene adhesive and sealer
- A few empty quart-sized zipper-seal bags (I don't hesitate to toss wet items back into the box so I keep all items that need to stay dry in these bags. They will disintegrate after about a year and must be replaced.)

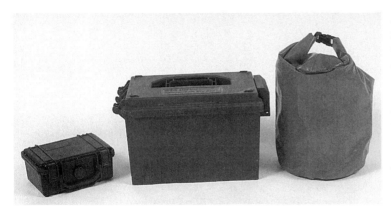

Diving is a wet sport. Small, waterproof Pelican boxes (left) are often used to keep C-cards, money, and keys safe and dry. These boxes are so commonly used that it's a good idea to mark yours to keep track of it. Larger boxes (middle) are good for keeping spares and incidental dive equipment. Bulky items such as T-shirts or towels are more easily kept in a dry bag (right).

DRY BAGS

Some items that are meant to stay dry are too bulky to fit into a dry box. Things like towels, dry clothes, and topside cameras are more easily kept in a dry bag.

Dry bags come in a variety of sizes, but they all work the same way. The bags are made from a plastic, waterproof material and are closed by folding the top over itself. The top is sealed by a Fastex clip that joins each end of the folded top. The result is a waterproof bag with a handle formed by the folded and clipped top.

Dry bags are not crushproof, so you must take care to stow them out of harm's way if breakable items are inside. The bags are not as easily opened and closed as a dry box, and it can be hard to find things inside. However, a dry bag is the only practical way to keep a towel or spare clothes dry on a small dive boat that does not offer any below-deck (dry) storage space.

Many dive shops carry dry bags as dive equipment. These bags can also be found in the camping section of some large discount stores (e.g., Wal-Mart) at a very reasonable price.

MEDICAL DIVE INSURANCE

Dive insurance is an important consideration for all independent divers. It typically covers any medical emergency that might arise from diving, as well as transportation costs to treatment areas.

The most established provider of dive insurance is the Divers Alert Network, more commonly known as DAN. The precursor of DAN came into existence in 1980, when a two-year NOAA (National Oceanic and Atmospheric Administration) and NIOSH (National Institute for Occupational Safety and Health, formerly OSHA) grant was awarded to Dr. Peter B. Bennett at the Duke University Medical Center. The grant allowed Bennett to set up an emergency medical call line for recreational divers under the name National Diving Accident Network. The network published its *Underwater Diving Accident Manual* the following year and implemented an additional advisory call line the year after that to answer nonemergency questions from recreational divers. The network switched to its current name, Divers Alert Network, in 1983 and launched a membership program to provide funding and support for its activities. By 1984, DAN was independent of federal funding and was supported entirely by divers and the diving industry.

DAN pioneered dive insurance for recreational divers in 1987 with an insurance policy designed specifically to protect them from the high cost of evacuation and treatment for diving injuries. Dive insurance became a popular idea, as most diving is done in remote areas, some diving injuries are life-threatening, and many dive injuries require immediate treatment.

For many years, DAN was the only show in town for medical dive insurance. Recently, however, additional organizations, including some of the scuba certification agencies, have introduced medical dive insurance plans. That's a good thing; the more players, the better. Additional carriers not only keep the burgeoning medical dive insurance industry financially competitive, but more input also inevitably leads to innovation and improvement.

I believe every independent diver should carry medical dive insurance. The industry has evolved to offer several types of coverage that are specific for different types of diving, but every recreational diver should at least carry insurance as protection from the cost of injury while engaged in recreational diving to established recreational depths.

Despite the newcomers to the industry, it's important to remember that the majority of scuba operators are most familiar with DAN. In fact, many offshore dive charters include a section on their waivers specifically for DAN information so that any injured diver can be expediently moved and treated. If you decide to purchase your dive insurance from a carrier other than DAN, remember that the dive operator might not be familiar with that carrier or its procedures. Make sure to give the appropriate emergency numbers to the boat captain or whoever is responsible for your care in the event of injury.

DIVE EQUIPMENT INSURANCE

Dive equipment may be covered by a homeowner's insurance policy, but many such policies will not cover equipment that is stolen, lost, or ruined during a dive trip. Divers who use delicate and expensive equipment such as underwater cameras, video lights, and strobes are especially vulnerable to loss by flooding.

THE NEIGHBORHOOD SHOE-REPAIR SHOP

OK, I'm not recommending that you go out and buy your neighborhood shoe-repair shop as a way to help your diving. However, shoe-repair shops are great at stitching and fixing bulky items such as dive gear. They're especially good at replacing zippers that rust or tear out of dive bags or dive booties. They can sew into tough items such as belt webbing to permanently attach things like Spare Air holsters to BC belts.

Many dive-gear repairs can be done while you wait at shoe-repair shops, and charges are usually minimal. I recently had a $100 dive bag with a broken zipper on the main compartment that rendered the bag useless. The zipper was replaced in a day by my local shoe-repair shop at a cost of less than $20, and the bag is as good as new.

Special dive equipment insurance was pioneered by Innovative Programs Group in 1996 with the introduction of its Divers Equipment Protection Program, commonly known as DEPP. DEPP premiums are based on the value of the equipment insured, and an additional premium is required for damage caused by flooding.

Several other carriers, including some of the scuba certification agencies, have introduced dive equipment insurance plans since the inception of DEPP. Dive equipment insurance is not for everybody, and divers should check their homeowner's policy to make sure this insurance is not redundant coverage. However, dive equipment insurance should be considered by any diver who owns particularly expensive dive gear or who habitually takes thousands of dollars worth of camera gear into the ocean. To paraphrase the DEPP slogan, flooding is not a question of *if*, it's a question of *when*.

CHAPTER 5

HOW TO
BUY EQUIPMENT

W E ' V E   S P E N T   A   L O T   O F   T I M E discussing equipment, because equipment questions are some of the first and biggest obstacles divers on their way to independence must face. Now that we've taken a look at the many options, it's easy to see how new divers can spend money without really knowing what they are buying and how they can waste money buying options they do not clearly understand. But the question remains: where and how do you get all this stuff?

BUYING NEW GEAR

Most new divers buy new gear (as opposed to used gear) for their first equipment purchases. This is because new divers have not been exposed to a wide variety of gear and need some guidance in their purchasing decisions even if they have a good, basic understanding of the types of gear available.

Your Instructor and Certifying Dive Shop

It is natural and good to look to your instructor for equipment advice. Assuming that your certification experience was a positive one, you've probably grown to know, respect, and trust your instructor. As most instructors are affiliated with a dive shop that can supply you with all the equipment you need, he or she will probably be glad to help you. In fact, there's a good chance that your instructor will become the salesperson for your equipment purchases and will earn a commission from the sale, and therein lies a subtle problem.

It's easy for the relationship between instructor and student to settle into a kind of comfortable subservience. The instructor knows best, the instructor is always right, and you do things because the instructor requests them. This relationship is easily upset as your status changes from student to equipment customer.

Some former students continue in their subservient role and buy whatever the instructor suggests. The vast majority of instructors have the best interests of their former students at heart, but it's a mistake to blindly follow the advice of another without some thought of your own. Your independence depends upon independent thought.

Unfortunately, some instructors do take advantage of their position of authority. I very recently walked into a dive shop and witnessed a sales conversation between a former student and his instructor regarding the purchase of a regulator. The instructor (and store owner, as it turned out) screwed up his face, looked at the regulator being considered, and said, "That one's not even *balanced*," as if to imply that the unbalanced regulator was prone to do wacky things or pee on the carpet, or that the former student was himself mentally unbalanced for even considering such a purchase. The former student, apparently ignorant of the differences between balanced and downstream regulators, backed off and immediately set the regulator aside to consider a more expensive model.

Maybe my feelings were hurt because the regulator so summarily dismissed happened to be the exact model I've used for many years. It is rugged and easily serviced; has consistently performed far beyond its price range in Scuba Lab tests; and has provided me with many years of competent, problem-free, and comfortable service.

Former students who question the suggestions of their instructors risk upsetting the comfortable relationship that has been established. Master might be offended if Grasshopper talks back. Of course, you are in the best position to know how your instructor would react to a genuine dialogue of ideas, and it's very possible he or she would serve very well as an equipment salesperson. However, if you have doubts, maybe you should continue to use your instructor as an advisor or mentor but opt for another salesperson for your actual equipment purchases.

There's an easy way to find out what gear the dive shop management really thinks is their most cost-effective, dependable, rugged, and easily serviced equipment without having to face the pressure of a salesperson at all. Simply take a close look at the gear provided by the shop for your pool work and open-water training dives or the gear available for rent. It won't be the most high-end stuff in the store, but it will be the most durable and cost-effective gear that the shop trusts for the hard use of its students.

It makes good sense to buy equipment from the people you're most familiar with, and those people are usually affiliated with the dive shop that served as the home base for your training. Take a good look around at what's available in the store, pay attention to the rental gear, take your time, and do your own research. Study the Scuba Lab tests of the brands and specific models of equipment available in the store. As you narrow your choices, try to actually use those choices in a pool before you buy.

Discount Catalogs and Online Providers

Dive equipment can be bought from a variety of discount catalogs and online providers. Some divers take advantage of their local dive shops by shopping and testing equipment in the dive shop and then saving a few bucks by buying the gear from a discount provider. If there is a better recipe for irrevocably alienating your local dive shop, I don't know what it is.

Scuba diving is a niche market, and most dive shops are small enterprises built from a passion for the sport. As such, most dive shops cannot stock every dive item from every manufacturer on their shelves, and the items that they do stock cannot be profitably sold at a discount (the industry joke is that the fastest way to end up with a million dollars in the dive business is to start with two million). However, the small amount of money you may save by buying from a discount provider will be more than offset by the service you receive from a dive shop. In fact, the services and courtesies you can expect from a dive shop will probably actually save you money in the long run.

Let's say that you buy a regulator from a discount provider for $50 less than the dive shop price. All is well until the regulator needs its annual maintenance. If you take the regulator into a dive shop that carries that brand of gear (as you must to get the proper maintenance parts), it's very possible that you will be advised to return the regulator to whence it came for servicing. Do you send it to the catalog? Do you send it back to the manufacturer? Can you get it serviced at all? Is this dilemma really worth a measly $50? Most dive shops will agree to service the regulator, but at a higher charge than for gear bought in their store. There goes your fifty bucks.

Of course, you shouldn't feel that your purchasing options are limited to the gear offered by your local dive shop, but that is the best place to start. If the local shop cannot provide you with specific gear upon your request, you are certainly free to look elsewhere. In many cases the local shop will help you with recommendations on where to buy the gear, but keep maintenance options in mind for any gear that requires regular servicing. If the shop doesn't carry it, it probably can't service it.

Discount providers do have their place. They are often a convenient and inexpensive way to buy incidental or disposable items—things like post clips, marker strobes, dive weights, dry boxes, or even dive lights. However, don't expect any kind of servicing to be available for items purchased from discount providers.

Life-support equipment such as regulators and buoyancy compensators should not be purchased from discount providers. If your home-base (certifying) dive shop does not carry a life-support item that you want, find another dive shop that does. The item should be serviced by the dive shop that sells it.

BUYING USED GEAR

Used scuba gear goes up for sale regularly, and there's nothing wrong with buying used equipment if you take a few precautions.

Masks, Fins, and Snorkels

There's no reason not to buy used masks, snorkels, and fins as long as you've done your research, you know what you're buying, and the equipment fits you perfectly. It always helps to try personal equipment such as masks and fins in the water before you buy. Remember that you will inevitably regret any purchase of equipment that does not fit, regardless of how much money you think you've saved. However, if it fits and works well in the water, go ahead and buy it.

Regulators

Buying life-support equipment such as a regulator involves more risk than getting a bad deal. You must literally trust your life or well-being to the quality and condition of the equipment you buy. However, you can safely buy a used regulator if you take appropriate precautions.

The first thing you must do before buying a used regulator is to independently determine that the regulator is one that you want to own. The mere fact that somebody else bought it first doesn't mean that the regulator is suitable for you, and the reduced price of used gear is no reason to buy a regulator that is not suitable. Do your own research, check the Scuba Lab reports, and make sure that the regulator is a good one for the kind of diving you plan to do with it.

Under no circumstance should you buy a used regulator without first having it checked and professionally serviced by a qualified technician. There is no way to determine the condition of a regulator simply by looking at it. Even if you have the assurance of the seller that the regulator has not been used since the last professional maintenance, internal materials may have deteriorated and O-rings may have flattened even if the regulator has been sitting on a shelf. So the second thing you must do when seriously considering the purchase of a used regulator is speak to a qualified technician who has access to all replacement parts. If the seller is a local diver, the easiest route is to go to the shop that originally sold the regulator to the seller. The staff there will be happy to help you.

If the seller did not originally buy the regulator locally, go to a dive shop that carries the brand of regulator in question and explain the situation. Dive shops should not be so sensitive that they will refuse to service gear not sold by them, but the charge for such service may be higher than for gear sold in their store.

Once a qualified technician has been located and the charge for service has been established, the cost of the service should become part of the sales negotiations between the buyer and the seller. A typical compromise is for the buyer and seller to split the cost of service if the regulator checks out and the buyer buys it, for the seller to pay the entire cost if the regulator does not check out, and for the buyer to pay the entire cost if the regulator checks out but the buyer decides not to buy.

If a technician qualified to service the regulator in question cannot be found in your area, you should not consider buying the regulator.

Buoyancy Compensators

Many of the same precautions that apply to the purchase of a used regulator also apply to the purchase of a used BC. The biggest difference is that you can do much of the servicing of a BC yourself.

Once again, the first thing you need to be sure of is that the BC in question is one that fits you perfectly and has the quality and features you need. It's easy to convince yourself that you can "make do" with a BC that doesn't fit quite right just because it's one that happens to be for sale at a reduced price. If the BC isn't convenient and comfortable, you won't use it for long. The result is that you will have wasted money on an item you can't use—money that could have been spent buying a new BC that fits. Do your own research, check the Scuba Lab reports, and try to use the BC in the water before you buy.

If you decide that the BC is a good fit for you, here are a few tests you should do before you buy:

- Inflate the BC, immerse it in water, and check for bubbles that indicate leaks in the air cell. If the BC loses air overnight, don't buy it.
- Carefully overinflate the BC with a power inflator until the overpressure relief valve functions. The relief valve should release air if the internal pressure exceeds 2 psi. If the overpressure relief valve doesn't work, well, you might blow out the air cell of the BC. Discuss this possibility with the seller before performing this test, but don't consider buying a BC unless you are certain the overpressure relief valve works.
- Test the function of all dump valves, preferably while wearing the BC in the water. The valves should function smoothly and dump air efficiently.
- Test the power inflation valve for smooth operation. However, I recommend that you replace the power inflation valve on any used BC you buy unless the valve contains an integrated alternate air source device.
- If the BC in question is equipped with an integrated alternate air supply, have the air supply serviced before you buy. Follow the same procedures outlined above for servicing a used regulator.

Tanks

You shouldn't hesitate to buy a used scuba tank that has a current hydrostatic test stamp, but the amount of time left before the next required hydrostatic test should affect the price. Even if the tank has a current VIP sticker, have the tank VIP-inspected again to make sure the tank and valve are clean and undamaged before you buy. Do not purchase aluminum tanks manufactured by Luxfer prior to 1988, as the aluminum alloy used in those tanks has been implicated in tank failures, and those tanks have been recalled by the manufacturer.

Exposure Suits

Exposure suits are, perhaps, the most common type of dive gear found on the secondhand market. People change sizes.

There is no reason not to buy used noninsulating suits such as dive skins. As dive skins are fairly cheap even when bought new, make sure the price is right.

Neoprene wet suits are another matter. As we discussed in chapter 2, when neoprene is subjected to a number of dives, it loses its ability to insulate as the neoprene cells break down from repeated compression. Thus, wet suits are subject to "mileage." It is possible for a wet suit to look nearly new but be worthless for keeping you warm in the water.

A wet suit with fifty dives should provide at least fifty more before it loses a significant amount of its insulating properties. A wet suit with a hundred dives has probably lost some insulation. A wet suit with significantly more than a hundred dives will not function properly to keep you warm. You'll have to trust the seller's word on wet-suit mileage.

Dry suits require more caution. The neck seal of any dry suit you buy will undoubtedly need to be replaced and cut to your exact size. The power inflation valve and exhaust valve must work perfectly, and the seals and zippers must be waterproof. Once the neck seal has been cut to fit, try the dry suit in the water to test the integrity of the wrist seals and zippers. A small amount of leakage around the wrists is normal.

Unless you are very familiar with dry suits and dry-suit diving, I recommend that you take a dry-suit diving course before you use the suit.

Personalizing Your Gear

Once you've accumulated your basic diving gear (your "kit," as it's sometimes called), practice with it at home. Prominently mark your gear with your name, as scuba gear on dive boats often becomes mixed with other divers' gear. Wear your BC around the house and get used to where all the dump valves are. Give some thought as to the best way to retain your regulator hoses so that you can easily read your gauges. Prepare your BC and incidental items so that the items can be conveniently clipped to the BC whenever they are needed. In short, transform the components of your gear into a comprehensive dive system that makes sense to you.

The dive site is not the place to start trying to figure out how the tank band cam on your BC works. Becoming familiar with your gear and tailoring it to your personal preferences is fun and involves a thought process that will make you a better diver.

CHAPTER 6

KINDRED SPIRITS AND FIRST TRIPS

T HE BUDDY SYSTEM has been a fundamental cornerstone of dive safety since the inception of the established certifying agencies. However, finding suitable dive buddies often can be a source of frustration for many new divers. Here are some things to consider when shopping for a dive buddy.

FINDING DIVE BUDDIES

The Value of an Established Buddy

Finding a true buddy who shares your passion for diving will add immeasurably to your own diving enjoyment. A good buddy is a person you can rely on not only during dives but also to show up on time and ready to go, a person who is able and willing to dive as actively as you want to dive.

A good dive buddy is one with whom you have a personal rapport, common underwater interests, and similar diving experience. Even if you start with little in common other than your passion for diving, the memories of shared adventures that you will accumulate with a steady dive buddy will help you to form a lasting friendship.

An established dive buddy simplifies diving. Communication underwater becomes intuitive, and the comfort of diving with someone you've grown to know and trust underwater reduces stress. Simply put, diving with an established dive buddy makes diving safer and more fun. However, good dive buddies are surprisingly hard to find.

Let me introduce you to a scenario that you will likely encounter as you become known as an active scuba diver. You will have a chance meeting with someone you know as a diver. Naturally, the conversation will turn to diving, and the friend's closing comment will be something like, "Great to see you; call me and we'll go diving."

If you happen to be looking for a dive buddy, you might say, "Hey, I'm planning a trip for this weekend. Why don't you join me?"

This request will be met with, "This weekend? Well, uh, I'd really like to, but I can't make it this weekend."

If you want to press a little, you could offer the following weekend, and you'd get the same response. In fact, you could offer to let the friend consult a calendar and agree to go diving on any weekend of their choosing. There'd be no weekend to go diving.

You might be left wondering what all the dive talk was about the first time a version of this scenario is played out. You might wonder why half the cars on the road sport a "diver down" front license plate but you can't find anybody to go diving with you.

There are lots of what I call "fantasy divers" running around. They are certified divers, they subscribe to all the dive magazines, and they swell the ranks of dive clubs. They embrace every facet of the active-diver lifestyle except for one thing: they rarely if ever actually go diving.

I don't disparage the fantasy divers. Quite the contrary, I usually enjoy their company, as they generally have a genuine passion for the underwater world and diving seems to be the only thing they want to talk about. However, they are not potential dive buddies. As you prepare to embark on a life of active diving, here are some places to look for kindred spirits:

Classmates

If you've recently completed dive training, there was probably at least one person in the class with whom you found common ground. It may have been the person with whom you were paired for pool and open-water work, or maybe the person to whom you naturally gravitated during breaks. If you had a natural buddy during class, chances are good that this person will become a dive buddy after certification.

If you do not know how to contact a former classmate, your instructor or certifying dive shop will certainly have contact information. Give the person a call and plan a trip.

It's good to begin your career as a certified diver with a person of similar experience. The two of you can help each other without either party feeling that he or she is holding the other back. Plus, since both parties have similar experience, they will be more likely to develop their own dive skills instead of relying upon or becoming dependent on the other.

Dive Shop Personnel

If you've been diving for a while and have become friendly with certain staff members at your dive shop, it may be appropriate to approach them as potential dive buddies. Most dive shop personnel are avid divers, and they may be looking for dive buddies as

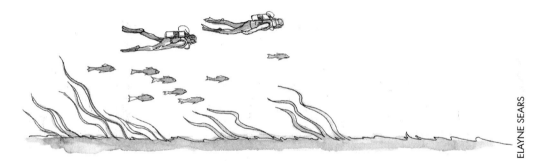

ELAYNE SEARS

well. Remember that the dive shop staff does not want to be "on the job" for their own recreational diving. You should be fully prepared to pull your own weight on any dive trip that you make with dive shop staff members.

Dive Clubs

Dive clubs are a good way to meet local divers, and your local dive shop may sponsor such a club. If the shop doesn't sponsor a club, the staff probably know of any clubs in your area. Most dive clubs are constantly on the lookout for new members, and they will welcome you with open arms. Dues are minimal.

Dive club meetings are typically held monthly and usually include a formal program. Programs vary in subject matter, but look for a dive club that includes reports of local diving in its agenda. Arrive at meetings early or stay after the formal program to meet the membership. If the meeting program is on a subject that interests you, approach the speaker and introduce yourself. Chances are good that the speaker could use a potential dive buddy. Express your interest in the subject of the talk and exchange contact information.

Dive clubs usually attract large numbers of fantasy divers. There's nothing wrong with that. Fantasy divers may even serve as the club's officers, and they may perform more than their share of the work necessary to make the club a success. Even though the fantasy divers are not prospective dive buddies, the club will attract a number of active divers who are probably eager to meet you. A dive club is a good place to form a call list of dive buddies from which to draw whenever a dive buddy is needed.

When Nobody Can Go

Even if you have managed to involve yourself with a pool of potential dive buddies, there will be times when you simply cannot find a suitable buddy for a dive trip that you want to make. It's hard enough to find suitable buddies to make the kinds of dives you want to make, harder still to find them during the specific times you can make those dives. So there you are—it's the perfect weekend for you to go diving, but you can't find anybody to go with you. What can you do?

Assuming that the diving you want to do is based from a commercial dive boat or dive operator, I suggest that you declare your independence and strike out on your own. Call the dive operator to make your reservation and tell them you will be arriving alone. Honestly describe your dive experience and tell the operator that you are willing to buddy up with other divers on the boat upon your arrival. The operator will then be on the lookout for other divers in similar situations with whom you can pair.

If you do not feel comfortable with the prospect of diving with a total stranger, ask the operator if a divemaster will be accompanying the dive party and if the divemaster would be available to dive with you. Dive operators are usually anxious to please

THE DIVE SHOP BS COUNTER

Dive shops are hubs of local diving activity, and Saturdays are often days when a large percentage of the local dive community passes through. Hanging out at the dive shop is a good way to meet local divers and get to know them. Some dive shops maintain bulletin boards of divers looking for buddies for upcoming trips. If your dive shop does not have such a dive buddy clearinghouse, maybe you could offer to set one up. Even if you don't personally meet any potential dive buddies, the shop staff will get to know you and may recommend you to other people who are looking for suitable buddies.

The local dive shop is not just a good place to meet divers. Active divers entering the store invariably have something to say about where they've been diving and what conditions were like. The shop is a good place for learning about local diving possibilities as well as meeting the local divers who are taking advantage of them.

If it sounds like I'm recommending the dive shop as a kind of pickup bar for divers, I guess I am. I've never used the line "Let's go diving if I'm wrong, but have we met before?" in a dive shop, but it might be worth a try. Seriously, don't be too shy to introduce yourself to a group of divers discussing their latest adventure. Divers are generally friendly folks, and most will welcome you into their group.

Dive shop management usually encourage social activity in their store. They are passionate about diving, and they know that active divers mean business for them. The shop personnel will be glad to talk to you about dive opportunities, and your certifying shop will be familiar with your skills, experience, and interests. Remember, though, that they are in business to sell things. Don't tie up salespeople with idle chat when customers are in the store, and try to spend a few dollars during your stay.

potential guests, and they will do their best to accommodate you. If the operator seems unwilling or unable to help you, look for another operator.

If you dive with a divemaster from the boat or operator, remember that he or she is only responsible to you as a good dive buddy. You are no longer a student, and you should not be dependent on the divemaster for the dive.

Single divers are typically identified during the dive briefing if no prior arrangement has been made to dive with a divemaster. The divemaster will ask if all divers have buddies or for any divers without a buddy to raise their hand. If you are the only person with a raised hand, the divemaster may offer to dive with you. However, it is more typical that a request will be made to see if any buddy pairs would be willing to form a threesome with you. If a buddy pair agrees to dive with you, take some time to get to know them and be frank about your level of experience and dive plan. If the match is not a good one, let the divemaster know so that a better arrangement can be made.

You will probably not be the only single diver on the boat or dive staging area. You will likely see another hand being raised by a person who looks and feels as sheepish as you do, and the two of you will be paired. Introduce yourself to your new prospective buddy and plan your dive together. Let the divemaster know if you are uncomfortable with the pairing.

Many lasting friendships have been established by two people who meekly raised their hands as single divers. The mere fact that you meet a person in this way suggests that the two of you have quite a bit in common. You are both active divers unwilling to allow the schedules of others to dictate your lives. You are each where you are based on a personal decision to strike out on your own to see what you may find, and you each ended up at the same dive site. The fact that you found each other was more likely than coincidental.

WHERE TO GO

Once your training is completed, it's time to go diving on your own. Some divers have the luxuries of time and money to travel to and dive at celebrated destinations around the world. For most of us, though, it's far more practical to find diving closer to home.

Checkout Dive Site

Your open-water training (checkout) dives were probably made a reasonable distance from your home. The diving was probably not world-class, but if you found it interesting, it may serve as a good local destination to get some dives under your belt.

The site of your open-water training dives is usually the most convenient and cost-effective diving in your area. It will probably be possible for you to tag along on future checkout trips with your certifying dive shop as a certified diver. By taking advantage of the routine established by the dive shop, you can save money on both diving and lodging. You must always remember, though, that even if you are in the company of your former instructor, you are diving as a certified diver and should not be dependent on the shop personnel for your diving.

As you become more familiar with the site and with the dive operator, it will become easier to arrange your trips around a schedule most convenient to you. Your open-water training site is a great place to start your independent diving career.

Where Do the Dive Shop Personnel Dive?

The fact that there's a dive shop in your community is a good sign that somebody is going diving, and there's a good chance that the people who are diving are affiliated with the dive shop. As you get to know the dive shop staff, ask them where their favorite diving is.

You will find that some dive shop staffers travel internationally for their diving. Some, though, are probably making dives within driving distance from your town. Most will be glad to talk to you about their diving. You might even be invited to come along on the next trip.

Local Specialties

Many areas of the country are known for specific kinds of diving. For example, the Louisiana coast is known for oil rig diving and spearfishing; the eastern and Great Lakes states are known for wrecks; and the California coast is known for its forests of kelp.

Chances are good that the dive shop personnel are involved with whatever local diving specialties are close to your area and they will be glad to tell you about them. Even if you do not feel any compulsion to participate in the specialty, the dive infrastructure that will have evolved to accommodate the specialty divers is something that you might be able to take advantage of. For example, even if you are not trained, prepared, or interested in wreck-penetration diving, you and a like-minded buddy might be able to join a wreck-diving party for a dive trip and limit your diving to established recreational-diving activities.

Continuing Training

Your open-water certification should be enough to start you on your way to a life of active, independent diving. However, additional formal dive training is a good way to boost your confidence, meet other divers, be exposed to different types of specialty diving that interest you, and gain more information about dive sites. Continuing formal training is also an excellent way to keep you actively diving if you have trouble organizing your own trips. The following are some training classes that I feel are most beneficial:

Advanced Open Water
Courses for Advanced Open Water certification vary slightly among the established certifying agencies, but they all revolve around the simple curriculum of making more open-water training dives under the supervision of an instructor. You will be introduced to underwater navigation, perhaps night diving, perhaps basic search and recovery. The main thing, though, is that you will make dives. By doing so, you will meet new people and be exposed to new sites—things you can build upon as you pursue your goal of becoming an independent diver. Don't let the "Advanced" distinction

IS SPEARFISHING ETHICAL?

The prospect of taking game from the sea was a major motivation in the invention and development of scuba. In fact, a few lobsters were taken during the very first scuba dive in June 1943, as described by Jacques Cousteau in his thrilling book *The Silent World*, and spearfishing and game collection was a mainstay of the sport of scuba in its formative years.

I do not believe that Captain Cousteau foresaw the reckless exploitation that followed his invention and his example in the middle part of the twentieth century. Divers obsessed with taking game virtually denuded many areas. Some early divers set out to "conquer the sea" with their spearguns, and they left a chilling and bloody wake.

As Bob Dylan proclaimed, the times they were a-changin' by the 1960s. Global ecology became a mainstream science and popular-cultural concern, and the public perception of hunting and hunters changed dramatically. Hunters were no longer seen as daring adventurers dueling with the dangers of nature. Hunters were either depicted as the embodiment of evil (the faceless hunters in Walt Disney's *Bambi*) or as dim-witted buffoons (Elmer Fudd). *Nimrod*, a word traditionally used to denote a gentleman hunter, assumed a connotation more like "bonehead." The idea of benevolence toward all living things became a cultural icon, and this idea persists to the present.

I personally like the idea of benevolence toward all living things. However, it is a fundamental fact of life that our individual existence comes at the expense of other living things. No one, not even the strictest vegetarian, is excluded from this fact. The farms that produce the vegetables we eat cause the demise of many living things due to destruction of habitat. This fundamental fact is no cause for self-loathing. Rather, it is an affirmation of our place in the ecology of the world.

So where does this leave spearfishers? Does spearfishing violate some sort of sacred trust between divers and the inhabitants of the sea? Should spearfishing be banned because it is primitive and unnecessary?

Responsible spearfishing is, perhaps, the most ecologically friendly way to obtain seafood. As opposed to the significant waste and by-catch of the commercial fishing boats that supply your local seafood market or restaurant, spearfishing only affects the fish or creature to be consumed, and the impact on the environment or habitat is nil. It is true that spearfishing is not necessary in our modern world, but it is not primitive either. We all participate in the food chain. Spearfishing is a way for divers to participate directly and naturally, and the buoyancy control and diving skills acquired by good spearfishers enable them to dive with far less impact on the diving environment than most divers.

Spearfishing equipment and techniques vary around the United States. California spearfishers typically fish in open water by free diving (diving without scuba). Their spearguns are attached to buoys or floats on the surface. Southern spearfishers typically hunt deep within the semi-overhead environments of oil rigs and often use scuba. (An overhead environment has a solid barrier that separates divers from the surface; oil rig beams aren't solid, but still impede access to the surface, and thus are termed semi-overhead environments.) Their spearguns are not attached to floats on the surface, and they must deal with speared fish underwater. Eastern spearfishers often hunt near deep wrecks and use equipment and techniques similar to those of the southern spearfishers.

All spearfishers must conform to the same season, limit, and size laws that pertain to ordinary rod-and-reel fishers. Many dive shops near areas in which spearfishing is popular offer instruction. Also, NAUI (National Association of Underwater Instructors) offers a specialty in hunting and collecting, your local PADI instructor may offer spearfishing as a Distinctive Specialty, and your local SSI (Scuba Schools International) instructor may offer spearfishing as a Unique Specialty.

go to your head. You may be an advanced open-water student, but you will still be a newbie independent diver even after you have attained your Advanced Open Water certification.

Local Specialties

Many types of local specialty diving such as kelp diving, wreck diving, and spearfishing require knowledge and techniques beyond what you'll get in either Open Water I or Advanced Open Water training. The established training and certifying agencies do not generally provide courses for local specialties, but local dive shops usually provide formal training. Ask your dive shop about such training. The more you know about the local specialty, the better prepared you will be to take advantage of it. If you live near cold water, see about taking a course in dry-suit diving. If your local diving involves technical diving such as deep New England wrecks or Florida caves, your local training could last a lifetime and transform you into one of diving's elite.

Rescue Diver

The established training and certifying agencies offer Rescue Diver courses. These courses focus on diving medicine and emergency procedures that every independent diver should be familiar with. Not only will you learn techniques that will enable you to assist other divers in distress, but you will also become more attuned to your own diving safety.

Training Agency Specialties

The established agencies offer a wide range of diving specialty courses such as Underwater Photographer and Underwater Naturalist. Find out what courses are available from your dive shop. These courses are typically rudimentary, but they may shorten

SPECIALTY COURSES BY CERTIFYING AGENCIES

SSI SPECIALTY COURSES

Boat Diving
Computer Diving
Deep Diving
Diver Stress & Rescue
Dry Suit Diving
Enriched Air Nitrox
Equipment Techniques
Navigation
Night & Limited Visibility Diving
Search & Recovery
Underwater Photography
Unique Specialties[1]
Waves, Tides & Currents
Wreck Diving

NAUI SPECIALTY COURSES

Advanced Scuba Rescue Diver
Cave Diver
Cavern Diver
Deep Diver
EANx Diver
Hunter & Collector
Ice Diver
Night Diver
Scuba Rescue Diver
Search & Recovery
Training Assistant
Underwater Environment
Underwater Photographer
Wreck Diver (External Survey)
Wreck Diver (Penetration)

PADI SPECIALTY COURSES

Altitude Diver
AWARE[2]–Coral Reef Conservation
AWARE–Fish Identification Diver Program
Boat Diver
Cavern Diver
Deep Diver
Dive Propulsion Vehicle Diver
Distinctive Specialties[1], Drift Diver
Dry Suit Diver
Emergency First Response
Enriched Air Diver
Equipment Specialist
Ice Diver
Master Scuba Diver
Multilevel Diver
Night Diver
Peak Performance Buoyancy
Project AWARE Specialty Course
Search and Recovery Diver
Semiclosed Rebreather[3]–Dolphin/Atlantis
Semiclosed Rebreather–Drager Ray
Underwater Naturalist
Underwater Navigator
Underwater Photographer
Underwater Videographer
Wreck Diver

[1] Unique Specialties (SSI) and Distinctive Specialties (PADI) are special courses written by instructors of the respective agencies and approved by the respective agencies. They can cover a wide range of topics.
[2] Project AWARE is an international foundation dedicated to conservation of the oceans (www.projectaware.org).
[3] Rebreathers are scuba devices that allow exhalations to be rebreathed after adding oxygen and removing carbon dioxide. The different specialties pertain to different rebreather manufacturers.

Sources: www.padi.com, www.naui.com, and www.ssiusa.com.

the learning curve regarding special interests that you may have. More importantly, you will meet people with similar interests and you'll go diving.

Nitrox Diver

Nitrox, sometimes more properly called enriched air nitrox, or EAN, is a gas mixture that contains a higher percentage of oxygen and a lower percentage of nitrogen than air. The main purpose of diving on nitrox is to extend bottom time with respect to decompression sickness, and the additional bottom time can be substantial at moderate depths. Nitrox certification involves a bit more classroom work than most advanced certifications, but the payoff can be significantly more time for each dive. Nitrox diving presupposes a serious commitment to diving, and the people you'll meet in a Nitrox certification class will likely be active divers. The certification is not complete until you have made a number of dives on nitrox, so you'll go diving if you take this class.

Master Diver

The Master Diver certification is the highest attainable from the established certifying agencies before entering the teaching certifications such as Divemaster or Instructor. Prerequisites for the class include many of the certifications I've mentioned in this section. Master Diver certification involves substantial classroom work, and it is completed with open-water training dives. The people you'll meet in this class are committed divers, and many will be on their way to becoming Divemasters or Instructors upon completion of their Master Diver training.

Dive training should not be an end in itself. The point of dive training should be to make you a better diver and to better prepare you to independently pursue the kinds of diving that interest you.

CHAPTER 7

An Introduction to Mother Ocean

Water Weight and Density

BONNIE CARDONE

Y OU, AS A CERTIFIED DIVER, are fully prepared to deal with the physics, techniques, and equipment that allow you to thrive for a few minutes beneath the surface of the water. Your certification class has adequately trained you for that. Unfortunately, most certification classes do not spend much classroom time discussing the water itself.

Many certification classes seem to be designed to teach students how to dive only in a swimming pool. That's good enough for dive destinations that feature pool-like conditions. Consistently easy diving is the hallmark of the destinations celebrated in the dive magazines. They're great and they're easy, but they're out of reach for many of us for most of our diving.

Most of us must venture a little farther out into the ocean and be prepared to encounter conditions a little less predictable in order to get our dives in. For that reason, it's important that you understand a few things about the ocean beyond the dive resorts.

THE CHARACTERISTICS OF OCEAN WATER

In this section we touch on several major aspects of the ocean that directly affect you as a diver. Many of the things we talk about apply to the benign conditions of the dive resorts as well as to the more challenging conditions you'll encounter elsewhere.

Water Weight and Density

Water is heavy. How heavy? Well, the accepted standard weight of a cubic foot of seawater is 64 pounds. Similarly, the accepted standard weight of a cubic foot of fresh water is 62.4 pounds. Since the weight of seawater is greater than the weight of the same volume of fresh water, we can say that seawater has greater density than fresh water. A little arithmetic $[(62.4 \div 64 - 1) \times 100]$ reveals that the difference between the densities of seawater and fresh water is 2.5 percent. Why is seawater denser than fresh water? Because seawater contains dissolved salts and minerals that have greater density than the water into which they have dissolved.

Remembering Archimedes from the old high school physics class, we know that any object fully or partially submerged in a fluid will be buoyed up by a force equal to the weight of the fluid displaced by that object.

Given these few facts, you might think that because seawater has greater density than fresh water, the weight of the volume of seawater displaced by a fully or partially submerged object would be greater than the weight of the same volume of fresh water, so seawater can "float" a denser object than fresh water can.

Guess what? You'd be exactly right. The buoyant force of seawater is greater than the buoyant force of fresh water. How much greater? We've already figured that out. Seawater has 2.5 percent more buoyant force than fresh water.

Salinity

So far we've been talking about two distinct kinds of water—seawater and fresh water. What happens when the two mix, such as when a freshwater river empties into the sea? As you might imagine, the resulting mix is neither fresh water nor seawater. The amount of salts and minerals dissolved in water is known as the water's salinity, and salinity varies in coastal waters (the average salinity of seawater also varies slightly from ocean to ocean, but we'll leave that alone). Water that is somewhere between seawater and fresh water in salinity is called brackish water. Brackish water flows from the coast into the ocean, where evaporation and absorption of salts and minerals eventually transform it into seawater. Brackish water has greater density than fresh water, but less density than seawater.

Haloclines

So what does all of this talk about water density have to do with you as a diver? If you dive near the coast, it can affect you in lots of ways.

We've seen that brackish water near the coast has less density than the seawater farther from shore. We've also determined that if an object weighs less than the volume of water it displaces, it will float. If you consider the less dense brackish water as an object, what do you think might happen when it moves over denser seawater offshore?

Brackish water floats on seawater until evaporation and absorption of salts equalize its density with seawater. Near areas of freshwater runoff, such as near the mouths of major rivers, this layer of brackish water spreads out over the ocean. The layer may be up to 50 feet thick, and it is moved around by the wind.

This floating mass of brackish water is usually very murky. This is due to several factors, including the fact that it contains sediment from the river from whence it came. Additionally, suspended particulate (more reasonably known as "stuff in the water") that would float atop denser seawater remains suspended in less dense brackish water and reduces underwater visibility to practically nil.

If you find yourself on a dive boat anchored or moored within this floating mass of brackish water offshore, you may question the point of diving in it. While it's true that the diving might be poor, it's also possible that the surface layer of ugly water is only a few feet thick. Divers who brave the dirty surface water descend until they pass through the interface between the brackish water and the seawater upon which it is floating. This interface is called a halocline.

Haloclines are dramatic. The interface between the two types of water may be very thin, and water visibility may increase from mere inches to 50 feet or beyond. It's as if the ocean opens up to welcome you. Visibility at the halocline itself is distorted—almost like looking through a windshield in the rain with the wipers off.

Even though the seawater beneath the halocline generally has much greater transparency, the murky water above will have absorbed much of the sunlight. Diving beneath a halocline is like entering a world of perpetual twilight. It's a world of steely blue light with little color. It's breathtakingly beautiful.

Divers who frequent offshore sites near areas of freshwater runoff are very familiar with haloclines. The surface layer of brackish water is typically called the murky layer, and local divers keep abreast of how far offshore it reaches and how deep they must go to dive beneath the halocline. As the murky layer is distorted and moved by prevailing winds, its position and thickness change from day to day. Obtain current local information regarding the murky layer before you dive such sites.

Thermoclines

Salinity is not the only thing that affects the density of water. Water density is also affected by temperature.

Cold water is denser than warm water of equal salinity, so cold water sinks. Take a moment to doff your hat to this fact, for it is one of the fundamental principles that drives the ocean engine that moderates our global climate and makes our world habitable. Now that we've taken care of that, we'll get to the more important issue of how water temperature affects our diving.

Seawater stratifies by temperature, with the warmer water floating atop the colder water. In areas where haloclines exist, it is common during summer months for the brackish surface water to be warmed by the sun, further reducing its density. When this happens, the interface between the waters of disparate densities demarks a pronounced temperature change as well as a change in water salinity and clarity. The interface between waters of different densities due to temperature is called a thermocline.

Thermoclines are also dramatic. Water temperature may fall 10°F within just a few feet of depth. A thermocline combined with a halocline is more dramatic still, as divers move from warm, murky water into the cold, clearer water beneath. Passing through such a demarcation almost feels like jumping into the water all over again.

Of course, a thermocline may develop without an accompanying halocline. Such a temperature interface is invisible but no less dramatic (though the effect of the thermocline might be visible if you count the goose bumps on your buddy). Make a point to get local information regarding thermoclines and the water temperatures you are likely to encounter before you travel to a site. Wear exposure protection appropriate for the water temperature beneath the thermocline.

Since thermoclines are caused by a density disparity due to temperature rather than salinity, they also form in freshwater lakes and quarries. Thermoclines in these relatively small and contained bodies of water are generally seasonal, but they can be even more dramatic than their ocean counterparts.

The surface waters of lakes and quarries are warmed by the sun in summer months, which forms a warmer and less dense surface layer called the epilimnion. A cold, dense layer of water called the hypolimnion remains beneath. A thermocline separates the two layers. Several thermoclines may develop if the water is deep.

As the surface layer of lakes and quarries cools during the fall months, the disparity in temperature between the epilimnion and hypolimnion diminishes. The thermocline disappears as the body of water approaches a common temperature—a condition called isothermal. Further cooling of the surface layer combined with wind results in a mixing of the layers of water and is known as the fall turnover. The former epilimnion sinks as it cools. This may force nutrients up from the oxygen-poor hypolimnion and cause an algae bloom that greatly reduces underwater visibility.

An interesting phenomenon occurs if the surface temperature of a lake or quarry approaches the freezing point in winter. As water molecules approach the freezing point, they organize themselves in a way that reduces density (that's why ice floats). When this occurs, the freezing or near freezing water near the surface is less dense than the warmer water beneath, and a reverse thermocline develops. The cold water is on top and warmer water is beneath.

Another turnover occurs in lakes and quarries in springtime as the surface water is warmed significantly above the freezing point. The cold surface water becomes denser than the warmer water beneath, and it begins to sink. This mixing continues until the surface water is warmed to the point that the temperature stratification begins anew. After an isothermal period, a thermocline develops, with warm water on top and cold water beneath.

Thermal stratification in lakes and quarries affects oxygen distribution, which in turn affects fish and wildlife distribution. Temperature also affects the development and distribution of plankton, which affects visibility. Isothermal conditions are generally best for diving in lakes or quarries.

Personal Buoyancy

As we've seen, the buoyant force of water is affected by its density, and masses of water of differing densities stratify in layers. We've seen a variety of ways that these layers can affect your diving experience, but we haven't covered the most intimate effect of all. How does the density of water affect your personal buoyancy?

The differences in water densities that cause thermoclines and haloclines in open water are subtle. Their effect on your personal buoyancy will generally go unnoticed by you. If you notice any effect at all, it is usually as you ascend back into the layer of less dense water near the surface. You always need to remove air from your BC as you ascend to shallower depths, but you may need to dump a bit more air as you move into warmer or less-saline water.

Diving in the extremes of salinity is a different story. Your buoyancy is affected if you move from true fresh water to seawater, and vice versa. Many open-water training (checkout) dives are conducted in freshwater lakes, springs, or quarries as a matter of convenience. Divers who have weighted themselves in these freshwater environments must make an adjustment to dive in seawater.

As seawater is denser than fresh water, divers must increase their own density to dive in seawater. Simply put, you increase in density if you increase your mass (weight) without increasing your volume (size). OK, maybe that wasn't so simply put. Better put, you need to add weight to your weight belt if you dive in seawater wearing the same equipment and exposure suit you used in fresh water.

How much weight should you add? We've determined that seawater has 2.5 percent more buoyant force than fresh water. Some divers figure that all they have to do is add 2.5 percent more weight to their belt and all will be fine. For example, if they wore 10 pounds of weight in fresh water, all they would need to add is 2.5 percent more—a scant quarter of a pound—to make up the difference. Those divers are wrong.

The buoyant force of water affects all of you—not just your weight belt. The buoyant force affects your entire body and all the equipment you are wearing.

To figure out how much additional weight you need to dive in seawater, you must first determine your entire weight when diving in fresh water. If you weigh 160 pounds and you wear 10 pounds on your weight belt in fresh water, you're up to 170 pounds. Add another 50 pounds for your tank, BC, and regulator, and you weigh 220 pounds. Now we're getting somewhere. Add 2.5 percent to this total weight, and you'll find that you need to add 5.5 pounds to your weight belt to counter the additional buoyant force of seawater ($220 \times 0.025 = 5.5$).

How Water Density Affects Light

Now that we've talked about the different densities of water, let's address some of the effects caused by the tremendous difference between the density of air and the density of water.

Air has density and weight. A cubic foot of air at sea level weighs about 0.075 pounds. That means that the air compressed into a full 80-cubic-foot scuba tank weighs about 6 pounds ($0.075 \times 80 = 6$). If you don't believe me, pick up a full aluminum-80 with one hand and an empty one with the other hand. You'll feel the difference. Some experienced divers (especially dive shop personnel who fill tanks daily) can roughly estimate the amount of air in a scuba tank simply by feeling the weight of the tank.

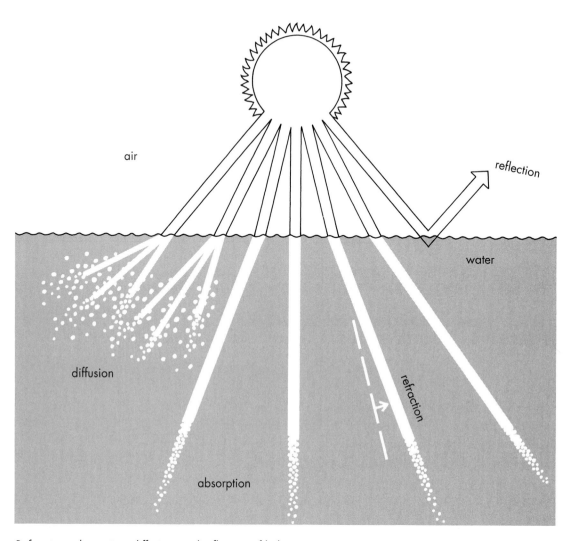

Refraction, absorption, diffusion, and reflection of light in water. JIM SOLLERS BASED ON AN ILLUSTRATION FROM NAUI MASTER SCUBA DIVER

As a bit of an aside, you were trained to ballast yourself with dive weights to the point that you could maintain neutral buoyancy at a depth of 15 feet with a near-empty tank and little or no air in your BC. This was to ensure that you could maintain neutral buoyancy for your safety stop at the end of your dives, when your tank would be nearly empty. Your instructor made the point that your buoyancy be set with a near-empty tank because the empty tank reduces your weight (by as much as 6 pounds with a standard 80-cubic-foot tank) and affects your personal buoyancy.

So air has density. However, comparing the 0.075-pound cubic foot of air against the 64-pound cubic foot of seawater (or the 62.4-pound cubic foot of fresh water—the difference is negligible in this context), we can figure that water is about 850 times denser than air. This disparity of densities affects light in four major ways: refraction, reflection, color absorption, and diffusion.

Refraction

I like to watch new divers returning to a mooring or anchor line after a dive. They arrive cool, calm, and confident after their adventure. But something happens when they glide to a stop and casually reach for the line to officially end their dive. The line isn't there! An expression of consternation flashes across their faces as they reach again, a bit more frantically this time. The line isn't there! Is the boat moving away from them? Have they been caught in some mysterious current? Are they moving backward? Coolness and calmness be damned, they shoot forward with a powerful kick of their fins and slam into the line. It makes me giggle every time I see it. What makes the divers behave so strangely?

The density of water causes light to slow down by 25 percent. If the light moves from the air to the water (or from the water to the air in your dive mask) at an angle, the light bends. This slowing and bending of light is called refraction.

Refraction is the reason you need a dive mask to see clearly underwater. Your eyes are designed to refract (bend) light moving in air in order to focus. Light moving in water is traveling too slowly to be affected enough by the lens (another refractor) in your eye, so the light does not bend enough to come into focus. That's why everything is blurry underwater unless you're wearing a mask. The mask provides an air space for the light to resume its speed in air before entering the lens of your eye.

We're all familiar with the refractive effect of water. A pencil leaning in a glass of water appears to be bent at the waterline, and the portion of the pencil underwater appears larger. Similarly, it appears that a person's butt and legs are overly large if they're wading waist deep in a pool, but this last observation is usually best kept to yourself.

We are not as good at recognizing the refractive effect of water when an object is totally submerged. The object looks normally proportioned even though the refractive effect is still at work.

When we're underwater and have an air space in front of our eyes (as with a dive mask), refraction causes objects to appear to be 25 percent closer than they actually are. This explains the strange phenomenon of the vanishing anchor line. The returning divers were programmed to recognize their distance from the line in air, but underwater, the line appeared to be 25 percent closer than it actually was. When the divers reached out to grab the line that they thought was 3 feet away, it was actually 4 feet away. They missed it by a full foot.

The magnifying effect caused by refraction similarly alters your perception of an object's size underwater. This explains serious reports of 10-foot barracuda (they really only grow to about 6 feet in length). The effect is more serious for underwater hunters, who must adhere to strict size limits of their game.

Reflection

A portion of the light moving in air does not penetrate the surface of the water at all but simply bounces off the water. This bouncing of light is called reflection, and we're all familiar with it from looking in mirrors. Light penetration into water is greatest when the light strikes the water at a 90-degree angle, and reflection increases (light penetration diminishes) as the angle moves away from 90 degrees. As a result, underwater visibility is usually best when the sun is highest in the sky.

The surface state of the water also affects reflection and light penetration and therefore affects underwater visibility. Steep waves alter the angle of the light striking the water and increase reflection when the sun is high overhead. Perfectly smooth water also increases reflection if the sun is not directly overhead. Generally speaking, decreases in underwater visibility due to reflection are minimized when the surface of the water is slightly rippled.

Reflection is greatest when the sun is low on the horizon, as virtually all light will be reflected if the angle becomes too small. When the angle becomes critically small, the underwater world will be in near total darkness even though it may be light enough to see comfortably above. Underwater, dawn and dusk are fleeting.

The reflective quality of the interface between air and water also affects light moving from the water to the air. Night divers who aim their dive lights at an angle to the surface may see their light beam bounce from the "ceiling" and reflect back into the water. It's neat to see.

Color Absorption

As you'll remember from your grade school science class, light is radiant energy of varying wavelengths. Visible light is composed of the range of wavelengths that can be detected by the human eye. We see all the wavelengths combined as white, we see the lack of any wavelength as black, and we detect the individual wavelengths as color. Wavelength can be thought of as energy, so we can say that the colors we see depend upon the energy of the wavelength of light entering our eyes. Long wavelengths have less energy; short wavelengths have greater energy.

You can divide and see the spectrum of visible colors in white light by passing the light through a prism, which separates the different wavelengths starting with the longest (least energy) and progressing to the shortest (most energy). The order of the colors (by decreasing wavelength) is red, orange, yellow, green, blue, indigo, and violet. The mnemonic "Roy G. Biv" is often used to remember the order of the colors.

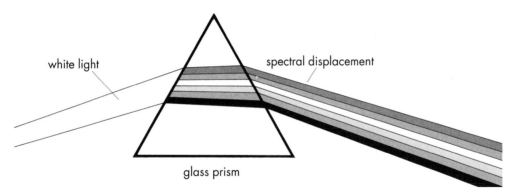

white light

spectral displacement

glass prism

The spectrum of colors in white light can be seen by passing it through a prism. JIM SOLLERS BASED ON AN ILLUSTRATION FROM NAUI MASTER SCUBA DIVER

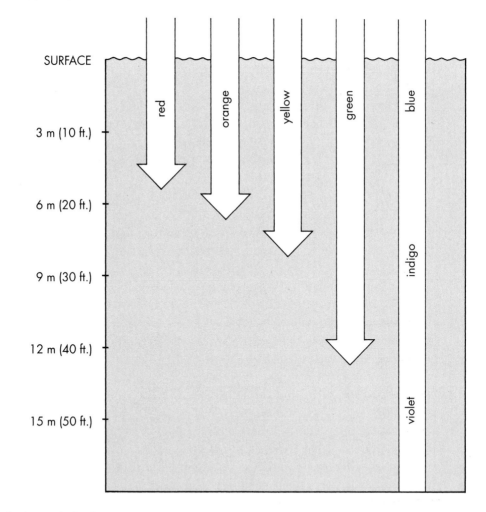

SURFACE

DEPTH

red

orange

yellow

green

blue

indigo

violet

3 m (10 ft.)

6 m (20 ft.)

9 m (30 ft.)

12 m (40 ft.)

15 m (50 ft.)

Color loss with depth. JIM SOLLERS BASED ON AN ILLUSTRATION FROM NAUI MASTER SCUBA DIVER

An Introduction to Mother Ocean

Wavelengths of light that are longer than red (infrared) or shorter than violet (ultraviolet) cannot be seen by the human eye.

So, visible light is made up of different wavelengths, the wavelength with the least energy is seen as red, and the wavelength with the most energy is seen as violet. What do you think happens to these wavelengths (colors) when they travel through the dense medium of water?

Underwater, wavelengths of light are absorbed and color, starting with red, disappears. Orange, yellow, and green disappear in order as depth increases, until only shades of blue moving toward violet are visible.

The disappearance of color occurs rapidly with depth. Red disappears at a depth of only about 20 feet, orange at about 25 feet, and yellow at about 30 feet. I guess you could say that "Roy" is completely out of the game at a depth of only 30 feet. Green disappears at around 40 feet, and all colors deeper than that are seen as shades of blue.

In chapter 2, we mentioned that some divers wear masks with faceplates tinted red or orange. These faceplates are designed to enhance as much low-energy light as possible to give the diver a more natural view of colors underwater. However, they cannot enhance a wavelength of light that has been completely absorbed by the water. A red mask faceplate will help bring out the color red in shallow water, but it will have no effect on color at a depth where the wavelength we see as red does not exist.

Diffusion

Diffusion is not so much an effect caused by the density of water as are the other effects on light we've discussed. Rather, diffusion is the scattering of light caused by stuff suspended in the water. Like absorption, diffusion acts to limit the depth to which light can penetrate into water.

The diffusion caused by light striking suspended particles in the water and scattering in random directions reduces underwater visibility. The amount of particulate suspended in water is called the water's turbidity. The more turbid the water, the less you will see. Diffusion caused by turbid water not only reduces available light at depth, but the scattering effect also acts to reduce visibility in the remaining light.

HOW WATER DENSITY AFFECTS SOUND

The density of water affects sound in the opposite way that it affects light. While light is radiant energy that is slowed or absorbed by a dense medium, sound is a pressure wave that moves faster and more efficiently as the density of the medium increases. Water is far denser than air, so sound moves faster and more efficiently in water than it moves in air.

The fact that sound is a pressure wave also reverses the order in which varying wavelengths of sound are absorbed. Sound is the transference of energy (vibrations) from a source to a receptor. As such, the wavelengths that required the most energy to produce are the first to dissipate over distance. We hear high-energy wavelengths (high frequencies) as high pitch. Low frequencies (low pitch) travel farther. That's why you mostly hear the bass line when a lowrider passes on the street with the stereo blaring.

Since the speed of sound varies significantly depending on the density of the medium through which it passes, it's hard to put a finger on how fast sound travels in air and in water. This is because the density of air changes with altitude, temperature, and humidity, and, as we've seen, the density of water changes with salinity and temperature. When the general speed of sound is discussed, averages or standards must be used. The standard speed of sound in air is accepted to be 1,080 feet per second. Likewise, the standard speed of sound in water is accepted to be 4,725 feet per second—more than four times faster than the speed of sound in air.

Many creatures of the sea take advantage of the efficiency of sound underwater. Some fish grunt or croak; shrimp and barnacles click and pop. Some types of shrimp can actually use sound to stun or kill their prey. But the creatures that push sound to its limits underwater are the cetaceans—the porpoises, dolphins, and whales.

Dolphins and porpoises use sound to communicate with each other, to navigate, and to locate their prey. Their echolocation ability enables them to detect items buried in sand and to determine the size, shape, distance, and physical makeup of those items. It's sort of like X-ray vision through sound.

Whales produce underwater sounds that travel great distances. The famous "songs" of humpback whales can be heard by divers up to ten miles away. The songs can be detected by other humpback whales at distances approaching a hundred miles. Blue whales, the largest whales and the largest creatures ever to inhabit the earth, produce tremendous sounds at frequencies too low to be heard by the human ear. As we've seen, low-frequency sounds travel the farthest. Calls of blue whales have been detected by sensitive hydrophones from distances approaching a thousand miles. With a holler like that, who needs a telephone or long distance?

Many divers attempt to take advantage of the efficiency of sound underwater to communicate with their buddies. On the shelves of your dive shop, you'll find all kinds of shakers, bangers, and clackers designed to attract attention through sound. In fact, the most common use of the dive knife for most divers is to bang it on a tank to make an attention-getting sound. However, you may have noticed that I did not recommend any sound producers in the gadgets chapter of this book. Why not?

Our senses have evolved to work in air, and sound travels far more slowly in air than it does in water. Sound reaches each of our ears at different times, and in air, our brains can calculate this time difference to tell us the direction from which the sound came. But our brains can't keep up with sound traveling four times faster than normal. Sound underwater moves so fast that the directional programming in our brains can't discern any difference between the times the sound reaches each of our ears. Because of this, we simply can't determine the source of sounds underwater. We hear it, but we can't tell where it's coming from.

So even though we can hear the bangers and clackers clearly, we have no idea if the sound came from our buddy swimming 5 feet to our right or from another diver swimming 20 feet behind us and to our left. Because of this confusion, I personally find sound-makers to be more of an annoyance than a benefit underwater—especially if there are divers in the water other than you and your buddy.

If you're diving with a good-natured buddy on your next dive, you might want to have some fun with this little experiment: Position yourself above and slightly behind your buddy and yell a falsetto "Yoo-hoo" through your regulator. Your buddy will stop, look right, look left, look down, look up, look all around, and probably never find you. If the buddy gives up too easily, call the buddy's name through your regulator. They'll recognize their own name and the game will begin anew.

This exercise may be more than a silly game. It's a good idea to decide on a vocal call to be used only by you and your buddy to get each other's attention underwater. If you hear the call, you'll know it's your buddy, and you should have a good idea of where your buddy is. It's a way to share discoveries with your buddy without clanging and causing every diver within a hundred feet of you to stop, look left, look right, etc.

CHAPTER 8

THE WEATHER

WIND AND WAVES, STORMS, AND CURRENTS

DAVID BREIDENBACH

139

I F Y O U W E R E T O A S K A N O N D I V E R what his biggest concern would be at the prospect of taking up scuba and going diving, the answer would probably have something to do with marine creatures with bad reputations like sharks or jellyfish. A new diver's answer to a question regarding concerns about her next dive trip would probably revolve around dive skills like buoyancy or air management. But if you were to ask an experienced, independent diver to define his biggest concern regarding his next dive trip, the answer would almost invariably be the weather.

There's no doubt about it—weather will affect your diving in more ways than any other variable. In this chapter we discuss some of the common ways that weather affects diving, as well as ways to deal with less-than-perfect dive conditions caused by weather. However, we, as independent divers, can never lose sight of the power of weather. In a battle between weather and the best diver in the world, the weather will always win.

You will encounter all kinds of weather as you continue your exciting journey as an independent diver, and the experience you gain with various weather conditions is as important to your development and safety as anything you'll learn underwater. You should become a student of the weather and how it affects the conditions of prospective dive sites. Talking about the weather is far more than a casual pastime for divers.

Take a moment right now to come to grips with the fact that you will have to forfeit some dive trips due to bad weather. Don't worry about it. Just accept it.

Even if you give the weather proper respect, as you continue to pursue your diving career, the day will eventually come when you'll have a thought that you never thought you'd have. You'll be on a dive trip, you'll be engaged in diving, you'll be living your passion, but then the weather will take a bad turn, the boat will start to rock and roll, the spray will fly, and this will suddenly occur to you: you'll wish you were back home cutting the grass. No kidding.

WIND AND WAVES

Barring a seismic event such as an earthquake, waves on water are caused by wind and generally move in the same direction as the wind. The size of waves depends on wind speed, wind duration, wind fetch (the distance the wind blows over the water), and water depth.

Waves are described by their height, wavelength, and period. The height of a wave is a vertical measurement from the wave's crest (highest point) to its trough (lowest

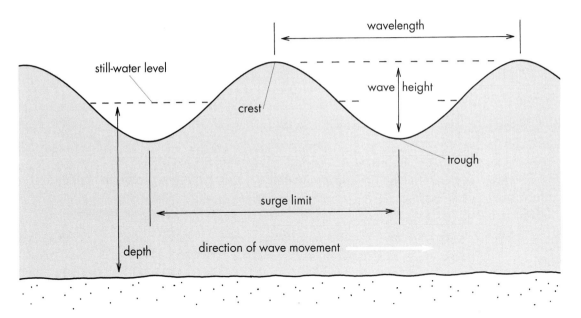

Wave terminology.

point). The wave's wavelength is a horizontal measurement between crests (or troughs), and the period is the time it takes for two successive crests to pass any given point. The surface of the water develops what is called a sea state as wind blows over it, and the resulting waves are called seas.

Seas are unstable waves in the act of formation. Once waves are formed, they may continue to move in a stable form for hundreds of miles. These stable waves generally have a long wavelength and are known as swells. Swells are more gently rolling waves that pose far less danger to boaters than do unstable seas.

Water Movement in Waves and Surge

Nonbreaking waves do not transport water. Rather, waves are an energy force moving through water. Water within a wave moves in an orbit as the wave moves forward, then returns almost to its original position once the wave passes. Therefore, a diver will not be swept away by wave action in the open sea. However, objects on the surface of the water may be moved by currents and by the wind that causes the waves.

Surge

Surge (see sidebar, next page) affects divers underwater by moving them back and forth in the pattern of the orb. If the water is shallow, the orb of moving water

WATER MOTION

Water moves in an orbital path within a wave, and the diameter of the orbit on the surface is equal to the height of the wave. In fact, you could say that the orbit of water at the surface is the wave. However, the wave also affects water beneath it, and smaller orbs of water movement occur underwater as a wave moves above.

Orbs of water moving beneath a wave are called surge. The surge caused by a wave moving on the surface diminishes with depth until it dissipates completely. The depth at which surge becomes negligible is approximately equal to half the wavelength of the wave that caused it. For example, if waves are moving 30 feet apart, surge will cease at a depth of about 15 feet.

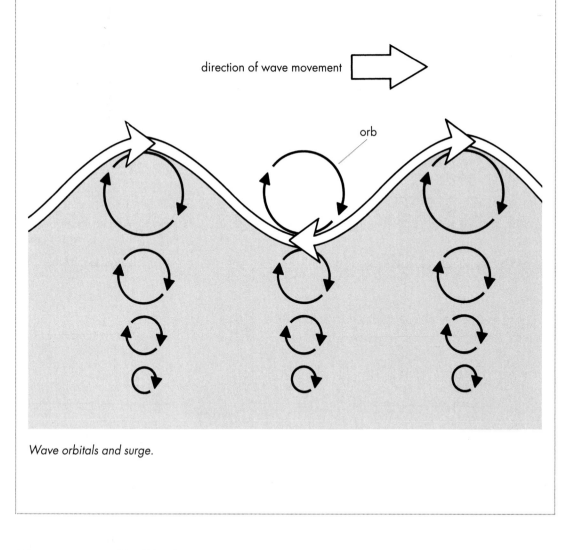

Wave orbitals and surge.

flattens and elongates into an elliptical shape, which lengthens the to-and-fro movement of anything (you, for example) in the water. If the water is shallower than half the wavelength of the waves moving on the surface, it will be impossible for a diver to descend beneath the effect of the surge. Surge is at its worst when waves are large, wavelengths are long, and the water is shallow.

Diving in heavy surge can be dangerous and disorienting. The back-and-forth movement of the water can be an irresistible force, and it may be impossible to avoid crashing into formations on the bottom. The disorienting view of the bottom caused by this motion may cause some divers to become ill.

On the positive side, surge does not seriously inhibit swimming, even though it feels like it does. Although a diver will be pushed backward by returning surge even while kicking, the backward movement is offset by the forward push of the surge. As with the movement of waves on the surface, the water is not transported by the surge and an object in the water will not be swept away by it. If a diver continues to swim within the back-and-forth cycle, she will make almost the same progress that she would if there were no surge, although she will move backward at regular intervals. Progress is one step back, two steps forward.

Shallow water also affects the height and movement of waves. When the orbs of water that form waves become flattened by the bottom, the effect causes more than surge. Shallow water causes the waves to slow down, which increases their height and shortens their wavelengths. The waves get bigger and closer together.

If the water shallows to the point that it is roughly twice as deep as the waves are high, this slowing and growing becomes dramatic. The wave grows until it becomes unstable and collapses—surf conditions. Waves that break due to a shallow bottom transport water and move objects in the water in the direction of their break.

Wave Size

The ultimate size of waves is determined by the speed of the wind, the amount of time the wind blows, and the expanse of water over which the wind blows (fetch). We've seen that wave action does not really affect divers underwater unless the water is shallow. The problem is that all dives begin and end at the surface.

Wave size is the most common weather culprit for canceling dive trips involving boats. Simply traveling on a boat in heavy seas can be uncomfortable and dangerous. Anchoring or mooring the boat can become even more dangerous, and diving from a boat in heavy seas can be impossibly dangerous. A confrontation between a 200-pound diver and a 20-ton boat, each moving violently and uncontrollably in close proximity to each other, is not a pleasant one to contemplate.

Since waves are caused by wind, wind is the nemesis of ocean divers. That's easy to understand from an academic standpoint, but how much wind does it take to ruin your dive trip? If you know the velocity of the wind, how can you predict the sea state that the wind will produce? Answers to these questions depend on things like water depth, bottom formation, and wind fetch. Assuming a fetch of 20 miles, a water depth of 100 feet, and a 100-foot commercial dive boat, here's a very general idea of what kind of seas various winds will produce and how those seas will affect your diving experience.

HOW WIND AFFECTS DIVE CONDITIONS

Wind	Seas	Diving Prospects
Wind variable, 5 to 10 knots	Seas less than 2 feet; surface may be mirror smooth in places	The perfect diving day. Boat will pound gently or not at all when under way, rock gently or not at all at anchor.
Steady direction, 10-knot wind	Seas 2 feet	A great day for diving. Boat will pound gently when under way, rock gently at anchor. Periodic heavier rocking may occur as the boat moves in sympathy with the waves.
Steady direction, 10- to 15-knot wind	Seas 3 to 5 feet	A marginal day for diving. A small-craft advisory may be issued. Boat will pound uncomfortably when under way, rock at anchor. Rocking may be severe when the boat moves in sympathy with the waves. Boarding the boat may be difficult.
Steady direction, 15-knot wind	Seas 5 feet	A difficult day for diving. Conditions severe enough for most commercial operators to cancel a trip. Boat will pound heavily when under way, rock heavily at anchor. Rocking will be severe when the boat moves in sympathy with the waves. Boarding the boat will be difficult and dangerous.
Steady direction, 20-knot wind	Seas 7+ feet	A good day to stay home and cut the grass.

Remember that this table is based on a 100-foot boat; many commercial boats are half that size or less. While the sea affects smaller boats more violently, the table is a good rule of thumb for them as well.

But wait a minute! You may have done some diving from an island resort where the wind constantly blew more than 15 knots and the diving was great. You may have dived from a small boat with little regard to the sea state even though the wind practically blew you off the beach. What gives?

If you look at a map of almost any popular island dive destination, you'll notice that virtually all of the established dive sites are off one side of the island. The side of any land mass (or any other object, for that matter) that is away from the direction of the wind is called the leeward side, while the side that faces the wind is called the windward side. Dive destinations that are subject to prevailing winds always develop more dive sites on the leeward side because the water is far calmer there.

Even though an island or land mass may block some wind, the reason that the water is calmer near a leeward shore is not due to reduced wind speed but because there's not enough fetch for large waves to develop.

Diving near a leeward shore—sometimes called a lee shore, or, more simply, a lee—is often the only way to salvage an ocean or large-lake dive trip when the wind is blowing forcefully. Become familiar with the lay of land masses near dive sites to determine possible lee shores in various wind directions. Remember that wind direction is given as the direction from which the wind is blowing. For example, if a north wind is forecast, look for a lee off the southern side of a land mass.

Forecasting Wind and Waves

Wind direction and velocity are obviously good things to know before you embark on a dive trip. Some coastal weather forecasts include winds and sea state in local radio and TV broadcasts, but many don't. A forecast of winds from coastal towns provides a very general idea of conditions at the coast, but it does not normally provide a clear picture of what conditions will be like offshore.

The Internet is a powerful tool for obtaining good information about sea conditions. Web sites notoriously come and go, but the National Oceanic and Atmospheric Administration (NOAA) has been providing excellent weather information for divers and boaters at www.nws.noaa.gov/om/marine/zone/usamz.htm for many years, and hopefully will continue to do so. NOAA is responsible for offshore weather forecasting for mariners, and it maintains many offshore weather buoys for this purpose. Once you access the site, simply click the area of the map where you want to go. The site provides good data for all major bodies of water within or near the continental United States. Coastal marine forecasts typically give information on wind speed, wind direction, and sea state from the coast to twenty miles offshore.

Many other Internet sites provide offshore weather information. If your chosen dive site has a presence on the Web, chances are good that the site provides applicable weather information. Many boating sites also provide good reports. Have a look at www.motorboating.com or www.wunderground.com/MAR/ for information on weather and sea state.

THUNDERSTORMS

Wind and waves are not the only weather concerns for divers. What may be a refreshing afternoon shower on land may be a dramatic or even dangerous event at sea.

Thunderstorms are likely to develop during a day at sea even in the absence of any front or weather system, as the sea itself and the energy of the sun combine to cause storms. In the very simplest of terms, here's what happens:

Thunderstorms are born when the sun heats the air near the surface of the water. When the surface air heats to the point that it loses density, it becomes unstable and begins to rise—a phenomenon known as an updraft. When the warm, moist sea air rises to an altitude of between a half mile and two miles, the coldness of the air at altitude causes the water vapor within the rising air to condense. This condensation forms a puffy cloud called a cumulus cloud. Cumulus clouds look like cotton balls floating in the air, and their presence may indicate a fine diving day with little wind. However, they are not as benign as they look, even though they pose no danger at this stage.

Those pretty cotton-ball clouds are actually storm engines. As more moist air rises from the sea and condenses within one of these clouds, the condensation process releases heat. The puffy cumulus cloud gets warmer, which causes it to grow taller. The cloud continues to increase in height as long as there is an updraft to supply it with warmth and moisture, until it reaches a height where something makes it stop.

To understand what limits the height of cumulus clouds, we must first learn a few things about our atmosphere. Just like water in the ocean, the air in the atmosphere is stratified by density. The relatively dense layer of air that covers the ground is called the troposphere. Temperature decreases with altitude within the troposphere.

The layer of air above the troposphere is called the stratosphere. The stratosphere contains a layer of ozone that absorbs much of the ultraviolet radiation from the sun (does this sound familiar now?). As a result of this absorption, temperature increases with altitude within the stratosphere. The combination of high altitude and increased temperature results in a layer of air with very low density. That's why the stratosphere "floats" atop the troposphere like warm water floats atop cold water. The interface between the troposphere and the stratosphere is called the tropopause. You can think of the tropopause as a kind of thermocline in the sky if you promise not to tell your science professor I said so. The height of the tropopause varies depending on latitude and the time of year, usually somewhere between four and ten miles. The greatest height is near the equator.

So if our growing cumulus cloud reaches the tropopause (most don't get that high, but some do), the rising air hits the less dense layer and stops. The tropopause becomes a ceiling for the rising air. If the cloud continues to grow, the upper part flattens out against the ceiling of the tropopause and gives the cloud the trademark anvil shape of a powerful thunderstorm. Our former cotton ball is now called a cumulonimbus cloud, and it has transformed itself into a beast. It could be ten miles high.

Bad things happen inside the cumulonimbus cloud. The condensed water and ice near the top of the cloud begin to fall. As the water and ice fall, a downdraft is produced that becomes more powerful as frictional drag pulls cold air downward. Evaporation causes additional cooling. If warm air from the updraft continues to enter the system, it rises quickly within the cooling cloud. Static electricity is produced by frictional forces that are not completely understood, and the result is lightning. When the updraft diminishes and the downdraft remains, the cloud finally produces rain.

Now that you know something about how thunderstorms are produced, it should be easier for you to predict when and where they will occur. Since the formation takes time and is started by the heat of the day, most thunderstorms become mature in late afternoon. Also, since the first step involves heating the surface, thunderstorms are most likely to develop near the coast or in shallow water on hot days.

Thunderstorms endanger divers in four major ways. The first is by the wind and wave action they can produce. Winds in excess of 25 knots are not uncommon within fully mature thunderstorms, and the seas they can produce are large, steep, and dangerous.

The second major danger of a mature thunderstorm is lightning. All boat antennae should be lowered to decrease the possibility of a lightning strike.

The third major danger is reduced visibility caused by heavy rain, which could lead to collisions with objects or other boats at sea. However, heavy rain may also act to calm seas produced by the wind of the storm.

The fourth major danger of a mature thunderstorm at sea is the rarest but perhaps the most terrifying. Thunderstorms may produce wall clouds—tornadoes. A tornado at sea is called a waterspout, and waterspouts are seen far more often than their landlocked counterparts. Due to the weight of the water within the funnel, waterspouts are not as powerful as land tornadoes. However, they are capable of capsizing a boat. A storm that produces one waterspout will sometimes produce many.

Thunderstorms often develop near shore in late afternoon, even in the absence of a weather system or front, and conditions that form one storm will sometimes produce many. What may be a nice afternoon shower on land can be a dangerous event at sea in a small boat.

Tornadoes at sea are called waterspouts. Waterspouts seldom contain winds as fierce as their landlocked counterparts, but they occur more frequently and are very dangerous events. Any strong thunderstorm is capable of producing a waterspout, and divers should monitor developing storms carefully.
DAVID BREIDENBACH

The Weather

147

So there you have it—all the bad news about thunderstorms at sea. The good news is that it is usually easy to watch for the formation of these storms throughout the day and to avoid them altogether. Boat captains and dive operators always keep a keen eye on developing cumulus clouds and alter their plans accordingly.

Coastal marine forecasts usually include thunderstorm information. A forecast for isolated storms indicates a fine day that will produce a few storms. Widely scattered storms bear closer attention and increase the likelihood that dive plans might be altered sometime during the day due to a thunderstorm. A forecast of scattered storms might indicate an approaching weather front, and a forecast of numerous storms should keep you at home.

CURRENTS

Just as atmospheric weather affects divers at the surface of the water, currents can dramatically affect divers under the surface of the water. Currents, the "underwater winds," are created by tides, gravity, and atmospheric wind.

The velocity of a current is expressed in nautical miles per hour, commonly referred to as knots. The distance of a nautical mile is determined by dividing the circumference of the earth into 360 degrees, then dividing each degree into 60 minutes. One minute of the arc of the circumference of the earth is equal to 1 nautical mile. The distance of a nautical mile works out to be about 1.15 statute miles, so a velocity of 1 knot is about 1.15 miles per hour.

The velocity of a current is called its drift, and the direction a current is flowing is called its set. So a current's set and drift might be described as north at 2 knots, meaning that the current is moving toward the north at 2 nautical miles per hour. It's important to remember that the set of a current is the direction toward which the current is moving. This is the opposite of the way winds are described, as wind direction refers to the direction from which the wind is coming. A north wind and a north current move in opposite directions.

That's all good, but how does current affect divers? The certifying agencies have determined that the maximum sustainable swimming speed of a physically fit, fully equipped diver is approximately 1 knot. I like to think that the average independent diver can do a little better than that, but a current of only 1 knot will tax even the best underwater swimmer.

The two most precious commodities of any diver are air and energy. Currents work to rob a diver of energy, which effectively diminishes the diver's air supply. Currents also complicate underwater navigation, as they can significantly skew a diver's course underwater. Currents are a force that must be considered for every dive you make.

To estimate a current's drift from the shore or from a stationary boat, watch debris in the water to see how it moves. If you're on an anchored boat and you know how long the boat is, you can calculate the amount of time it takes for an object in the water to drift the length of the boat. Once you know the time, you can calculate how fast the object is moving in feet per second (divide the length of the boat in feet by the number of seconds it took the object to travel that distance). Multiplying feet per second by 0.6 will give a very general idea of the drift of the current in knots. For example, if you're on a 30-foot boat and it takes a chip of wood 35 seconds to drift the length of the boat, the chip was moving at about 0.857 feet per second (30 feet divided by 35 seconds). Multiplying 0.857 by 0.6 yields a current drift of close to 0.5 knot. This is a quick, dirty, and rather ugly calculation, but it will give a decent estimation of a current's drift.

Currents can be divided into two broad types: near-shore and offshore. We'll tackle near-shore currents first—what causes them, where they're likely to be, and what to do about them.

Tides

Tides are bulges of water pulled upward primarily by the gravitational force of the moon. The sun's gravitational pull also contributes to the tides, but even though the sun is far more massive than the moon, its effect on tides is only about half that of the moon due to its great distance from the earth.

Tides are regular, rhythmic, and predictable on seacoasts. Most points on the globe experience semidiurnal tides, which means that two high tides and two low tides occur each day, with a tidal change approximately every six hours.

Tidal currents are the periodic movements of water associated with tides. Tidal currents caused by water moving toward the coast due to a rising tide are called flood tides. Currents caused by water receding from the coast due to a falling tide are called ebb tides. The brief period between tides when the water is neither rising nor falling is called slack tide or slack water. Slack tide may be the only possible time to make shore dives in areas where tides are strong.

The force of tides depends upon the alignment of the sun and the moon, the configuration of the coast, and the latitude. When the earth, sun, and moon are in alignment, the gravitational forces of the sun and moon combine to produce a powerful spring tide. Spring tides (they have nothing to do with the season of the year) usually occur twice each month, when the moon is full and when the moon is new.

When the earth, sun, and moon are out of alignment, the gravitational forces of the sun and moon counteract each other to produce a mild neap tide. Neap tides usually occur twice each month, on the first and third quarter moon. Shore divers concerned with tides should watch the phases of the moon and plan dives during times when the moon is in its quarter phases.

The moon does not travel in a perfect circle around the earth, so its distance from the earth varies during the year. Of course, the moon's distance from the earth affects tides. Tides are more pronounced when the moon is closest to the earth (at perigee) and lower when the moon is farthest from the earth (at apogee). When spring tides coincide with perigee, the tides are the highest of the year. When neap tides coincide with apogee, they are the lowest of the year. (To find local tide information, local tide charts are the best bet. Many calendars give phases of the moon, and the Weather Channel gives local times for tides in a pinch.)

The force of tidal currents is affected by the configuration of the coast. The best way to visualize how coastal configuration affects tidal currents is to think of water running through a garden hose. What happens when you block the opening?

Coastal restrictions greatly amplify the force of tidal currents. Straits, sandbars, harbors, channels, and rivers all represent restrictions that amplify the force of tides. In many coastal areas near channels or straits, diving is only possible during the fifteen to twenty minutes of slack tide.

Tides are more powerful at higher latitudes. This means that tidal forces increase as you move northward in the Northern Hemisphere. Some of the most powerful tides in the world occur off the eastern Canadian coast, while tides are almost nonexistent in the Caribbean.

Tide tables are readily available for coastal sites, and divers must be familiar with the tides and plan their dives accordingly in areas where tides are powerful. Slack tide is the time to dive, and most coastal divers plan to start their dive slightly before the slack tide that precedes a flood tide. By doing this, the divers can ride the fading ebb tide away from the shore, make their dive in slack water, and catch a bit of a ride back to shore with the incoming flood tide.

Diving in areas of powerful tidal currents is serious business, and the penalty for being caught downstream of a powerful tide is severe. Tidal currents may be far too powerful to swim against, and divers should not exhaust themselves trying to do so. If you are caught downstream from your planned exit point in a tidal current, here are some possible solutions:

- If air supply, energy, and bottom time permit, descend to the bottom and attempt to pull yourself hand over hand upstream toward your planned exit point.
- If a land mass exists, swim perpendicular to the current toward land and an alternate exit point.
- If circumstances prohibit you from reaching an exit point, then surface; inflate your BC; inflate your safety sausage; attempt to signal to shore by waving your hands, blowing your whistle, or using any other signaling device; and wait for assistance. Always leave your dive plan and planned time of return with someone onshore when you're diving in areas of powerful tides so a search-and-rescue operation can be rapidly initiated if necessary.

Longshore Currents

Longshore currents are wind-driven currents that run parallel to a coast. However, since waves seldom run parallel to a coast, the existence of a longshore current may be easy to overlook.

We've learned that shallow water slows waves, so when a wave enters shallow water near shore, the part of the wave that encounters the shallow water first slows first. This causes the wave to turn at an angle toward shore. The wave is refracted by the shallow water in the same way that light is refracted when it slows down in water.

The result is wave action that approaches the shore at an angle, and a current that continues to move past the shore in the original direction of the waves. This current is called a longshore current. The speed of longshore currents is usually 1 knot or less, but when waves are large and the current is strong, the current may be too powerful to swim against.

Longshore currents work to move divers down the beach. The danger of these currents is that divers may be moved to a place that does not offer a safe exit point. Longshore currents are strongest within the surf zone and diminish farther offshore. Underwater visibility is diminished where the current is strongest, because the current carries sediment.

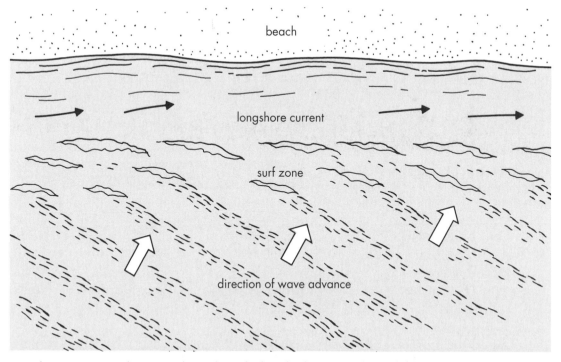

Longshore currents work to move divers down the beach. They pose a hazard if the divers are moved to an area that doesn't offer a safe exit point.

A strong longshore current may be a factor in ruining a shore-diving day, as the surf will usually be large when strong longshore currents are produced.

Rip Currents

Rip currents are anomalies because they are neither wind-driven currents nor tidal currents. They are caused by wind, surf, and gravity.

We've learned that breaking surf actually carries water. We also know that wind moves water. As a result of surf and wind, water may "pile up" on a shore. Sandbars or other obstructions work to contain this buildup of water. When this happens, a basin of water that is slightly above sea level is formed near the shore. Gravity causes water to seek its own level, so the water within the near-shore basin must ultimately move back offshore. This movement of water is a current that moves from the beach to the open sea, and this type of current is called a rip current.

The force of rip currents depends upon the buildup of water and the ease with which it can move back offshore. If water is allowed to move freely offshore, little current develops. However, if the returning water is channeled through a restricted underwater path, rip currents can become dangerously powerful.

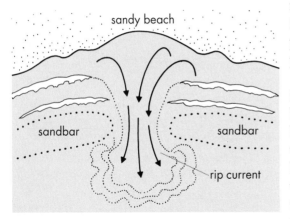

Rip currents occur when water returns to the sea after being piled up on a beach by surf. They can be greatly intensified when moving through restrictions.

An easy way to visualize a rip current is to imagine a bowl with a hole in its side sitting beneath a running faucet. If the hole in the bowl is very large, the water from the faucet will flow out of it evenly and little water will be held by the bowl. However, if the hole is very small, water will fill the bowl and leak through the small hole with force. Similarly, if the faucet is opened up to produce more water (as if the wind and surf were strong), the movement of water through the hole in the bowl will be increased.

There are four distinct types of rip currents: permanent rips, fixed rips, traveling rips, and flash rips. They're all caused by a buildup of water near shore that moves back offshore through a restricted channel.

Permanent rips are caused by permanent structures that restrict the flow of water. Piers, rock channels, jetties, and any other subsurface obstructions that do not change are responsible for them.

Fixed rips are caused by obstructions that change little over time. A hole or channel in the bottom can create a rip current that can last hours, weeks, or even months. The current will remain until the bottom topography that causes it changes.

A traveling rip is caused by a strong longshore current that moves the basin of trapped water down the beach.

The type of rip current that is perhaps the most dangerous to divers is the flash rip. Temporary in nature, flash rips may be produced by a large buildup of surf over a short period of time. Similarly, a flash rip will develop if a section of the basin that

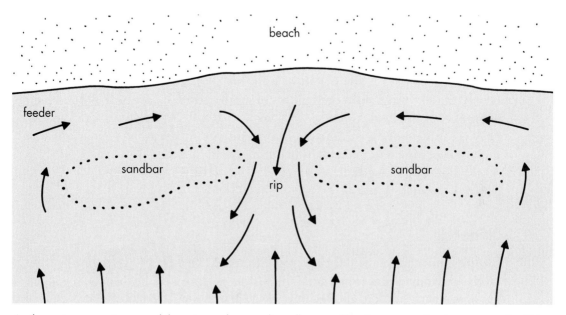

As the water moves in around these two submerged sandbars and begins to move back out to sea, it will be channeled with some velocity between the two bars.

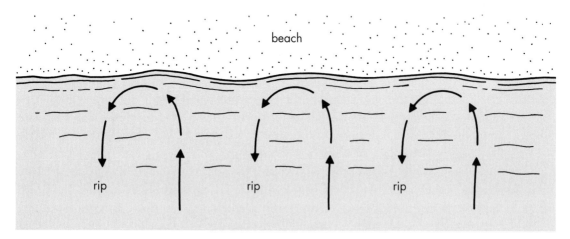

Along straight beaches, rip currents can appear in several places. Normally this occurs because a trough forms, and the water may be a little deeper at the point of the rip current.

holds the buildup of water suddenly gives way—such as when a section of a sandbar offshore suddenly breaks and forms a narrow channel through which the water can flow. The danger of flash rips is their unpredictability.

The distance a rip current can flow varies from just a few yards to a half mile or more. Rip currents are the leading cause of surf rescues of swimmers and can pose a danger to divers. Always get local information regarding permanent or fixed rip currents when planning a shore dive where surf is possible, and always be aware of the possibility of flash rips.

There is a direct relationship between the size of the surf and the intensity of rip currents. Large surf indicates a stronger rip current. A fan-shaped buildup of water on the beach, a stream of dirty water extending offshore, foam on the surface extending beyond the surf zone, and a distinct lack of surf in a contained area are all indications of the existence of a rip current.

It is usually possible to swim out of a rip current by swimming perpendicular to it until you've swum past the underwater restriction that caused the current. If the rip is accompanied by a longshore current, swim out of the rip by swimming downcurrent with the longshore current.

Undertow

It's easy to imagine how the concept of an undertow current—a current that pulls divers or swimmers downward from the surface near the beach—began. Anyone who has stood on a beach and allowed waves to wash over their feet has felt the swash of the returning waves running down the slope of the beach and pulling downward on their ankles. However, no such current exists underwater. Undertow currents are a myth, and you can tell your mama I said so. It is possible for current-driven downwellings of water to occur over reefs or deep obstructions, but they do not occur at the surface near a beach.

River Currents and Lake Seiches

The ocean is not the only place to dive. Rivers and lakes provide interesting and sometimes exciting alternatives, especially for underwater treasure hunters and fossil collectors. While river currents and lake conditions vary greatly depending on the location, a few general things can be said about them.

River currents, caused by gravity as water flows from an elevated origin, range from near stagnant to rapids to waterfalls. Needless to say, powerful river currents can be extremely dangerous to divers. Divers who plan to dive in river currents exceeding 1 knot should receive training specific to river diving.

River currents are usually strongest in the middle, on the surface, and on the outside of bends in rivers. The current is usually less severe at depth and near the shore.

Rain is the weather nemesis of river divers, because it washes sediment into the river and reduces underwater visibility. The addition of rainwater to rivers also acts to increase the prevailing current. Changing water level due to heavy rain may also alter exit points.

Rivers that empty into the sea may be affected by the tides near the seashore, and the effect may be dramatic. Local tide charts must be observed when diving in tidal rivers, and the river should only be dived at slack tide.

Water also moves in lakes, harbors, and other large, enclosed or partially enclosed bodies of water. The force that moves the water is usually the wind. When strong winds blow over a period of time, they act to "pile up" water on one side of the water basin. Once a buildup of water occurs, a wave with a very long wavelength is produced. This wave, called a seiche (pronounced *saysh*), oscillates within the water basin.

The best way to visualize a seiche is to imagine a bowl of water that has been tipped until the water begins to slosh in the bowl. The water sloshes to one side, then bounces off the side of the bowl and sloshes to the other side. That's what a seiche is. A seiche is water sloshing back and forth in a lake, harbor, or bay. The period of oscillation of a seiche is unique to each body of water and depends on the depth and size of the basin. The oscillation period may exceed twelve hours.

Seiches also affect divers. They reduce visibility and alter the water level at any given point in the water basin. The effect of a seiche on a large basin like one of the Great Lakes can raise the water level on the downwind side by as much as 10 feet, with a corresponding lowering of the water level on the windward side.

The Gulf Stream

All of the currents we've discussed to this point have been currents that occur near the shore. Offshore divers must also deal with currents.

An amazing and wonderful thing happens at the western boundary of every ocean basin in the world. Prevailing atmospheric winds (trade winds) blow from east to west near the equator, but from west to east nearer the poles. These constant winds are powerful enough to move the water and cause a rotation of the oceans. Of course, a rotation of the ocean creates a current, and the current is narrowed and intensified by the earth's rotation on the western boundary of each ocean basin. These currents are called, imaginatively, western boundary currents, and they are responsible for moderating the earth's climate. The currents bring warm water from the equator to areas nearer the poles.

The trade winds of the northern latitudes of the North Atlantic Ocean blow from west to east, toward northern Europe, and the southern westerlies of the North Atlantic blow from east to west, toward the Caribbean. As these winds push the ocean's waters, the entire North Atlantic Ocean circulates in a clockwise direction. The resulting western boundary current of the North Atlantic is called the Gulf Stream, and it moves northward through the Caribbean, loops through the Gulf of Mexico, gains momentum in the Florida Strait, and heads northward up the eastern coast of the United States. The Gulf Stream is one of the deepest, fastest, and largest western boundary currents in the world.

The Gulf Stream splits as it swirls through the islands of the Caribbean. The more western split is channeled through the Yucatán Channel (between Cuba and the Yucatán Peninsula), where it is known as the Yucatán Current. As the current continues and loops through the Gulf of Mexico it is known as the Loop Current, and then it becomes known as the Florida Current as it rushes through the Florida Strait (between Cuba and Florida). This western split of the Gulf Stream reunites with the eastern split (called the Antilles Current) as it rounds the tip of Florida. It's all the same current despite the variety of names.

The Gulf Stream directly affects divers where it moves closest to shore in restricted areas. Two prominent areas where the current is consistently and directly felt by divers are near the Yucatán and near the tip of Florida. Divers in these areas (Cozumel near the Yucatán; West Palm Beach in Florida) have developed a style of diving called drift diving to deal with the current. The divers simply go with the flow while the boat follows above.

The Gulf Stream varies in intensity and distance from shore as it moves up the eastern coast of the United States, and coastal diving may or may not be affected by

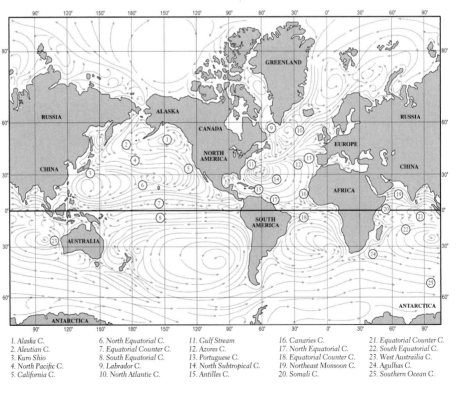

Major ocean currents of the world. Notice the clockwise rotation of the oceans in the northern hemisphere. The Gulf Stream off the eastern coast of the United States is the western boundary current of the North Atlantic Ocean, and is one of the most powerful currents in the world.

1. Alaska C.	6. North Equatorial C.	11. Gulf Stream	16. Canaries C.	21. Equatorial Counter C.
2. Aleutian C.	7. Equatorial Counter C.	12. Azores C.	17. North Equatorial C.	22. South Equatorial C.
3. Kuro Shio	8. South Equatorial C.	13. Portuguese C.	18. Equatorial Counter C.	23. West Austrailia C.
4. North Pacific C.	9. Labrador C.	14. North Subtropical C.	19. Northeast Monsoon C.	24. Agulhas C.
5. California C.	10. North Atlantic C.	15. Antilles C.	20. Somali C.	25. Southern Ocean C.

the warm, clear, moving waters of the current. Divers off the eastern coast must stay apprised of the current's location and plan their dives accordingly. The Gulf Stream accelerates as it reaches the waters off Cape Hatteras, North Carolina, then moves eastward into deeper water farther offshore, where it is unlikely to be encountered by coastal divers.

I know what you've been thinking while I've been talking about these western boundary currents. If there are western boundary currents, there must also be corresponding eastern boundary currents. There are, but they are much wider, shallower, and slower moving than their western counterparts. The eastern boundary current that affects divers in the United States is the current on the eastern boundary of the Pacific Ocean, called the California Current, which runs from north to south along the coast of California. (The western boundary current of the Pacific is the powerful Kuroshio Current off the coast of Japan.)

The California Current seldom hinders divers with a strong current, but anybody who's stuck their toe into the water off a California beach has felt the effect of the California Current. The current brings cold water from the north.

Surface-Wind Currents

Surface-wind currents are the wild-card currents offshore divers must cope with. Surface-wind currents are caused by (you guessed it) surface winds that move the surface of the water. The movement of water at the surface is transmitted by friction to water beneath the surface, so these currents are strongest near the surface and usually decrease with depth.

Surface-wind currents move somewhat in the direction of the wind, but they are deflected by the rotation of the earth—a deflection known as the Coriolis force. The Coriolis force is more pronounced at higher latitudes and in deep water. Expect the direction of surface-wind currents to deviate clockwise (in the Northern Hemisphere) from the direction of the wind by about 15 degrees in shallow water, though the deviation can be as much as 45 degrees in deep northern waters.

The force of a surface-wind current depends on the strength, consistency of direction, and duration of the wind. A wind blowing in the same direction for at least twelve hours will produce a surface-wind current equal to approximately 2 percent of the wind speed.

Since the wind causes both waves and current, these effects will often combine to complicate offshore diving when the wind is blowing. However, even if the wind stops and the seas calm, the current may remain for quite some time. It is entirely possible to encounter surface-wind currents even when the wind and seas are calm. It is also possible for waves to develop before a current is produced, which results in heavy seas but little current.

Divers don't calculate the force of surface-wind currents by measuring the wind and standing on the boat with a calculator and protractor to figure the angle of the current. Once a boat has been stabilized in the water by an anchor or mooring, the force and direction of the current can be seen by watching how the water moves around the anchor line or mooring buoy, or around the boat itself, and by observing how the boat lines up with the anchor or mooring line. If no water backs up against the anchor line and the boat lines up directly downwind of the anchor, the current is light. However, if water surges around the anchor line and the boat settles downwind and off to one side of the anchor, the current is strong.

So how can you nail down the force of the current if one is detected? My preferred procedure is to watch debris drifting by the boat. If you follow a drifting object, you know that the speed you must walk to keep up with the object is the same speed that you must swim at the surface just to stay in place. If you know the length of the boat, you can more accurately gauge the current's speed by timing the object as it drifts alongside. As we covered at the beginning of this section on currents, once you know the velocity of the current in feet per second, multiply that number by 0.6 to get a rough approximation of its velocity in knots. Remember that the certifying agencies consider the maximum swimming speed of a fully equipped diver to be 1 knot, so a velocity of just 1.5 feet per second is an indication of a current that will be difficult to swim against.

Does a current of 1 knot mean that no diving can be done? No, but it does mean that precautions must be taken to mitigate the danger of the current. Offshore divers utilize configurations of lines (ropes) to negotiate strong surface currents by pulling themselves along with their hands. (See the Dive-Boat Rigging and Lines section in chapter 10 for more on this.) For this reason, you should always wear sturdy gloves when diving in currents.

Since surface-wind currents diminish with depth, it is very possible that a dive that begins in difficult conditions will be serene near the bottom. Surface-wind currents may coincide with haloclines or thermoclines, and the effect of diving beneath the murk and current can be dramatic.

How do you know how deep a surface-wind current runs? I know of only one way to determine this, and that's to jump in and find out. Commercial dive boats will send a divemaster down to check the current before the paying customers are allowed to dive, and information regarding the current will be included in the dive briefing. Of course, when there is a current, all dives should be made into the current, as you were taught in your certification class.

Surface-wind currents are transient. They may develop quickly, they may dissipate quickly, and they may change directions quickly. Bottom formations may deflect them so that they move in a direction at depth that is different from their direction at the surface. All divers should constantly monitor the current on every dive and always plan to stay upcurrent from their exit point.

CHAPTER 9

THE MARINE ENVIRONMENT

CAN'T THINK OF ANYTHING that will enhance your enjoyment of diving more than learning something about what you see underwater. It often happens that divers return to the beach or boat with very different opinions of their dives. One group may complain that they swam a great distance and didn't see anything of note, while another group from the same site will return from their dive with great excitement about what they found within a few feet of the entry point.

The difference in enjoyment is due to the knowledge and understanding of what the various divers witnessed. Many newly certified divers are only impressed by the obvious, and they may swim blithely by wildlife that would fascinate more knowledgeable observers. Learning at least a little bit about the marine environment is not an academic assignment—it will make your diving more fun, and having fun is what recreational diving is all about.

As each marine, lake, or river environment is unique, a detailed discussion of all ecosystems is beyond the purview of this book. It is up to each diver to take a long, curious look at his or her dive site. What wildlife makes the site their home? Why do the animals behave as they do? What is really going on beneath the apparently random interactions of the inhabitants?

The ocean is not the only diving environment where interesting underwater life can be found. Freshwater lakes and rivers also contain intricate ecosystems and fascinating creatures such as this spotted gar.

It's a good idea to buy a few reference books that cover whatever environment you decide to explore. Keep the books handy so you can reference them immediately after dives in order to identify what you saw.

While this handbook cannot provide all of the information you need, we can take a look at a few general things about the most common marine environments that divers encounter.

ORGANIZATION OF THE OCEAN

The Environments

There are two basic environments in the ocean. The benthic environment is the bottom of the sea, and the pelagic environment is the water above the bottom of the sea. That's simple enough, right?

The Zones

Each of these basic environments is divided into two basic zones. The benthic environment is divided into the littoral zone and the deep-sea zone. The littoral zone starts at the shore and extends out to a depth of 650 feet. The deep-sea zone is the bottom environment at a depth greater than 650 feet.

The pelagic environment is divided into the neritic zone near shore and the oceanic zone offshore. The boundary between these zones of the pelagic environment is arbitrarily set at the edge of the continental shelf, which is the underwater boundary of every continent on earth. That's kind of simple if you put your mind to it, right?

The Littoral Zone Regions

The littoral zone of the benthic environment is divided into three regions: the supralittoral, the eulittoral, and the sublittoral.

The supralittoral is the splash region on beaches where waves may reach.

The eulittoral region begins at the intertidal area of the coast (the area that is covered by water at high tide but exposed to air at low tide) and includes coastal water that moves with the tides. The outer edge of the eulittoral region is near the depth at which plants can no longer grow on the bottom, or around 130 to 200 feet. The width of the eulittoral region depends on the tidal range and on the slope of the bottom.

The sublittoral region of the littoral zone begins where the eulittoral region ends and extends to a depth of 650 feet, where the deep-sea zone of the benthic environment begins. That's marginally simple if you're a Dale Carnegie memory expert, right?

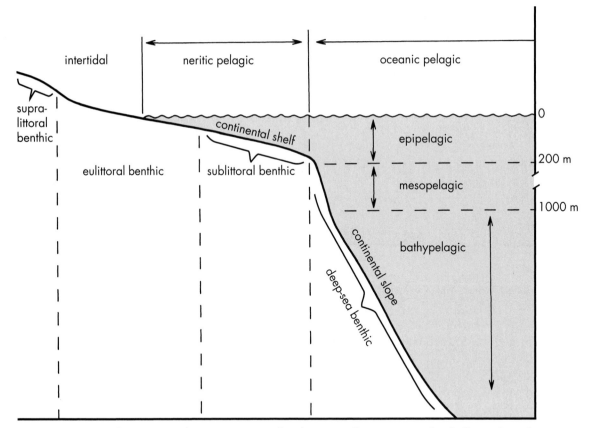

Scientists organize the ocean as shown. Recreational scuba generally occurs over the shallow eulittoral seabed. Note that the vertical scale here is greatly exaggerated. The continental slope angle is rarely more than 20 degrees, usually much less.

THE FOUR LIFE-FORMS

Divers divide the ocean's life-forms into four categories: littoral life-forms, benthos, nekton, and plankton.

Littoral life-forms are plants and animals that live in the intertidal zone. These animals must endure powerful water movement and temperature extremes and are subjected to the direct radiation of the sun during low tide. To survive in the harsh intertidal environment, many littoral creatures bury themselves in the sand or cling tightly to rocks and crevices.

The benthos, or benthic life-forms, are the plants and animals that live on the seafloor. They include animals that are attached to the bottom like anemones and sponges. Bottom-dwellers like crabs and shrimp are also usually considered benthic animals.

DIVER LINGO

So, you could say that most recreational diving occurs in the neritic zone of the pelagic environment near the eulittoral region of the littoral zone of the benthic environment, but would you really want to? Wouldn't you rather say that most diving is done in the water near the bottom close to shore?

Divers, with some help from the training provided by the established certifying agencies, have taken the formal designations of the marine environment and simplified them to the point that most marine biologists would hardly recognize them. However, it's important to know where the lingo came from. Accuracy aside, you never know when you might actually be talking to a marine biologist.

In diving lingo, the littoral zone is not separated into regions. When divers refer to the littoral zone, they are referring to the intertidal zone—the area that is covered by water at high tide but exposed to air at low tide. All references to the other regions of the littoral zone are conveniently discarded in divespeak. The littoral zone simply means the intertidal area.

Divers use the word *pelagic* when referring to deep water far offshore. This usage does not really correlate with either of the formal pelagic zones (neritic or oceanic), but it comes closest to describing the oceanic pelagic zone. When divers mention pelagic fish, they are referring to types of fish that ply the ocean's deeper waters far from shore—fish like tuna and any of the billfish. However, the diver's use of pelagic has no bearing in terms of the water's position relative to the continental shelf.

The word *benthic* remains unscathed by divespeak. The benthic environment refers to the seafloor in diving lingo just as it does in scientific nomenclature.

The nekton, or nektonic life-forms, are the free swimmers that can navigate in open water under their own power regardless of wind or current. Another fancy word for most of the nekton is *fish*.

The plankton comprise tiny plants (phytoplankton) and animals (zooplankton) that cannot purposefully swim against currents and wind, but instead drift with the currents and winds of the sea. Phytoplankton are the beginning of the ocean's food chain, and zooplankton feed on phytoplankton. Many marine animals start their lives in larval stages that cannot swim against the wind or current, and these tiny floating babies (meroplankton) are included in the planktonic life-form category.

When conditions are favorable, phytoplankton can reproduce at a prodigious rate. This occurrence is called a plankton bloom, and it seriously diminishes underwater visibility. Some of the phytoplanktons (dinoflagellates in particular) are reddish in color, and an extremely heavy bloom of these planktonic plants produces a phenomenon known as a red tide. These one-celled plants contain a toxin, so a red tide may decimate the local wildlife and may also contaminate edible animals like clams and mussels that feed by filtering plankton from the water.

ANATOMY OF A CORAL REEF

Coral reefs are the most popular diving environment for many divers, and rightly so. Coral reefs seldom fail to amaze with their beauty and abundance of life. The more you get to know about them, the more fascinating they become.

Coral Reef Formation

Coral is born as the result of mass spawnings on coral reefs around the world. On a few contiguous nights each year, corals of like species release eggs and sperm into the water en masse. These spawnings are timed by the season of the year and by the phase of the moon. For example, the coral spawning at the Flower Gardens Banks in the Gulf of Mexico (one of the places where this timing was first discovered) occurs on the eighth day after the full moon each August. Think about that for a minute. Corals that are living more than 50 feet beneath the surface of the sea coordinate their spawning by the moon. The results of these amazing mass spawnings are a soup of reproductive material in the water. Eggs are fertilized, and the embryonic coral drifts away in great numbers as a type of zooplankton called planulae. They continue to drift until they are consumed as part of the food chain or they settle in an area that is conducive to coral growth.

To grow and prosper, corals have three main requirements: a hard substratum to which they can attach, warm water, and sunlight.

A hard substratum can be almost anything, including the shore of a continent or island or the rocky formations that lie near such shores. Seamounts, which are mountainous anomalies on the seafloor that rise close to the surface of the sea, may also provide a good surface to which corals can attach. In addition to these natural surfaces, corals may attach to man-made surfaces as well. Shipwrecks, pier pilings, oil rigs, and other structures can support a coral reef if the other requisite conditions are met.

Coral reefs are classified according to the way they grow from the substratum that supports them. Reefs that connect directly to a shore or are separated from shore by a shallow lagoon are called fringing reefs. Reefs that form on a substratum near shore but are separated from shore by deep water are called barrier reefs. A reef that forms on a seamount in the open ocean is called a bank reef. Corals that attach to seamounts may grow to the point that a coral island is formed. These islands are called coral atolls (see illustration on page 166).

Corals cannot survive cold water, so most coral reefs are within 30 degrees of the equator. The water surrounding a coral reef can never drop below about 65°F.

The last necessity for coral survival is sunlight. As corals are animals, this requirement needs some explaining. Within each individual coral animal (polyp) reside algae called zooxanthellae. The surrounding skeleton of each polyp contains filamentous green algae. These algae need sunlight to live, and each coral polyp depends upon the algae for its survival.

The algae, through the process of photosynthesis, transfer some food energy directly to the coral polyp. Coral also feeds (usually at night) on zooplankton, which it filters from the water with its tentacles. Preying on zooplankton not only provides the coral with calories, but it also provides scarce nutrients—especially phosphorus. As digestion occurs, these nutrients are released to the algae. The algae and the coral then cycle these nutrients between them, which reduces nutrient loss to a minimum.

Any surface permanently submerged in warm, sun-drenched water over a period of time may serve as a substratum for a coral reef. These pier pilings are covered by sponges and soft corals. The long, skinny fish standing on its head in the center is a trumpet fish—a fierce reef predator despite its comic appearance.

The zooxanthellae that live within coral polyps contribute to the color of the coral. If the algae dies, the coral lightens in color—a phenomenon called coral bleaching. Coral bleaching is an indication of coral in dire distress, as the coral cannot survive for very long without the algae.

So corals depend on algae to survive, and algae need sunlight to survive. Since sunlight does not penetrate water to any great depth, coral reefs normally occur in shallow water. The clarity of the water also affects the amount of penetrating sunlight, so coral reefs normally occur in clear water.

Let's take one last inventory of the conditions that are conducive to coral growth—

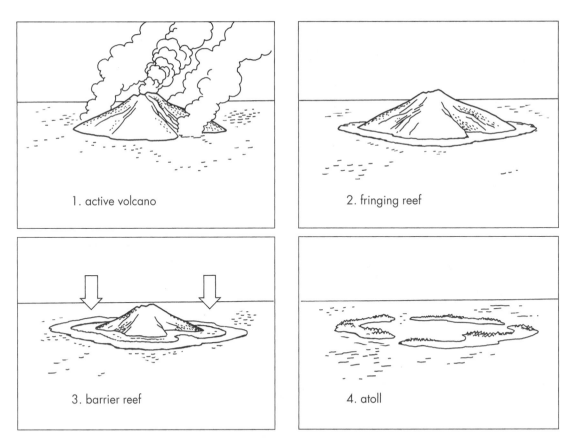

1. active volcano

2. fringing reef

3. barrier reef

4. atoll

Coral atolls are often the remnants of reefs that initially formed around a land mass that has subsequently disappeared.

A detail of star coral during the day reveals a stony appearance as the polyps hide inside their protective limestone casings (corallites).

The same coral seems to bloom at night as the polyps extend their delicate arms to feed.

Different species of corals colonize in wonderfully distinctive ways. This is elkhorn coral. I think it looks more like the horn of a moose, but nobody asked me.

a hard substratum beneath clear, warm, shallow water with plenty of sunshine. As these are conditions that are also conducive to the happiness of divers, is it any wonder that coral reefs are so popular as dive destinations?

Coral Colonization

Most corals form colonies once they've attached to a substratum in a supportive environment. The corals secrete calcium carbonate from the bottom half of the individual polyp, forming a skeletal cup called a corallite that anchors the polyp and provides a sanctuary into which the polyp can withdraw for protection.

Once a coral has established itself in a supportive environment, it begins to colonize through a process of asexual budding from the base or from the oral disc of each polyp. The colony grows in size as living polyps build on the deposits of their predecessors. Even though each polyp is an individual animal, the polyps are connected laterally by tubes that are extensions of the polyps' gastrovascular cavities. Food for one means food for all. The pattern of colonization and the fantastic shapes that the colonies form depend on the species of the coral.

Hard Corals and Soft Corals

Hard corals, sometimes called true corals, are the corals that form the stonelike formations that most people associate with coral. Each polyp of these corals usually has six, or a multiple of six, tentacles with which it captures its food. As such, these corals are also sometimes called hexacorals.

Soft corals are colonies of animals that are held together by fleshy secretions, as opposed to the calcium carbonate secretions of hard corals. Each polyp of soft coral usually has eight tentacles with which it captures its food, so soft corals are sometimes called octocorals. Soft corals include gorgonians and sea fans, sea rods, and other animal colonies that resemble plants. However, a coral reef is mostly a community of animals, and few plants other than algae are found on a coral reef.

Soft corals such as these deepwater sea fans may grow to spectacular lushness on deeper reefs.

Sponges

Although sponges can exist in colder water than corals and are not limited to coral reefs for habitat, they usually have a significant presence on coral reefs.

Sponges are the most ancient form of multicellular animal on earth. All major sponge groups alive today had representatives living 600 million years ago. When you see a sponge, you are looking at one of the great-granddaddies of the world's multicellular life-forms.

Sponges are water pumps, and they extract sustenance from the water that is pumped through them. Water enters a sponge via lateral incoming pores called ostia, is pumped through the body of the sponge by flagellated cells that fan the water through, then exits the sponge through a large exhaust-pipe-type opening called the osculum. Some sponges can build enough water pressure to shoot water a long distance from the osculum.

Between the outer porous cells and the inner flagellated cells lies a layer of supporting skeletal structures that are usually composed of spines called spicules. Sponges are not hard like hard corals; instead, they are fleshy like soft corals.

Sponges grow into distinctive shapes through a process of asexual budding. Some grow into shapes that look like stovepipes; others look like barrels and may grow larger than a human. The act of pumping and filtering water works to clean and clarify the water where sponges live.

Predation, Cooperation, and Competition

Within the structure of the reef live animals that are rivaled only by the animals of the rain forests in their diversity and numbers. Benthic animals such as anemones and hydroids attach to the reef; other benthic animals such as urchins, sea stars, and crinoids crawl about; various types of underwater worms and mollusks cover the reef, bury themselves in the sand, or attach themselves to the corals; shrimp and crabs hide, scurry, and feed among the other benthic life-forms of the reef.

Fish of every shape and description use the reef for food and protection. Butterfly fish pick algae with their tiny snouts; parrot fish bite off chunks of coral to feed on polyps and algae, then excrete the chewed coral as sand (a good topic of conversation

Sponges are some of the most primitive animals on earth. Essentially water pumps, they filter food from the water and work to keep the water clean and clear. This colorful sponge is called elephant ear sponge and can grow quite large.

when picnicking on a sandy beach); schools of tangs arrive like marauding outlaw gangs, wreak havoc on coral heads, then move on; squirrelfish and soldierfish seek refuge within the reef during the day; angelfish display their beautiful colors and nip

Some animals blur the line between benthos and nekton. Some crabs are purely benthic and never leave the bottom, but others such as this ocellate swimming crab can swim in open water.

Lobsters are familiar benthic creatures. They may move to deeper water during the storms of winter and return to shallow water in summer.

WEIRD SEX

Individual marine animals employ a variety of strategies—including the use of teeth, toxins, or camouflage—to ensure their personal survival. However, the strategies used by species to propagate their own kind are even more diverse and strange.

Many marine animals produce fertilized eggs in such quantities that survival of the species is ensured simply by overwhelming numbers. Even though only a tiny fraction of the brood survives to sexual maturity, the sheer mass of the brood is enough to keep the species going. This strategy is a kind of evolutionary lottery where the survival of the young is a matter of numbers, probability, and luck.

Other animals increase the probability of finding suitable mates by gender bending. Lower animals like flatworms and segmented worms may be hermaphroditic, which means that each animal possesses sexual organs of both sexes. Synchronous hermaphrodites can be either male or female simultaneously, although they do not typically mate with themselves. Hermaphroditism increases the chance of finding a suitable mate by a factor of two.

The distended abdomen of this longsnout sea horse indicates a pregnant male.

Several fish are successive hermaphrodites, which means that they are either male or female at different times of their lives. Groupers begin their lives as females and then transform themselves into males as they mature. This type of female-to-male successive hermaphroditism is called protogynous hermaphroditism. If a population of groupers does not have enough males, a dominant female will undergo a sex change and become a functioning male. This strategy ensures an optimum ratio of males to females for maximum reproduction.

Perhaps the most intriguing sexual strategy is employed by sea horses. Sea horses have traditional genders and typically mate for life. The mating ritual is a tender and complicated dance that culminates with the female depositing her eggs into a special brood pouch of the male—thus impregnating the male. The eggs are fertilized and develop within the male's brood pouch, and the male gives birth to live young at the proper time.

Fish are the most common form of nektonic life on coral reefs. These fish are called boga and form schools that may consist of thousands of individuals.

Fish that sleep at night are vulnerable to predators. Sleeping parrot fish often blow cocoons around themselves to mask their scent.

The competition for space on the reef is fierce and constant. Every square inch of substratum is covered by algae, corals, sponges, and tube worms in an explosion of pastel colors. To top it off, a golden crinoid (an echinoderm related to sea stars and urchins) has crawled atop this pinnacle, found protection in a hole, and extended its elegant arms to feed.

at sponges; moray eels stare myopically from their lairs within the reef by day and actively hunt by night.

Even the most cursory overview of the diversity and behavior of life on a coral reef is a book in itself and is clearly beyond the scope of this one. I enthusiastically recommend that you buy such a book and study it before you actually explore a coral reef. The better you understand the workings of the reef, the more fun you'll have. With that said, here are a few basic things to look for on a coral reef.

Snappers, groupers, moray eels, barracuda, and jacks are the largest and most commonly seen predatory fish on most reefs. However, peaceful coexistence is the rule between these predators and the smaller fish upon which they prey, except during feeding times, which usually occur during early morning and late afternoon. Moray eels and octopuses openly cruise and hunt the reef at night.

Porcupine fish, a common type of puffer fish, can inflate their bodies with water when threatened. When the body is inflated, the spines along the back become erect to discourage predators. This panic response is rarely seen unless the porcupine fish is molested.

The trumpet fish is a less obvious predator, as they are smallish and slender fish, but they are voracious feeders among the small fry of the reef. Other less obvious predators are the ambush hunters that rely on their stealth and camouflage in order to feed. Scorpion fish and frogfish are among these types of predators.

The coral reef is an underwater jungle, and the law of the jungle rules. It's an eat-or-be-eaten environment where life is cheap and violent. However, truces are formed within this jungle, and some animals cooperate with each other in fascinating ways. Relationships between animals of different species that benefit both animals are called mutualistic symbiotic relationships, and they are somewhat common on a coral reef.

The most intriguing mutualistic symbiotic relationships commonly seen involve the cleaning of large fish by shrimp or smaller fish. Large, predatory fish may allow small shrimp or small fish such as gobies or wrasses to climb into their gaping mouths to clean parasites and dead skin from them. The cleaners get a meal, and the larger fish are cleaned of unhealthy parasites and detritus.

The cleaners may advertise their services by waving antennae or swimming excitedly, and large fish wait patiently in line at these "cleaning stations" for their turn to be serviced. The fish being cleaned seem to enter a trancelike state as the cleaners in-

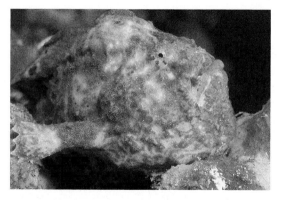

Frogfish are consummate ambush hunters of coral reefs. These strange-looking fish are common on many reefs, but are rarely noticed due to their excellent camouflage.

The longlure frogfish takes the art of camouflage ambush hunting to the next level. These fish are equipped with built-in "fishing poles" and "lures" that they dangle enticingly in front of their mouths.

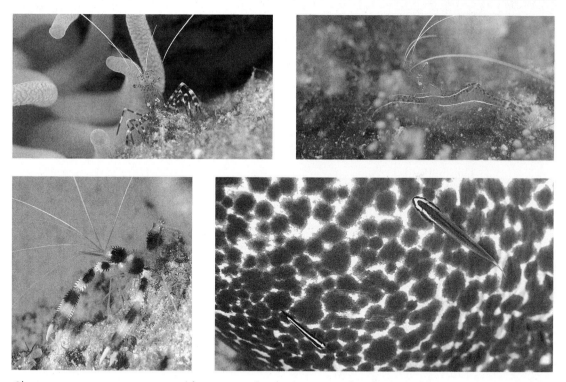

Cleaning stations are common and fascinating phenomena on coral reefs. Several species of shrimp and smaller fish establish mutually beneficial relationships with larger fish, feeding on parasites and detritus on the skin of the larger fish. The cleaners get a meal, and the larger fish are cleaned. Many cleaner shrimp have long antennae they can wave to attract the attention of a potential "client." Clockwise from top left: spotted cleaner shrimp, Pederson cleaner shrimp, gobies cleaning the skin of a spotted moray eel, and banded coral shrimp.

spect their skin, enter their mouths and gills, and comb every inch of their bodies for parasites. Cleaning stations are common on the reef, and observant divers may witness this spellbinding behavior on virtually every dive on a coral reef.

Beneath the struggle for life among the reef-dwellers, the fundamental corals and sponges appear beatific, stable, and constant. They're not.

The entire reef is a war zone for the limited substratum that provides the base of the reef. Corals and sponges compete with each other for space, with weapons both chemical and physical. Although chemical warfare is the norm among the animals of the reef, some corals of different species may actually physically attack each other at their boundaries. The violence of the struggle is disguised by the time frame in which it occurs, which lasts as long as the area supports corals, and reefs slowly change and evolve as corals fight each other for space and dominance.

Spooky and Potentially Hazardous Marine Animals

We have established that a reef is a complex ecosystem comprising competing animals and that many reef inhabitants rely on teeth or toxins for predation and for defense. It should not be surprising that some of these animals pose a threat to divers. Here is an overview of the most common threats, how to avoid them, and what to do if an unfortunate encounter occurs.

Corals

No, I'm not talking about any kind of "Attack of the Killer Corals" here. However, corals are the animals that produce the greatest number of diver injuries, and they do so by simply being there. The sharp, hard edges of coral can produce bruises, abrasions, or cuts on any diver who comes into contact with them. Coral abrasions and cuts are not usually deep or serious in and of themselves, but virtually all such cuts will be contaminated by organic materials and are prone to infection.

Corals belong to the animal phylum Cnidaria (along with anemones, hydroids, and jellyfish), and they contain tiny stinging cells on their tentacles called nematocysts. Think of nematocysts as tiny balls full of spring-loaded poisonous barbs that fly out in all directions if the nematocysts are molested. Nematocysts are used for capturing planktonic prey and for defense. Most corals are not toxic to people, but some may cause allergic reactions.

You can avoid injury from corals by exercising good buoyancy control and by wearing a dive skin or other protective covering. All divers should be careful to avoid the living corals of the reef, as contact injures corals as well as divers.

If stinging or an allergic reaction follows contact with coral, wash the wound with vinegar to disable the nematocysts. Immediately transport the patient to a medical facility if allergic symptoms develop. Otherwise, clean coral cuts with peroxide and apply a topical antibiotic.

Fire Coral

Fire corals are hydrocorals, which are hydroid colonies that secrete hard, calcareous skeletons. These corals contain very powerful batteries of stinging nematocysts on the tentacles of their tiny polyps. When bare skin comes in contact with fire coral, it produces a burning sensation that stings like the dickens for about a minute. Once the intense stinging subsides, welts or a rash may persist for several days and continue to produce pain and itching.

Fire coral in the Caribbean Sea is a mustard color with white tips and a smooth appearance. There are three distinct growth patterns. The colonies may grow into branches, with the branches usually aligned in a single plane. Blade-type formations may grow to look like a stiff, upside-down curtain with folds rising from the substratum. Box fire coral has a more compact form with a lower profile. Scientists differ on whether these growth forms represent different species or are simply different growth patterns of the same species.

Fire coral is an encrusting coral, and it has a sneaky trick of covering other objects and assuming their shape. Sea fans, other gorgonians, and even man-made objects may be encrusted. Fire coral can encrust mooring lines that have remained submerged for an extended period of time.

You can avoid fire coral stings by maintaining good buoyancy control and staying off the reef. Dive skins or other protective clothing will also protect bare skin from fire coral. You should wear gloves whenever you use a permanent mooring line for ascents or descents, as fire coral may encrust a permanent line.

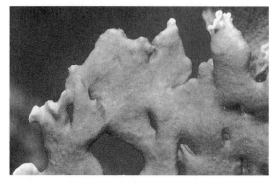

Fire coral is a common hazard on coral reefs. The initial sting usually lasts about a minute and may result in itching welts or a rash that can last for several days.

This detail of fire coral shows the thin filaments that contain the stinging nematocysts.

SNEAKING UP ON THINGS

As virtually all of the reef's inhabitants are subject to predation, they are naturally shy of large creatures that invade their domain—especially large creatures that blow noisy bubbles and have a fearful, Cyclops-like "eye." That is, most reef creatures are afraid of divers breathing on scuba and wearing a dive mask. In addition to being wary of the size and unusual physical characteristics of divers, reef inhabitants are sensitive to water-pressure waves and to shadows cast by large creatures.

In spite of these disadvantages, it is usually possible to get reasonably close to the animals of the reef through the use of dive skills and by avoiding actions that produce fear in the inhabitants. Here are some techniques that help bring the fascination of a reef to light by offering an up close and personal view of the residents:

Maintain good buoyancy. The art of getting close requires the skill of being still. Divers who must constantly swim or flail their limbs to maintain their buoyancy have no chance of getting close to shy animals. Pressure waves generated by sudden or jerky motions will spook marine animals. On the other hand, a diver who can float motionless in the water may fascinate some reef creatures and may even be approached by them.

Go slowly. You will not see the creatures of the forest by sprinting through the woods. Likewise, you will not see the creatures of a reef by sprinting through the water. The pressure waves that a fast-swimming diver produces will cause reef animals to seek shelter long before the diver arrives.

Know what you're looking for. Research the creatures of the reef and learn something about their preferred habitats. Many reef creatures rely on camouflage and are not easily seen unless a diver knows what to look for. The animals that rely most on camouflage are usually the easiest to approach once they are discovered.

Think small. Many of a reef's most interesting characters are miniatures.

Do not swim directly toward animals. Instead, slowly maneuver yourself until you are parallel with an animal and then slowly close the distance by moving laterally. It is usually easiest to approach animals from downcurrent, as moving against the current allows you to proceed more slowly and with more precision. Try to create the impression that you and the animal just happen to be swimming in the same ocean.

Many of a reef's most interesting creatures, such as this tiny spinyhead blenny peeking out from a hole, come in miniature sizes. It usually pays to think small when exploring a reef. The closer you look, the more you'll see.

Do not chase animals that move away from you. Instead, try to guess where the animal is going and slowly move to a point to casually intercept it.

Avoid eye contact. This is, perhaps, the most important rule. If an animal sees you looking at it, it will assume you are sizing it up for dinner. Observe the animal with peripheral vision until it becomes accustomed to your presence. Animals may only be approached if they think you are indifferent toward them.

Do not point your body at animals even if you are not moving toward them

Small creatures like this fingernail-sized hermit crab will brighten any dive. Divers who race through the reef miss most of what is going on around them.

or looking directly at them. Animals perceive a head-on posture as a preparation for attack.

If an animal gets the jitters and swims purposefully away from you, the game is up. That particular animal has decided you are a threat, and further attempts to approach it will most likely fail. However, if you remain calm and still, avoid eye contact, and give every impression that you are indifferent to the animal, the animal may return to you.

Be aware of your shadow when approaching tube worms such as Christmas tree worms or feather-duster worms that retract quickly within their tubes when threatened. As these animals depend heavily on light and pressure waves to detect danger, an approach that casts no shadow on the animal and sends a minimal pressure wave will have the greatest chance of success.

A school of fish is generally easier to approach than a solitary fish, as the schooling behavior gives the individuals confidence. However, you should follow all of the rules above to successfully approach even schooling fish.

Most fish move deeper when threatened. Avoid approaching fish from above. Instead, make your approach from slightly beneath and downcurrent from them. Schooling fish face the current, so they will be facing away from you when you approach from downcurrent. Do not attempt an approach from directly behind the fish. Slowly swim upcurrent until you are parallel to the school, and then slowly move laterally toward them.

Think back to the last time you were on a reef or dive site. Did a large group of divers cluster together and take off in an attempt to cover a large area? If interesting marine life was spotted, did divers clang on their tanks, point excitedly, or even sprint toward the animal in hot pursuit? Were divers within the group having trouble with buoyancy, swimming with their arms, or "bicycling" constantly with their fins? If you were part of such a group, do you think you saw much of the marine life in the area you dived?

continued on next page

Tube worms are common and beautiful creatures that add color to most coral reefs. The bodies of the worms are encased in special tubes that the animals construct around themselves and attach to the reef. The heads of the worms are crowned by featherlike appendages called radioles that act both as gills and as a means by which the worms can filter plankton from the water. These animals are very sensitive to pressure waves in the water or to shadows cast by larger creatures, and they will retract their radioles back into their casings in the blink of an eye if alarmed.

The feather-duster worm is a common type of tube worm. The colonial pink variety is shown here.

The detail of the radiole of a brown fan worm reveals a delicate marvel of engineering.

Another common type of tube worm is the Christmas tree worm.

Independent divers will see more wildlife and have more-interesting dives by pairing or swimming calmly in small groups. Interesting marine life can usually be found and observed a short distance from the entry point. Move slowly, be patient, be nonthreatening, know the area and its inhabitants, and work to become a part of the environment rather than a clumsy intruder.

Do not rub or wash fire coral stings with fresh water or soap, as the contact may cause any remaining nematocysts to fire their poisonous barbs and exacerbate the sting. Saturate the affected area with vinegar to immobilize any remaining nematocysts. Remember that most ear-flushing products are a mixture of vinegar and alcohol, so ear flush can be used to treat stings if pure vinegar is not handy. Meat tenderizer or baking soda is often recommended as a means to alleviate nematocyst symptoms, but clinical studies indicate that these substances are not effective for hydrocorals and may complicate the wound. Treat stings with ice for pain once the remaining nematocysts have been immobilized by vinegar. Apply a topical hydrocortisone cream to the resulting rash or welt.

Hydroids

Like corals, hydroids are cnidarians that group together by the thousands to form colonies. Hydroids have branched skeletons that usually grow in patterns that resemble ferns or feathers. Coloration is usually drab—whitish, gray, or brown. However, despite their delicate appearance, many hydroids possess very potent nematocysts that can sting as severely as fire coral.

Hydroids are so delicate and lacy that it is possible for a diver to brush against them without realizing that contact has been made. However, even a casual brush with a hydroid may result in a sting. Like fire coral stings, hydroid stings are intense for about a minute and may result in welts or a rash that lasts for days.

Avoid hydroids by maintaining good buoyancy and staying off the reef. Dive skins or other protective clothing will protect bare skin. Wear gloves whenever using a permanent mooring line for ascents or descents, as hydroids may attach to anything in the water.

Do not rub or wash a hydroid sting with fresh water or soap, as this may cause un-fired nematocysts to trigger. Saturate the sting with vinegar and then apply ice for pain. Topical hydrocortisone cream is good for any resulting rash or welt.

Sponges

Even a creature as benign as a sponge can injure careless divers. If a diver makes hard contact with a sponge or grabs or squeezes a sponge, the spicules that serve as the sponge's skeleton can become embedded in the skin. The spicules are difficult to remove and are susceptible to infection.

In addition to the possibility of a spicule injury from any sponge, some sponges are toxic to people. Fire sponge is a small orange or reddish sponge that lives in shallow water and can produce a painful sting or a severe allergic reaction in divers who come into contact with one. The touch-me-not (*Neofibularia nolitangere*—*nolitangere* is Latin for "do not touch") is a larger sponge that can produce the same reaction if it comes into contact with bare skin.

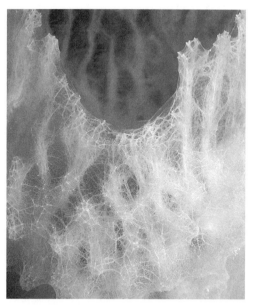

Some sponges are capable of producing a painful sting when touched, and all sponges contain supporting spicules that can puncture skin and lead to infections including tetanus. Divers can easily avoid sponges by maintaining good buoyancy and staying off the reef.

You can easily avoid injuries due to sponges by maintaining good buoyancy and by leaving sponges alone. Resist the temptation to feel or touch sponges. A dive skin or other protective clothing will protect bare skin from casual contact with toxic sponges such as the fire sponge or touch-me-not.

Treat sponge spicule injuries by removing as many of the spicules as possible. Sticky tape may be used to remove the small fragments. Saturate the affected area with vinegar. Tetanus-causing bacteria live in some sponges, so it's a good idea to make sure that tetanus immunizations are current if spicules puncture the skin. Stings from toxic sponges should be treated similarly with vinegar. Apply ice for pain. A topical hydrocortisone cream is good for any resulting welt or rash.

Anemones

Anemones are a common type of cnidarian found on coral reefs, and their presence is usually prominent. All anemones possess nematocysts, but many are either nontoxic to people or produce only mild effects. However, some may produce a painful sting. All divers should avoid touching anemones to avoid the possibility of a sting as well as to observe good reef manners.

Avoid anemones by maintaining good buoyancy and staying off the reef. Anemones are often beautiful creatures, but you should resist any temptation to touch or feel them. A dive skin or other protective clothing will protect bare skin.

As with the other cnidarians, first aid for an anemone sting begins with saturating the affected area with vinegar to disable unfired nematocysts. Apply ice for pain and a topical hydrocortisone cream for any resulting welt or rash.

The beautiful Caribbean giant anemone is the largest and most noticeable anemone on Caribbean coral reefs. Although all anemones are cnidarians and are equipped with stinging nematocysts, with which they defend themselves and capture food, most people are not affected by the Caribbean giant anemone. However, divers should avoid touching or molesting any marine life on the reef by maintaining good buoyancy.

The knobby anemone is a common resident of Caribbean coral reefs. While not as noticeable as the giant Caribbean anemone, the knobby possesses a potent sting. Divers can easily avoid anemones by maintaining good buoyancy and staying off the reef.

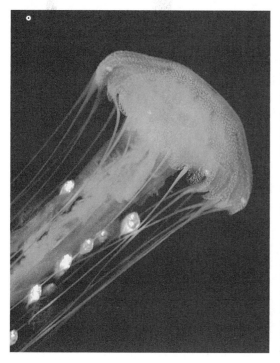

Jellyfish

Jellyfish are the cnidarians nondivers are most familiar with. There are two main types that commonly affect divers—the true jellyfish (unattached cnidarian medusae of the class Scyphozoa) and the siphonophores (cnidarians of the class Hydrozoa).

True jellyfish are translucent animals that swim in open water by pulsing contractions of their domes. Tentacles hang from the margins of the domes, and the tentacles contain nematocysts.

Siphonophores are hydroid colonies that use a gas-filled float to regulate their depth in the water. Tentacles containing nematocysts hang from the float. The tentacles can be contracted close to the float or relaxed until they extend a greater distance from the float. The Portuguese man-of-war is an infamous example of a siphonophore.

While many jellyfish are not toxic to people, it's a good idea to avoid all jellyfish. This is sometimes difficult to do, as some of the most potent characters are less than 3 inches in length and are nearly transparent. The most potent species can produce stings severe enough to require medical attention, but most toxic types produce stings comparable in severity to those of fire coral and hydroids.

It is important to note that another group of animals, the ctenophores (phylum Ctenophora), are commonly mistaken for jellyfish

While not all jellyfish produce stings that affect divers, most do, and you should avoid any unfamiliar jellyfish. This jellyfish, called a stinging nettle, is a potent stinger. The little fish are not prey; they are juvenile jacks that are risking using the jellyfish's deadly tentacles as cover against other predators. Always be on the lookout for jellyfish when making a safety stop in a current, as they are most common near the surface.

due to their gelatinous bodies. Ctenophores are commonly called comb jellies. These animals have no domes, are usually oval or pear-shaped, and have either two or no tentacles. Their tentacles contain no nematocysts, and these animals are completely harmless to divers.

Comb jellies have eight rows of hairlike cilia that run the lengths of their bodies. The cilia (called combs) are the comb jelly's only means of locomotion. The beating action of the cilia looks like iridescent lights moving along the animal's body and is quite beautiful to see.

So, not all gelatinous creatures in the sea are jellyfish. If the animal has a dome, a gas-filled sack, or prominent tentacles, it should be avoided. If the animal has no dome or gas-filled sack but instead has cool-looking lights moving down its sides, it is not dangerous and is worth a closer look.

Jellyfish are usually encountered near the surface, and divers performing their safety stops at 15 feet should keep their eyes peeled for jellyfish drifting in the surface current. A dive skin or other protective clothing will protect bare skin from jellyfish stings.

Stinging "no-see-ums," which are usually stinging zooplankton or larval hydroids called hydromedusae, may also be drifting in the current. These tiny animals can produce stings on sensitive skin, particularly the lips. If your lips begin to burn during a safety stop, simply place your hand over your mouth and regulator. The tougher skin on the back of your hand is usually impervious to no-see-um stings.

Treatment for jellyfish stings is the same as for stings of the other cnidarians. Saturate the sting with vinegar. Use ear flush if no pure vinegar is handy. Vinegar may not be effective for siphonophore stings (Portuguese man-of-war), and these stings should be rinsed with salt water. Treat pain with ice after the remaining nematocysts have been washed away or immobilized. If the sting is severe or if allergic symptoms develop, treat for shock and transport the patient to a medical facility. Treat rashes or welts with a topical hydrocortisone cream.

Urchins

Sea urchins belong to the phylum Echinodermata. Echinoderms have five body sections of equal size that are arranged around a central axis, and the phylum includes such animals as sea stars, brittle stars, and crinoids. Most echinoderms have hundreds of small feet called podia that serve to move the animal around and to capture food.

The defensive strategy of sea urchins is obvious. They are like miniature underwater porcupines, relying on a body covering of sharp spines for protection. The spines of most sea urchins are sharp enough to easily puncture human skin. To complicate matters, the spines are also brittle and are prone to break off once they are embedded in tissue. Tiny hooks on the shafts of the spines work to keep the spines embedded once they puncture and break off.

Here's a prickly, sticky combination. An urchin has crept up behind a feathery hydroid. The urchin's defense is obvious—contact with the spines can result in a painful puncture wound with broken spines embedded in the skin. Stinging nematocysts on the fronds of the delicate-looking hydroid will produce a painful sting that may result in an itchy welt that lasts for days. Divers can easily avoid urchins and hydroids by maintaining good buoyancy and staying off the reef.

Sea urchins commonly hide in recesses of the reef during the day but begin to move around and feed at night. It is easy to avoid them during the day by maintaining good buoyancy, staying off the reef, and refraining from putting your hands into holes or places that you cannot see. Dive skins offer little protection against sea urchin spines, but thicker wet suits may offer some protection.

Urchins may move to shallow water during the night, and they may come right up to the shore or beach. Night divers diving from shore should examine their entry and exit points carefully for sea urchins. Urchins feed on algae, and they may climb onto permanent ladders at established shore-diving areas. Always check permanently submerged ladders for urchins before using them.

Since sea urchins may be present in shallow water, where surge is sometimes powerful, it is important to check for sea urchins whenever surge is present. If sea urchins are numerous and if the surge is powerful, divers may opt to swim on the surface to deeper water before diving in order to avoid being swept into urchins by the surge.

Treat sea urchin punctures by removing as many of the spines as possible. Contrary to popular dive lore, spines should not be crushed to facilitate healing. Remaining spine fragments will usually be absorbed by the body or work their way out of the skin within twenty-four hours, but the process may take as long as three weeks. Spines that enter the body near joints can be especially problematic and should be examined by a doctor as soon as possible. Also see a doctor if large spines or large portions of spines remain embedded in the skin, if nerve damage is suspected, or if the wound becomes infected.

Stingrays and Scorpion Fish

Stingrays and scorpion fish are common reef residents that contain venomous spines that are used strictly for defense. Lionfish have similar venomous spines. Though lionfish are found primarily in the Pacific Ocean, they seem to have somewhat established themselves along the southern Atlantic coast of the United States, so local divers should be aware of them.

Stingrays and scorpion fish rely on camouflage to hunt their food and to avoid their enemies. As such, these animals are reluctant to move out of the way of unsuspecting divers. They are not aggressive, but they can be difficult to see. Any diver who either unwittingly or intentionally molests these animals is at risk of a painful and dangerous injury from the poisonous spines.

Stingrays carry their spines near the middle of the tail. Scorpion fish carry their

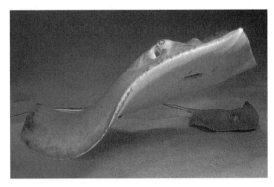

Stingrays are graceful inhabitants of sandy areas, where they often sit almost completely buried in the sand. Although they possess a venomous, barbed stinger near the middle of their tails, they pose no threat to respectful divers. However, any diver wishing to settle onto the sand should be certain that no stingray is hiding there.

Here's looking at you, kid. Scorpion fish rely on their excellent camouflage to avoid detection, and they will often hold their ground. They are harmless unless molested either intentionally or inadvertently through not being seen. Their pectoral and dorsal spines contain a toxin that produces a very painful wound. Divers can easily avoid scorpion fish by maintaining good buoyancy and staying off the reef.

venom in the spines of their fins, with the dorsal spines being the most prominent.

Avoid stingrays and scorpion fish by maintaining good buoyancy and staying off the reef. Stingrays typically inhabit sandy areas and bury themselves in the sand. Scorpion fish typically sit on the bottom near rocks or coral areas, or they may sit atop the rocks or coral. Divers who never come into contact with the bottom or with the reef are at no risk of injury from stingrays or scorpion fish. Divers who choose to settle on the bottom must be careful of where they do so.

Stingrays often bury themselves in sand while lying on the bottom. While not aggressive, they pose a threat to any diver who unwittingly settles onto one.

Spooky stuff aside, since stingrays and scorpion fish rely so completely on their camouflage and are so reluctant to move, they may be approached closely for inspection once they are discovered.

Any diver who reads the dive magazines or has visited Grand Cayman Island is familiar with an attraction called "Stingray City"—a shallow area off Grand Cayman where stingrays are fed, petted, and generally played with as if they were puppies. Keep in mind

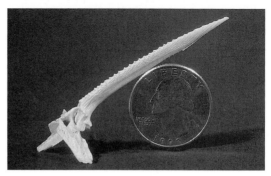

Even without the venom, the barb of a stingray is a nasty weapon designed to produce maximum hurt. Divers accustomed to playing with acclimated stingrays at dive attractions like "Stingray City" (Grand Cayman Island) should never lose sight of the fact that a frightened or threatened stingray is capable of inflicting a serious injury.

that stingrays encountered elsewhere are not accustomed to people and may perceive any physical contact as a threat. Never touch, prod, or molest stingrays or scorpion fish.

Stingray and scorpion fish wounds are traumatic, extremely painful, and serious. Treat patients for shock. The venom of these animals is composed of proteins that break down quickly when heated. Soak the wound in nonscalding hot water for thirty to ninety minutes and seek professional medical attention.

Fireworms

Fireworms are segmented worms that belong to the same phylum as the common earthworm, but fireworms are somewhat more flattened in appearance. They are

normally 4 to 6 inches long but may grow to a foot in length. They may be seen crawling over the reef at any time, but they generally stay more hidden during the day.

Perhaps the most distinguishing characteristics of fireworms are the tufts of fine bristles that they carry on each body segment. Although fireworms may be reddish or greenish in color (they're actually quite beautiful), the bristles are white. The bristles are sharp, venomous, detachable, and produce a painful and long-lasting irritation if they come into contact with bare skin.

The beautiful bearded fireworm is capable of delivering a nasty sting that can leave bristles embedded in the wound and cause an infection. Divers can easily avoid them by maintaining good buoyancy and staying off the reef. This is especially important at night, when these worms are most active.

You can easily avoid fireworms by maintaining good buoyancy and staying off the reef. If you must touch or hold any portion of the reef, make sure to avoid any living creatures. A dive skin may not protect bare skin from fireworm bristles, but a wet suit probably will.

Treat fireworm stings by removing as many of the bristles as possible. You can use sticky tape to pull the fine bristles from the skin, but some bristles will inevitably remain. Saturate the wound with vinegar. When the wound is clean, apply topical hydrocortisone cream. Be alert for any allergic reaction to the sting, and transport the patient to a medical facility immediately if allergic symptoms such as hives or difficulty in breathing occur.

Moray Eels

Moray eels come in a wide variety of sizes ranging from small and benign to thicker than a man's thigh and 8 feet in length. They have mouths full of long, needle-sharp teeth, and the larger ones are clearly equipped to cause serious injury to divers. The medium-sized spotted moray and the imposing green moray are the moray eel species that most commonly pose a threat to divers on Caribbean reefs, and several Pacific species are equally capable of mayhem.

Moray eels inhabit holes or recesses in the reef during the day. It is common to see their heads peering from their lairs, but it is just as common to see only portions of their bodies through the honeycomb network of the reef. Morays actively hunt at night and are often seen completely out of their holes as they forage for food after the

Moray eels are common residents of coral reefs. They are often seen peering out from their lairs during the day. Sometimes only portions of their bodies may be seen through the honeycomb structure of the reef. Morays actively hunt at night, but they rarely swim more than a few inches above the reef even when foraging. All morays have mouths full of needle-sharp teeth, but they are not aggressive unless molested and pose no danger to respectful divers.

The green moray is the largest eel commonly seen on Caribbean reefs; it may reach a length of up to 8 feet and be as thick as a man's thigh.

The spotted moray, seen even more frequently than the green moray, is about half the size of the latter.

The attractive golden-tail moray is also a common sight on the reef, but it only reaches a length of a foot or two.

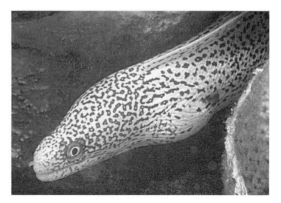

Golden-tail moray eels sometimes come in reverse colors, with yellow bodies and dark markings.

sun sets. They seldom swim more than a few inches above the reef even when they are actively hunting.

Moray eels feed on fish and crustaceans and have no interest in divers as a food item. However, morays are protective of their territories, and they may defend their hole against a perceived intruder. A diver foolish enough to reach into a hole may be bitten if a moray eel is in residence.

Some divers feel a need to interact with the animals of the reef by feeding them.

Feeding moray eels is dangerous. Morays have weak eyesight but a keen sense of smell. The scent of bait will incite the eel to feed, but it is entirely possible that it will not be able to see the difference between a piece of bait and the hand that is holding the bait. If the scent of food is heavy in the water, the moray's eyesight is poor enough to mistake a hand for a fish even if the hand is not holding the food.

Morays are competitive with each other and fight for dominance, females, or lairs. Moray eels are sometimes seen with terrible injuries on their bodies, almost always the result of a disagreement with another moray eel. It is important for underwater photographers and videographers to keep this competitive behavior in mind when photographing moray eels. If a camera is held close to a moray eel, the eel may see its own reflection in the lens or video port and react aggressively toward the "intruder." If you are photographing and you see a moray coming out of its hole in a threatening manner, keep the camera between you and the eel, back away, and tilt the camera so that the eel can no longer see the reflection.

Divers who keep their hands out of holes, who do not carry bait, and who do not place reflective items in front of moray eels are in no danger from them.

A bite from a moray eel is traumatic and may be very serious. Although the bite is not venomous, it carries a large load of bacteria and is prone to infection. Bites to the hand may cause tendon or nerve damage. Carefully clean bite wounds with fresh water and remove any embedded teeth. If the injury is severe, treat for shock, control bleeding, and seek professional medical care.

Sharptail eels are commonly seen on sandy areas of reefs, and they can travel beneath the sand. These harmless eels are sometimes mistaken for sea snakes due to their snakelike appearance. There are no sea snakes on Caribbean reefs.

Barracuda and Groupers

Barracuda and groupers are predatory fish of the reef that are large enough to cause injury to divers. The barracuda has an unwarranted reputation for aggression that probably arose from its formidable dentition. Barracuda and groupers often display curiosity toward divers and may follow divers at a discreet distance.

Divers who feed fish may possibly be bitten by either of these fish in the resulting feeding melee. Groupers are the more aggressive feeders of the two, and they feed by rapidly opening their large mouths and sucking prey in. If a diver chooses to feed large groupers, it is possible for the diver's hand to be drawn into a grouper's mouth by this powerful sucking action.

Groupers and barracuda pose no threat to divers who do not feed fish.

Clean bites with fresh water and seek medical attention if the bite is severe.

Barracuda are common residents of reefs. Although they are equipped to inflict serious damage and may show interest or curiosity toward divers, they pose no threat unless they are molested or fed.

Territorial Biters

Some small fish of the reef will defend their territories even against a creature the size of a loitering diver. The damselfish are the most common attackers. Fortunately, damselfish are too small to cause damage, although they may surprise divers with their aggression and fearlessness. It has been said that if damselfish were 6 feet long, nobody would go swimming in the ocean.

Ocean triggerfish may also show aggression toward divers. These fish are larger than damselfish, and their

Groupers are among the top predators of the reef. This large black grouper would seemingly have little to fear (what would argue with a face like that?), but something has bitten off one pectoral fin and left a wound behind the fish's right eye.

bite is capable of breaking the skin. However, their bite cannot really be classified as dangerous.

Fish that defend their territories by biting cannot usually be discouraged. The only defense against them is to move to another area of the reef that is not so zealously protected.

Bites from damselfish or triggerfish do not usually require any first aid. If the bite breaks the skin, clean it thoroughly and apply a topical antibiotic cream.

Sharks

No fish has historically captured the imagination of or terrified humanity more than the shark, and there is one good reason for this: No other fish in the sea may perceive a healthy human being as a food item. While only a handful of species actually do this, the rest of the species are guilty by resemblance or association. The media has cashed in on the entertainment value of this terror through movies like *Jaws* and its sequels and knockoffs, and until very recently, sharks were considered to be mindless, demonic, bloodthirsty killers—the absolute bane of the oceans.

A recent and concentrated effort by environmentalists (an effort of which I wholeheartedly approve) has served to some extent to educate the public about the role of sharks in the oceans and to plead their case against overfishing and mindless persecution. These efforts have made an impact on public perception. However, when the pendulum of public opinion swings, it seldom swings evenly. Here's a personal story:

A tourist was attacked a few years ago by an unidentified shark off a beach, and the tourist lost an arm in the encounter. As the beach is a popular vacation destination for folks in my neck of the woods, the local media went into a frenzy of coverage. I was asked by a local TV station to provide underwater video of a shark for their coverage of the story.

I met with the TV crew and gave them some pretty footage of a nurse shark swimming languidly through a school of fish. Some of my friends were interviewed on camera, and they offered reasonable information about sharks. As my friends and I were concerned about a story that might incite the public against sharks, we were careful to avoid depicting sharks as mindless demons.

When I watched the newscast later that evening, this is what I saw: An attractive newswoman gave the facts of the incident—that a man had been attacked and had lost an arm to a shark. Then she began to talk about sharks and their role in the sea as my pretty footage rolled in the background. Then came the shark-sympathetic commentary of my friends. The newswoman returned on-screen and spoke a few more kind words about sharks, and then she ended the story by describing sharks as "these gentle creatures of the sea."

I was dumbfounded. In our attempt to defuse an emotionally explosive incident regarding a shark attack, my friends and I had contributed to an equally unreasonable depiction of sharks. There was no headline on the story, but had there been, it might have been something as unlikely as, "Man Has Arm Ripped Off by Gentle Creature of the Sea."

Sharks are not demons, nor are they saints. Sharks are wild, carnivorous predators that behave according to stimuli that we are only beginning to understand, and some of them are capable of causing us serious injury or death. However, while sharks must always be respected, I believe that their threat to divers is negligible. Here's my take on the most commonly encountered species, beginning with the relatively less dangerous one.

Sharks are seldom seen during dives, and the vast majority of those encountered by divers pose little or no threat. The most commonly seen shark on Caribbean or Bahamian reefs is the nurse shark *(Ginglymostoma cirratum)*—a species that is usually seen lying motionless on the bottom beneath coral or rocky overhangs. They may reach a length of over 10 feet, and they have somewhat blunt snouts and distinctively pale eyes. Nurse sharks have no interest in divers, but their benign reputation may tempt some foolish divers to take liberties with them. Nurse sharks may bite when molested or cornered, and they may hang on tenaciously once they bite. Divers who do not molest nurse sharks are in no danger from them.

The second most commonly seen shark on Caribbean or Bahamian reefs is the Caribbean reef shark *(Carcharhinus perezi)*. This is the type of shark that usually shows up at Caribbean or Bahamian shark-feeding dives, and they are powerful and

Nurse sharks are the most commonly seen sharks in many areas. They are usually observed lying on the bottom beneath some sort of cover. They are not dangerous to divers unless they are fed or molested. Touching or cornering a nurse shark is a form of molestation and may result in a serious and tenacious bite despite the animal's benign reputation.

beautiful fish that may approach 10 feet in length. Caribbean reef sharks near shark-feeding areas may show interest in divers as possible sources of handouts of food. However, they do not see divers themselves as food. They are seldom seen if no bait is in the water. In the absence of bait in the water, Caribbean reef sharks generally act with wariness or indifference toward divers and pose little threat, although they command respect, caution, and good judgment.

Sand tiger sharks (*Odontaspis taurus*—also known as the gray nurse in Australia or the ragged-tooth in Africa) are sometimes seen around wrecks, oil rigs, or reefs. They are large (up to 10 feet long), heavy-bodied sharks with long, sharp, prominent teeth that they use to catch fish. Sand tigers are the large sharks most commonly seen in aquariums, and they are an imposing presence. Predators the size of sand tigers command respect, caution, and good judgment, but they pose little threat to divers unless molested or in the presence of bait.

Blue sharks (*Prionace glauca*) may be seen on shark-feeding dives off the coasts of New England and California. Blue sharks are beautiful, slender, supple sharks that live in deep water. They may grow slightly over 10 feet in length. Blues attracted to bait may approach divers, and encounters with them in the three-dimensional world of deep water can be challenging. Blue sharks command respect, caution, and good judgment, but they pose little threat to divers unless there is bait in the water.

Scalloped hammerhead sharks (*Sphyrna lewini*) are sharks with the distinctive hammer-shaped head that sometimes congregate in great numbers over seamounts. They are generally 5 to 10 feet in length. Beautiful to see, scalloped hammerheads are generally very skittish and difficult to approach. They pose little threat to divers unless bait is in the water.

Greater hammerhead sharks (*Sphyrna mokarran*) also have the distinctive hammer-shaped head, but the "hammer" has a smoother front edge than that of the scalloped hammerhead. Greater hammerheads can reach 15 feet in length. They are imposing sharks with impressively high dorsal fins, and they may show up as unexpected guests at shark feeds. Greater hammerheads command respect, caution, and good judgment, but they are generally wary of divers. However, they may show interest in spearfishers if bait and blood are in the water. In the absence of bait, greater hammerheads pose little threat to divers.

All the sharks described above are large, powerful predators that are rarely seen unless they have been intentionally attracted by baiting. Although they are all potentially dangerous to divers, they do not consider divers as food items and dives can usually be safely made in their presence. Following are four species of shark that are even less likely to be seen, but their reputation for aggression toward divers should put divers on maximum alert and dives should be aborted in the unlikely event that they are encountered underwater.

Anyone who has seen the movie *Jaws* is familiar with the formidable appearance of the great white shark (*Carcharodon carcharias*). These sharks can grow to lengths of

20 feet or more, and they are the largest predatory fish in the sea. Great whites normally live in temperate waters, where they feed on seals and other pinnipeds. The coast of California is a suitable habitat for great whites, and they are sometimes seen there. Great white sharks may mistake divers for their normal prey, or they may consider divers to be a food item. Great whites seem to be in serious decline worldwide, but any dive should be immediately aborted in the extremely unlikely event that one of these magnificent fish is sighted.

The oceanic whitetip shark *(Carcharhinus longimanus)* will not be seen by divers on reefs. Oceanic whitetips are deep-ocean sharks that may be seen near the surface around seamounts or by blue-water spearfishers in temperate or tropical waters. These sharks can grow to lengths exceeding 10 feet and have distinctively large dorsal and pectoral fins. The fins have large, blotchy white spots near the tips. The pectoral fins are so long that the shark's "wingspan" is nearly as wide as the shark is long. Oceanic whitetip sharks are notoriously aggressive toward anything in the water with them. Since oceanic whitetips are usually encountered near the surface, a dive can usually be easily aborted in the unlikely event that an oceanic whitetip is encountered.

Tiger sharks *(Galeocerdo cuvier)* may be seen in open water or on reefs worldwide. They may reach lengths exceeding 15 feet. Tiger sharks have large heads and mouths, and their snouts are somewhat square and blunt. They have distinctive dark bars or blotches on the upper sides of their bodies. They are voracious feeders and include turtles, fish, and seabirds in their diet. Although they are usually shy toward divers unless bait is in the water, I recommend that any dive be aborted in the unlikely event that a tiger shark is seen.

Bull sharks *(Carcharhinus leucas* — also known as the Zambesi shark in Africa) are the most common of the sharks I consider to be the most dangerous, especially in waters near the state of Florida. Bull sharks may grow to lengths of 10 feet or a bit more. They are heavy-bodied and have no distinctive markings. The tops of their bodies are brown or gray, and their undersides are pale. There are no markings on the fins. Their short snouts and heavy bodies give them a blunt look. Bull sharks may be encountered in murky, shallow water, where they may mistake a diver's skin for fish, and many shark attacks off Florida beaches have been attributed to them. Bull sharks are normally shy or indifferent toward divers unless bait is in the water, but I believe a dive should be aborted if a large bull shark is sighted.

Shark Dives
Back in the dark ages when I first began my travels throughout the Caribbean, resorts and dive operators meticulously avoided the S-word for fear of frightening the tourists. Cryptic references to sharks were sometimes made as "the man in the gray suit," but the word *shark* was strictly taboo. It was as if the resorts thought they could guarantee a safe absence of scary sharks simply by pretending that sharks did not exist.

Things have certainly changed. Many resorts now come close to guaranteeing shark sightings on some of their dives through the practice of chumming or feeding. The Bahamas are the epicenter of shark-feeding dives, but many Caribbean destinations also offer shark feeds on their dive agendas. Operators out of California (primarily San Diego) have offered shark dives for many years, and some operators off the coast of New England have followed suit. The California and New England shark dives attract significant numbers of large blue sharks in deep water and offer the protection of shark cages. The sharks on these dives are "chummed close" (attracted by food), but they are not usually directly fed. Bahamian and Caribbean shark dives typically attract Caribbean reef sharks and do not involve the use of shark cages even though the sharks are usually directly fed.

The safety record of shark dives worldwide is excellent. However, a fierce struggle occurred in 2001 between dive operators and shark-feeding detractors regarding shark-feeding dives in Florida. The detractors argued that shark feeds alter the feeding behavior of sharks and create a dangerous association in sharks between people and food. The detractors won, and shark-feeding dives are currently banned in the state of Florida.

Should you participate in shark dives? Of course, as an independent diver the choice is yours alone, but I believe that shark dives are reasonably safe and I personally enjoy them. Here are some things to consider about shark dives:

- Shark dives involve wild and potentially dangerous animals, and dive operators have little control over what will occur during the dive. You will be asked to sign a liability waiver that practically states that you have decided to commit suicide by diving with sharks. The reward of such dives is the unique opportunity to view these magnificent animals up close. However, the risk is real, and each diver should make a conscious and personal decision as to whether the reward is worth the risk.

- Pay close attention to the predive briefing and follow all procedures precisely.

- Shark dives in the Bahamas or Caribbean typically require divers to kneel on the bottom. Consider adding a few pounds to your weight belt to make this easier and more comfortable. Shark dives in New England or California typically involve the use of a shark cage. A few extra pounds of lead on your belt will also make cage diving easier.

- Exposed skin may look like bait to sharks in the chaos of a feed. Cover your entire body with a dive skin or wet suit. Keep your hands close to your body. If you intend to use a camera, cover your hands with gloves if gloves are allowed during the dive.

- Sharks possess special sensors called ampullae of Lorenzini on or near their snouts that enable them to detect very faint electrical impulses, so they may be attracted to video cameras or camera strobes. Dive lore abounds with stories of divers losing cameras to sharks, but I've never personally witnessed this nor have I spoken to anyone who has. I have, however, personally experienced very close attention from sharks while my camera strobe recharged.

Being surrounded by large sharks in the open sea is a nightmare that keeps many nondivers out of the water, but some divers actually seek out the experience through well-planned, commercially operated shark dives. These are Caribbean reef sharks—the type most often seen on shark dives in the Caribbean or Bahamas. Even when encountering sharks attracted to such dives, divers must remember that sharks are wild and potentially dangerous animals and that all large sharks should be observed with respect and caution. Get out of the water if sharks show any signs of aggression or inordinate interest.

- If shark feeding occurs near the bottom, visibility will be compromised by silting caused by the commotion. Avoid any movement that might contribute to the silting. If the water near the bait becomes murky, you might get a clearer view of approaching sharks by watching for them behind or above you. Some operators allow divers to swim freely as long as the divers do not approach the bait. If this is allowed, consider moving away from the bait in order to see approaching sharks in clearer water.
- Resist the temptation to touch passing sharks.
- Continue to pay attention to the divemasters during the dive and be prepared to end the dive in the prearranged manner when instructed.

It is true that the feeding behavior of sharks is altered by regular shark feedings. Sharks that take advantage of these feeding opportunities become accustomed to the presence of divers and may allow themselves to be seen or act less warily in the presence of divers. Sharks may begin to congregate in the feeding area as soon as they hear a dive boat approach. I find this quick adaptation and Pavlovian-type response to be remarkable. However, I do not believe that sharks depend on these feedings for their survival or that divers who carry no food are in great peril from sharks accustomed to these feedings.

Perhaps the greatest residual danger of shark-feeding dives is the cavalier attitude that some shark divers develop toward sharks. Established shark feeds are manufactured encounters with acclimated animals. It is good for divers to see sharks and to gain a better understanding of them. However, it is not good for divers to develop disrespect for the potential danger of sharks based on these manufactured experiences.

Shark Aggression and Bites

Most sharks that approach divers are simply curious. Sharks may be discouraged by reversing the rules for sneaking up on fish. Stay calm, descend to the bottom if possible, and establish firm eye contact. Let the animal know that you see it, that you are not prey, and that you are perhaps sizing *it* up for *your* dinner. This technique works in the vast majority of these rare encounters. However, if a large animal persists, discretion is the better part of valor. Retreat to an exit point and get out of the water.

Shock and blood loss are the immediate threats to divers bitten by large sharks. Because blood loss cannot be monitored or controlled while a diver is in the water, removing the stricken diver from the water is the first priority. If the bite is serious (some are not), stem the blood flow by applying pressure directly to the wound. A tourniquet should be applied only if the bleeding is massive, cannot be otherwise controlled, and is life-threatening. Treat for shock and transport the patient to a medical facility immediately.

CHAPTER 10

GOING DIVING

Most certification classes do a fine job of teaching new divers how to use dive equipment, how to make safe dives by understanding the physiological changes their bodies undergo underwater, and how to manage those changes and their air supply. The better classes practice buoyancy control, stress management, and dive safety. Newly certified divers are usually fully prepared to make safe dives within established recreational-dive limits, but most haven't a clue about how to actually go diving or what to expect at dive sites.

You already know how to dive. In this chapter we discuss how to go diving.

Diving from Charter Boats

Diving is often done from dedicated dive charter boats. Although each boat or operator may have its own rules, most boats operate in the same general manner.

Dive charter boats can be divided into two general types—those that can accommodate up to six paying passengers and those that can accommodate more than six. The smaller boats are commonly called six-packs. Why the distinction at six passengers? Charter captain license requirements are more stringent for carrying more than six paying passengers, so many captains are only licensed to carry six. The larger boats often carry ten or more divers, and they generally offer more stability and creature comforts than the smaller boats. However, the smaller boats are usually faster and, of course, allow fewer divers to be on the dive site.

Most dive charter boats supply tanks for your dives but do not provide any other equipment. However, some boats don't provide any dive equipment at all, and you must bring your own tanks (or rented tanks) for your diving. Make sure that you understand what is expected of you. If you are required to bring your own tanks, make sure that the boat can conveniently store the tanks you bring. Aluminum-80s are the standard, and it's a safe bet that the boat is set up to carry them. If the boat provides the tanks, they will most likely be aluminum-80s, so your BC should be set up for aluminum-80s before you board the boat.

You will be expected to bring all of your personal dive equipment, including a weight belt and weights. Drinking water is usually provided by the boat. If you decide to bring soft drinks, you will probably be asked to put them into a communal ice chest to save space.

The following apply to both smaller and larger boats.

Check-In

Although check-in may take place on board the boat itself, most charter boats handle this business in an affiliated dive shop or an onshore office. Check-in time is usually an hour before the boat is scheduled to leave the dock, but be careful to verify the appropriate time. It's better to be early than late, because check-in can take a while.

Arrive at the check-in fully prepared to dive, and bring your C-card, your DAN (Divers Alert Network) or other dive insurance card, your logbook if requested, and money to pay for the dive. The dive personnel will ask for your C-card and hand you a liability waiver in return.

Dive liability waivers are legal documents designed to place responsibility for all diving activities directly on the diver, which is you. The waiver will usually make the specific point that you have "assumed the risk" of all dive activities, and it will contain a "hold harmless" clause that absolves all parties of the dive operation from liability in the event that you are injured during the trip. This is a good and necessary document, and dive operators could not exist without them. Read the document carefully. You will not be allowed to board the dive boat unless the document is signed, dated, and (usually) witnessed.

The legality of dive liability waivers is usually upheld in court if challenged. Clauses that exempt the operator from liability even in cases of gross negligence on the part of the operator may be unenforceable in some instances, but you should consider the waiver to be a serious document that will limit any recourse you might otherwise have against the dive operator should something go wrong.

Once the business of payment has been completed and your C-card, liability waiver, and insurance have been recorded, you're done, unless you have other business such as equipment rental, nitrox tank sign-off and delivery, or other requests like the availability of tanks other than the standard aluminum-80s. You're ready to go to the boat unless procedure calls for all divers to caravan en masse to the dock.

Boarding the Boat

Arriving at a dive boat is like arriving at a party in a private home to which you've been invited. They're expecting you, but you don't just walk in and start throwing your stuff around.

Your first order of business is to get your gear on the dock near the boat. As parking is sometimes not available near the dock, it may be necessary to park in a loading zone temporarily, deposit your gear, and park your car somewhere else. Ask marina personnel about parking if you're not sure.

Once the car is parked, it's time to move your gear to the boat. Do not board the boat unless you are invited to do so. Many boats make more than one dive trip per day, and the turnaround is a busy time for the boat crew as they remove spent tanks, load fresh tanks, fuel the boat, add fresh water, clean up, or do any of the myriad things that are necessary to prepare a boat for a dive charter. Make sure that your gear does not block or hinder access to the boat. If you see dive personnel lugging tanks, you might offer to help them. However, boat turnaround is like a precision military drill for the personnel, and you should not participate without asking first.

The crew will invite you aboard when they're ready for you. Ask about procedures for stowing extra gear such as cameras. Most dive boats are configured with bench seats along each side and tanks racked behind the seats. Select a spot and place your dive gear beneath the seat. A mesh bag will fit easily beneath the bench, but a standard dive bag may not. If you must bring a standard dive bag aboard (I discourage this), remove the essential gear for your diving and place the gear beneath the seat. Store the dive bag belowdecks if possible.

Organization and cooperation are necessary whenever diving from a crowded charter dive boat. Divers should select a tank and set up their rigs before the boat hits open water, then sit on the bench in front of their tank with their personal dive gear stowed beneath the seat. The key is to keep your stuff together and out of everybody else's way.

Ask first, but most operators will encourage you to set up your BC and regulator onto a tank and replace the rigged tank in the rack behind your seat. Make sure that the rigged tank is secured in the rack by a bungee cord or by whatever means is used to secure the tanks. At this point, you will have staked your claim to your spot on the boat, and you should work to keep your gear in that small area and out of everyone else's way.

Once all guests are aboard, it is common for the captain or divemaster to give a briefing on boat procedures. This briefing will include safety information regarding life jackets and man-overboard procedures as well as matters of convenience such as how to use the marine head (toilet) or what areas of the boat are considered "dry" areas off limits to divers in wet clothing. It is important that all divers stop what they're doing and pay attention to this briefing. Stop and pay attention even if you've heard the briefing before. Other divers on board may be making their first trip, and, of course, it's just plain good manners to avoid making noise or interfering with the briefing.

The captain may depart the dock as soon as all divers are aboard. If your tank is set up and your gear is properly stowed under your seat, you should sit at your place on the bench and try not to contribute to the confusion caused by late arrivers who might still be setting up their rigs. Be careful to avoid blocking the captain's view, and leave the driving to the captain. Even if you are an experienced boater, refrain from "helping" the captain by fending the boat off pilings or interfering in any way. Of course, if you really are an experienced boater, you will understand that the captain might be pivoting the boat around a piling or that any unexpected alteration of the boat's movement will cause a problem.

The Marine Head

If the boat ride to the dive site is a long one, it is likely that you will feel the need to use the rest facility somewhere along the way. Don't expect this task to be as convenient and easy as it is ashore.

Marine heads (toilets) are notorious for their finicky operation, and chances are excellent that the head on whatever boat you're on is prone to malfunction. Head use is often discussed if any briefing on boat procedures is held before the boat leaves the dock.

The general rule for marine heads is that nothing should be placed in them that has not first passed completely and naturally through your body. Very small amounts of toilet paper may be an exception to the rule. Do not use the head for seasickness. Consult a crew member if you have any questions, as flushing procedures sometimes seem as complicated as driving a submarine. Also consult a crew member if the head malfunctions. It's embarrassing, but be assured that you're not the first and you won't be the last to have a problem with the head.

The Dive Briefing

Don't expect to suit up and jump into the water as soon as the boat arrives at the dive site. It may take some time for the crew to securely moor or anchor the boat and to prepare the boat for diving. Once the boat is ready for diving, a divemaster will take center stage and give a briefing on the site, water conditions, and objects of interest.

Too many divers treat the dive briefing as if it were the same tired speech given by airline flight attendants. Pay attention to the dive briefing. It may include important navigational information, and it will always contain information about dive conditions and procedures for exiting and reboarding the boat. It will also normally let you know how the crew is keeping track of the divers to make sure they are accounted for at the end of the dive.

It is not uncommon for a divemaster to actually enter the water and check the site before the briefing so that the information on the site and conditions is as accurate as possible. Information about wildlife or interesting formations will be included in the briefing, and this can make your dive more fun.

MAL de MER

Beware (and maybe stay upwind) of the diver who confidently states, "I don't get seasick." It may be true that some divers have never experienced seasickness, but virtually everyone is susceptible to seasickness if the motion is violent or disorienting enough for an extended period of time. Divers who have never been seasick usually have limited boating experience or at least limited experience on boats in rough weather. Seasickness can almost always be controlled by preparation and medication, but it is a possibility that must be considered whenever you venture far offshore in a dive boat.

Even though everybody gets seasick if conditions are right (or wrong, depending on your point of view), some people are more resistant to it than others. Seasickness is primarily caused by sensory confusion between the eyes and the balancing mechanism of the inner ear, although doctors are not sure exactly how or why such confusion causes nausea. Although some sufferers may wish that it could, seasickness will not kill you. In fact, the sensory confusion will eventually work itself out and the illness will pass. However, this may take more than a day to occur.

An interesting phenomenon occurs in divers who have either resisted or overcome seasickness while on a moving boat. The balancing mechanism of the inner ear seemed to give up and go with the flow. This relaxation helped these divers resist seasickness, but it may cause them to feel as if they are still rocking and rolling after they are back on dry and stable land. I suspect this phenomenon is a possible contributor to the "drunken sailor" stereotype, as sailors who make landfall after a time at sea will sway and stumble when they walk even if they haven't had a drop of spirits to drink. The effect may last for several hours.

Seasickness is a mercurial thing, and resistance to it varies from day to day for any given diver. I am convinced that mental attitude plays an important role in its resistance. Fear of the unknown or even fear of becoming seasick may contribute to its onset. Physical comfort is also a factor. The following are things that you should consider to ward off seasickness:

- Preparation for a day at sea begins the night before. Get a good night's sleep, eat sensibly, refrain from alcoholic beverages, and arrive at the boat refreshed and ready.
- Don't worry about becoming seasick. Involve your mind instead with the excitement of the opportunity to dive. Immerse yourself in the glory of the moment. If you get sick, you won't be the first and you won't be the last. Don't worry about it.
- Remain on deck and let your eyes see what's going on around you. Do not stare at the deck or at the people across from you. Watch the boat move on the sea and feel yourself as a part of it. Watch the horizon as a point of reference.
- If possible, stand up and face forward. On most boats, you may be able to brace yourself by holding onto braces of the awning above the dive deck. If this is not possible, you may be able to go to the rear of the boat and lean against the transom or gunwale. However, avoid exhaust fumes and only move to the back of the boat if the boat is moving and it is

safe to do so. Much of the motion of the boat will be absorbed by your hips and legs if you stand, and your head will stay relatively still.

- Avoid becoming too cold or too hot.
- Avoid reading or doing close work.
- Don't wear a dive skin, wet suit, or restrictive clothing.
- Once the boat arrives at the dive site, get ready and be one of the first to get into the water. The refreshing feel of the water and the excitement of a dive will help ward off seasickness. However, seasickness may complicate a dive if you already feel ill.
- Seasickness is contagious. Avoid other seasick divers.

If you succumb to seasickness, my advice is to move to a lee (downwind) rail and get it over with. Do not use the head (bathroom). Most people feel much better after vomiting, and your day of diving is not necessarily ruined. Try to get back into the spirit of things.

Some divers may succumb to seasickness while in the water. Disorientation caused by surge or being in wave action at the surface can produce sickness. It is possible to vomit through a regulator, and I recommend that you not remove your regulator in the event that you get sick underwater. Stay calm, don't panic, be careful not to aspirate water or liquid, and purge the regulator when it's all over.

Remedies for seasickness abound, and since seasickness involves the psyche, many remedies work as placebos. Some divers swear by the use of special wristbands placed over acupressure points; some eat honey or nibble on ginger crackers. If it works for you, by all means use it. However, studies have indicated that wristbands have no clinical effect. Ginger and honey may have some clinical effect on seasickness.

Of course, there are medications designed specifically for seasickness and other forms of motion sickness. These drugs work to raise the threshold of resistance, so they are much more effective for resisting motion sickness than they are for reversing sickness once it occurs. Thus, it is important to take them long before the motion starts. The medications come in two types—a prescription drug called scopolamine and over-the-counter antihistamines like Dramamine or Bonine.

Scopolamine is currently available only by prescription, and it is most often administered through the skin by means of a patch behind the ear. Scopolamine patches have proven in clinical tests to be very effective against motion sickness, and the patches last for several days. Apply the patch twelve to twenty-four hours in advance of boarding the boat. Side effects include drowsiness and dry mouth, and some people experience difficulty focusing their eyes for reading. It has also been reported that sudden removal of an active patch may cause nausea, so patches should be left in place until the drug gradually diminishes and is absorbed by the body. The patch looks like a little circular Band-Aid, and it is not inconvenient or conspicuous to wear. (Remember, if somebody at work the following day asks why you're wearing a Band-Aid behind your ear, always start the story with, "There were these five big guys . . .")

continued on next page

Most people are familiar with over-the-counter drugs like Dramamine, Bonine, and other antihistamines for motion sickness. These drugs have been proven by clinical tests to be very effective. Side effects include drowsiness and dry mouth. Begin taking these medications at least two hours before the motion starts.

So that's it, right? Slap on the patch, pop the pills, and forget about it. Well, not quite. There's a bit of a rub to using seasickness drugs while diving. Scopolamine has been reported to cause personality changes bordering on dementia in rare cases. All of the drugs cause drowsiness and may impair judgment, and there are serious questions about how the drugs react when under the pressures divers routinely encounter when diving. Some medical experts, including DAN, caution divers about the use of seasickness drugs while diving.

These concerns are a relatively recent development. I have personally used Dramamine for many years when conditions warrant, and I find it to be effective for me. I do not find that it makes me too drowsy or more stupid than normal. My wife Sharon, who is the dive partner I consider most likely to become seasick, uses Dramamine for day trips and scopolamine patches for longer trips such as live-aboards. Neither of us has ever consciously experienced any unexpected side effects from using these drugs while diving.

So there it is—the good, the bad, and the maybe. If you decide to use any medication for seasickness, experiment at home before you actually go diving. If the medication causes side effects that will significantly impair your judgment while diving, then of course you should not use it when diving. Remember that the possible side effects of these drugs when under pressure are still under study. Consider the use of seasickness medications as an additional risk when diving. The decision as to whether to use them is yours alone.

" . . . so don't worry, our diver recovery rate on this boat is up to almost 95 percent" (pause for chuckles). Pay close attention to the predive briefing even if you've heard all the jokes. Important information regarding navigation and conditions will be covered, as will tips on where to find interesting marine life at the site that will enhance your dive. Divemasters on charter boats often work for tips, so remember to do your part.

Mask Rinse Buckets and Camera Buckets

Most boats provide a bucket of seawater near the exit point that is convenient for rinsing masks immediately prior to diving. Some boats also provide a larger container of fresh water that is necessary for rinsing and flushing sensitive underwater cameras. Be careful not to rinse your mask in the camera rinse. Remember that many mask defoggers contain detergents. Most underwater camera housings or bodies contain O-rings that are carefully greased to ensure their suppleness for a waterproof seal. Detergent and grease don't mix very well. What may seem to be a harmless rinse of the mask could cause many thousands of dollars in damage to cameras due to flooding. Mask rinsing also needlessly contaminates the fresh water, which makes it less useful for rinsing expensive camera gear.

Dive-Boat Rigging and Lines

Dive boats typically have a complement of lines to assist divers in the water. These lines are most useful when the diving is from boats longer than 50 feet, when a surface current is present, or when seas are high. The following is a list and description of these lines and how to use them.

Unless the boat is tied to a divable structure—a structure suitable as a dive site such as a deep pier or oil rig—it will have a down line, which is the line that anchors the boat in the water and is connected to the bottom. It may be a permanent mooring line to which the boat is tied, or it may be an anchor line from the boat to the bottom. Down lines should be used for diver ascents and descents, and they should be used for safety stops if no other lines are available for that purpose.

Every boat should have a drift line (sometimes called a current line or a trailing line) that is connected to the stern and drifts behind the boat. A highly visible float should be attached to the end of the line, and the line may extend behind the boat for as far as 300 feet. This line is for divers who somehow get downcurrent from the boat and who may have trouble swimming against the surface current back to the boat. It is also useful for divers who have surfaced and are waiting their turn to board the boat.

Pulling yourself along a line such as a drift line seems pretty simple, but a mistake can be made. If you are wearing a regular weight belt, it's best to pull yourself with the line to one side rather than directly beneath you. If you "climb" the line with the line directly beneath you, it is very possible that the release buckle of your weight belt will get caught in the line, the buckle will snap open, and your weight belt will be lost.

Boats that are long enough to require a substantial swim to the bow (front) or are anchored in a significant current may use a tag line (sometimes called a granny line or a gerry line [for "geriatric"—aren't bold young divers funny?]). Tag lines are tied at one end to a stern cleat, run the length of the boat, and are tied to the down line at the other end. They are used by divers to pull themselves forward to the down line, where they can begin their dives. Divers usually exit the boat from the side when a tag line is used. Once the divers enter the water, they swim to the tag line and pull themselves forward along the outside of the line. Once again, pulling yourself with the line beneath you is a good way to lose your weight belt.

If the boat is large or if there is a large group of divers aboard, the boat may use hang lines (sometimes called deco lines—*deco* is short for *decompression*), which are weighted lines that hang from the sides of the boat to depths of more than 15 feet. The lines are used by divers during their safety stops to avoid the cluster of divers that inevitably ends up on the down line at the end of a dive. Sometimes two hang lines are connected by a length of plastic or aluminum pipe, creating a hang, or deco, bar. Hang bars allow several divers to spread out while holding on during their safety stops at the recommended 15-foot depth.

It is very important to remember that hang lines and hang bars are connected only to the boat. As the boat rocks and rolls, the line may be pulled dramatically upward. If you hold the line too tightly, you face the serious risk of being pulled rapidly upward toward the surface, which, of course, is a big no-no. Use hang lines only to prevent

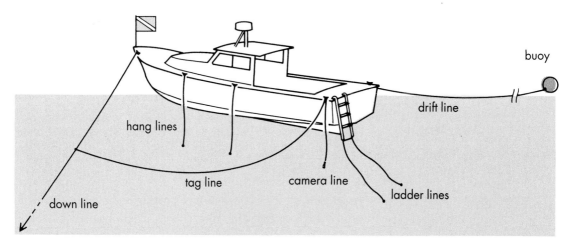

This is how many commercial dive boats are rigged for diving. Divers use the tag line to pull themselves to the bow of the boat before descending. The down line is used for descents and ascents. Divers can use the down line for their safety stops, but many boats also offer hang lines for safety stops to alleviate crowding on the down line. The drift line is used to assist divers who have somehow gotten downcurrent of the boat to return to the boat, and it may also be used by divers waiting to use the boarding ladder. In rough weather or from large boats, divers can remove their fins while holding a ladder line before using the boarding ladder. Cameras are attached to camera lines in rough weather or on large boats so divers don't need to approach the boat with bulky and sensitive camera gear. The cameras are hauled aboard by the crew. Smaller boats may not have this full contingent of lines, but all boats should have a minimum of a down line and a drift line unless conditions are extraordinarily calm. Many boats at dive resorts do not use drift lines because conditions are so consistently calm.

yourself from being swept laterally by the current. Hold them loosely so that they will slip easily through your hand should the boat rock. Use your own buoyancy control to maintain your depth.

Another consequence of a hang line's connection to the boat but not the bottom is its propensity to swing. As you hold the line at the recommended 15-foot depth, the increased drag of your body in the current may cause the line to swing, which reduces your depth. This problem is magnified if more than one diver is holding the line. Keep an eye on your depth gauge when holding a hang line in a current, and be prepared to move farther down the line to compensate for swinging.

Larger boats may use camera lines to safely deliver and recover sensitive underwater camera equipment to and from the water. These are usually short lines attached near the stern of the boat, and they typically have a brass snap hook on the end. Cumbersome but delicate equipment is lowered to divers in the water via the line, and the divers reconnect the equipment back onto the line at the end of their dives. The cameras are then hauled aboard by the crew. Recognize these lines and avoid using them for hang lines.

Lastly, some larger boats that typically offer diving in less-than-optimum sea conditions may use a ladder line. The ladder line is a relatively short line (10 feet or so) that is tied to the bottom rung of the boarding ladder and allowed to drift back in the current. These lines are convenient for pulling yourself rapidly to the ladder, and they are a godsend when boarding large boats in heavy seas. Read on for more-specific information regarding the use of ladder lines.

Battling the Beast: Dealing with Boarding Ladders

With the possible exception of weight belts dropped on feet, my observation has been that most diver injuries occur at the boarding ladder. Although a dropped weight belt may break a toe, boarding-ladder injuries can be far more serious, and they can occur in a variety of ways.

There are two basic types of boarding ladders: the familiar ladder with enclosed steps and handrails and the open-step ladder with no handrails that is designed to be climbed with fins on. Neither type is intrinsically safer than the other, and each is typically hinged at the transom so it can be swung out of the water while the boat is under way.

It is possible to be seriously injured in a boarding-ladder mishap even if you never come into contact with the ladder. Divers sometimes slip off the boarding ladder and fall back into the water. If another diver is approaching the ladder when a diver falls, a decidedly one-sided collision occurs. The approaching diver is commonly hit in the head or face by the tank of the falling diver, and the impact may be severe enough to knock him or her unconscious. An unconscious diver in the water is at serious risk of drowning. Even if the blow does not cause unconsciousness, any blow to the head from a falling diver may result in a concussion. The first rule of boarding-ladder safety is to stay well away from the ladder if someone else is using it.

It is nearly impossible to climb a closed-step boarding ladder with fins on, and even open-step ladders should not be climbed with finned feet unless conditions are very calm. Every diver I've seen fall off a boarding ladder was trying to climb the ladder with dive fins on his or her feet. The second rule of boarding-ladder safety is to remove your fins before putting your feet on the ladder.

The boarding ladder will not move in perfect synchrony with a boat that is rocking in waves. As the boat moves downward, the ladder will swing on its hinges and become separated from the back of the boat. When the boat rises with the next wave, the ladder will swing back into contact with the boat. This motion turns the boarding ladder into a giant pair of scissors that is capable of mangling anything that gets caught between it and the back of the boat. The third rule of boarding-ladder safety is to stay away from the side of the ladder unless conditions are perfectly calm.

However, some dive operations call for returning divers to swim to the swim platform behind the boat (where the ladder is) and hand their fins up to a crew member before boarding via the ladder. This common procedure not only puts divers dangerously close to the scissorslike effect of the ladder, but it's also a good way for fins to be dropped into the water. What should you do?

I approach all boarding ladders the same way—a way that is commonly used on dive boats far offshore in the Gulf of Mexico. Once the ladder is clear of other divers, I approach the ladder underwater and grab the bottom of it. Things are calmer underwater at the bottom of the ladder than at the surface, where waves are breaking, and I am at no risk of being caught in the "scissors" when holding onto the bottom. Grasping the bottom of the ladder with a stiff arm to prevent the ladder from hitting you as it moves is like holding a snake behind its head so it can't bite you.

Once I'm secure at the bottom of the ladder, I slide the heel strap of one fin off my heel and slip the fin off my foot with my free hand. As the fin is removed, I put my hand through the heel strap, which leaves the fin hanging from my wrist. I then switch hands and remove the other fin in the same way. This is very easy to do underwater. I seldom manage to put ice cubes in a glass without dropping a few cubes on the floor, but I've never dropped a fin doing this.

When both fins are removed and one is hanging from each of my arms, I simply put my feet on the bottom rung with both hands on the handrails and climb aboard. If anything unexpected happens and I fall off the ladder, I still have my fins and I can put them back on if necessary to start again. However, I have never fallen off a ladder even in the roughest conditions once I have established four-point contact, with both feet on a rung and both hands on the handrails.

That's it—a simple way to board any ladder that avoids all risks and allows you to keep control of all your gear. I consider this to be the only safe way to board a ladder when conditions are rough. If you practice the procedure during calm dives, it will be

This diver is preparing to remove her fins while holding the boarding ladder beneath the surface. She will loop her fin straps around her wrists before climbing aboard. This is the safest and easiest way to board a boat.

easier when the sea is up and you really need it. Of course, the procedure is impossible to perform with full-foot fins due to their lack of heel straps. The only way to board the boat with full-foot fins is to first toss them into the boat or hand them to somebody on deck.

Ladder lines come into play when you're boarding large boats in heavy seas. The forces involved in such conditions are extraordinarily powerful, and any attempt to approach a heaving boat of over a hundred feet in length is extremely dangerous. To board in such conditions, substitute the ladder line for the bottom of the ladder in the procedure described above. Remove your fins and loop them over your wrists while holding onto the ladder line instead of the ladder itself. Once your fins are removed and secured on each arm, study the ladder as it pounds in the water. Do not approach the ladder if it is moving violently. As soon as a period of relative calm occurs, pull yourself rapidly to the ladder and establish firm, four-point contact, with both feet on a rung and both hands on the handrails. You don't need any extraordinary measure of physical strength to ride out rough conditions once you establish this position on the ladder. Climb the ladder during periods of relative calm.

NAUI, one of the prominent certifying agencies, recommends that you "remain on your hands and knees unless otherwise instructed" once you climb the ladder and reach the swim platform. If you follow this advice, you may stay on your hands and knees for quite some time while the boat crew tries to figure out what's wrong with you. Once you've exited the water, walk back to your place on the bench. The dive crew may help stabilize you as you walk.

Surface Intervals

Many charter-boat excursions involve more than one dive. Surface intervals usually last around one to two hours if the diving is deeper than 50 feet or so. The dive operator will usually set a minimum surface interval, but the dive planning for your multiple dives will be up to you. Even if the dives are made as a group and a leader must be followed, you, as an independent diver, have sole responsibility for the planning and safety of your dives and should never delegate that responsibility to anyone else.

The first order of business after reboarding the boat during a multitank trip is to change tanks. The dive deck is usually a chaotic place immediately after the first dive, so you might want to wait until all the divers are back on board before you begin to fool with your equipment. Even so, I like to get my tank changed while I'm still wet and before I get too involved in conversations or other business like filling out a dive log.

Most divers keep their regulators and BCs connected as a unit when changing tanks between dives. Unhook your regulator from the tank and replace the dust cap on the regulator, but keep the regulator attached to the BC via the power inflator connection and the octopus keeper. Most dive operations distinguish full and empty tanks by leaving the valve caps off empties, so don't replace the valve cap on your used tank.

Make sure that the tank you select for your second dive is full. Full tanks will have valve caps in place and will be noticeably heavier than empties. If you're not sure, this is a good time to pull your stand-alone pressure gauge out of your dry box and check the tank before you go through the trouble of hooking it up. Once you're sure the tank is full, remove your BC/regulator unit from your spent tank and put it on the full tank, then hook the regulator to the new tank and check the air if you haven't already done so with a stand-alone gauge. Replace the complete rig in the tank rack, secure it with a bungee, and you're ready to visit, log the dive, take a nap, or do whatever you want during the surface interval.

Often the boat will move to a new site during the surface interval—usually a shallower dive closer to port. If you took care of your tank-changing duties immediately after the first dive, you can enjoy the ride by watching the procrastinators search for fresh tanks and wrestle with their gear while the bouncing boat is under way.

Heading Back and Tipping

I recommend that you pack your gear as soon as all the divers are aboard after the last dive of the day. Dive decks typically become messier and more cluttered throughout the day, and it's very easy to lose small items such as gloves, masks, or booties in the confusion. After your gear is packed, you are free to visit, log your dive, or occupy your time any way you wish during the ride back to port.

Make sure that you are seated on the bench to afford the captain an unobstructed view when docking the boat. Docking is a finely tuned drill for the crew, so leave the procedure to them. Don't handle lines or participate in any way unless specifically asked to do so.

It is considered good manners to tip the crew once the boat has returned to the dock. Tipping should be 10 to 15 percent of the cost of the charter and is typically about $10 per diver for a day of diving. If you've developed a rapport with a helpful crew member or divemaster, go ahead and give the money to that person. However, tips are often distributed evenly among the crew. Many divemasters or crew members are not paid by the boat operator and rely solely on tips for their pay.

It is not considered good manners to loiter on the boat once you've returned to the dock. Resist the urge to chat for too long with the crew. They have work to do. Paying customers may sometimes form a bucket line to help unload tanks, and you should feel free to join in if you want to help.

It's a good idea to carry a large, plastic bin (Rubbermaid bins are a good choice for this) in your car whenever you go diving. Place your mesh bag full of wet gear in the plastic bin to protect your car and to keep the mess to a minimum.

DIVING FROM PRIVATELY OWNED BOATS

Few things can excite an adventurous spirit more than striking out with like-minded compatriots in a privately owned boat and going diving. Almost any kind of boat that can accommodate four divers and their equipment and is appropriately seaworthy for the dive site can be used as a dive platform. If a boat is suitable for fishing, it's suitable for diving, and diving from a privately owned boat is a bold affirmation of your status as an independent diver.

It is important to remember, though, that diving from a privately owned boat usually involves greater risk and personal responsibility than diving from a professional dive boat. It usually means diving without the safety net of professionally trained dive personnel and special dive-safety equipment.

Safety Considerations

Virtually all dive charter boats carry basic medical equipment specific to dive-related injuries. One of the most basic dive emergency kits contains a quantity of pure medical oxygen and the means to deliver it to a diver afflicted by a pressure-related dive injury such as decompression sickness. Such kits are available for purchase from providers such as DAN, but the kits require specialized training in their use.

It is most likely that emergency oxygen will not be available on a privately owned boat. This doesn't necessarily mean that you shouldn't dive from such a boat, but it does mean that you should be very aware of the deficiency and plan your dives accordingly. Depths and times for dives should be planned extra conservatively whenever there is no emergency oxygen on the boat.

Even if emergency equipment is on board, the equipment is useless unless somebody on the boat is trained in its use. And even if the boat owner or dive leader is properly trained, who's to say that that person is not the one who will need assistance? All divers in the dive party should discuss the possibility of something going wrong and procedures to deal with problems. However, it is most likely that if you dive from a privately owned boat, you will not have the benefit of possible assistance from a person professionally trained and practiced in dive emergencies. Not only must you plan your dives without any assistance from a dive professional, but you will not have the assistance of a dive professional in the event that you make a mistake. Once again, divers from privately owned boats must be aware of this deficiency and plan their dives accordingly. Add a pinch of paranoia to your conservatism when planning dives from a privately owned boat.

Privately owned boats will not typically be designed specifically for diving, so diver assistance lines will usually not be as elaborate as those found on professional dive boats. However, some effort must be made to make the boat suitable for diving. At the very least, a drift line and float should be set to assist any diver who gets downcurrent from the boat.

Boarding ladders on privately owned boats are not typically as sturdy as the ladders used by professional dive boats, and divers on privately owned boats may opt to hand all of their equipment (including fins, weight belt, tank, and BC) to someone on the boat before boarding. Before diving, your party must establish some procedure for safely boarding the boat from the water.

Of course, the boat should never be abandoned. Always leave at least one person on board; that person should be competent to handle the boat and its equipment and also be familiar with all dive and emergency procedures. The person on board should keep a constant watch for divers surfacing far from the boat. The boat should be minimally equipped with a marine radio and a GPS (global positioning system) unit. The GPS will not only keep you from getting lost, but it may be very useful in letting authorities know your exact location in the event you must radio for help. An ordinary cell phone will often work from boats close to shore, and it can also be very helpful if a problem arises—like having to call home to let somebody know you'll be late for dinner if the diving is particularly good.

The keys to safely diving from a privately owned boat are planning, communication, a keen awareness of the risks and each diver's limitations, and common sense. Despite the increased risk and personal responsibility of such independent diving, diving from a privately owned boat is as safe as you make it and is usually a ton of fun.

However, it's especially important to keep peer pressure in check when diving with friends from a privately owned boat. The dive/no dive decision is always yours alone.

Legal Considerations

Of course, any boat must be in compliance with all federal and local licensing and registration, but boats used for diving also have a legal requirement to fly an appropriate dive flag whenever divers are in the water.

If you are familiar with boats and international boating procedures, you might know that lights and day shapes (flags) are required for any boat over 38 feet in length. However, dive boats are specifically mandated to show the appropriate signal regardless of length. If you're diving from a boat, you must fly the correct flag even if the boat is nothing more than a glorified bathtub toy.

The flag required for diving activities according to COLREGs (International Regulations for Preventing Collisions at Sea) is the Alpha (A) flag, which is blue and white. The familiar red flag with the diagonal white stripe is not recognized by international rules.

Now that you know that, push it to the back of your mind. Although the red-and-white flag is not recognized by the international rules, it is far better understood by other boaters than is the Alpha flag, and most states require that it be flown on boats used by divers in state waters. It doesn't hurt to fly both flags, but most boaters do not recognize the blue-and-white Alpha flag as a dive flag or as a warning to stay clear of a

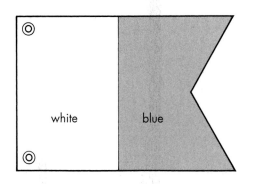

international "A" or "Alpha" flag

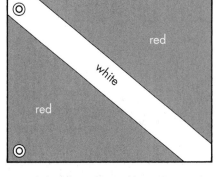

recreational dive flag required by U.S. state laws

Various laws require boats involved in dive operations to display a flag to warn other marine traffic to steer clear. Part A, Rule 27 (e) (ii) of the International Regulations for Preventing Collisions at Sea (COLREGs) requires the blue-and-white Alpha flag (left) to be displayed. The more familiar red flag with the diagonal stripe (right) is required by most states to be flown in U.S. waters, and this flag is more recognized worldwide for scuba activities.

boat flying that flag. Research local laws regarding dive flags and follow them, but always fly the familiar red-and-white flag when diving from a boat. Not only is flying the correct flag in the correct way an important safety device, but failure to comply could also result in a stiff fine. A dive flag painted on the side of the boat is not a legal substitute for flying the flag.

Even if divers fly the correct flag, it is important for them to realize that many boaters have no understanding of any flag. In fact, some boaters may ignorantly approach a boat flying a dive flag just to see what's going on. Don't get me started about the sad fact that any yahoo with a down payment can immediately take to the water in a powerful and dangerous boat, but it's important for all boat divers to plan for dangerous boat traffic even if they are flying the proper flag.

The appropriate flag should be flown beneath the anchor light when diving from a boat at night. If the boat has no anchor light, the flag must still be flown and it must be illuminated in some way. A spotlight should also be aimed on the water in the direction of the divers.

It's sensible for divers to share expenses with the boat owner for the costs of a trip. However, an owner who demands compensation beyond a share of expenses is acting as a charter captain and must possess the required license. A trip on a privately owned boat normally places no special duty of care on the owner for anything that may happen to you while you are aboard the boat or diving, and no liability waiver is required. You have sole responsibility for your own safety and well-being when diving from a privately owned boat.

DIVING FROM SHORE

Shore diving doesn't require an expensive boat, and it offers a great opportunity for independent diving. No matter where you live, there is probably an ocean or lake within a day's drive from your home that is suitable for shore diving. All you need is a buddy and a plan.

Safety Considerations

Like diving from a privately owned boat, diving from shore usually means diving without the assistance of a dive professional and without emergency equipment such as an oxygen kit to deal with pressure-related injuries. However, most shore diving is relatively shallow, and conservative dives can usually be planned and executed.

Another safety concern that is unique to shore diving is the possibility that nobody except your dive buddy will know that you've gone diving. Always let somebody on shore know of your dive plans and your expected time of return; this will facilitate a search-and-rescue effort in the event that you run into trouble.

Boat traffic is an important concern of shore divers, especially near a channel or harbor. Shore divers should be on the constant watch for personal watercraft (Wave Runner–type craft)—a dangerous type of toy boat that seems to have been specifically designed to expose any juvenile-delinquent tendencies of its driver.

The difficulty of shore diving runs the gamut from completely benign to dangerously challenging. Many lakes, quarries, and springs offer swimming-pool-like conditions and require little planning and no special skills. However, some ocean shores offer something more akin to washing-machine-like conditions and require local information and special skills before they can be safely dived. Like all diving, shore diving requires planning, risk assessment, and common sense to be done safely.

Tides and Currents

As we covered in the section on tides in chapter 8, the farther a coast is from the equator, the more pronounced the tides will be. If tides are a factor in the area you want to dive, you must plan your dives around them. Consult local tide tables to get the times of the tides.

Most shore dives in areas of prominent tides are made during the slack tide between the outgoing (ebb) tide and the incoming (flood) tide. This slack time may be only fifteen or twenty minutes in duration, and it only occurs twice each day. Study the tide tables to find a day when this slack time occurs at a convenient time to dive.

Remember that nontidal currents such as longshore currents or rip currents may be present on any ocean coast at any time. Study the water at the planned entry point for evidence of such currents. Dives are often canceled due to strong currents, and a careful appraisal of currents should always be part of your independent dive/no dive decision.

Surf

Surf is a diving condition unique to shore diving, and high surf can be dangerous. A breaking wave only 2 feet high is powerful enough to knock most people off their feet, and larger surf may cause serious injury—especially if the wave is large enough to lift a diver upward and then slam him or her into the bottom.

The presence of heavy surf often also means the presence of a strong longshore current, and heavy surf also creates a buildup of onshore water that is conducive to powerful rip currents. Even if the surf itself can be managed, heavy surf is often a reason to cancel a dive. A careful appraisal of surf conditions should always be part of your independent dive/no dive decision.

If you decide to dive from a shore with surf, you face the challenge of getting beyond the surf zone and into deeper, divable water. Local techniques for accomplishing this vary, and it's a good idea to get local information about how to negotiate surf on any particular shore. Underwater obstructions such as banks or rocks affect the surf, and local information may help you to either avoid such obstructions or use them to help you get safely past the surf zone.

Many divers are taught to enter the surf wearing all their dive equipment and to walk sideways or backward in the water with their fins on their feet. That may be necessary when the surf is powerful and breaking very near the shore. However, I've watched divers entering perfectly calm water and walking backward with their fins on, turning awkwardly every now and then to see where they are going, and generally tripping all over themselves for no good reason. That's silly.

I've found it easier to wade forward into relatively calm water wearing my dive equipment but carrying my fins in my hands. If the surf is breaking over a bank or sandbar some distance from shore, I usually find it possible to wade near the area where the waves are breaking. I can also usually turn sideways and squat to brace myself or duck beneath waves that have already broken ("foamies") as they continue toward shore in the shallow water. If I fall, well, I get back up.

Surf is not constant and usually comes in a series of three large waves called a set. As I approach the breaking waves or as I get into water above my waist, I study the sets of waves and try to time my passage over whatever is causing them to break. Only then do I put my fins on and start swimming. I can usually swim right over the breaking area without having to contend with any large, breaking waves.

It's easy for buddies to become separated when negotiating the surf zone. Once past the zone, stay on the surface until you reunite with your buddy before starting the dive. Consider a plan of inflating safety sausages to make it easier to find each other if seas are high.

Of course, you must also negotiate surf when returning to shore. End the dive and surface beyond the area where the waves are breaking. Inflate your BC and study the waves as they approach, move beneath you, and then break. Time your return to shore after the last wave of a set. It is usually possible to swim over the breaking point without having to contend with a breaking wave.

Legal Considerations

Some states require divers near shore to tow a dive flag. Shore-diving flags are typically the traditional red flag with the diagonal white stripe, and they are connected to a float with a weight on the bottom to keep the flag upright when floating. A length of nylon line is attached to the weight on the bottom of the float, and the line is usually wrapped around a spool device that enables you to let out more line as you descend and to wind the line back onto the spool as you ascend. Buddy teams are usually allowed to share a flag, but check local laws concerning dive flag requirements for shore divers at your selected site.

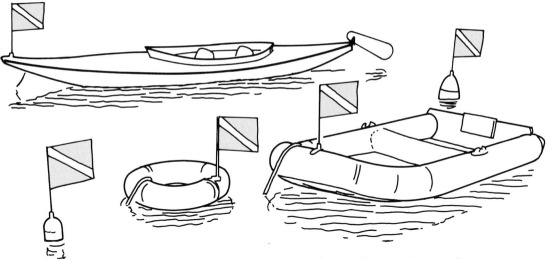

The dive flag hangs from a pole that can be attached to either a small buoy, inner tube, surf mat, surfboard, or small boat. Floats can be resting stations during the dive, and larger floats are good places to store equipment.

Personal dive flags are mandatory when diving from shore or when diving from a boat near shore in shallow water. This is a popular model. The flag is weighted at the bottom to keep it upright in the water. The length of line is let out as the diver descends and wound back onto the reel upon ascent to keep the line neatly out of the way.

It's a good idea to tow a dive flag whenever you are diving near boating traffic, even if local law does not require it. Remember, however, that many boaters are ignorant of the flag's meaning, and some may actually be attracted to the flag. You will hear boats as they approach, but you won't be able to determine the direction of the sound. Look toward the surface if the sound of a boat seems close. Hold the dive flag spool loosely in case a boat runs over the dive flag. As always, be especially aware of children of all ages on Wave Runner–type watercraft.

Carrying a dive flag through the surf zone complicates the process. It's usually easiest to let out some line and tow the flag behind you as you move through the surf. Expect a significant tug on the line whenever a foamy hits the flag. Push the flag ahead of you when returning to shore to prevent the flag from being pushed by a wave and hitting you in the head.

Practical Considerations

It is sometimes impossible to get a vehicle close to a shore-diving site, which means you might have to carry your gear some distance from the car to the site. The easiest way to carry dive equipment any significant distance is to wear it. Assemble your

BC/regulator/tank unit at the car, put on your weight belt, put on the BC, and start walking while carrying your fins and mask in your hands. If you don't plan to dive immediately once you arrive at the site, it's best to carry your exposure suit rather than wearing it, to avoid overheating.

Sand is a nemesis of dive gear, and it can be a problem whenever you dive from a sandy shore. If your dive begins at a sandy beach, I recommend that you start the dive at the car and wear your gear directly into the water. Placing a regulator or BC on a sandy beach is asking for equipment trouble due to sand in the regulator's second stages (primary and octopus) or in the BC power inflator. Carefully wash your gear after diving in a sandy area.

You can lock valuables in the trunk of the car, but what to do with keys to an unattended car sometimes poses a dilemma for shore divers. One solution is to place the keys in a lockbox with a combination lock. However, there is no guarantee that the lockbox itself won't be taken unless it is also chained to the car in some way.

Another solution is to simply put the keys in a BC pocket or attach the key ring to a D ring on the BC. The metals used for keys are usually noncorrosive, and they won't be damaged by salt water. However, it's a good idea to rinse the keys with fresh water and to dry them before inserting them into a car's ignition.

Small, waterproof containers that are designed to be worn around the neck may also accommodate car keys during a dive, but these containers may be dislodged and lost. Divers who want to carry their keys but keep them dry can place them in the battery compartment (with batteries removed, of course) of a dive light.

Shore diving usually involves driving to and from the site in a car. Buy a large, plastic container and keep it in the car. When the diving is done, put the wet and sandy gear in the plastic bin to keep the car reasonably dry and to keep the mess to a minimum.

DRIFT DIVING

Drift diving is a type of boat diving that is typically done in areas where currents are strong, and it is sometimes the only way to dive in a strong current. The distinguishing characteristic of this type of diving is that the boat is never moored or anchored. Divers enter the water and drift with the prevailing current, and the boat follows above. Drift diving is easy and relaxing and offers an opportunity to see a large area of a reef. However, it is different from regular diving in some important ways.

Types of Drift Diving

Drift diving is done in two general ways. The way that is recommended by the certifying agencies involves the use of a highly visible dive float (with flag where required by law) that is towed by the leader of the dive. The dive leader enters the water first with the float, and the other divers quickly follow suit and congregate around the dive leader. The divers then descend as a group and dive as a group while the boat follows the dive float.

The divers ascend as a group at the end of the dive. If there are only a few divers, they can use the tether to the dive float as an ascent line, but drift diving often involves making a controlled ascent and safety stop without the benefit of an ascent line. The boat approaches the divers only when all the divers have surfaced. If the dive group is small, the boat may drift in the current with engines out of gear until all have boarded. If the group is large, it may be necessary for the divers to approach and board the drifting boat in pairs, and for the boat to move and maneuver close to the remaining drifting divers once again after a pair has boarded.

Drift diving was popularized by commercial dive operators on the Mexican diving mecca of Cozumel—an island off the coast of the Yucatán Peninsula that is subject to the powerful Yucatán Current, which is a diversion of the Gulf Stream. Interestingly enough, the drift diving done in Cozumel does not typically involve the use of a dive float. Divers enter the water as a group and follow a divemaster in this second type of drift diving, but the divemaster is not tethered in any way to the surface. The boat follows the divers by watching their bubbles.

Drift diving in Cozumel is more loosely organized than drift diving in some other areas. Divers who run low on air before the rest of the group are sometimes allowed to surface independently of the group and are picked up by the following boat. However, the group generally dives together, performs their safety stop together, and is picked up together.

Safety Considerations

Drift diving is usually safe and easy, but there are some special safety concerns. It is important to stay reasonably close to the divemaster or dive leader during drift dives. If you become separated from the group, there is a chance you could be stranded. Should this occur, surface independently, inflate your safety sausage, attract attention to yourself by blowing your whistle or air horn, and wait to be seen and picked up.

The boat driver may lose track of the divers, especially if no diver is towing a highly visible float. Wind ripples or rain can make bubbles nearly impossible to see. Carry a safety sausage whenever drift diving with a commercial operator that does not use a surface float.

Drift diving usually involves swimming in close proximity to other divers. Awareness and good buoyancy control are necessary to avoid collisions. If you decide to stem the current to stop for any reason, it is likely that the diver drifting behind you will not stop and a collision will occur. Likewise, it is difficult to avoid any diver in front of you who has suddenly stopped. Underwater diver collisions are usually not serious, but be prepared to perhaps have your mask dislodged by another diver when drift diving.

It's also important to remember that drift divers continue to move down the reef even when they are not swimming. Distracted divers may collide with the reef itself if they don't watch where they're going. Collisions with the reef can be serious both to the reef and to the diver, and divers should not become so enthralled by the diving experience that they lose track of where they are in relation to the reef.

Ascent lines are usually not available to drift divers, and the divers must rely on their own buoyancy control for their ascents and for their safety stops. The ability to hang comfortably and accurately at 15 feet for at least three minutes without the aid of a line is an important skill for drift divers.

Drift diving involves close cooperation between the divers and the boat operator. Commercial operators are very practiced in this type of diving, but private boat owners probably are not. Always use the towed-float technique if you decide to try a drift dive from a privately owned boat, and make sure that the diver-pickup procedure is perfectly understood by both divers and boat operator.

Practical Considerations

Drift diving is usually lots of fun and offers an exhilarating opportunity to "fly" with the current and see a large area of a reef. However, it is somewhat of a team effort, and some independence while diving is lost. Don't expect to be able to swim off with a buddy and explore on your own or to linger at points of interest along the way. Being a part of a large group of divers is not the best way to have intimate encounters with marine life. As drift divers generally dive as a group, bottom time is usually limited by the air-consumption rate of the least efficient diver in the group.

Some divers like to be the first or the last to enter the water to avoid the chaos of a gaggle of divers waiting to exit the boat. Since drift divers dive as a group, they must exit the boat as quickly as possible as a group in order to stay together. You should expect to be one of the crowd while you're on the boat, in addition to diving as part of a group once you're in the water.

Lastly, drift diving usually requires divers to spend more time on the surface before and after the dive than other types of diving. Divers using loosely fitting BCs or back-inflation BCs are at a bit of a disadvantage when bobbing for an extended time on the surface.

NIGHT DIVING

Nighttime is a great time to dive. Few things offer the excitement and adventure of plunging into inky-black water to explore a reef at night, and the reef itself undergoes an amazing transformation when the sun sets. The diurnal (daytime) creatures of the reef go to bed, and the nocturnal (nighttime) creatures come out to hunt and feed.

Skittish creatures that cannot be easily approached during the day can often be closely observed at night, and fascinating creatures that cannot usually be seen at all during the day are commonly seen at night. Even the structure of the reef is transformed, as corals extend their tentacles to feed. Diving a reef at night is like seeing the reef for the first time all over again.

Night diving may be intimidating at first, but there is no reason for independent divers to be afraid of the dark. However, night diving does require some special equipment and procedures to be safely accomplished.

Yoke Lights

Yoke lights are small personal lights that a diver attaches to the regulator yoke when night diving. They come in a variety of types, but they are all used to make the diver visible in the water.

Cyalume sticks are commonly used as yoke lights. These are plastic tubes filled with chemicals that glow when mixed. The chemicals are separated in the tube by a thin partition. Bending the tube breaks the partition, and the tube begins to glow as

What can stoke the fires of adventure more than anticipating the excitement of a night dive? While the rest of the crew take their places at the bar or settle in for the night, night divers prepare for the best dive of the day.

Brittle stars are sea stars (starfish) with disc-shaped bodies and long, slender arms that they can move surprisingly quickly. While brittle stars may sometimes be seen during the day, they are commonly seen during night dives when they crawl out to feed. This brittle star has crawled atop a colony of beautiful golden zoanthid.

soon as the chemicals are allowed to mix. Cyalume sticks come in a variety of sizes and colors, but the ones used most frequently by night divers are 6 inches in length and produce a lime-green glow that lasts for several hours. Cyalume sticks are most commonly attached to the regulator yoke by none other than the surprisingly low-tech and low-cost plastic ties.

Cyalume sticks are cheap, but they are one-use items and must be discarded after they are used. Some popular dive destinations have banned the use of Cyalume sticks due to the plastic and chemical waste they produce.

Battery-powered lights are another common type of yoke light, and they are available in a baffling variety of colors, shapes, and types. The lights are usually powered by a single AA battery, and the light they produce is usually similar in intensity to the light given off by Cyalume sticks. Colors are usually white, yellow, green, or red, and the lights may blink or remain constantly on.

Battery-powered yoke lights are inexpensive and are more cost-efficient than Cyalume sticks over the long run, and they are permitted at all dive destinations. Since battery-powered yoke lights come in a variety of shapes and colors, it is usually easier to identify a particular diver underwater by his or her light—a distinction that makes buddy diving easier if several divers are in the water.

Regardless of the type they use, all divers should wear a yoke light when night diving. Some divers carry an extra yoke light in a BC pocket, to be used in the event that they must surface far from the boat or exit point. Many safety sausages are equipped with a small pocket near the end that will hold a Cyalume stick or battery-powered yoke light, which will make the diver visible when on the surface.

Dive Lights

Every night diver should carry at least two dive lights—a primary light and a secondary light to use in the event that the primary light fails. Most divers carry a large light as their primary light and a smaller light for their secondary light, but many divers (including me) simply carry two lights of the same size.

Normal primary night-diving lights (as opposed to cave-diving lights, which are beyond the purview of this book) are powered by four to eight C cells, and they are designed as either a pistol-grip or a straight-grip flashlight. Pistol-grip lights look like spotlights, and generally they are powerful lights that cast a wide beam. Straight-grip lights look pretty much like ordinary flashlights and generally cast a narrower beam. Either type of light works well as a primary dive light, but I've found that straight-grip lights are easier for me to carry and use.

Some divers carry a much smaller light powered by AA batteries as their secondary light. Many of these lights have no proper on/off switch and are turned on and off by tightening or loosening the bulb housing. These small lights have their purpose—they are useful for looking into dark holes on any dive—but I do not think they are appropriate as either primary or secondary night-diving lights. They don't produce a wide enough beam of light to be very useful when night diving, and the tighten/loosen mechanism that turns them on and off is prone to flooding—especially when turning the light off by loosening the bulb housing underwater. Both lights (primary and secondary) should be appropriate night-diving lights. Each should be powered by at least four C-cell batteries and should have an on/off switch that does not involve tightening or loosening the bulb cap.

Some manufacturers offer dive lights that are mounted on the head by means of an elastic band or are mounted to the mask strap. These hands-free lights seem like a good idea, but I've found them to be problematic for a variety of reasons.

The first drawback of head-mounted lights is that they're hard to aim accurately. My experience has been that the light strikes objects that are above my natural view and that I must roll my eyes to see where the light is falling.

Many night creatures are sensitive to light and will withdraw or move away if a light is shined directly on them. You can easily maneuver a normal dive light to cast just enough light on these creatures to allow you to see them without spooking them. Head-mounted lights, however, are always shined directly where you are looking.

Just as gnats and bugs are attracted to a lightbulb at night, many small, free-swimming marine organisms are attracted to dive lights at night. These small, wiggling, wormy animals (collectively called squigglies in common, scientific diving lingo) are sometimes present in great numbers, and they sometimes swarm dive lights. A horde of squigglies around a head-mounted light can be quite a distraction.

The last drawback of head-mounted lights is the problems they cause for the buddy of the diver who uses one. It is considered poor form to shine a dive light directly at a buddy, as the light will ruin his night vision for several seconds. A buddy's yoke light or dive light is easy to see at night, so you can monitor your buddy without ever having to shine a light on her. However, it's impossible to look at other divers without blinding them when using a head-mounted light.

Marker Strobes

Marker strobes are small but intense strobe lights that are usually powered by one or two AA batteries, and they are primarily used during night dives as navigational aids to mark important navigation points or exit points. Using marker strobes is like leaving an easily followed trail of bread crumbs to lead you back to where you started in the somewhat disorienting realm of the underwater world at night.

Marker strobes are highly visible underwater at night, and their use greatly simplifies night diving. Shore divers typically leave a strobe at the exit point, and they can set another strobe on the reef to mark the exit turn if the reef does not form directly from the exit point. Night divers diving from a boat usually set one strobe at the anchor and another strobe about 15 feet up the anchor line, where it will be visible to divers

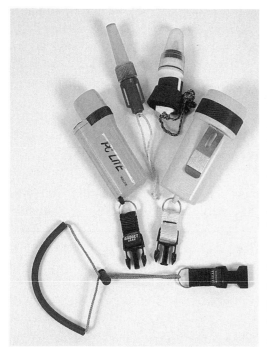

This is the array of lights needed for a normal night dive. From left to right: medium primary light, battery-powered yoke light, marker strobe, medium backup light. A wrist lanyard with a Fastex receptor is at the bottom of the photo, and Fastex clips are attached to each light. It is a simple matter to move lights from Fastex clips on the BC to the wrist lanyard whenever necessary.

within a large radius of the anchor. By keeping the blinking lights in sight throughout the dive, night divers are comforted by the knowledge that the dive is under control and all is well.

An extra marker strobe can be carried in a BC pocket, to be used in the event that a diver must surface far from the boat or exit point. The strobe will make the surfaced diver highly visible at night, and placing it on top of a safety sausage will make the diver even more visible. Of course, being visible is important not only to facilitate pickup but also as a safety measure in areas where boat traffic might be hazardous.

Some divers get the idea that a marker strobe would make a good yoke light. It won't. Marker strobes are far too bright to be used as yoke lights, and they will temporarily compromise the night vision of any diver in close proximity who looks directly at one. Perhaps more importantly, a strobe worn by a diver might be mistaken for a navigation marker by other divers. Many yoke lights are designed to blink, and that's fine. A blinking yoke light does not emit an intense enough light to be confused with a strobe light.

Many commercial dive boats do not allow individual divers to use their own marker strobes during night dives. The boat crew will set marker strobes on the anchor, anchor line, and hang lines to help divers return to the boat. Strobes set by individual divers are prohibited because they might cause confusion among the other divers in the dive party.

Marker strobes generally last several hours on fresh batteries. The strobe continues to fire when the batteries get low, but a greater time elapses between blinks. Of course, it is important to keep strobes well maintained and to load fresh batteries whenever you use them as navigational aids, and always keep in mind the possibility that they might fail. Night divers should never rely completely on marker strobes for their navigation.

Many marker strobes are not equipped with a proper on/off switch, and they are turned on and off by twisting the cap. As such, they are prone to flooding when turned off underwater. Maybe I'm just clumsy, but I've flooded so many strobes by loosening the cap to turn them off that I now never turn off these types of strobes underwater. It's easy to hold a blinking strobe in the hand in such a way that the strobe is not blinding.

If I have to pick up more than one strobe on my way back to the boat or exit point, I put them in a BC pocket without turning them off. There's little danger of forgetting to turn them off and running down the batteries once I've exited the water. The strobes in my pocket make me blink like a neon sign in Vegas.

Safety Considerations

Although night diving may seem spooky the first few times, it does not really involve much more risk than diving during the day. However, the reduced visibility will affect the dive in a few ways.

It is standard procedure to become familiar with a dive site during the day before making a dive at the site at night. However, as dive lights shine on the reef and cast their eerie shadows, even familiar sites take on a whole new ambience and appearance at night. Plan your dive conservatively, and be careful with your navigation even if you use marker strobes.

Night divers can only see what is illuminated by the narrow beam from their dive lights, so their first order of business when descending on a reef or dive site is to orient themselves to the area. This means that, before approaching the reef, they should look beneath them, look to either side, and look behind them for anything with which they might come into contact. Night divers should monitor their position throughout their dives to avoid coming into contact with the reef. Divers should always avoid contact with the reef, but it is even more important at night. Urchins and fireworms, which normally hide during the day, will more likely be out at night, and contact would be unfortunate both for the diver and the animal.

Good buoyancy is an important skill for any dive, and its importance is magnified at night. Divers have a tendency to dive closer to the reef at night to better see what their lights are illuminating, and night divers have no peripheral vision of their surroundings. It's very easy for your fins, shins, or knees to come into contact with the reef unless you carefully maintain your buoyancy. In addition to protecting yourself from scrapes, stings, and bruises, it's your responsibility to protect the underwater environment from damage.

Buddy contact can also be compromised at night. It's easy to maintain contact and close proximity to a buddy at night if you are the only pair in the water, but it can become confusing when you are diving with a group or when several independent buddy pairs are in the same area. Night divers all look pretty much the same underwater. Make a point of remembering the shape and color of your buddy's yoke light when several divers are in the water. If your buddy's yoke light is indistinguishable from the yoke lights of other divers, become familiar with the type of fins your buddy is wearing. You should always avoid shining your dive light toward another diver's face, but illuminating another diver's fins does no harm and is a good way to identify your dive buddy in a crowd.

Underwater communication with a buddy is different at night, but it's not really more difficult than communicating during the day. If fact, it's often easier to get the attention of a buddy at night than it is during the day. The established method of getting a buddy's attention at night is to aim the beam of your dive light within her field of vision and move the light back and forth rapidly. This is often done to show her something of interest. Once you have your buddy's attention, you can simply shine your light on the object of interest to share the experience.

The established certifying agencies teach light signals to communicate with buddies underwater. For example, if you wanted to do an "OK" check, you would move your dive light in the shape of an O and wait for a return signal from your buddy. I don't like this method, because it usually results in lights being shined in divers' faces and ruining their night vision.

If you want to communicate with your buddy at night, I recommend that you first get his attention in the established way of moving your light beam back and forth in front of him. Then, instead of shining your light toward your buddy and making some sort of signal, you should shine your dive light on yourself. Of course, you should not blind yourself by shining the light at your face, but your buddy will look at you if you shine your own light on your chest. You can then communicate with your buddy by making established hand signals and illuminating your hand with your dive light. Your buddy can then respond in the same way. This method of communication should be discussed and established before the dive, but I've found that it works far better than underwater semaphore with blinding lights.

If two divers are close to each other and also fairly close to the reef, the reflection of their lights from the reef will usually make them somewhat visible to each other. If you can see your buddy, it is usually possible to communicate without having to use your dive light to illuminate your hand.

There is one important exception to my rule against using dive lights as communication devices when underwater at night. In the event that you are in difficulty and need the assistance of your buddy, you should shine your light toward your buddy and wave it above your head in an arc. This is an emergency signal, and you should not use it to simply get your buddy's attention.

Dive lights are also important signaling devices in the event that you must surface far from the exit point or dive boat. Observers on the boat or shore who see a diver at the surface will immediately want to know one thing: Is the diver in distress? If you surface far from an exit point and you are OK, you should signal the shore or boat by shining your dive light and moving it in a deliberate and controlled O motion. If you are not OK, you should wave the light above your head in an arc. If you are OK and you move your light too rapidly in the prescribed O, it is possible that the signal could be confused with the signal for distress, so be careful with the "OK" signal.

If you surface far from the exit point or boat and are not in distress, but you cannot swim back to the exit point or boat, give the "OK" signal with your dive light to let ob-

HAND SIGNALS

Buddy teams who frequently dive together often develop communication signals that can range from the identification of common marine animals to gossip about their fellow divers. New buddy teams, however, generally limit their communication to signals that directly relate to the dive. These photos show some common signals. Make sure that you have your signals straight whenever planning a dive with a new buddy.

I'm OK/Are you OK?

Danger.

Check your gauges.

I'm out of air/Let's share air.

Let's surface.

Let's continue the dive at a shallower depth.

Let's go back to the boat/ Where is the boat?

My planned air supply is half gone/Let's turn the dive according to our plan.

servers know that your predicament is not an emergency, then inflate your safety sausage and shine your dive light on the top of the sausage. This will indicate that although you are not having an emergency, you request a pickup. Illuminating a safety sausage also makes you visible to potentially hazardous boat traffic.

Practical Considerations

The thing I enjoy most about night diving is the opportunity to approach animals closely and to see animals that hide during the day. Many fish sleep at night and can be seen lying in crevices or on the bottom. Parrot fish may secrete a mucous cocoon around themselves to mask their scent while sleeping. The opportunity to closely observe these sleeping animals is exciting, but night divers should be careful not to disturb them with their dive lights or by approaching too closely. Dive lights can be as blinding to the animals of the reef as they are to a dive buddy, and a temporarily blinded animal is at great risk from marauding predators on the reef. Take advantage of the unique opportunity to observe the wildlife, but be courteous to them.

Underwater photographers also enjoy the opportunity to closely approach animals at night, and many photo opportunities are only available at night. Of course, a camera strobe fired at an animal at night will cause temporary blindness. An underwater photographer should stay close to her subject after taking photos and act as a protector until the subject regains its vision and composure.

Octopuses are common residents of reefs worldwide, but they are rarely seen during the day. The possibility of observing one of these intelligent creatures is a reason in itself to go night diving.

Predators on some reefs have learned to use night divers and their dive lights as hunting aids. It is fairly common for large fish to follow divers at night on Caribbean reefs that are popular for night diving. The large fish wait until a potential meal is illuminated by a dive light and then rush in and gobble the highlighted animal. This remarkable adaptation is commonly used by tarpon, which are large, silver fish with very reflective scales. A large tarpon is so reflective that divers may be blinded by the reflection of their own lights if the tarpon comes close. Not only can this event scare the bejesus out of an unwary diver, but divers should also be aware that their lights may be a death sentence for some animals on the reef. Avoid shining a light on prey animals for extended periods of time.

Of all the animals that can be seen at night but not during the day, my favorite is the octopus. Octopuses are common on reefs at night, and the sight of one always makes my dive. Octopuses are mollusks (related to snails), are highly intelligent, and are so different from us that it amazes me that they and humans inhabit the same planet.

The orange ball corallimorph is one of the most exquisite animals of the sea. These jewels of the reef may grow to the size of a man's fist when fully extended, and the brilliant orange balls on the tips of their translucent tentacles appear to float without support. Orange balls shun the light of day, and they will begin to retract even if directly illuminated by a dive light. Only night divers have the opportunity to see them. Look for these beautiful creatures at depths of 30 to 35 feet on Caribbean reefs at least an hour after the sun fully sets.

Orange ball corallimorphs are another nocturnal favorite. Like corals and anemones, corallimorphs are cnidarians. They are virtually invisible during the day. Orange ball corallimorphs resemble small anemones (they are often called orange ball anemones, which is a misnomer) and have brilliant orange balls on the tips of their translucent tentacles. They are jewels of the reef at night, and I consider them to be some of the most beautiful animals in the sea.

The entire reef seems to come alive at night. Corals seem to bloom as they extend their tentacles to feed. Moray eels leave their lairs and cruise for food. Eyes of small shrimp reflect dive lights and create the distinct impression that you are being watched at every turn. Regardless of your personal wildlife preferences, you will be enthralled by the beauty and excitement of a reef or dive site at night.

CHAPTER 11

STAYING OUT
OF TROUBLE

I'M STUPID. This is no revelation to those who know me well, but it's amazing how that admission has simplified my life. I no longer must struggle to rationalize the stupid things I do, and whenever I commit a blunder and the inevitable question, "What's the matter with you, buddy, are you stupid?" is asked, I can respond with all the confidence and assurance of the guy in those old beer commercials, "Yes, I am."

The fact that I've managed to dive for more than thirty years without serious mishap is a testament to the safety of our sport and to the fact that even I can figure out a few things if given enough time. Even so, I've had my share of anxious moments underwater and I've seen my share of dive problems. Most of the problems I've witnessed were not terribly serious and resulted in embarrassment rather than injury, but some were serious situations involving exhausted and panicky divers far from the boat or exit point and out of air.

It's easy to make a list of dos and don'ts based on the end results of dives gone bad. Don't run out of air, don't surface far from the boat, don't panic, etc. However, most dive problems involve a series of errors, and the end result could usually have been avoided had the diver interrupted the error chain at any point. So rather than concentrating on the ending catastrophe (nobody wants to run out of air), it makes more sense to start at the beginning of the chain.

So what is the beginning of most dive problems? Well, it doesn't involve equipment failure, shark attacks, or any of the things that new divers seem to worry most about. Most dive problems begin with divers getting lost.

Amazingly, most certification classes do not adequately cover underwater navigation, and many newly certified divers get lost underwater simply because they make no effort whatsoever to navigate. They just jump in, swim around, and then rely on a divemaster or dive buddy to get them back to where they started. This kind of dependence is dangerous and often results in the gut-wrenching realization that your dive buddy is as lost as you are and was depending on *you* to get home.

Learning to navigate underwater is an important step toward becoming an independent diver. All of the rules you learned in your certification class regarding when to turn dives and how to manage your air are meaningless unless you know where the dive ends.

UNDERWATER NAVIGATION

Underwater navigation is an inexact science that is influenced by the mere fact that it occurs underwater. Many dives do not follow a straight path, and currents can significantly alter a course. However, the small distances traveled underwater usually mitigate the imprecision of navigation at least to a tolerable level. With diligence and practice, anybody can develop underwater navigation skills that will greatly increase their safety and independence when diving.

Starting at a Fixed Point

Underwater navigation does not necessarily involve compasses, headings, bearings, or any of the other complicated-sounding things you might have heard about. However, it always involves starting from a meaningful fixed point to which the navigator hopes to return. Red-flag warning number one and the first cardinal rule of underwater navigation is this: An anchored boat is not a fixed point, and returning to the point where the boat was at the beginning of the dive might not be meaningful at the end of the dive. A boat at anchor can swing in a circle around its anchor, and boats often change their position around the anchor as wind and surface conditions change during a dive. How far can the boat move?

Boat anchors don't work by gravity; they work by digging or hooking into the bottom. An anchor dropped directly beneath a boat will not have a sufficient angle of attack to dig in and will simply drag across the bottom rather than anchoring the boat.

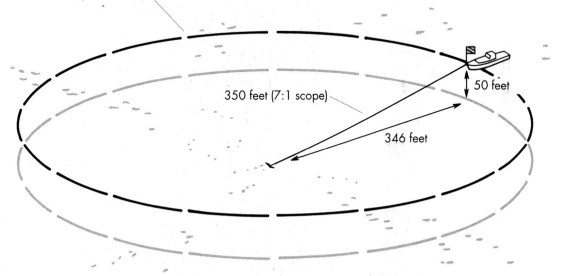

circle of possible boat movement has 346-foot radius

350 feet (7:1 scope)

50 feet

346 feet

A boat anchored in 50 feet of water using an anchor scope of 7:1 will have an anchor line 350 feet long (not to scale). The boat will be able to swing on this anchor line in a circle with a radius of 346 feet. All boat divers must begin their dives at a fixed point, such as the anchor itself, in order to navigate back to the boat.

Once the anchor is on the bottom, extra line must be let out from the boat to the anchor to achieve a reasonable angle of attack for the anchor to work. The ratio of water depth to the length of line that must be let out to achieve the proper angle is called scope. A scope of 5:1 is considered minimal, but most boat captains typically use a scope of 7:1 when anchoring in normal conditions. What does that mean? A scope of 7:1 means that 7 feet of anchor line (called a rode in nautical lingo) is used for every foot of water depth. For example, if the water is 50 feet deep, the anchor line should be 350 feet long in order to properly position the anchor to hook or dig into the bottom and securely anchor the boat (7 x 50 = 350).

If you thought you'd never really use the Pythagorean theorem in the real world, here's your chance. The boat, anchor, and water depth form a right triangle. The length of one side is 50 feet (the water depth), the length of the hypotenuse is 350 feet (the length of the anchor line), and the unknown length of the third side of the triangle is easily calculated to be a little more than 346 feet. We've just determined that a boat anchored with a scope of 7:1 in 50 feet of water can swing in a circle with a radius of 346 feet. To use that most-American standard of measurement, that's more than a football field.

Now imagine that you've just jumped off the back of such a boat. You descend to the bottom under the boat and start your dive. Your navigation is perfect, and you return to the exact spot on the bottom where your dive began. However, the surface breeze has changed direction and is now blowing the opposite way from when you started your dive, and the boat has swung to the opposite side of the circle around the anchor. Although your underwater navigation was perfect, you're still 692 feet (twice the radius of 346 feet) from the boat. In other words, you're lost. Even if the boat only swings a small arc of the circle, the result is the same. You're still lost.

Always begin navigation from the anchor on the bottom. No matter how the wind blows, the anchor will not move and will be there when you return, so you can follow the anchor line back to the boat. Although a boat tied to a permanent mooring will not typically involve as much scope as a boat using its own anchor, the circle of swing is still more than enough to defeat navigation that is begun beneath the boat. Always start navigation from the mooring anchor or U bolt (U bolts are often set into the bottom, and mooring buoys are tied to them) whenever you dive from a boat moored to a permanent mooring.

Sight Navigation

If visibility is good and the diving is interesting near the anchor or other fixed exit point, the easiest way to make sure that you can return to the anchor or exit point is to keep it in view throughout the dive. The circle of swing of an anchor line close to the anchor is very small, and it is often possible to complete a dive without ever losing sight of it. Divers who stay close enough to the anchor to keep the anchor or anchor line in view can spend their bottom time concentrating on observing marine life rather than swimming and navigating, and dives that do not involve swimming and navigating are often the most enjoyable.

I often make dives without ever losing sight of the anchor or anchor line, and I have made this simple observation about diving close to the anchor: the whale shark/mermaid/interesting marine creature that will make a dive memorable has the same chance of swimming 30 feet from the anchor as it does of swimming 300 feet from the anchor. There is usually no good reason to venture far from the anchor or exit point to enjoy a dive.

Buddy teams who dive close to the anchor or exit point usually have longer bottom times, have dives that are more relaxing, see as much as the long-distance swimmers, and never have to worry about where the boat or exit point is.

The Dive Briefing

If you plan to lose sight of the anchor or anchor line during the dive, pay close attention to the dive briefing. The briefing will usually contain important information regarding the lay of the reef and how the boat is anchored in relation to it. Some divemasters will actually draw a little map of where things are. Make notes on your slate before entering the water. Even if you've visited the dive site before on the same boat, the boat's orientation to the site may be significantly different than the last time, because surface conditions can swing the boat on its anchor or mooring. Pay close attention to the dive briefing even if you know all of the divemaster's jokes by heart.

Navigating Boat Dives on Walls and Reefs

Boat dives on walls and reefs usually involve anchoring the boat in the shallows and then swimming from the shallows to the reef to make the dive. These types of dives are typical of dive resorts, and they pose, perhaps, the most common navigation problem that most divers will face. Boat dives on walls or reefs can be easily navigated without the use of a compass. However, you will need another important navigational tool to make sure that you return to the boat's anchor, and that is your depth gauge.

Divers usually follow the wall or reef in one direction, which is into the current at the beginning of the dive. When it's time to turn the dive, they follow the wall or reef back to the boat. But since the boat is actually anchored not on the reef or wall but in the shallows closer to shore, how do you make sure that you don't overshoot the boat on your return? This is a serious mistake that will result in your being lost downcurrent from the boat and low on air.

It's easy to forget the first cardinal rule of navigation when diving from a boat over a reef. It often happens that the boat will swing over the reef from its anchor, and divers exiting the back of the boat will see the reef directly beneath them and immediately begin their dives. The reef is right there, the boat is hanging right over it; what could go wrong? As we've discussed, the boat might swing on its anchor during the dive, the divers will not be able to see the boat from the reef or wall when they return to the spot where their dive began, and they'll keep going with the current until they realize they've missed the boat. By that time they're usually far downcurrent from the boat and low on air. Oops.

The first order of business when diving from a boat over a reef is to go to the anchor. This often involves swimming away from the reef and goodies at the beginning of the dive, which usually means swimming away from the rest of the divers as they begin their dives. Once you find the anchor, make a careful note of its exact depth with your depth gauge and remember the depth or write it down on your slate. You and your buddy are now ready to begin your dive. If you can't see the reef from the anchor, it will be where the water gets deeper.

Once you begin your return to the boat, ascend into the shallows at the depth of the anchor well before you reach the boat. Returning to the boat at the shallower depth makes good decompression sense, and chances are very good that you'll swim right back to the anchor. You'll see the anchor line even if you're a bit off.

Natural Navigational Aids

Natural navigational aids are ways to mark your way without the use of a compass. We've already talked about one natural navigational aid—the contours of a reef or wall. Similar natural aids on a reef might be unusual or distinctive formations or sedentary marine life such as anemones.

Water depth is another navigational aid we've already discussed. Of course, water depth usually decreases close to shore, and it's usually possible to follow the contour of a shore by maintaining a constant water depth.

Sand ripples are another natural navigational aid that are very useful when swimming over shallow, nondescript areas. Sand ripples generally run parallel to a beach and become steeper and closer together closer to shore. It is easy to swim in a reasonably straight line by keeping your angle to the sand ripples constant, and it is usually possible to swim out a considerable distance from shore and return close to where you started simply by orienting your body to sand ripples on the bottom.

It is sometimes possible to use your shadow on the bottom as a navigational aid. Unless your shadow remains directly beneath you (at midday), you can orient your body to your shadow and use the shadow in the same way you use sand ripples.

It is possible to swim in a straight line and return to a starting point without a compass even over unremarkable terrain by using a method of three-point navigation. Once you have determined your desired direction, line up a stationary object behind you and another stationary object in front of you in line with your present position. The stationary objects can be anything, such as clumps of grass or seashells on the bottom. Swim to the object in front of you, and then orient yourself to your last position, which will now be behind you. Find another stationary object in front of you that is in line with your present position and the object behind you and proceed again. This will keep you swimming straight, and the constant checking of objects behind you will help orient you to the return route. As with all navigation skills, practice is the key.

Using a Compass Underwater

As we've learned, many dives can be navigated without the use of a compass. However, a compass is an important navigational tool, which you'll need whenever you swim over terrain that doesn't have natural aids or when you need more accuracy than can be achieved with imprecise natural navigational aids like shadows or sand ripples. Some divers seem to think that compass use involves some sort of voodoo or high intellect, but compasses are simple devices that can be used by anyone.

Most dive compasses are of a type known as needle direct compasses. The compass has a magnetic needle (the needle is usually painted onto a card that rotates inside the compass casing) that points north and a bezel that can be rotated around the needle. The bezel is marked from 0 to 360 degrees in a clockwise direction. The compass also has a lubber line, which is a line on the face of the compass that is used to make sure that the compass is pointed in the same direction that the navigator is going.

Most divers have some sort of compass, but underwater navigation is only easy if a good one is used. Little compasses on watchbands or small compasses on consoles are usually insufficient. A high-quality compass will be large enough to see clearly and will be liquid-filled to dampen the motion of the needle, and the rotating bezel will be marked by a prominent notch at 0 and another mark at 180. Some good compasses have a window on the side that enables the navigator to read a heading directly from the needle card, and some have a leveling bubble within the liquid-filled casing to help make sure that the compass is level when navigating. Expect to pay close to $100 for a good compass, and don't expect a cheap compass to be easy to use.

Compasses are used in two fundamental ways: to determine the direction the navigator is going to allow turning around and returning to the starting place, or to follow a predetermined heading toward a specific destination. Here's how to do each:

Suppose that you've just jumped off a boat that is anchored within a field of rubble that spreads out in all directions. Once you've descended to the anchor and are ready to begin your dive, you orient yourself into a slight current that is running on the bottom. You decide to start your dive into the current to explore the rubble. How do you determine which way you're going so you can return to the anchor?

The first thing you must do is align the compass to the direction you plan to go. If you wear the compass on your left wrist (as many are worn), the certifying agencies recommend that you extend your right arm in the direction you want to go, bend your left arm at a 90-degree angle, and hold your right arm at the elbow with your left hand. The compass will then be lined up in the direction you want to go and you'll look like a schoolchild raising your hand. I should say as an aside that this method is not very comfortable for me and I don't use it. The important thing is that the lubber line of the compass must be accurately lined up with the direction you want to go, and the method you use to accomplish this should be consistent. Some divers strap their compass onto a dive slate and orient the compass by holding the dive slate in both hands. This is a good way to orient a compass, and the dive slate is useful for making navigational notes.

The second thing you must do is make sure the compass needle is swinging freely. If the compass is tilted at an angle, the needle card will jam within its casing and the compass will be useless.

Before we continue, let's go over those two points again. Compass-navigation problems commonly stem from either failing to properly line up the lubber line in the direction you want to go or holding the compass in such a way that the needle card

This diver is demonstrating a mistake commonly made when orienting a compass worn on the left wrist in the manner often taught in navigation classes—a method I find rather awkward. She has tilted the compass too far in order to see the compass's face. The compass card will jam against the casing if the compass is tilted this much, and a compass with a jammed card is useless. Experiment with ways to consistently orient your compass without jamming the card. It doesn't matter how you do it, as long as the compass is oriented accurately and consistently.

cannot swing freely. Be careful. I've found that aiming the compass in the way prescribed by the certifying agencies makes it hard to see the compass unless it is tilted, which, of course, is likely to jam the compass card. Feel free to experiment with ways to hold the compass that are comfortable for you as long as the compass is accurately oriented and the needle is swinging freely.

So now you're at the anchor on the bottom, you are pointing in the direction you want to go, your compass is properly oriented toward that direction, and the compass needle/card is swinging freely. Let's say that the compass needle is pointing at about a 45-degree angle to the right of where you want to go. Simply rotate the bezel until the 0 mark on the bezel aligns with the compass needle. Since the 0 mark usually has a notch, you can accomplish this by rotating the bezel until the needle is in the notch. You can now read your heading (the direction you want to go) by looking at the mark on the bezel that is lined up with the lubber line. In our example, where the needle is off to the right at a 45-degree angle, your heading will be something like 300. As long as you keep the compass needle in the notch of the bezel at "0" and the compass continues to be properly oriented and freely swinging, you'll stay on a heading of 300.

Now let's say that you've swum for a while and want to return to the anchor. The easiest way to turn around is to rotate your body and compass until the compass needle points to "180" on the bezel, which is usually also marked in some way. By keeping the needle lined with "180" on the bezel, you'll retrace your path and swim back to the anchor, following a course that is the exact opposite of your original course. This is called a reciprocal course.

The actual reciprocal course can be calculated by subtracting 180 from the original heading if the original heading is 180 or greater or adding 180 to the original heading if the original heading is less than 180, but would I ask you to do that? Hell, no. Simply look at the bottom of the lubber line that is pointing back toward your body and read the marking on the bezel. In our example, where the original course was 300, you can see that the return heading is 120, with no math required. If you want to follow that heading with the needle in the notch, rotate the bezel until "120" is aligned with the top of the lubber line, rotate your body and compass until the needle is once again in the notch at "0," and you're on your way. Right now is a good time to pick your compass up and experiment with this. It's not hard.

By following a compass heading out and returning in a straight line via a reciprocal course, you can perform a type of compass diving called spoke diving. Once you've returned to the anchor, you can set out again in a different direction, explore for a while, and return. Making forays from a fixed point like the spokes on a wheel is a great and easy way to explore an area with a compass.

Now let's imagine that you're standing on a shore with a treasure map. According to the map, a pirate chest of gold doubloons can be found by swimming out at a heading of 240. That's easy. Simply rotate the compass bezel until "240" lines up with the lubber line. Rotate your body and compass until the compass needle is in the notch at

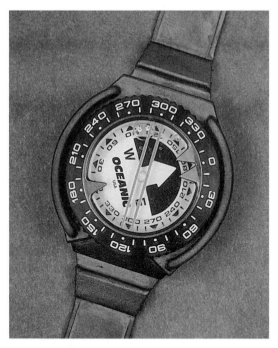

The lubber line on this compass is the double red line on the face. The bezel has been rotated until the "0" mark on the bezel is in line with the arrow ("in the notch"), which is pointing north. The lubber line is in line with a heading of 300.

"0" on the bezel, and you're ready to follow the heading of 240. A quick look at the bottom of the lubber line will give your return heading of 60, with no math required.

You can now use a compass to swim in a straight line, to return accurately to where you started, and to follow a predetermined course. These simple skills will greatly enhance your independence as a diver. Compass use is a skill that can easily be practiced on land. If you live near a playground or other open area, take your compass and practice walking and returning to a fixed spot while looking only at the compass.

Estimating Distances Underwater

Navigation involves distance as well as direction. Underwater navigators determine the distances they travel by counting the number of fin kicks they use to get from one place to another. One complete kick of both legs is called a kick cycle, and you count kick cycles by counting the number of times one foot reaches the top of the kicking motion. It doesn't matter which leg you choose to count as long as you always count the same leg.

Once you add distance to the navigational scheme, you can swim patterns other than reciprocal courses. For example, by swimming thirty kick cycles at a heading of 0 degrees, then thirty kick cycles at a heading of 90 degrees, then thirty kick cycles at a heading of 180 degrees, then thirty kick cycles at a heading of 270 degrees, you will trace a square that should return you close to the place you started. This is useful for reconnoitering an area, and it works even if you don't know the precise distances covered. As long as you use the same number of kick cycles on each leg of the trip, you should return to the starting place.

You can follow a rectangular path by making 90-degree turns and swimming the same number of kick cycles on the parallel legs. Write the number of kick cycles on each heading on your slate to keep them straight.

You can trace triangles by swimming an equal number of kick cycles on three legs. Add 120 degrees to your previous heading for each of the two turns required to make the triangle. For example, swimming thirty kick cycles at a heading of 300 degrees, thirty kick cycles at 60 degrees (300 + 120 − 360 = 60 — if the sum is greater than 360, you must then subtract 360 to get the proper heading), and then thirty kick cycles at

180 degrees (60 + 120 = 180) will return you to your starting place. Make sure to write the headings on your slate before you begin, as mistakes in arithmetic will get you lost.

Practice these patterns on land by substituting paces for kick cycles, and then give it a try underwater.

Of course, having some idea of the actual distances covered is useful. Every diver will travel a slightly different distance with each kick cycle, and divers should determine the distance covered by their kick cycles by counting them over a measured distance. This can be done in a swimming pool or any other body of water that can be precisely measured. Try to make the measured distance at least 100 feet and swim the distance at least three times while counting the kick cycles needed to cover the distance. If there is a possibility of a current in the body of water you use, make sure to swim the measured distance in both directions. Average the number of kick cycles from all runs, and then divide the distance by the average number of kick cycles required to cover the distance to determine the distance each kick cycle covers. For example, if a diver counts thirty-three kick cycles to cover 100 feet, then each kick cycle covers about 3 feet. It's important to wear full scuba gear and to swim underwater when making this measurement, as equipment drag significantly affects the distance traveled by a kick cycle. Variables like currents, drag, and even the diver's energy level also affect the distance, and estimations of distances traveled based on kick cycles are always imprecise. However, a general idea is better than no idea at all.

Let's go back to our pirate treasure example. No self-respecting treasure map will contain only a heading to the treasure—it'll also contain a distance. If the map says to start at a certain point and swim at a heading of 240 for a distance of 150 feet to the treasure, start by rotating the compass bezel until the lubber line is aligned with the "240" mark on the bezel. After you've rotated your body and compass until the compass needle is in the notch at "0" on the bezel, you'll be facing the correct heading of 240. If you've determined that your personal kick cycle covers a distance of 3 feet, you'll know that you will need about fifty kick cycles to cover the 150-foot distance to the treasure. However, you should probably slow down and start looking for the treasure chest after about forty kick cycles and keep kicking until you've finished about sixty kick cycles to give yourself a fair chance of finding the treasure.

Navigating in Currents

Currents can significantly hinder underwater navigation, and a current can affect both distance and heading.

Swimming directly into a current or directly downcurrent has the greatest effect on kick cycle distances but has no effect on the direction traveled. The difference the current makes in the speed of travel is difficult to accurately determine, but you should be aware of the current and make allowances for how it affects your progress underwater.

Swimming at an angle to a current affects the direction of travel and can seriously impair navigation. Heading is usually more important than distance in finding your way, and the effect of a current on your heading should be minimized as much as possible.

The best way to minimize a side current's effect on a heading is to employ a navigation method known as point-to-point navigation. Instead of swimming constantly on the compass heading, secure yourself so you are motionless on the bottom and locate a stationary object that is directly in line with the heading you want to follow. The object can be anything that doesn't move, such as a clump of grass or a shell on the bottom. Swim to that object, stop again, and orient yourself to another object directly in line with your heading. By following a string of stationary objects, you'll stay on course far better than if you swim constantly and allow the current to push you off course, and you'll remember many of the objects if you return on a reciprocal course. This method is similar to the three-point navigation discussed earlier, but this time you use a compass instead of a third point to keep you on a desired heading.

Point-to-point navigation is not limited to navigating in currents. It's often a good way to navigate when visibility is good to avoid spending a great portion of a dive staring at your compass.

Currents complicate navigation, and the potential effect of currents on navigation should influence your independent dive/no dive decision. A possible compromise is to make the dive but keep the distance you travel from the anchor or exit point to a minimum. The shorter the distance you travel, the less accurate your navigation needs to be.

Compass Variance and Deviation

Compasses are magnets, and they always point to magnetic north. However, magnetic north is often not true north, and the difference between the two varies depending on where on earth you are. The difference between magnetic north and true north is called variance (sometimes called declination), and mariners and other long-distance navigators must make allowances for it.

Underwater navigation does not involve distances great enough for compass variance to be relevant, so underwater navigators need not make any allowance for compass variance from true north. Now that you know what compass variance is, you can forget about it for underwater navigation.

Compass deviation is another matter. It occurs when the magnetic compass needle is affected by nearby metal. The tank of a buddy can cause compass deviation if it is close enough, and divers often dive near shipwrecks, oil rigs, or other metallic structures that can cause it as well.

There is no way to adjust for compass deviation, and the only solution to the problem is to move the compass away from whatever is causing the deviation. Most metals must be within about 3 feet of a compass to cause deviation, but large masses of metals such as iron can cause deviation from twice that distance.

So there you are on a metal shipwreck, and you want to go back to shore—what can you do to properly orient yourself on a true course? If you know the general direction of the course toward your exit point, you can simply swim 10 feet or so from the wreck, orient your compass, and go home. If metallic rubble near the wreck creates a magnetic field that continues to cause deviation in your compass, you can always ascend until your compass is free of the influence of the metal. An ascent of only 6 feet or so is usually enough to accomplish this.

Advanced Underwater Navigation

We've touched upon what I believe are the basics of underwater navigation, which will enable divers to independently venture out and return safely. These simple skills can be built upon to enable far more complicated navigation, such as courses that involve several legs and turns or courses that cut corners to return to the starting place without taking a reciprocal course. While each step of a complicated course only requires the simple techniques we've discussed, the accumulation of heading changes and distance measurements increases the likelihood that an error will occur. Compass navigation is a skill that requires practice, and navigation should be kept simple until your confidence grows through practice in the water.

Some divers get much of their diving satisfaction from their ability to navigate accurately. Most advanced compass-navigation techniques used by terrestrial navigators apply to underwater navigators as well, and books on the subject abound. If you are interested in honing your underwater compass-navigation skills to their fullest potential, consider this handbook as a mere introduction to the subject. Most of the certifying agencies offer specialty courses in underwater navigation. I recommend taking such a course if underwater navigation is new to you or if you really want to develop your skills beyond the basics.

The Fine Art of Being Lost

Even if you have good navigation skills, it's awfully easy to become disoriented underwater—especially when diving over repetitive or unremarkable terrain. It can happen in a million different ways and it often happens quickly.

So there you are with your buddy—you've followed some fascinating creature, you've turned around a few times, or you've been happily swimming with your noses to the reef when it occurs to you that nothing looks familiar and that you suddenly seem to be the only divers in the ocean. You stop the dive, ascend a few feet, and take a careful look around without seeing anything or anyone that gives you a clue as to where you are. You're lost, and the first link of the error chain has been forged. Now what?

I've heard the stories of lost divers so many times that I no longer even have to ask what happened when divers are rescued far from their boat or exit point. Here it is—the ugly link-by-link chain of errors that is replayed time and again by lost divers:

Error #1: The divers get lost in the first place. It happens.

Error #2: Each diver assumes that the other is not lost, and the dive continues.

Error #3: Even after they determine that they're lost, the divers have plenty of air and bottom time left and are enjoying the dive, so they decide to worry about it later. The dive continues—often in a direction that moves the divers farther from the boat or exit point. The thinking is, "We can't be very far off course, so we'll figure it out at the end of the dive."

Error #4: The dive continues, and the divers push the fact that they're lost to the backs of their minds. The thinking is, "My buddy doesn't seem to be worried about it, so why should I?" Diver ego has become part of the problem.

Error #5: One of the divers has consumed half of his or her air supply. It's time to turn the dive, but turn it to where? After a session of confused hand signals and shrugging of shoulders, one buddy thinks that the boat or exit point is in a certain direction. The other buddy is relieved that a decision has been made, and the divers set off in the chosen direction. The lost divers have a 1 in 360 chance of swimming back toward the boat or exit point. Unless they use a compass, it is unlikely that they will swim a straight course.

Error #6: After swimming aimlessly for some time, one of the divers is down to 1,000 psi. Things are getting dicey. The diver who is low on air indicates that they should surface to see where the boat is, but the buddy resists this possibility. Egos have become a larger part of the problem. Neither diver wants the fact that they're lost to become known, but both are becoming increasingly stressed about their situation. The divers are probably angry at each other for getting lost, which contributes to the stress.

Error #7: After they change course a few times in the futile hope that they will somehow stumble across the boat anchor, one of the divers frantically indicates that his air supply is down to 500 psi. The dive is over and the jig is up. The divers must surface.

Error #8: The divers begin their controlled ascent. They pause at 15 feet and perform their safety stop while staring at their gauges or at each other. They are unaware that they are drifting in a surface current that was not present on the bottom. The diver who is lowest on air watches as his SPG creeps toward zero. The safety stop is cut short, and the divers ascend the final 15 feet to the surface.

Error #9: The divers surface and look for the boat. It's not there. They turn until the boat comes into view. It looks very small and far away. How could they have gotten so far from the boat? Panic begins to take hold of the divers, and they remove their mouthpieces to fuss at each other and discuss their predicament. A wave sloshes over them and one diver swallows a gulp of seawater. The grip of panic tightens. The divers remain fixated on each other, stare fearfully at the distant boat, and begin to signal frantically to get the attention of anyone on the boat. They began the day wanting to dive; now they just want to get home.

If the divers are diving from a commercial dive boat, chances are good that an observer on the boat realized that something was wrong soon after the wayward buddy pair's bubbles veered off course. Consternation on the boat grew as the buddy pair continued their dive far from the boat. If the boat is equipped with a rescue dinghy, the dinghy was put into the water and prepared long before the lost divers surfaced. Once the divers finally surface, the dinghy is launched while an observer on the mother boat keeps the divers in view and directs the dinghy toward them. The exhausted, panicky, and embarrassed divers are then picked up and returned to the boat, where they face an interrogation about what went wrong and an examination to determine if they've suffered any sort of pressure-related injury. They face the ire of the divemaster and captain plus the curious stares of the rest of the dive party once their physical well-being is established. Chances are good that the wayward pair will be banned from diving for the rest of the day.

If the wayward pair are diving from a commercial dive boat not equipped with a rescue dinghy, the boat must wait until all the other divers are on board and accounted for before it can pull its anchor and move to pick them up. This may leave our lost divers in the water for a long time. When the boat finally arrives to pick them up, they face the wrath not only of the divemaster and captain but also of the rest of the diving party for messing up their diving day. Chances are excellent that the wayward pair will be banned from diving for the rest of the day.

If the divers are diving from a privately owned boat, they can only hope that their buddy on board is not fishing, taking a nap, or reading a book. If the divers are diving from shore, they can only hope that the person with whom they left their dive plan remembers and takes appropriate action. In either case, the divers must compose themselves and either prepare for a long swim or inflate their safety sausages and settle in for a long wait.

An exciting day of diving has turned into a nightmare of stress, danger, and embarrassment for our buddy pair of divers. What steps could they have taken to avoid their final predicament? Let's take another look at each link and consider what could have been done to break the chain:

Error #1: The divers got lost. It happens.

Error #2 and Solution: Each diver assumed that the other was not lost. That's silly. It is the responsibility of all independent divers to keep track of their dive and to know the way back. It makes good sense to consult with a buddy if you become disoriented, but you must personally know the way back even if your buddy assures you that he or she knows the way. Your dive buddy must reorient you to the dive site so that you know where you are and how to return to the boat or starting point independently of your buddy. This may involve returning to the anchor or entry point and starting again.

No independent diver should delegate the responsibility for navigating a dive to a buddy. You are dependent as long as you don't know your way back, and dependency is anathema to an independent diver. Independent navigation should be agreed upon by the dive pair before the dive begins, and each buddy should be prepared and willing to return the other to a familiar spot should either become disoriented.

Some dive resorts require divers to follow a divemaster, and the divemasters often follow courses that are familiar only to them. Of course, you should not expect the divemaster to orient you during such dives, but you must recognize that you are a dependent diver during those dives and stay with the divemaster for the duration.

Error #3 and Solution: The divers did nothing to solve their problem even after they knew they were lost. That's more than silly; that's stupid. Being lost is a problem that must be solved before the dive can continue, and the problem cannot be solved by swimming randomly on the bottom. Swimming lost will exacerbate the problem in several ways. The divers will use precious air and bottom time, and they will most likely move farther off course.

So you're lost and you shouldn't swim randomly around on the bottom in an attempt to figure out where you are. What should you do? You should surface and find the boat or exit point as soon as you know that you are good and lost. This requires some planning and technique to do safely. Ascending in open water can be disorienting, and it's easy to become caught in a surface current without feeling it or knowing it. Pausing for a safety stop in a current can move you a significant distance downcurrent from the boat.

Ascending divers should try to keep a reference point in sight to avoid being moved by a current as they approach the surface. If the water is shallow or the visibility is good, you can usually keep the bottom in sight as you ascend. A patch of sand will reflect the most light and be the most visible as you ascend above it. Keep the point of reference directly below you as you pause for your safety stop.

If the divers cannot keep the bottom in view for the entire ascent, they may be able to station one diver where he or she can see the bottom while the other diver ascends to a shallower depth, keeping the stationed buddy in sight. This procedure requires preplanning and cooperation between the buddies, and at no point should they lose sight of each other. Once the shallower buddy is oriented to the surface current by using the deeper buddy as a reference, he or she can signal the deeper buddy to ascend, and both divers can perform their safety stops together while stemming the surface current in the direction established by the first ascending diver.

Both divers should surface together at the end of their safety stops and immediately signal the boat that they are OK by placing their hands on the tops of their heads in the accepted "OK" signal. This will notify the boat personnel that the buddy pair is still together, both divers are accounted for, and both divers are fine.

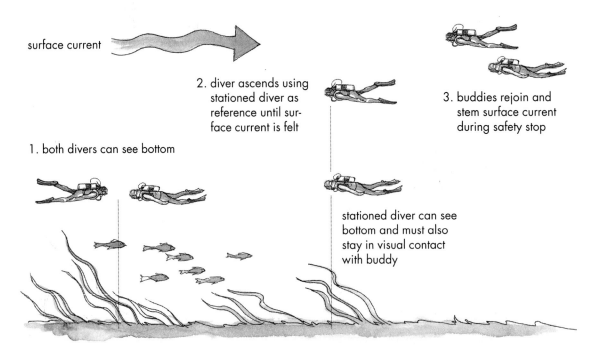

surface current

2. diver ascends using stationed diver as reference until surface current is felt

3. buddies rejoin and stem surface current during safety stop

1. both divers can see bottom

stationed diver can see bottom and must also stay in visual contact with buddy

If the water is clear and the divers can see the bottom from their 15-foot safety stop depth, they can use the bottom as a reference in order to stem a surface current. If the divers lose sight of the bottom before the safety stop depth is reached, it may be possible to station one diver who can see the bottom and have the other diver use the stationed diver as a reference. However, at no point should the divers lose sight of one another. If the divers can't use the bottom as a reference, they should study the movement of their ascending exhalation bubbles in an attempt to discern the direction and velocity of a possible surface current. ELAYNE SEARS

What should happen next depends upon how far the divers are from the boat and upon prevailing conditions. If the divers are far from the boat or if conditions are severe, the dive is over and the divers should work their way back to the boat. However, if the divers aren't far from the boat (and they often aren't if they surface as soon as they know they're lost), it may be possible for them to take a bearing on the boat and swim back to it underwater.

Taking a bearing simply means aiming your body and compass toward a desired destination, rotating the compass bezel until the needle is in the notch at "0," and proceeding on the heading that lines up with the lubber line in order to reach that destination. However, the divers must not make the cardinal mistake of taking their bearing on the boat itself. Remember that the boat will swing on its anchor and is not a fixed point. The divers must take their bearing on a point in front of the boat where the anchor line or anchor will be found.

Even after the divers have surfaced and seen the boat, signaled the boat personnel that they are together and OK, and taken a good heading back to the anchor or anchor

Divers surfacing away from the boat or exit point will alarm boat personnel or support personnel on shore, so the first thing they should do is to let everyone know whether they're OK or in trouble.

The accepted signal for "OK" is to place the hands on top of the head.

If only one arm is available, as when carrying a camera or other equipment, the alternate "OK" signal is one hand placed atop the head.

Waving one's arms is a signal of distress and should only be used to request immediate assistance. Failure to give any signal will usually be interpreted as an emergency and will initiate rescue procedures. If a buddy team must surface to find the boat, both divers should surface together and both should signal. This lets the boat personnel know that the buddy team is still together and that both divers are OK.

SUDDEN STRESS

Even a simple dive plan is a complicated activity that is dependent on a wide array of equipment and the vagaries of natural forces. Masks leak; fin straps break; tanks come loose from the tank band; regulators free-flow; surge or currents come and go for no apparent reason; unexpected or alarming marine life is encountered. The stress caused by these bumps in the road is amplified by the alien nature of the underwater world.

Dive plans also often go a bit awry. Divers become confused about their navigation; buddy teams become temporarily separated; air is consumed at an unexpected rate; decompression status becomes a factor in the dive sooner than anticipated. The stress caused by these common little mistakes is also amplified when diving.

How you deal with the normal stresses of diving can be the difference between a forgettable inconvenience and an unforgettably serious event.

You were probably introduced to sudden stress in your certification class, and you were probably instructed to deal with sudden stress using the three-part process of STOP, THINK, and ACT. That's a good strategy, but actually dealing with stress during a dive involves a bit more than being able to repeat the process from memory. The fact that so many dangerous situations involving panicked divers begin with simple stress-causing incidents is a good indication that many divers are unprepared to deal with sudden stress. Here are some things to think about before and during your dives to help you deal with sudden stress:

- Anticipate problems. Take it for granted that every dive won't go perfectly, and don't be surprised when the dive takes an unexpected swerve. Minor problems during dives are normal.
- Don't dive independently of a dive professional dedicated to taking care of you unless you have confidence in your basic dive skills. A dislodged mask or broken fin should not give you any reason for alarm.
- Recognize problems and deal with them as soon as they occur. Many divers tend to deal with navigation or even air-supply problems by convincing themselves that the problem is not happening. Never assume that your buddy can get you back to the exit point or that your air supply is sufficient simply because you have as much remaining air as your buddy. Independent diving means independent thought and independent problem solving. If a situation causes you stress, take immediate steps to alleviate the stressful situation even if it means calling the dive and returning to the boat or exit point. Ignoring a problem until it's too late to correct it can lead to panic.
- Communicate with your buddy about your problem. Divers' egos sometimes prevent them from letting anybody know that they're having a problem, and this compounds stress. I've seen too many divers wait until it is too late to let their buddies know they are hopelessly lost. I've seen too many divers resort to sharing air with their buddies at the end of a dive simply because they didn't want to be the first one to turn the dive due to

their air supply. A dive is not a competition, and all divers should leave their egos on the boat or shore.

- Sudden and unexpected traumas such as losing a mask or having the mask dislodged; being stung by a jellyfish, fire coral, or hydroid; or becoming entangled are events most likely to trigger panic in divers. These kinds of events can be disorienting, and divers are often initially unaware of exactly what has happened to them. This is where the STOP part of the STOP, THINK, and ACT trilogy comes into play. Unless your air supply has been affected, you have time to figure out what has occurred (THINK) and do something to fix the problem (ACT). Resist the urge to act randomly or reactively to problems you don't fully understand.
- Keep problems in perspective. Losing a fin is a bummer, but mindlessly chasing it as it sinks and putting yourself into a decompression situation for which you are not equipped or prepared is far worse. Don't become so focused on a small problem that you lose control of your dive.
- Be properly equipped. The addition of a redundant emergency air supply (Spare Air or pony bottle) and a good safety sausage will do wonders for your peace of mind.
- Dive well within your comfort level. Keep the anchor or exit point in view for the duration of dives in areas you are unfamiliar with unless navigation is straightforward and simple. Use your bottom time and air supply conservatively so you can deal with unexpected problems. There will always be another dive, and there's no good reason to push dives to the limit.

line, they are still lost until they actually reach the anchor or anchor line. Only at that point should they consider continuing their dive with their remaining air and bottom time.

As we've seen, the chain of errors that results in lost divers surfacing dangerously far from their boat or exit point should be broken after the first two errors are made. Those first two errors are that 1) you got lost and 2) your buddy got lost. Once you've determined that you've made those errors, it's time to stop making errors and start coming up with solutions, and the best solution for lost divers is to surface together and find their boat or exit point without delay.

BUDDY PROBLEMS

It has become somewhat fashionable in recent years to disparage the buddy system as a way to make diving safer. I do not agree with this trend. I believe that diving with a competent and supportive buddy adds an obvious measure of security to any dive.

However, the buddy system involves more than simply diving in proximity to another diver, and divers who rely on the buddy system as a panacea for their own lack of confidence or preparation place themselves in a dangerous situation.

Independent divers should practice the buddy system with an attitude of mutual support and assistance but should never rely on anyone other than themselves for the safety of their dives.

For the buddy system to work, each diver of a buddy pair must be immediately available to the other to offer useful assistance. Unfortunately, this is seldom the case in real-world diving, and, consequently, divers who perceive their buddies as guardian angels are flirting with peril. The fact is, unless your dive buddy is an instructor or dive professional who has dedicated his dive to taking care of you, he is probably far more interested in his own dive than in yours.

You are solo diving whenever you cannot realistically expect immediate and useful help from your dive buddy during a dive. Isn't that a scary revelation? Before you rail against me, please understand that I am not recommending that ordinary recreational divers should practice solo diving. I am, however, facing the fact that many ordinary recreational divers already practice solo diving without being fully aware of it.

Common Solo-Diving Scenarios

Most divers conjure an image of a lone figure entering the water from a deserted beach or a single rogue diver back-rolling from a boat in the open sea when the subject of solo diving is mentioned. These are, indeed, examples of solo divers, but ordinary buddy divers should be aware that solo diving is much broader than these extreme examples. A diver is solo diving whenever she has no reasonable expectation of immediate and useful assistance from another diver. This definition encompasses a broad spectrum of common diving situations, and it's clear that most solo diving occurs when there is more than one diver in the water.

Perhaps the most common scenario in which solo diving occurs at some time during a dive involves the buddy pair of friends who dive together often and pursue interests such as photography, exploration, or naturalism during their dives. These divers enter the water together, pursue their interests once the dive begins, check on each other from time to time, and exit the water together—a good example of the "same day, same ocean" buddy team. Although the two divers are not usually very far apart at any time during the dive, their attentions are so distracted by their own interests that neither could reasonably be considered to be immediately available to the other for assistance. If this sounds like the way you typically dive with your best dive buddy, it's time to face the fact that you habitually practice solo diving for at least some portion of many of your dives.

Another common scenario that involves solo diving is the buddy team of strangers who are arbitrarily paired. This often happens when two single divers end up on the same dive boat, and I've already mentioned that it's a good way to meet fellow divers with similar interests. However, diving with a stranger allows no reasonable expectation of his or her capability to offer useful assistance in an emergency. You should consider yourself a solo diver whenever you dive with anyone you don't know well enough to trust with your life. If you've ever been arbitrarily paired with another diver on a dive boat, you made a solo dive within the broad definition of solo diving.

Consider the experienced diver who agrees to take a nervous neophyte on a dive. Although the neophyte is totally dependent on the more experienced diver, the neophyte is buddy diving while the more experienced diver is probably not. Unless the experienced diver can reasonably expect immediate and useful assistance from the neophyte in the event of a mistake or emergency, the experienced diver is solo diving.

So, unless an individually competent pair of divers are holding hands and constantly checking on each other throughout their dive, chances are excellent that they are each solo diving at some point during the dive.

Independent Buddy Diving

Independent divers should consider every dive as a solo dive even when they are diving with a buddy. You should practice the buddy system and plan to make yourself immediately available to your buddy in the event of a mistake or emergency, but you should not rely or plan on receiving such assistance yourself. Think of your relationship with your buddy as a one-sided affair—your buddy can count on you but you cannot really count on your buddy. In this type of buddy pair, each diver should be willing and able to assist the other, but each should also be fully prepared to deal with mistakes or emergencies without aid.

Many techniques of more extreme diving have been adopted by recreational divers to make their dives safer. For example, the cave-diving "rule of thirds" for air management calls for divers to use one-third of their air supply for the dive, use one-third for the return to the boat or exit point, and hold one-third in reserve as a safety measure. The fact that many recreational divers use this technique (I recommend it) does not make them cave divers.

Likewise, independent buddy divers should adopt some of the techniques of solo divers engaged in the more extreme definition of solo diving. Solo divers must have a supreme confidence that the dive can be made safely and without assistance, and must carefully monitor the dive in terms of navigation and air management. Every independent buddy diver should be fully prepared to safely complete a dive without any prospect of assistance from another diver even if another diver is in close proximity. If a diver is not fully prepared and confident that he can make the dive without assistance, then he should be diving only with an instructor, dive professional, or more experienced buddy who is willing and able to accept total responsibility for the nervous or unprepared diver.

CAN YOUR DIVE BUDDY SUE YOU?

Dive boats and dive operators have carefully crafted waiver documents designed to protect them against lawsuits brought by divers or the families of divers who are injured or die while diving. However, dive buddies typically have no such protection. If your dive buddy is injured during his dive with you, can he sue you? If your dive buddy dies during or because of the dive, can her family sue you?

Sadly, in our litigious culture the answer is an emphatic yes. All concepts of personal responsibility and assumption of risk go immediately out the window once the worst occurs. Lawsuits will fly like confetti if a diver is seriously injured or dies. The dive boat/operator waiver will be challenged; boat captains, boat owners, and divemasters will be personally named. And, of course, you will be right in the middle of the legal mess as the injured or deceased diver's dive buddy. Even if you and your dive buddy are the best of friends and wouldn't consider suing each other, you have no assurance that your dive buddy's family won't sue should an accident occur.

There's not much you can do to avoid being sued if your dive buddy is injured or killed during your dive together. However, an understanding of your legal obligations to a buddy can help you lessen the possibility that you will be judged legally responsible for something that happens to your dive buddy.

There are four parts to the type of suit (a tort) that might be brought against you as a dive buddy. It must be established that you had a duty of care toward your buddy, that the duty was breached by something you did or failed to do, that the breach of duty was the proximate cause of the injury to your buddy, and that damage occurred to your buddy because of the breach of duty. Let's take a quick look at each part.

The courts seem to be pretty good at deciding the duty of care owed by instructors and dive professionals to the divers in their charge. However, the duty of care between ordinary dive buddies is vague, although it does exist. In the most general of terms, dive buddies have a duty to help and support each other in accordance with accepted diving procedures to the best of their abilities in the absence of any compelling reason not to do so. For example, a diver has a legal duty to share air with a buddy in an out-of-air emergency, but if both divers are critically low on air, there may be a compelling reason for neither diver to share air with the other. It is possible that a diver with extensive training and experience might be held to a higher duty than a diver with minimal training and experience.

Breach of duty occurs when one diver lets the other down in a critical situation. The breach may be an act of commission (something you did that you shouldn't have done) or of omission (something you didn't do but should have done). Abandonment or not being available to help is a gray area (who abandoned whom if divers get separated?). Goading or enticing a buddy into a bad situation, such as leading her into an overhead environment for which she is not equipped or prepared, may be determined to be a breach of duty.

Courts like to use a test of "reasonableness" when considering conduct that may be construed to be a breach of duty.

Causality, or determining that the breach of duty caused the injury, is usually easier to prove in court if the alleged breach of duty involved an act of commission as opposed to an act of omission. For example, if you released a buddy's weight belt and he suffered an embolism because of the buoyant ascent that followed, it's easy to identify the released weight belt as a direct cause of the injury. On the other hand, if the buddy drowned before you got him to the surface without releasing his weight belt, it is a matter of conjecture as to whether the failure to release the belt directly caused the tragedy.

A determination of damage is the last part of the suit. Most dive-related lawsuits involve some sort of actual physical injury to the suing party, but nonphysical injuries such as mental anguish are not out of the question. Remember that the suing party (plaintiff) can sue for anything they want, but they have the burden of proof concerning both the breach of duty that caused the injury as well as the extent of the damage. As the person being sued (defendant), you do not have the burden to prove your innocence but only must defend yourself against charges of a breach of duty.

Is it time to have another "get to know you" chat with the stranger with whom you've been arbitrarily partnered as a dive buddy? The prospect of being sued by a dive buddy is a disagreeable thing to contemplate, but it is a fact of modern life. As onerous as a lawsuit may be, all divers must remember that their own survival is the most important factor in any emergency situation. It's far better to be a live defendant than a dead buddy.

Extreme solo diving involves more than attitude, preparation, and care—it also usually involves special equipment. Extreme solo divers carry a completely redundant air supply whenever they are diving at twice the depth to which they can comfortably free dive. Obviously, this is to ensure that they can safely make an emergency swimming ascent in the event of an out-of-air situation caused by a catastrophic equipment failure.

Independent buddy divers should not consider an emergency swimming ascent as a part of their dive plan. Therefore, all independent buddy divers should consider carrying a 100 percent redundant air supply regardless of the depths of their dives. A 100 percent redundant air supply (sometimes called a type II or 2 alternate air source) is an air supply that is completely independent of the main scuba tank and also has its own regulator; it can be used in an out-of-air emergency to get the diver to the surface without assistance from another diver. I believe that carrying a redundant air supply is a good technique that independent buddy divers can adopt from extreme solo divers.

The most common and readily available redundant air supply is the Spare Air, marketed by Submersible Systems. The Spare Air is a small (the standard model

DIVE BUDDY CHECKLIST

You were taught in your certification class to do a buddy check before each dive to make sure that all equipment is secure. However, a buddy check should be much more than that. Here are some things to consider during a buddy check:

- Know your buddy's physical and mental fitness to dive. If you know your buddy personally, it's OK to simply ask if he feels up to the dive. However, as many independent divers are paired with dive buddies that they don't know well, it's important to look for any signs of uneasiness in your buddy that could lead to problems in the water. Watch how your buddy assembles her dive equipment to make sure that she is familiar with the equipment and competent to use it. Chat with your prospective buddy and get to know a little bit about her. Excessive talking, boasting, or humorous questions might be attempts to conceal serious misgivings. Alternatively, quietness, fumbling, or delaying tactics might also be signs of uneasiness. If you suspect that your prospective dive buddy is not ready for the dive, gently ask him if he's OK. If your suspicions are not assuaged, talk to the divemaster or boat captain to see if a more suitable buddy is available.

- Inform your buddy of your own physical and mental fitness to dive. Let your prospective buddy know if you are unfamiliar with the area and plan to dive ultraconservatively. Even if your buddy assures you that she very familiar with the area, do not subjugate yourself to a buddy you don't know and trust unless the buddy is a dive professional affiliated with the trip and is willing to dedicate her dive to showing you around. If your prospective buddy is simply another paying customer who plans to dive a route that only he is familiar with, find a more suitable buddy for yourself. Stay in control of your dive, or don't dive at all. If you decide not to dive, let your buddy know so he can find another buddy.

- Plan the dive. Talk to your buddy about navigation and safety factors and consider all options. For example, you might decide with your buddy that the two of you will check bottom conditions at the anchor before deciding if you will lose sight of the anchor during the dive. If the dive is on a wall or reef, the plan will likely be as simple as starting the dive into the current and following the reef at a predetermined depth until you reach a predetermined air supply or decompression status, at which time the two of you will ascend to a shallower depth and return downcurrent to the starting point.

- Get your signals straight. Go over hand signals to make communication easy.

- Help suit up and do a gear check with your buddy. Make sure that your buddy's air is on, that her tank is secure, that no hoses are dangling, and that computers are on.

- Have fun. The "plan your dive and dive your plan" cliché works in most cases, but your dive is not a military exercise. Your only mission is to enjoy yourself. If an unexpected distraction that does not compromise the safety of the dive occurs once the dive has started, forget the original plan and form a new one on the fly with your buddy.

contains 3 cubic feet of air; older models contain 2.7 cubic feet of air) tank with its own integrated regulator that is easily carried and convenient to use (see chapter 4 for more information on this device). However, considerable controversy rages regarding the suitability of a Spare Air as a redundant air supply for extreme solo divers. Many solo divers consider its very limited air supply to be inadequate and opt instead for larger pony tanks with independent regulators. Pony tanks are far less convenient to carry and use.

I consider the Spare Air to be a reasonable compromise between convenience and suitability for independent buddy divers making dives within the accepted recreational limits. However, I encourage you to do your own research and make your own decision based on the depths and types of dives you intend to make. If you decide on the Spare Air, you must be aware of its very limited air supply and never consider it as an air source for any part of a dive. The Spare Air is an emergency device to be used only to reach the surface from unimpeded recreational-diving depths. The addition of this simple device will significantly reduce your dependence on a buddy in your role as an independent buddy diver.

Bad Buddy Tricks

I am convinced that the buddy system is an important cornerstone of dive safety, but I also realize that buddies can sometimes be the source of problems rather than the solution to them. Detractors of the buddy system are quick to point out that your buddy can become your worst enemy in a panicked out-of-air situation, and popular dive lore is filled with stories of divers being drowned by their panicked buddies in their frantic attempts to save themselves from real or imagined crises. Actual case studies indicate that while these tragedies have been known to occur, they are extremely rare.

More common buddy problems involve situations where the buddy dives in a manner for which you are not prepared or equipped. For example, what if your buddy dashes off immediately upon entering the water from an anchored boat without first checking the location of the boat's anchor? What if you've planned a dive in confusing terrain without a compass and agreed to keep the anchor line in view throughout the dive, but your buddy swims off and vanishes into the blue? What if your buddy goes too deep, swims too far, or enters overhead environments for which you are not prepared or equipped? Buddy pairs should communicate frankly and plan their dives carefully to avoid these problems before entering the water, but plans are often forgotten or dismissed once the excitement of the dive begins.

These kinds of common buddy problems present a dilemma: Do you adhere to the buddy system and follow your buddy, or do you abandon the buddy system and dive in the manner that involves acceptable risk? Are you duty-bound to follow a wayward buddy, or should you abandon your buddy to take care of yourself? Or, as your mama probably put it, should you jump off a bridge just because your friends do it?

The answer, of course, is that you should never knowingly place yourself at unacceptable risk to follow the whim of a buddy. Who's to determine what risks are unacceptable? You are. As a good buddy, you should do your best to dissuade a wayward buddy from straying into unacceptable danger and you should make it clear that you will not follow. Your buddy needs to know that he or she is going it alone if the dangerous whim cannot be resisted and that you will not be available to help if trouble occurs. However, you must not allow peer pressure or a sense of duty to knowingly drag you into a bad situation.

Your independence does not end as soon as you enter the water with a buddy. Quite the contrary, your independent decision-making process becomes even more important once a dive has begun. It's your dive, and you must set your own risk limits independently of your buddy.

Of course, abandoning a buddy means that you are, indeed, solo diving by the most extreme definition. As an equipped and prepared independent buddy diver, you are far safer returning to the boat or exit point on your own than allowing a buddy to lead you into known danger.

Does that make you a big chicken? I don't think so, but it may be a step in your evolution toward becoming an old, un-bold diver like me. The vast majority of buddy teams complete their dives with a common spirit of safety and adventure, and the mutual cooperation and support of buddy teams usually add to the enjoyment and safety of diving. However, you have no duty to share the consequences of dangerous buddy behavior.

It's fine if you don't agree with my opinions on these matters. What's important is that you think about them before they happen and decide what your personal course of action will be.

CHAPTER 12

WHEN A GOOD THING GOES BAD

BASIC RESCUE PROCEDURES AND DIVER PROBLEMS

ALL OF THE ESTABLISHED CERTIFYING AGENCIES offer courses on rescue procedures, and I strongly recommend that you take such a course before considering an attempt to rescue another diver in serious distress. Even after taking such a course, unless you've actively and recently practiced the rescue procedures, you are probably unprepared for an actual rescue. In fact, even if you've taken a course and you *have* actively and recently practiced the procedures, chances are good that you are unprepared for a real-world emergency involving a panicked diver. As would-be rescuers sometimes place themselves at great risk, an unprepared attempt to remedy a bad situation can often make the situation twice as bad. That said, all independent divers should at least be aware of rescue procedures and of the symptoms and causes of serious dive injuries, if only so they can monitor themselves and their behavior in order to avoid injury or recognize the possibility of an injury, increasing the chances that diver assists can be performed with little risk to the assistant.

Fortunately, the quality of training and equipment available to divers today makes diving safer than it has ever been, and the likelihood of serious injury is very low.

RATIONAL-PATIENT SURFACE ASSIST

The vast majority of diver assists involve divers who are tired or have recurring cramps that cannot be stretched out. The fatigue or cramps often result from other problems such as getting lost or equipment trouble. Some divers become distressed at the surface immediately upon entering the water. This is sometimes caused by breathlessness due to overly tight wet suits or from stress due to feeling unprepared to make the dive. Rational patients can often solve their problems by self-assistance if they are encouraged to do so. Here is a step-by-step plan of action for assisting a rational diver in distress:

1. Call out to the patient and ask him what is wrong. Instruct him to inflate his BC and drop his weight belt if necessary to establish comfortable buoyancy at the surface. If cramps are the problem, instruct him to stretch the cramped muscle. Calves, hamstrings, and foot arches are common cramp areas on divers, and cramps can often be alleviated by holding the fin tip of the affected leg and straightening the leg to stretch the muscle. Maintain a safe distance of 10 feet between you and the rational patient if you are in the water together. Reassure the ra-

RESCUE NOMENCLATURE

Before we begin to talk about specific procedures, we must first become familiar with rescue nomenclature. Here are some basic definitions:

- **Assist:** Action taken to prevent, interrupt, or solve a conscious, functional diver's problem or difficulty.
- **Rescue:** Action taken to remove an unconscious or helpless diver from danger to a place where necessary care can be given.
- **Self-Assistance:** Action taken by a diver to recognize or correct a personal condition that is developing into a problem or difficulty.
- **Patient:** A conscious or unconscious person in distress who is breathing and has a heartbeat. A living person in distress.
- **Victim:** An unconscious person who is not breathing and has no heartbeat. A dead person. The distinction between a patient and a victim can become very important when calling for assistance. For example, the coast guard may not respond as quickly to a report of a "victim," since a "victim" has already expired and the situation is no longer life-threatening.
- **Sign:** Any physical or behavioral manifestation of a problem that can be detected by another person. You detect signs in other people.
- **Symptom:** Any sensation experienced by a person that is a departure from his or her normal mental or physical state. You detect symptoms in yourself.
- **Rational Patient:** A patient who knows that there is a problem but is not overwhelmed by it. A patient who is functional and can respond to instructions.
- **Passive Patient:** A patient who is effectively unconscious although possibly not clinically so. An unaware and helpless patient who cannot act to remedy a problem and who requires assistance.
- **Panicky Patient:** A patient who is totally overwhelmed by a situation, is unresponsive to reason, and is out of control. Panicky patients may be extremely dangerous to approach.

tional patient and encourage him to self-assist if practical. Make sure the rational patient keeps his mask on and his regulator securely in place.

2. If the rational patient cannot swim back to the boat or exit point, attempt to throw a line to her if you are on board or onshore. If this is not possible and if you are not already in the water with her, you must decide if you are ready and capable to enter the water in order to assist.

3. If you decide to enter the water to assist the rational patient, you must first enlist the help of someone on the boat or shore to act as a spotter. The spotter should direct you to the patient and let you know when you approach to within 10 feet. You

must wear a mask, fins, and snorkel as a bare minimum. Enter the water and swim with your head out of the water to see where you're going and to keep the rational patient in view if possible.

4. Stop at least 10 feet from the rational patient to avoid being grabbed, and repeat the procedures listed in step 1. Encourage the patient to self-assist by following you back to the boat or exit point. Be a cheerleader. Make sure that she is comfortably buoyant at the surface and has her mask and regulator in place.

5. If the rational patient cannot self-assist by swimming back to the boat or exit point, you must decide if you are ready and capable to assist. If you decide to assist, tell the rational patient that you will assist by means of a fin push. The fin push is the easiest way for an assistant to move a scuba diver through the water. Have the rational patient, with his mask and regulator securely in place, float on his back and put his heels on your shoulders. Hold the diver's feet in place by holding his ankles or shins and push him through the water by swimming forward. Talk the patient through this procedure if he is not familiar with it. Push the patient back to the boat or exit point and enlist help if necessary to get him out of the water. Once the patient has been moved to safety, you should take immediate steps to account for the patient's dive buddy unless you are the patient's buddy.

The rational-patient assist involves minimal risk to the assistant and is the most common type of diver assist.

The easiest way to move a tired or cramped diver through the water is by the fin push. Once both divers are positively buoyant at the surface, have the distressed diver relax on her back with mask and regulator in place and put her fins on your shoulders, then push her through the water by swimming forward. Pushing is a lot easier than towing, and the distressed diver can carry any bulky item that either of you might have used during the dive. Barring a dire emergency, this is the only kind of assist you should attempt unless you have completed a Rescue Diver course from one of the established certifying agencies.

Passive-Patient and Panicky-Patient Surface Rescue

Some divers in distress are noncommunicative and cease to function in a reasonable way. These distressed divers are sometimes so fixated on an incidental task that they cease to communicate, or they have given up trying to help themselves and have reached a point of resigned stupor or catatonia. In any event, these divers are in trouble and are not likely to be able to work their way out of it themselves.

Failure to communicate is a sign of panic. Divers exhibiting more-advanced signs of panic will have wide eyes, strain their head and neck to keep them as high as possible, cough and sputter, hyperventilate, and slap the water with their hands. Panic is a primitive response to an overwhelming feeling of being out of control, and panicked divers will not hesitate to save themselves by any means possible or imagined. If you approach a panicked diver in the water, the diver may see you as an island of salvation and try desperately to climb onto you.

Attempting to rescue a passive or panicky patient may involve serious risk to the rescuer. The rescuer has no idea what the patient might do if the patient is not communicating. Stop and think before you rush into action. Know your own limits, assess the situation, don't attempt a rescue beyond your capabilities, pace yourself, and always have a plan to abort the rescue attempt if things get too crazy. You naturally want to help, but you must remember that the most important person in any rescue scenario is you. Use the least hazardous method possible, and avoid getting into the water with a passive or panicked patient unless absolutely necessary.

In the unlikely event that a passive or panicky diver is in the water and will not respond to instructions, that you have assessed the situation and your limitations and have decided that a rescue is possible, and that you are the most qualified person to attempt such a rescue, here are the steps you should take:

1. If you are already in the water with the passive or panicky patient, skip to step 3.
2. If you are onshore or aboard a boat, enlist the help of a spotter before you enter the water. The job of the spotter is to direct you and to let you know when you have approached to within 10 feet of the patient. Do not enter the water without the minimum equipment of mask, fins, and snorkel. If you are wearing an exposure suit, you must also wear a weight belt that will allow you to easily surface-dive. Wearing full scuba gear is best.
3. Swim to the patient with your head out of the water and maintain visible contact if at all possible. Situations involving passive or panicky patients change rapidly. Stop at least 10 feet from the patient.
4. Call out to the patient calmly but forcibly. Yell the patient's first and last names in an attempt to get his attention. Instruct the patient to inflate his BC and drop his weight belt. Instruct him to keep his mask and regulator in place, but make no attempt to replace them if he has removed them. Be prepared to swim away if the

WHEN CRAMPS ATTACK

Most divers experience the problem of muscle cramping sometime during their diving careers. Cramps are involuntary contractions of muscles due to fatigue, dehydration, or cold. Cramps often come upon divers suddenly and unexpectedly, and they can be quite debilitating.

The most common muscle cramps experienced by divers occur in the backs of the legs or in the arches of the feet. The calves are, perhaps, the most commonly afflicted areas, but hamstring and foot cramps are almost as common. A cramp feels as if a powerful vise has clamped down on the affected area, and further attempts to use the affected muscle are cripplingly painful.

The best way to deal with muscle cramps is to make every attempt to avoid them. The three factors of fatigue, cold, and dehydration work in combination, and measures you take to minimize these factors will help to prevent cramping. The very act of diving contributes to all three factors, and cramping usually occurs after you have made a few dives during the day. The more dives you make, the more fatigued you will become and the more the chilling effect of water will accumulate. The dryness of the air that you breathe from a scuba tank contributes significantly to dehydration, which results in blood chemistry that is conducive to cramping. The likelihood of cramping can be minimized by resting, stretching, staying warm, and drinking plenty of fluids between dives.

You can take steps to ward off cramps even after the dive has started. Cramps are usually caused by a repetitive motion such as kicking with fins. Varying the kicking motion from time to time during a dive will decrease the possibility that a cramp will occur, especially if a long swim or swimming into a current is part of the dive plan.

Sooner or later, though, in spite of all efforts to avoid them, a cramp is likely to occur. Stretching the affected muscle is the best way to alleviate a cramp. Since most cramps occur in the back of a leg or foot, the best way to stretch the muscle is to hold the fin tip in both hands and straighten the affected leg until you feel the stretch in the muscle. Stretching in this way will usually relieve the cramp, but the

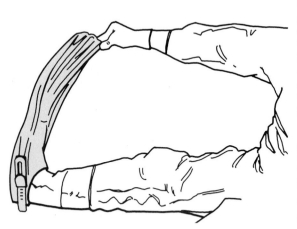

Cramps can usually be alleviated by stretching the affected muscle. Holding a fin tip and straightening the leg is a good way to stretch muscles in the back of the leg or in the arch of the foot, areas where cramps most commonly occur.

factors that caused the cramp will remain. Make a conscious effort to avoid the kicking style you were using when the cramp occurred. Once a muscle cramps during a dive, it will be very susceptible to further cramping until the dive is over and you can rest, stretch, warm up, and rehydrate. It's no surprise that cramps often occur during night dives when divers are tired, chilled, and dehydrated after a full day of diving.

If cramping becomes a recurring problem for you, take a look at your fins. Fins with large blades can contribute to the fatigue that leads to cramping. Consider using fins that are designed to minimize resistance during the upstrokes of your kicks.

patient moves toward you. Continually instruct him to inflate his BC, drop his weight belt, and keep his mask and regulator in place, while maintaining a distance of 10 feet. Tell the patient that you will not help him unless he inflates his BC, drops his weight belt, and keeps his mask and regulator in place.

5. If the patient responds and begins to take action to help herself, encourage her to self-assist by following you back to the boat or exit point. If she begins to communicate in a reasonable way, follow the procedures for assisting a rational patient. If the passive or panicky patient still takes no action to help herself or communicate, prepare to surface-dive by deflating your own BC if you are wearing one.

6. Surface-dive and approach the patient from below. Dive to his left side and release his weight belt with your right hand. Surface behind him while grabbing the BC collar behind his head. Keep your arm stiff to keep the patient away from you and to prevent him from grabbing you. You have now attached yourself to a person who may possibly drown you in his attempt to save himself.

7. Begin to tow the passive or panicky patient back toward the boat or exit point. Continue to instruct her to inflate her BC and to keep her mask and regulator in place, but make no attempt to perform these tasks for her. Be constantly wary of any attempt by the patient to grab you. If the patient does grab you, you must go the only place she won't follow, and that is beneath the surface of the water. Release the patient and dive immediately if she grabs you or begins to gain control of you. You must fight for your life should this occur, and all bets for a rescue are off until you are safely away. Reassess the situation once you escape.

8. Tow the patient back to the boat or exit point. Drop your own weight belt if it is hindering you in any way. Continue to instruct and reassure the patient. Enlist help to remove the patient from the water. Unless you are the patient's dive buddy, take immediate steps to account for the buddy.

So now you're a hero, right? In my thirty years of active diving, I've performed rational-diver assists a few times and I've witnessed several others. The assisted divers were uniformly grateful for the assistance.

I've never attempted a passive- or panicky-diver rescue, and I've only witnessed it twice. The patients recovered fully in both instances, and in both instances they developed interesting attitudes once the danger was past. They were both mad as hell and treated their rescuers like meddling miscreants. One of the former patients demanded payment from his rescuer for the cost of the weight belt that was dropped. So much for the hero stuff.

UNCONSCIOUS-PATIENT SURFACE RESCUE

When a person in the water is unconscious, it is a dire situation indeed. However, it is important to remember that a diver who appears to be unconscious may still present a serious danger to a rescuer. In the event that you should encounter this highly unlikely and tragic scenario, think before you act and resist the temptation to jump blindly into a situation you might not fully understand. If you decide that a rescue is possible and that you are the person best qualified to attempt such a rescue, here's what you should do:

1. If you are already in the water with the unconscious patient, skip to step 3.
2. If you are onshore or aboard a boat, enlist the help of a spotter to direct you and to let you know when you have approached to within 10 feet of the patient.
3. Swim toward the patient with your head out of the water to see where you are going. Keep the patient in view if at all possible. Stop no closer than 10 feet from the patient and call out to her. Shout her first and last names. Instruct her to inflate her BC and drop her weight belt. Follow the procedures for passive or panicky patients if the patient responds in any way.
4. If the patient does not respond and appears to be unconscious, cautiously approach him and give a gentle shake. Turn the patient over on his back if he is floating face-down in the water. If the patient is, indeed, unconscious, drop his weight belt and drop your own weight belt if you're wearing one. Move to the patient's side and hold him in a do-si-do fashion (right shoulder to right shoulder, or left shoulders touching).
5. Remove the patient's mask and regulator. Do not remove your own mask and regulator. Turn the patient's head toward you and put your ear next to her mouth. Look at the chest. *Look, listen,* and *feel* for ten seconds for signs of breathing. You should be able to see the chest rise and fall, feel the breath on your cheek, and hear the breathing if the patient is breathing. If she is breathing, tow her to the boat or exit point immediately.
6. If the patient is not breathing, pinch his nose, turn his head toward you, press your mouth over his, and inflate him with two full breaths. A device called a pocket mask will make mouth-to-mouth easier, but it requires practice to use. Also, don't waste

time looking for a pocket mask unless it is immediately available. Remove all scuba gear from the patient and tow him to the boat or exit point. You must inflate the patient with a full breath every five seconds while towing him to the boat or exit point.

7. Once you reach the boat or exit point, enlist help to remove the patient from the water. You must continue to ventilate the patient with a full breath every five seconds no matter what else you are doing. Ventilate the patient with two full breaths when you are ready to remove her from the water. You have fifteen seconds before you must ventilate the patient again.

8. Once the patient has been removed from the water, continue rescue breathing and take steps to account for the patient's dive buddy if you are not his buddy. As soon as possible, make an emergency call on channel 16. Remember to refer to the patient as a "patient," not as a "victim."

Unconscious Patient on the Bottom

The worst of any rescue scenario involves an unconscious diver on the bottom, and it is likely that the diver will cross the line between patient and victim before he can be returned to the boat or shore. In the event that you are faced with this tragic situation, here's what you should do:

1. If you encounter the unconscious patient on the bottom, skip to step 3.
2. If you are onshore or aboard a boat and are attempting to locate a diver who is overdue or who has surfaced in distress and sunk again, enlist the help of a spotter to direct you to the diver's last known position before you dive. Begin a search pattern appropriate to the area and surface periodically to enable the spotter to guide your search.
3. Approach the patient on the bottom cautiously and shake her gently to check for consciousness. Turn the patient faceup if she is facedown. If she is indeed unconscious, your first priority is to get her to the surface as quickly and as safely as possible. Do not spend critical time trying to minister to the patient on the bottom.
4. Prepare to bring the patient to the surface by holding him from the left side. Some certifying agencies recommend that you release the patient's weight belt at this time, but I disagree. Control the patient's buoyancy by operating his BC from the left side. Make a controlled ascent. If the patient's regulator is not in his mouth, don't waste precious time trying to replace it. However, if the regulator is still in his mouth, hold it in place during the ascent. The patient may begin to breathe again as the ambient pressure decreases during the ascent. In the event that the patient becomes too buoyant to hold even with all the air out of his BC, spread-eagle the patient on his back and let him go. Do not allow the patient's buoyancy to cause you to ascend too fast and risk injury to yourself.

5. Release the patient's weight belt as well as your own weight belt and, when you reach the surface, follow the procedure for rescuing an unconscious patient at the surface.

Emergency procedures must continue after an unconscious diver is returned to the boat or shore. Seek help. Pass the patient off to the person or authority most qualified to minister to him or her and call for emergency help. If the patient dies, gather all of the victim's equipment and quarantine it, as it is now evidence. Always account for the patient's or victim's dive buddy unless you are the buddy.

In the event that you must minister to the patient, it is up to you to perform CPR (cardiopulmonary resuscitation) if he or she is not breathing. CPR is a skill that must be learned and practiced in order to be effective, and I recommend that all independent divers take a Rescue Diver course from an established certifying agency that includes instruction and practice of this skill. The bare basics of CPR include clearing the patient's airway, compressing an area just below the patient's sternum with the palms of your hands at a rate of about three compressions every two seconds for fifteen compressions, and ventilating the patient with a breath of air after every fifteen compressions. The object of the procedure is to force blood out of the heart by compressing the area below the sternum, to allow the heart to refill with blood by completely releasing the pressure, and to provide oxygen to the blood by ventilating the patient's lungs with your own breath. It is an emotionally and physically taxing procedure that I'm glad I've never had to perform in earnest.

Decompression Sickness

Now that we've discussed some procedures for removing stricken divers from the water, let's talk about some of the most serious causes of diver distress.

Decompression sickness, often called DCS or "the bends," is the most studied pressure-related malady of diving, and a significant amount of time during your open-water certification class was dedicated to it. Even so, much is still unknown about its exact mechanisms and contributing factors. Decompression sickness causes physical damage in a variety of ways that are not completely medically catalogued. However, the root cause of DCS is well understood.

The tissues of your body absorb inert gases from the air you breathe, and they absorb more inert gases from the pressurized air you breathe as you dive. These gases continue to be absorbed into your body's tissues as long as you breathe pressurized air at depth. Since virtually all of the inert gas in air is nitrogen, decompression sickness is caused by the absorption of nitrogen into your tissues when you dive on air. The deeper you dive and the longer you stay at depth, the more nitrogen your tissues absorb from the air you breathe.

Nitrogen in your tissues is not a problem in and of itself. The problem arises if the pressure on your tissues is released faster than the excess nitrogen can be removed from the tissues through the mechanics of breathing. Should this occur, the nitrogen will form bubbles in your tissues rather than being released through your exhalations. The bubbles in your tissues are the problem. The rate at which pressure is released from your body tissues is determined by the rate at which you ascend from depth.

So, whether decompression sickness occurs is based on the rate at which nitrogen is absorbed and the rate at which pressure is released. Depth and time each contribute to the amount of nitrogen absorbed, and ascent rate is the sole determinant of the rate at which pressure is released. Therefore, the three primary contributing factors to decompression sickness are depth, time, and ascent rate.

Of course, you are very familiar with the tables and computers that divers use to compute safe depths and times for their dives, and you are probably very careful to avoid violating the time or depth parameters for any dive. However, my experience has been that many divers are not nearly as diligent about their ascent rates as they are about depths and times.

You know from your certification class that the recommended ascent rate is 30 feet per minute. That's very slow. Since the pressure on your body is reduced by half (from 2 atmospheres to 1 atmosphere) when you ascend from 33 feet to the surface, ascent rate becomes especially critical as you approach the surface. It should take a full 30 seconds to ascend from a safety stop at 15 feet. Mark off a distance of 15 feet on the floor and practice walking it while watching your watch to give you a better idea of how slowly you must move to cover 15 feet in 30 seconds.

Whether or not some tiny nitrogen bubbles form in your body during every dive is a matter of some dispute among the experts, but it is clear that microbubbles that do not produce any symptoms often form. Decompression sickness only occurs when bubbles large enough to cause symptoms form.

In addition to the three primary factors of depth, time, and ascent rate, secondary factors related to the individual state of your body may also predispose you to DCS. These risk factors are not well understood, but they include dehydration, fatigue caused by lack of sleep, cold, alcohol intake, hot baths or showers following dives, and strenuous exercise a short time before or after diving. Repetitive diving over a period of several days also increases the likelihood of DCS even if all the individual dives are performed within the accepted limits of the current decompression models.

Speaking of models, it is important to remember that dive tables and computers are not real reflections of the state of nitrogen in your body but are only models based on time, depth, and ascent rate. Simply put, a projection of your decompression status derived from a dive table or computer is only a guess based on what has occurred in other people at similar depths, times, and ascent rates. How do you know how you measure up to the model human being from whom the tables and computer programs were calculated? You don't. Avoiding DCS is an inexact science, and you should use the models conservatively to lessen the risk of decompression sickness.

Types and Symptoms of Decompression Sickness

Although great technological strides have been made to help you avoid DCS, you cannot be absolutely sure that you have succeeded even if you've dived within the safe parameters of the dive tables or your computer. That's tricky, but things get even trickier. Symptoms of decompression sickness can be rather vague and may not manifest until many hours after the dive.

Decompression sickness is always caused by bubbles of nitrogen (or other inert gases if you're diving on a gas mixture other than air) in tissue, but the symptoms vary depending on where the bubbles form. The joints are commonly affected in recreational divers, and bubbles in the joints produce what is called limb bends, sometimes referred to as Type I DCS. The shoulders and elbows in particular are commonly affected. The symptom is pain in the joints, and the pain may be mild and vague or piercing and severe. The affected area usually looks normal and is not tender to the touch.

Bubbles may also form in the brain or spinal cord and produce what is called neurological bends, sometimes referred to as Type II DCS. The symptoms of neurological bends vary greatly and may include vague effects such as weakness, numbness, "pins and needles" sensations in the limbs, headache, or extreme fatigue. Extreme symptoms include visual disturbance, incontinence, paralysis of one side of the body, mental or emotional changes, changes in personality, or difficulty concentrating.

Other manifestations of decompression sickness include a rash or marbling of the skin, typically on the torso. This is commonly called skin bends and can be an indication of a serious DCS problem. Vertigo caused by problems in the inner ear, commonly called "staggers," is another symptom. A manifestation more common in aviators but sometimes seen in divers is called "chokes," which is caused by bubbles in the pulmonary system. Chokes is characterized by difficult breathing, pain beneath the sternum, coughing, and a feeling of being choked.

While some of the symptoms of DCS are dramatic and severe, some are not. Add the possibility that symptoms may not develop until several hours after the dive and the fact that DCS may result from a dive that is deemed safe according to dive table or computer, and we're left with some serious questions. Is that pain in your shoulder a symptom of DCS, or did you just strain a muscle climbing up the boarding ladder? Do you need a dab of Ben-Gay or a dash to the emergency room? Did your foot go to sleep from sitting too long on the boat bench, or are there bubbles in your brain? Or, to sum it up, if you can't be sure you've avoided DCS based on your dive profile and if your symptoms are vague, how do you know if you have DCS or not?

I know that I've pounded home the fact that some cases of DCS occur even when

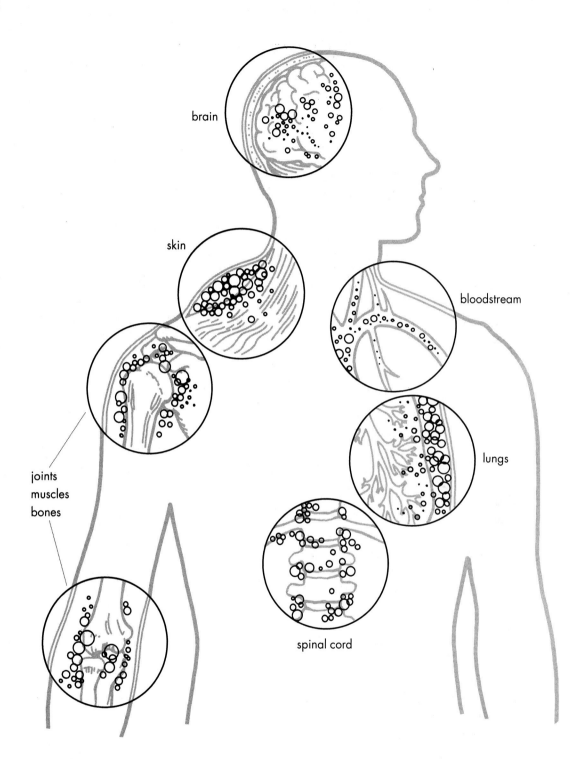

Bubble formation.

dives are made within dive-table or dive-computer parameters, but these instances are rare. Such an occurrence is called an "undeserved hit" because the diver has done nothing wrong and has followed accepted decompression procedures but has still ended up with decompression sickness. Undeserved hits of DCS may be caused by physiological abnormalities on the part of the diver. One such abnormality that has been associated with undeserved DCS hits is a condition called patent foramen ovale, or PFO, which is an incomplete fusion between areas of the heart. Regardless of the cause, an undeserved hit presents a serious problem for any would-be diver and should disqualify a person from future dives unless the cause of the DCS can be determined and corrected.

The vast majority of cases of decompression sickness result from unsafe diving and decompression practices ("deserved hits"), and the dive profile should be the first thing considered if symptoms of DCS occur. If the dive profile suggests the possibility of DCS and symptoms are present, treatment for decompression sickness should be sought immediately. It should be noted that if symptoms follow a dive that was made to the limits of the dive table or computer, it suggests the possibility of DCS—especially if secondary risk factors such as dehydration or multiday repetitive diving are present.

That's the best we can do at present for the diagnosis of decompression sickness, and it is far from perfect. There is little doubt that many divers unnecessarily endure the treatment for DCS from an abundance of caution. However, a new development may work to take the uncertainty out of DCS diagnosis. It has recently been reported that a correlation exists between DCS and bubbles in the tear film of the lower eyelid. Tests are ongoing, but early indications are promising. The development of a cheap, portable, and reliable field test for decompression sickness would be almost as revolutionary as the development of the dive computer itself for enhancing the safety and convenience of recreational diving.

First Aid and Treatment of Decompression Sickness

First aid for decompression sickness is immediate administration of 100 percent oxygen and transportation to a medical facility equipped with a hyperbaric chamber. The best way to administer oxygen is with a demand mask that covers the patient's face and delivers the oxygen whenever the patient breathes. If the patient will not tolerate a demand mask, a nonrebreathable mask can be used with the oxygen flow set at 15 liters per minute. Keep the patient on 100 percent oxygen until you can reach a hyperbaric chamber or until the available oxygen supply is exhausted. Do not use less than 100 percent oxygen as a way to prolong the oxygen supply. The Divers Alert Network (DAN) offers a variety of oxygen kits for divers, as well as training in their use, and I encourage all independent divers to take a Rescue Diver course and become familiar with the use of these kits. If you plan to dive often from shores or boats that are not equipped with emergency oxygen, consider purchasing such a kit for your own use.

It's always a good idea to have the telephone number and address of the hyperbaric chamber nearest to where you plan to dive. However, obtaining this information can be difficult. If you don't know and an emergency arises, call the patient's dive insurer and ask them to help you locate the nearest chamber. However, insurers typically will not provide such information prior to a dive, as the availability of hyperbaric chambers changes rapidly. If you do not know the location of the nearest manned and operational hyperbaric facility and you do not know if the patient has dive insurance, transport the patient to the nearest trauma facility and call DAN at 1-919-684-8111 for further advice.

Prompt hyperbaric treatment is very important to the recovery of the DCS patient. If, once you reach a hyperbaric facility, you anticipate a long wait, explain to the medical personnel that the patient is suffering decompression sickness from scuba diving and encourage prompt treatment.

Hyperbaric treatment consists of recompressing the patient until the nitrogen bubbles in the tissues are forced once again to go into solution. The pressure is then slowly released in a medically controlled process until the excess nitrogen is expelled from the patient's body. Most cases of decompression sickness can be cured with no permanent damage if 100 percent oxygen and hyperbaric treatment are administered promptly.

LUNG OVERPRESSURE INJURIES

Lung overpressure injuries, sometimes called pulmonary (lung) barotraumas (pressure injuries), are some of the most serious injuries in diving. They occur when a diver holds his breath while ascending or when air is trapped in the diver's lungs by congestion or restriction while he ascends after breathing pressurized air.

Your lungs are lined with a layer of tiny and delicate air sacs called alveoli. Your regulator must deliver air at the pressure necessary to overcome the pressure of the water around your diaphragm in order for you to breathe underwater, so your regulator is always delivering pressurized air to your lungs. As long as the pressure inside your lungs is equal to the pressure outside of your lungs, all is well with the lining of alveoli. However, if air is trapped in your lungs as you ascend, either because you hold your breath or because of a restriction (like mucus from a cold, or asthma), the pressure around your lungs decreases while the pressure inside them remains constant. Of course, greater pressure inside than outside the lungs causes the lungs to expand, and they may expand to the point that the alveoli are damaged. Bubbles of air may escape the damaged alveoli and wander off into parts of your body where no air should be.

How far must you ascend while holding your breath for this injury to occur? The difference in pressure of only 4 feet of water can cause a lung overexpansion injury. In other words, you can kill yourself by holding your breath with pressurized air and ascending from water that is hardly more than waist deep.

The escaped air typically moves to one of four places in the body: the pulmonary veins, after which it passes through the left side of the heart and into the arterial circulation system; the space in the chest between the lungs and the sternum; the space between the skin and the neck; and the space between the lungs and the chest wall. Although the cause of the air bubble is the same, its consequences vary considerably depending on where it goes.

Arterial Gas Embolism

Arterial gas embolism, often called AGE or simply an embolism, is the deadliest consequence of lung overexpansion. It occurs when the escaped air from the damaged alveoli enters the arterial circulation system. As the bubble leaves the heart, it will likely interrupt blood flow to the brain as the blood vessels become smaller. Alternatively, it may restrict or block blood flow to various other organs, including the heart itself. We're talking very bad business indeed.

Symptoms of AGE resemble stroke if the bubble blocks blood flow to the brain, and heart attack if it blocks blood flow to the heart. A diver with AGE usually exhibits symptoms within ten minutes of surfacing, and often immediately upon surfacing. AGE should be suspected for any unconscious diver at the surface. Symptoms include out-of-character behavior, confusion, sudden unconsciousness, dizziness, headache, convulsions, unilateral or bilateral paralysis, numbness and tingling, weakness, loss of sensations of taste and smell, chest pain, speech and visual disturbances, and nausea. The symptoms may pass and recur as the bubble moves throughout the patient's body.

First aid for arterial gas embolism is immediate administration of 100 percent oxygen and transportation to a hyperbaric fa-

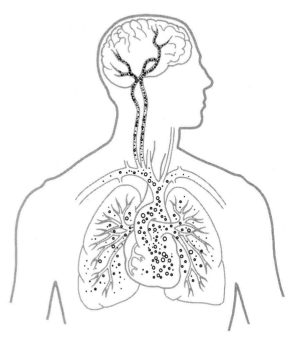

Air bubbles move from the lungs, to the heart, to the brain.

cility, or a trauma center from which DAN can be called. CPR must be performed in the event the patient stops breathing. Administration of oxygen and CPR are skills that must be learned and practiced, and the best way to become proficient is to take a Rescue Diver course from an established certifying agency.

Mediastinal Emphysema

Emphysema is the term used to describe any abnormal distension of body tissues with air, and mediastinal emphysema occurs when the air bubble settles into the area of the middle chest beneath the sternum. As with all lung overexpansion injuries, symptoms occur quickly after the diver surfaces and include pain beneath the sternum, breathing difficulty, shock, weakness, crepitation (crackling sounds), and faint heart sounds.

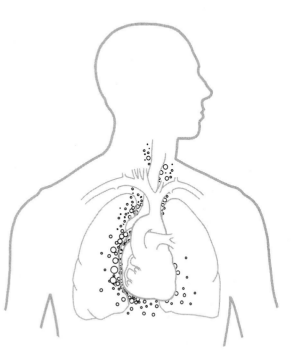

First aid for mediastinal emphysema is immediate administration of 100 percent oxygen and transportation to a hyperbaric facility, or a trauma center from which DAN can be called.

Air bubbles move from the lungs into space between the lungs next to the heart and the windpipe.

Subcutaneous Emphysema

An air bubble beneath the sternum may rise into the neck area and cause subcutaneous emphysema, which is air beneath the skin of the neck. Symptoms include swelling of the neck and collarbone areas, breathing difficulty, swallowing difficulty, and voice change.

First aid for subcutaneous emphysema is administration of 100 percent oxygen and transportation to a hyperbaric facility, or a trauma center from which DAN can be called.

Pneumothorax

Pneumothorax is another name for collapsed lung, and it occurs if the air bubble settles between the lung and the outer chest wall. Symptoms include sharp chest pain,

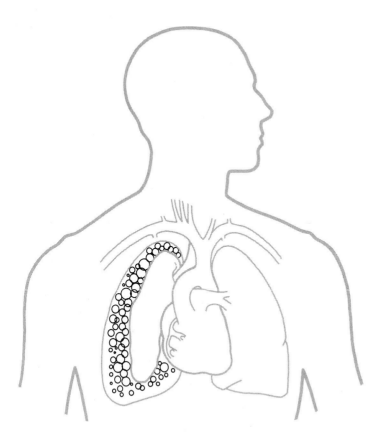

Air bubbles travel from the lungs in between the lungs and a moist membrane called the pleural lining.

shortness of breath, coughing, uneven chest rise, deviation of the trachea (windpipe) to one side, shallow and rapid breathing, shock, anxiety, and diminished lung sounds.

First aid for pneumothorax is immediate administration of 100 percent oxygen and transportation to a medical facility (not a hyperbaric facility).

SOME PROBLEMS OF BREATHING UNDER PRESSURE

I'm not talking about difficulty in breathing here. In fact, this section is not about any sort of diver injury per se. Here we'll discuss problems caused by the way divers breathe at depth and some of the negative effects of pressure on the air we breathe.

Oxygen Toxicity

Oxygen is the fuel that runs the engines of our bodies, but it is toxic when breathed under high pressure. The symptoms of oxygen toxicity may include convulsions and loss of consciousness, which usually means death by drowning to a scuba diver at depth.

Fortunately, the danger of oxygen toxicity is not a concern for recreational divers breathing normal air, because the oxygen in the air we breathe will not become toxic at the pressures of recreational-diving depths. Oxygen comprises 21 percent of air, and oxygen toxicity does not normally occur until it is breathed at a partial pressure of 1.6 atmospheres (the recreational limit is 1.4 atmospheres). A diver breathing air would have to descend to a depth of 220 fsw (feet in seawater) to achieve the 1.6-atmosphere limit, or 187 fsw to achieve the 1.4-atmosphere recreational limit. Of course, recreational divers do not dive to those kinds of depths.

Nitrox divers, on the other hand, breathe an oxygen-enriched mixture of gases. A large part of nitrox training involves learning to manage the percentage of oxygen being breathed and knowing the depth at which that percentage of oxygen may become toxic. You'll learn all about it should you decide to pursue nitrox training, but all divers should at least be aware of the possibility of oxygen toxicity.

As with many pressure-related phenomena, the exact pressure at which oxygen may become a problem for a given diver is rather vague, but no problem should occur at a partial pressure of oxygen of less than 1 atmosphere. The partial pressure of oxygen in air at a depth of 130 fsw is 1.04 atmospheres. The possibility of oxygen toxicity is not the sole reason that 130 fsw has been established as the recreational-diving depth limit, but it's more than a coincidence that this limit happens to be the point at which the partial pressure of oxygen in air exceeds 1 atmosphere.

Carbon Dioxide Toxicity (Hypercapnia)

Our bodies normally keep levels of carbon dioxide in our blood within a very narrow range. The production of carbon dioxide increases with exercise, and the gas is normally expelled through our exhalations as we breathe harder during exercise. However, divers sometimes experience a buildup of carbon dioxide that can lead to problems.

There are several possible reasons why levels of carbon dioxide may be elevated (a state called hypercapnia) in divers. Some are directly related to the way divers breathe underwater. Divers may breathe shallowly to conserve air or to maintain buoyancy. Some divers "skip-breathe" (pause between breaths) as a way to conserve air. Hypercapnia may also result from the higher partial pressure of the oxygen being breathed limiting the body's natural function of breathing harder to expel excess carbon dioxide.

Extreme effects of hypercapnia may include respiratory distress, diminished mental faculty, stupor, or even sudden unconsciousness. However, most cases of hypercapnia among divers are noticed after the dive in the form of a headache or nausea. Breathing fresh air is a quick cure. If you commonly experience postdive headaches that are not related to sinus problems, try breathing more deeply during your dives. Of course, you should avoid intentional shallow breathing or skip-breathing.

The flip side of hypercapnia (too much carbon dioxide in the blood) is hypocapnia (not enough carbon dioxide in the blood). Hypocapnia can occur after hyperventilation. Some free divers hyperventilate to engorge their blood with oxygen. This expels most of the carbon dioxide, and carbon dioxide in the blood is the natural trigger for breathing. The result is that a free diver can, indeed, make a long dive without feeling the urgent need to breathe. As the free diver ascends, the fall in the partial pressure of carbon dioxide (as well as all other gases) can continue to give her the false impression that she does not need to breathe. This can lead to a sudden blackout due to oxygen deprivation, even though the diver never feels an urgent need to breathe. Blackouts in free divers caused by lack of oxygen are often called shallow-water blackouts because they usually occur near the surface. Do not hyperventilate to extend your free-diving time.

Nitrogen Narcosis

Unlike the toxic effects of oxygen and carbon dioxide, nitrogen produces a narcotic effect when breathed under pressure. Your Open Water I certification class probably touched on the subject of nitrogen narcosis, but it deserves another mention here.

The effects of nitrogen narcosis are well documented but poorly understood. The narcotic effect varies greatly from diver to diver and even from dive to dive. However, the effect can be compared to that of alcohol intoxication, characterized by reduced mental agility and impaired judgment. In fact, divers sometimes refer to Martini's Law when discussing nitrogen narcosis. The "law" variously states that nitrogen narcosis produces the same effect as one martini every 33 fsw, every 50 fsw, or every additional 15 feet starting at 100 fsw of depth, depending on whom you ask and who's mixing the martinis. The point is that the narcotic effect of breathing nitrogen increases with pressure, which means it increases with depth.

Nitrogen narcosis is a serious problem. It is insidious, in that the impaired diver might not recognize the impairment. It can occur in some divers at depths as shallow as 50 fsw, and almost all divers are at least somewhat affected at a depth of 100 fsw. Distortions of reality can range from euphoria to apathy to a sense of dread or foreboding. Many divers describe the effect of nitrogen narcosis as limiting their thinking to the immediate present with no thought of the future. For divers on a strict plan of depth and time, this kind of thinking can obviously lead to problems. Nitrogen narcosis is another important factor in the 130 fsw depth limit for recreational diving.

All divers should be aware of nitrogen narcosis and plan for it. For example, if a dive plan calls for a pattern based on compass headings, the plan should be clearly written on a dive slate before the dive begins. The simple arithmetic needed to compute compass headings to swim a box or triangle pattern may be very difficult to do at depth, and kick cycle numbers might easily be forgotten. The rule regarding nitrogen narcosis is to plan to be stupid and to take precautions to prevent mental impairment from leading to trouble.

The effects of nitrogen narcosis are immediately alleviated by reducing depth.

HYPOTHERMIA

We've learned that heat is transferred from the body twenty-five times faster in water than in air, so it should come as no surprise that hypothermia (cold) can become a serious problem for divers. The clinical definition of hypothermia is a reduction of the core body temperature (as opposed to skin temperature) to 95°F. However, it is possible to become incapacitated by cold without becoming clinically hypothermic.

The effects of hypothermia occur as a matter of degree, so to speak, and the body needs as much as twenty-four hours to recover from exposure to the cold. Repetitive dives over several days have a cumulative chilling effect, and you should be prepared for this by wearing extra exposure protection when making multiple dives over a period of more than a day. Other factors that contribute to hypothermia are dehydration, improper wet-suit type or fit, low body fat, and, of course, simple overexposure to cold water. Wearing a wet exposure suit after diving, particularly a noninsulating suit like a dive skin, also contributes to hypothermia.

Mild and Moderate Chilling

You can feel cold even with a normal core body temperature, and a drop in core temperature of only 1°F will result in mild chilling. Symptoms are feeling cold, shivering, and making clumsy hand movements, but speech is only minimally affected. Moderate chilling occurs when the core body temperature drops to 97 to 95°F. Symptoms may become more severe and include confusion, apathy, uncooperativeness, difficulty with speech, weakness, and closed body positioning (fetal position or huddling).

First aid for mild or moderate chilling is exiting the water, removing the wet suit, getting dry, bundling up in dry clothes, and moving to a warm place. Drinking warm, noncaffeinated, nonalcoholic beverages will help.

Hypothermia and Severe Hypothermia

True hypothermia occurs when the core body temperature reaches 95°F. Shivering slows or stops at this point, and the symptoms of weakness, apathy, and confusion intensify. Drowsiness and slurred speech are pronounced. Divers who reach this state of chill are said to have the "umbles"—they stumble, mumble, fumble, and grumble. This is a serious medical condition.

Severe hypothermia occurs when the core body temperature falls below 90°F. Shivering stops, and symptoms include the inability to walk or follow simple commands, visual disturbance, a paradoxical feeling of warmth, and confusion and loss of function leading to coma.

True hypothermia and severe hypothermia are medical emergencies. The heart is sensitive to cold, and truly hypothermic divers must be treated gently to avoid cardiac arrest. Be prepared to administer CPR in the event that the heart and breathing stop. Prevent further heat loss by covering the patient with warm layers, and transport him or her to a medical facility where he or she can be rewarmed in a clinically controlled setting. Take great care to avoid jostling or jarring the hypothermic patient during transport.

HYPERTHERMIA

Hyperthermia means overheating. Divers don't only get cold; they get hot, too. Diving is often done during the hot months of summer in the humid air on and around the sea, and hot, humid air is conducive to hyperthermia.

Overheating

Overheating is common among divers who are planning dives in cool water on a hot day. The most common cause is donning a wet suit too soon before diving. Avoid sitting on a boat with a wet suit on for any length of time. If the day is hot and you must wear a wet suit, try dipping it in the water before putting it on.

Staying cool is an important comfort consideration, and remember that dehydration from sweating is a secondary risk factor for decompression sickness. Drink plenty of water and avoid the direct sun whenever you dive on hot days.

First aid for overheating is going to a cool place and drinking cool, noncaffeinated, nonalcoholic beverages. Water works. If your wet suit is already on and you don't feel like taking it off, a quick dip in the water is refreshing and will work to cool you. However, a cool swim will not replace fluids you've lost to sweating. Drink plenty of water.

Heat Exhaustion and Heatstroke

Heat exhaustion and heatstroke require medical care. If a diver becomes severely overheated, symptoms such as fatigue, drenching sweats, dizziness, nausea, weak pulse, rapid breathing, low blood pressure, and confusion are indications of heat exhaustion.

Heatstroke is more dangerous. It typically occurs abruptly, and its symptoms include headache, high fever, rapid pulse, confusion, and hot, flushed skin. Some sweating may still occur, but the sweat will not be drenching. Patients in the final stages of heatstroke collapse into an unconscious or semiconscious state. A patient who is unconscious or semiconscious due to hyperthermia constitutes a medical emergency. Serious and sometimes permanent damage to vital organs can occur, and there is a possibility of permanent brain damage.

First aid for heat exhaustion or heatstroke is immediate transportation to a medical facility. Give cool fluids along the way unless the patient is unconscious or semiconscious. Keep the patient in a reclining position to reduce shock. Cool the patient by splashing water or fanning, but do not cause chilling. Monitor the airway and breathing at all times.

Are you ready to give up diving yet? We've covered the most serious kinds of diver trouble, and, thankfully, they very seldom occur. You can expect to finish a long diving career without ever having to use any of the rescue skills we've discussed except, perhaps, a tired-diver assist or two.

On the other hand, it's always good to prepare for the unexpected, and all independent divers should be trained in rescue procedures by taking a Rescue Diver course from one of the established certifying agencies. Classes are instructional, they are fun, and they present an opportunity to meet other divers who are as serious about their diving as you are. Plus, all things considered, I prefer to dive with a buddy who is trained to pull my butt from the fire should the need ever arise.

CHAPTER 13

DIVING IN THE UNITED STATES

L ET'S REVISIT A PHENOMENON that we touched upon in chapter 6—the phenomenon of the "fantasy diver." Lots of people become fascinated by the underwater world and by the idea of flying unfettered through the liquid domain through the use of scuba. Based on the simple fact that you are a certified diver, you are one of those people.

Lots of people also prepare for a life of active diving by continuing their diving education, purchasing equipment, and becoming involved in the local diving community. Hopefully, you are also one of those people.

Unfortunately, of the people who become so interested in diving that they become certified divers and immerse themselves in the diver lifestyle by purchasing equipment and joining dive clubs, many never really get past the starting point. I call these people "fantasy divers," but they could just as accurately be described as "theoretical divers." These people are often very knowledgeable about diving physics and theory, exotic dive sites, and dive medicine, although they very seldom actually go diving. Why not?

I don't presume to know why all of these theoretical divers seldom get into the water, but I have a good idea why many of them don't. Many divers limit their diving to sites that are far away and expensive to reach, and the constraints of time and money restrict their diving. Don't get me wrong; the exotic dive sites regularly covered in the dive magazines are fantastic places that are wonderful to dive and visit. However, chances are good that you can enjoy unique diving adventures within a day's drive of your home with just an investment of energy instead of a major expenditure of time and money.

Too many divers consider the clear, blue water of the celebrated international destinations as the only diving worth doing. I disagree. In fact, some of the most interesting diving I've ever done was in water with limited visibility that bore very little resemblance to the great blue vistas displayed in the dive magazines, yet the dive experience was fun and productive. Here's a quick story:

I was on a live-aboard boat in the Bahamas a few years ago with some friends. The diving was great, and we all marveled at the warm, clear, blue water. Because we were planning to dive in a river in South Carolina to search for fossils when we returned to the United States, we naturally made daily comments about how different the conditions would be. One of the divemasters on the live-aboard boat became interested in our plans.

We returned from our Bahamas trip and met again in South Carolina for our planned river diving, and who do you think showed up? It was the divemaster from the live-aboard. He had taken a vacation from his daily grind of gin-clear water and sun-shine to dive in a river where visibility is measured in inches, and he said afterward that he hadn't enjoyed diving so much in years.

The point of the story is that there is more to diving than swimming on reefs in clear water, and while local destinations might not measure up to blue-water diving in terms of visibility or photo opportunities, local diving is often just as interesting and just as much fun. You'll find that interesting dive opportunities abound if you abandon the idea that all dive sites must look like the photos in the dive magazines.

Road Trip

What can be more exhilarating to an adventurous diver than tossing the dive bag in the car and setting off for a day or two of diving? Driving and diving is a great way to go, as it offers maximum flexibility and independence.

Assume that you leave your home for a road trip at the same time an air traveler leaves home. The air traveler has about a twenty-minute drive to the airport, then must spend more time to unload luggage and park the car. He or she then must stand in line to check in at least an hour before the scheduled flight. All things considered, about two hours will have passed from the time the air traveler left home to the time the plane taxies away from the gate.

You, on the other hand, have traveled nearly a hundred and fifty miles toward your destination before the air traveler even leaves the airport. You have not been standing in line; you have not had to endure that patiently condescending, disembodied airport voice reminding you of all the things you're not allowed to do. You have not lost control of your luggage, and the only limit to the luggage you carry is how much you can stuff into the car. While the air traveler has been herded like a head of cattle and treated suspiciously, you've had the freedom to sing show tunes at the top of your lungs, stand fifty feet away from your luggage, fire up a stogie, and accept candy from strangers if you are so inclined.

Now let's say that the air traveler has a one-hour flight, lands, then must collect luggage and arrange for ground transportation to the final destination. There goes another two hours.

You're another a hundred and fifty miles down the road. You have not been cramped in a tiny seat. You have not been breathing stale airplane air. If you've become uncomfortable at any time, you've had the opportunity to stop, sprawl out on a rest-stop picnic table, and sip a frappuccino to refresh yourself.

It takes about four hours for an air traveler to make a nonstop one-hour flight. Chances are good that a dive site worth exploring exists within a four-hour drive from your home. If not, well, it'll take longer to get there. Cruising to a dive site is a day well spent.

The return trip for the air-traveling diver is even worse. Divers should wait a full twenty-four hours before flying after diving, which adds a nondiving day to the trip. Road travelers face no such penalty and can be on their way home before their hair dries. Even if the trip requires more than a day of driving, you'll still get home at around the same time as the air traveler.

So driving and diving is a good idea. It keeps you in control of your life and can be easily canceled in the event of bad weather or other unforeseen contingencies. That's great, but where should you go?

I can't possibly direct you to the nearest river, lake, or quarry that may offer good diving. However, I can make some suggestions that might pique your interest of what I consider to be the most intriguing sites along the coastal areas of the United States.

THE GULF COAST

The United States is often seen as a bicoastal country. Well, don't look now, but we also have a Gulf Coast that stretches for more than a thousand miles along the Gulf of Mexico, and some of the best diving in the country can be found off its shores.

The Flower Gardens National Marine Sanctuary:
Coral Mountains in the Middle of Nowhere

A hundred fifty million years ago, within a shallow sea that covered most of the land of the world, a slow process began off the coasts of present-day Louisiana and Texas. Continuous deposits of sediment over salt layers, combined with internal pressure within the salt, caused isolated pockets of layered salt to be pushed upward through the deposited sediment. This, in turn, caused portions of the seafloor to bulge upward in distinct domes. The process ended during the last Ice Age, or only around ten thousand years ago, and the resulting mountainous bulges are called salt domes.

Although these domes were separated from the nearest living coral reefs by a distance of more than four hundred miles, the Loop Current diversion of the Gulf Stream apparently brought coral larvae to the area from the reefs of present-day Mexico. These lucky coral larvae found solid substrate in the form of the domes, as well as warm water and sunshine—the three main prerequisites of a viable coral reef. These reefs in the middle of nowhere have evolved over the past ten thousand years, and today they are considered to be the northernmost living coral reefs in North America.

The most well known salt dome reefs in the Gulf of Mexico comprise the Flower Gardens National Marine Sanctuary. The Flower Gardens Banks lie a hundred and ten miles south of the Louisiana–Texas border. Made up of two separate banks that are twelve miles apart, the Flower Gardens Banks contain 350 acres of living coral reef at depths of only 60 to 75 feet in the open waters of the Gulf.

A photographer frames a loggerhead turtle at the Flower Gardens in the Gulf of Mexico. The Flower Gardens Banks are considered to be the northernmost living coral reefs in North America, and trips to the Flower Gardens are an excellent opportunity to enjoy some live-aboard blue-water diving over a weekend.

The banks are home to two hundred species of fish more commonly seen in the Caribbean Sea, and they also attract mantas and turtles year-round. Scalloped hammerhead sharks congregate around the banks in winter, and whale sharks may also be encountered.

The third salt dome in the Sanctuary, Stetson Bank, is too far north to harbor hard corals due to the cooler water temperatures in winter. However, sponges and encrusting corals abound, as do large numbers of fish ranging from angelfish to bull sharks. Bare layers of sediment give Stetson Bank a stark, moonlike appearance, and many divers of the Sanctuary consider the diving at Stetson Bank to be the very best.

Freeport, Texas, is the starting point for most Flower Gardens trips, and three large boats currently offer a variety of multiday trips from Freeport. As might be imagined for a dive site more than a hundred miles from the nearest land, the diving ranges from sublime to challenging and the diversity of life on the banks seldom disappoints. Flower Gardens diving is blue-water diving, with visibility typically in the 80- to 100-foot range.

Weather is the limiting factor for Flower Gardens diving. The most consistent weather occurs in mid- to late summer.

Although the Flower Gardens are the most well known salt dome reefs in the Gulf of Mexico, they are by no means the only such domes in the Gulf. Sonnier Bank (more colorfully called Candy Mountain by Louisiana divers) lies eighty miles south of the Louisiana coastal town of Pecan Island, and smaller banks such as Geyer Bank lie nearby. Expeditions to explore these banks are sometimes organized by recreational scuba divers, and many banks have never been seen by human eyes. It is possible to dive virgin reefs in the United States, and the place to do it is in the Gulf of Mexico off the coasts of Texas and Louisiana.

Mantas are a signature sight at the Flower Gardens, and it is possible to see them throughout the year. An encounter with one of these flying carpets of the sea is an unforgettable experience.

Louisiana Oil Rigs: 3,000 Totally Tubular Reefs

The first offshore derrick in the world was erected in 1947 off the shore of the Mississippi River near New Orleans, and more than three thousand oil rigs have been placed in the Gulf of Mexico off the Louisiana coast since that time. Originally the bane of environmentalists, these oases of steel in the open Gulf have become so important to the recreational and commercial fisheries of Louisiana that the state now offers monetary incentives to the oil companies to leave the structures in place even after they cease to be productive for oil. They are one of the most extensive conglomerations of artificial reefs in the world.

Louisiana oil rigs did much to establish the new sport of scuba diving in the 1950s and 1960s as spearfishers flocked to the port of Grand Isle south of New Orleans to have a crack at the large and abundant fish that swam in and around the rigs. In fact, one of the most prestigious awards currently distributed by the scuba industry to barons of the sport, the NOGI award, was named for a Louisiana spearfishing tournament—the New Orleans/Grand Isle Invitational. Spearfishing remains the prime attraction of the oil rigs to divers, and dive clubs with names like Helldivers and Pneumatic Nailers abound in New Orleans and along the Louisiana coast.

The underwater environment of an oil rig in the Gulf of Mexico has a cathedral-like ambience.

It pays to look for the details even when in environments as vast as oil rigs. Anemones, sponges, and hydroids combine to provide a subtle explosion of color on an oil rig piling.

Although the Louisiana oil rigs are one of the most productive bastions of the sport of spearfishing in America, they offer more to visiting divers than the opportunity to spear large fish. Dive conditions are usually affected by freshwater runoff from the Mississippi River and Atchafalaya Basin, and the visibility runs the gamut from gin clear to murky green. However, the structures are covered with a wide variety of interesting marine life. In addition to big fish, expect to see arrow crabs, sponges, soft corals, and blennies galore on the pilings.

Trips to the Louisiana oil rigs are provided by independent boat operators that typically affiliate themselves with dive shops in New Orleans, Baton Rouge, Lafayette, or Lake Charles. Trips originate from the ports of Venice or Empire near the mouth of the Mississippi River, from the ports of Grand Isle or Port Fourchon south of New Orleans, or from Pecan Island on the coast west of Lafayette. Divable rigs are typically found twenty or more miles from shore. It's a wild place, a wild ride, and wild diving.

The Florida Panhandle:
The Emerald Coast

The Panhandle of Florida has long been famous for its blinding-white beaches and spring-break parties, but it also offers good diving. The algae-rich, green water that gives this area its emerald moniker is home to an eclectic assortment of junk on the bottom that serves as habitat for a wide variety of marine life. There are large ships, Liberty ships, supply boats, bridge rubble, scrap steel rubble, barges, and airplanes littering the bottom off the coastal towns of Pensacola, Destin, and Panama City. It is even possible to dive some oil rigs that have been towed from Louisiana for the purpose of establishing artificial reefs.

The oil rigs off the coasts of Louisiana and Texas in the Gulf of Mexico are best known for large fish and the spearfishers who pursue them. However, the pilings of the rigs are covered by tiny blennies that live in abandoned barnacle shells. Blennies are intriguing characters with growths called cirri on their heads that look like punk-rock haircuts. This seaweed blenny looks like it was surprised to be seen.

Leopard toadfish are commonly seen on dives deeper than 50 feet along the coast of the Florida Panhandle. Look for these odd fish in holes or beneath rubble near wrecks.

There is more to see on the Florida Panhandle than man-made reefs. A natural ledge in the limestone bottom is accessible to divers fairly near shore. Diving depths are typically in the 70- to 100-foot range, and visibility varies from murky green to pristine blue depending on the distance from shore and prevailing conditions. Regardless of conditions, unusual fish like toadfish and batfish can often be seen.

The Florida Panhandle also offers a rarity for Gulf Coast diving—shore diving. The rock jetties that protect passes to the Gulf offer interesting shallow-water diving, specifically the Fort Pickens jetties at Pensacola Pass, the East Pass jetties near Destin, and the St. Andrews State Park jetties near Panama City. It is fairly common to see or hear bottle-nosed dolphins near

Who says the only good diving is in crystal-clear, cobalt-blue water? This bottle-nosed dolphin was encountered off a jetty on Florida's Emerald Coast. You can hear the whistles and clicks from these magnificent animals long before you see them.

these jetties. To be picking around the jetties and suddenly hear the clicks and whistles of these magnificent animals is a magical experience.

Florida Springs and Rivers: Timeless Clearwater Pools

Although not strictly on the Gulf, several inland springs and rivers offer excellent diving. There are few places in the world where the inner workings of mother earth are exposed to exploration. The aquifer of northern and central Florida is one of those places. Freshwater springs lead to a flooded underground labyrinth of tunnels and caves that cuts through the limestone that forms the substratum of the state.

It's easy to imagine why Ponce de León mistook these springs for fountains of youth when standing beside them in midsummer. The stifling heat of the Florida sun is like a tangible weight that lowers the head and stoops the shoulders, and there in the middle of the dust and pines lie pools of water so cool and clean that they must be a tonic. These beautiful springs can be dived year-round, and the water is always about 68°F.

Florida spring diving means cavern and cave diving. Cavern diving (diving in ambient sunlight within sight of the opening to the surface) is taught in a popular specialty course offered by the established certifying agencies, and it's safe, interesting,

Excellent diving exists year-round in Florida's myriad springs. Cavern diving, or diving within sight of sunlight, is a popular specialty, and certification is easily obtained. However, cave diving, or diving deep within the earth in complete darkness, requires a great deal of training and experience.

THE LOWDOWN ON CAVE DIVING

The aquifers of northern and central Florida and the Yucatán Peninsula of Mexico are well known for cave diving. Freshwater pools and sinks lead to labyrinths of underwater tunnels and caves that cut through the limestone substrate of those areas, and the lure of the exciting possibilities for discovery has led many divers to a tragic end. The first recorded cave dive in Florida occurred in 1952, and an estimated four hundred divers have perished in underwater caves since 1960.

In the 1960s and 1970s, a mathematician named Sheck Exley undertook to determine how and why divers die in caves as a way to make underwater cave exploration reasonably safe, and Exley is considered to be the father of modern cave diving. Tragically, Exley himself met his demise during a deep cave dive in 1994.

Cave diving has been a somewhat closed society since that time. Two agencies have emerged with systematic curricula for Cave Diving certification—the National Speleological Society, Cave Diving Section (NSS-CDS) and the National Association for Cave Diving (NACD). Cave Diving certifications offered by the recreational certifying agencies are based on either of these two curricula. Cave Diving certification is achieved through the following progression of courses:

- **Cavern Diving:** Cavern Diving is an introduction to overhead environments. Open-water divers may take this course, and the only special equipment they need is a minimum of two dive lights. Cavern divers explore underwater caverns that are lit by daylight. Should untrained open-water divers enter such a cavern, it is recommended that they do not bring any lights; this will discourage them from penetrating into a cave system that could quickly lead to trouble.

- **Introduction to Cave Diving:** Prospective cave divers get a chance to really test the waters in this course, as they leave the zone of daylight and actually make their first linear explorations into well-known cave systems. Special equipment and major revisions to the standard scuba setup are required. Divers in Introduction to Cave Diving courses make several dives over a period of two days. The course includes special skills and basic emergency procedures.

- **Apprentice Cave Diver (NSS-CDS only):** The Apprentice Cave Diver course represents the first half of Full Cave Diver certification by NSS-CDS. Upon successful completion of the course, the student will receive a one-year training card while continuing the exacting training toward Full Cave Diver. More special equipment and modifications to the traditional open-water scuba setup are necessary.

- **Full Cave Diver:** The Full Cave Diver course is the final step toward Full Cave Diver certification. The course includes a refinement of skills with an emphasis on complex navigation.

A cave diver sets markers deep within a cave. ART MALONE

Cave diving is so significantly different from open-water diving that almost everything cave divers do and the way they do it seem foreign to open-water divers. The most obvious difference is equipment configuration. Cave divers typically use double tanks that are combined by a dual-orifice isolation manifold that allows redundant regulators to be attached. Second-stage regulator hoses are typically 7 feet long to enable divers to share air when moving in single file within narrow corridors, while other hoses are very short to prevent entanglement. Snorkels, large dive knives, and any other gadgets that could possibly lead to entanglement are absent on cave divers. Cave divers do not use split-blade fins, as they may snag a safety line and are not very efficient for the silt-reducing kicks that cave divers employ. Special equipment such as reels and lines or markers is confined within pockets. Nothing is left to dangle. Long hoses are kept close to the body with bungee cords. Everything is designed for simplicity, redundancy, and streamlining.

All of the cave-diving course levels require many dives over a period of two to several days in a variety of caves and conditions, and these courses are intense both in attitude and equipment. The standards for achieving Cave Diving certification are stricter than those required for most recreational dive certifications, and the significant expenditure of time, effort, and money required is no guarantee of successful completion. The Full Cave Diver certification is a badge of honor that signifies a diver with unusual skills, knowledge, and competence.

and fun. However, cave diving (diving where the sun don't shine) is a fearfully dangerous technical-diving specialty that requires years of training. As in all technical diving, trained cave divers take the sport of scuba to its scary limits.

Popular springs that offer recreational scuba are Vortex Springs and Morrison Springs on the Panhandle; Ginnie Springs near High Springs on the Peninsula; Blue Grotto and Devil's Den near Williston farther south; and Rainbow River near Dunnellon near the Gulf Coast. However, the entire state is pocked with springs, and it would take a lifetime to dive them all.

Diving Florida's springs and spring-fed rivers offers more than a beautiful swim among the wildlife that inhabits them. These clear, cool bodies of water were important to the Native American tribes endemic to the area, and artifacts are commonly found. All finds must be reported, but most isolated finds (those not part of a comprehensive site of archaeological importance) such as spear points, arrowheads, and pottery shards may be kept by the finder.

The spring-fed rivers of Florida are also productive for fossils. Mammal fossils such as prehistoric tapir teeth and even mammoth bones are not uncommon and must be reported to the state, and a small fee must be paid in the (probable) event that the finder is allowed to keep the object. Prehistoric shark tooth fossils are not regulated and may be kept by the finder with no red tape involved. The Chipola River near Marianna on the Panhandle is a popular river for fossil or artifact diving, and the prospect of finding treasures from the distant past adds an extra measure of excitement to any dive.

Crystal River and Homosassa Springs, Florida: Manatee Mecca

West Indian manatees are fascinating creatures. Legend has it that early Spanish explorers mistook them for mermaids—an observation that did not reflect kindly on their female contemporaries. The average adult manatee is 8 to 10 feet long and weighs 800 to 1,000 pounds. However, in defense of the lovely ladies of Spain, legend also has it that Columbus himself, when he first saw a manatee, noted that mermaids were not nearly as comely as previously reported.

Manatees certainly do have their charms, irrespective of these opinions. The combination of a puppy-dog face and a sweet disposition invariably works to endear manatees to anyone who sees them.

There are only twenty-five hundred to three thousand manatees still living in the United States, and a few more survive farther south. They range as far as the Carolinas and Louisiana in summer, but the cool waters of winter drive them into the warm, shallow, spring-fed waters of Florida each year. The waters near the Florida towns of Crystal River and Homosassa Springs, which are only ten miles apart near the Gulf Coast west of Orlando, attract large congregations of manatees from October through March.

It's not often that divers have the opportunity to interact with large and endangered species, but that is consistently the case near Crystal River and Homosassa Springs in winter. You cannot use scuba to dive with the manatees, but you may easily approach them on snorkel. Manatees can be found in water less than 10 feet deep, and they spend much of their days lying quietly on the bottom with their backs near the surface. This behavior has been their undoing, as many animals are killed or injured by boat propellers. Few adult manatees are free of scars from run-ins with boats.

Observing manatees in the wild is a thrilling experience. They often congregate in

groups that look like minefields of huge baked potatoes on the bottom. Adults generally surface to breathe every five to eight minutes, while youngsters surface more frequently. Young manatees often approach divers, and some will spend time right at the boat, where they seem to enjoy playing with anchor lines.

A trip to dive with the manatees is a great way to break up the doldrums of winter with an amazing dive experience. The Rainbow River spring is a short drive away, as are the Blue Grotto and Devil's Den springs, so making a few tank dives should also be on the agenda for a manatee trip.

A trip to the central Gulf Coast of Florida to have a swim with the manatees that congregate there is the perfect way to break up the doldrums of winter, and an encounter with these endearing and endangered animals will melt the heart of even the most jaded diver. This youngster is smiling coquettishly near the security of its mother's massive back.

Venice, Florida: The Shark Tooth Capital of the World

Sharks have cartilage skeletons, which are not conducive to fossilization, but they are essentially tooth factories and produce hundreds of teeth throughout their lives. As the entire southeastern coast of the United States was periodically underwater during the Pliocene and Miocene epochs, or about 2 million to 25 million years ago, this region is now one of the most fertile areas for marine fossils in the world, and shark teeth are some of the most commonly found.

Some of the sharks from the Miocene and Pliocene were not your common, everyday sharks. Several gigantic species of sharks lived in those times, the largest of which was the legendary *Carcharocles megalodon*, popularly known as the megalodon shark. The megalodon shark was the largest predatory fish ever to inhabit the oceans. It grew to lengths of 60 feet or more and might have weighed an astonishing 20 tons, and fossils of its massive teeth measuring over 6 inches long and weighing over a pound have been found. Originally thought to be an ancestor of the modern great white shark, megalodon is now believed to be an evolutionary dead end.

Another huge shark, the extinct mako *Isurus hastalis*, also lived and died along the southeastern United States during the Miocene and Pliocene epochs, and it is suspected that this shark was the true evolutionary ancestor of the modern great white. Teeth from this monster may measure over 4 inches in length, but they lack the mass and serrated edges of megalodon teeth.

The town of Venice, Florida, which lies south of Sarasota along the Gulf Coast, claims to be the shark tooth capital of the world. That's a hard claim to objectively substantiate, but the argument certainly has a point, so to speak. You can find fossilized teeth from a wide variety of modern sharks including sand tigers, bull sharks, and lemon sharks, as well as the occasional teeth from megalodons and extinct makos, by diving in only 20 to 30 feet of water. Surfaced divers have a clear view of the high-rise condos on picturesque Caspersen Beach. It's an intriguing dichotomy of time.

Spring and early summer are the best times for fossil hunting near Venice. Winter storms work to expose fossils, but fossil collectors, both private and commercial, work the bottom during the summer months. They cannot possibly pick the area bare of fossils, but their efforts do have an effect.

Venice fossil diving does not resemble the blue-water photos in the dive magazines. Visibility can be fairly good (10 feet or more), but the search area is mostly gray sand, grass or gravel beds, and algae. That does not diminish the fun and excitement of searching for fossilized shark teeth, and the thrill of discovery can be relived every time you pick up, feel, and examine the tooth at home. Even I can consistently find fossils that have been lost for millions of years in these waters—not bad for a guy who can put down his car keys and be unable to find them again thirty seconds later.

The Florida Keys and Key West: America's Favorite Reef

Few places offer the history, romance, and adventure of the Florida Keys and Key West. The history of the Keys includes the Spanish Main, treasure-laden galleons, and pirates. More recent history and the modern Keys include a diverse cast of characters such as writers, free spirits, musicians, artists, treasure hunters, and street performers. The past meets the eclectic present in a colorful collision of cultures and ideologies in the Florida Keys.

The Florida Keys comprise more than two hundred separate islands, stretch two hundred miles from Biscayne Bay to the Dry Tortugas, and contain the only living barrier reef in the continental United States. U.S. Route 1 is known as the Overseas Highway for the 126-mile stretch connecting the Keys from Biscayne Bay to Key West, making "island-hopping" a breeze. The Keys are one of the most visited dive areas in the world, with about 6 million visitors annually. More than a million of them are divers—many of whom are making their open-water training dives or visiting a coral reef for the first time. Much of the reef throughout the Keys lies four to six miles from shore and offers convenient, shallow diving.

The Florida Keys can be divided from north to south into five major areas: Key

Largo, Islamorada, Marathon, Big Pine Key and the Lower Keys, and Key West. Many divers consider the Keys to be beginner diving due to the shallow reef conditions and to the fact that so many operators in the Keys cater to the beginner. However, excellent diving for all levels of divers exists throughout the Keys.

The Florida Keys were ahead of the times when the John Pennekamp Coral Reef State Park off Key Largo was established in 1960. The park was formalized in 1975 when a 103-square-nautical-mile area off Key Largo was declared as the nation's second national marine sanctuary. Another national marine sanctuary in the Keys was established in 1981, which protected an area of over 5 square nautical miles around Looe Key Reef off Big Pine Key in the Lower Keys. Congress finally took the next logical step toward protecting the Keys in 1990 when it designated the Florida Keys National Marine Sanctuary. The marine sanctuary extends about two hundred and twenty miles southwest from the southern tip of Florida.

As a result of these various protective actions, some areas of the Florida Keys have been protected for more than forty years and the entire ecosystem has enjoyed federal protection for more than a decade. Consequently, great concentrations of fish and marine life are easily approached. Given a choice between interesting diving that is shallow and easy or interesting diving that is deep and difficult, I'll choose shallow and easy every time.

In addition to large schools of approachable fish on shallow reefs, the Florida Keys offer several large wrecks that were intentionally sunk to serve as artificial reefs. Most of these wrecks are in deeper water, and some operators require a diver to have a minimum of Advanced Open Water certification from one of the established certifying agencies to dive them.

Diving in the United States

ARTIFACT HUNTING: FINDERS KEEPERS OR FINDERS WEEPERS?

Artifact hunting and collecting is a popular activity among wreck divers, and most hard-core wreck divers have a porthole, binnacle, or other shipwreck artifact proudly displayed somewhere in their homes. But is artifact collecting legal?

The greatest artifact hunter of modern times was Mel Fisher, the man who searched for sixteen years for the wreck of the Spanish galleon *Nuestra Señora de Atocha*, which sank in 1622 near the southern tip of Florida. Florida state officials claimed ownership of the wreck from the moment the first coins were found early in the quest. Fisher fought through more than one hundred lawsuits before the U.S. Supreme Court finally determined that all finds were his.

The Supreme Court ruling that gave Mel Fisher his treasure was based on the time-honored maritime law concept of "the law of finds." The concept simply means that if a ship and its contents are abandoned by the owner, then whoever finds them is entitled to ownership. Therefore, the single most important determination in deciding who owned valuable sunken artifacts was whether the ship and its contents were, indeed, "abandoned" by the owner. Because insurance companies that pay claims as a result of shipwrecks become the owners of the wrecks, cases usually revolved around whether a given ship was abandoned by the insurance company that covered it.

Federal and state governments were pretty much left out of the picture. Wrecks belonged either to whoever owned them before they were found, or, if abandoned, to whoever found them.

Governments don't like to be left out of the picture—especially if the picture involves hundreds of millions of dollars worth of treasure, as the *Atocha* find did. With a wave of the bureaucratic pen, Congress passed the Abandoned Shipwreck Act of 1987, which gave states ownership of all abandoned shipwrecks found in their waters. The act specifically says that "the law of finds" does not apply to abandoned shipwrecks in state waters.

Does this mean that the porthole on your mantel, the one you recovered from an abandoned wreck with your own hands, actually belongs to the state in whose waters you found it? As a technical matter, if the artifact was found after 1988, the state does have a claim of ownership. Some states may grant ownership only after finds are reported though the state bureaucracy. Other states allow artifact recovery except in specific areas designated as archaeological sites. Yet others require permits or licenses to recover an artifact from any shipwreck in state waters. However, in the vast majority of cases, governments seem to be content to let shipwrecks languish and deteriorate in their waters unless a diver finds something of unusual value, and ordinary artifacts are unlikely to incite their custodial zeal.

Of course, wrecks in state parks, wrecks in marine sanctuaries, and wrecks designated as archaeological sites are off-limits to artifact collecting, and a significant number of divers feel that all wrecks should be left intact for other divers to enjoy.

Shipwreck artifacts aren't the only items that divers seek. Many divers search rivers for other archaeological artifacts such as Native American tools and pottery; other divers search the sea and rivers for paleontological artifacts (fossils). Who owns those?

Most states claim ownership of all archaeological or fossil finds made on state lands. Currently, objects found on privately owned land belong to the landowner, but some states are making moves to claim even these finds.

South Carolina and Florida (the states where many fossils and Native American artifacts are found) have developed bureaucracies that grant reasonable freedoms to artifact collectors while maintaining the states' custody of important finds. You can acquire a hobby license from the South Carolina Institute of Archaeology and Anthropology (SCIAA) for a small fee, which entitles you to recover reasonable amounts of fossils, archaeological artifacts, or shipwreck artifacts in South Carolina waters.

You must obtain written permission from the Florida Bureau of Archaeological Research department of the Division of Historical Resources before you can commence artifact-recovery activities in Florida waters. However, the rules exempt "isolated finds," which are artifacts that have become displaced from their original archaeological context and, as such, offer little archaeological insight. Isolated finds include stone tools and points, bottles, coins, and other small objects that have become displaced over time in Florida's rivers and coastal waters. However, isolated finds do not include fossils, and a special permit is required to collect fossils in Florida's waters. These permits are not expensive, and it should be noted that prehistoric shark teeth are exempt from all regulations. If you find a shark tooth, it's yours.

Although it is legal to recover an isolated find in Florida waters, the finder does not have ownership of the find unless it is granted by the state. The find must be reported to the Bureau of Archaeological Research. The bureau may grant ownership of the artifact to the finder, or it may determine that further study of the artifact is in the best interest of the state.

You should be aware of all state regulations that apply to whatever waters you plan to search. Chances are good that all legal requirements have been satisfied if you dive with an established operator for such dives. However, if you plan to dive on your own, it is your responsibility to know the law.

Many historic wrecks litter the Keys, some of which are several hundred years old. Some of these are the legendary galleons that struck the reefs on their way from Havana to Spain during the glory years of the Spanish Main. Treasure has been found, and is still sought. While these old wrecks hardly resemble ships anymore, the fact that they still exist and can be seen makes for a thrilling and tangible connection to that fabled time.

Dive operators in the Keys have also been busy creating artificial reefs with a number of intentionally sunk ships. These wrecks usually lie in deeper water offshore from the reef, and they offer interesting and more challenging dives to more advanced divers. Popular wrecks of this type are the coast guard cutter *Duane* and the 510-foot *Spiegel Grove* off Key Largo; the 287-foot freighter *Eagle* off Islamorada; the World War II cable layer *Thunderbolt* off Marathon (so named because it also served later duty as a lightning research vessel); and the 180-foot buoy tender *Cayman Salvager* off Key West. Most of these wrecks have been submerged for many years and offer mature artificial reefs with loads of marine life.

The Florida Keys and Key West are a fabulous domestic resource for U.S. divers. To borrow a phrase from their ad campaigns, they are the tropical reefs you can drive to.

THE EAST COAST

West Palm Beach, Florida: Riding the Gulf Stream

Most divers think of the Mexican island of Cozumel when they think of drift diving in the warm, clear, moving waters of the Gulf Stream. However, the confluence of the Florida Current and Antilles Current deflections of the Gulf Stream that occurs near West Palm Beach, Florida, offers a drift-diving opportunity that is second to none.

In addition to featuring clear and warm water, the Gulf Stream is also a conveyor belt of marine life. You can see several different species of turtles on sites a scant mile from shore near West Palm Beach, and you may encounter unusual species of fish like batfish or Goliath grouper.

Drift diving requires cooperation and teamwork among divers, but it is one of the most relaxing ways to dive. Save some pesos and give drift diving a try in West Palm Beach, Florida.

The Cooper River, South Carolina: The Tomb of Monsters

We've touched on the fact that giant sharks plied the shallow waters that periodically submerged the present-day southeastern coast of the United States between 2 million and 45 million years ago, and we've noted that the largest of those sharks was the fearsome megalodon, which lived during the Pliocene and Miocene epochs, or about 2 million to 25 million years ago. Megalodon was the last in a line of three gigantic species of sharks, each larger than its predecessor. Each lived on a diet of whales, and it is theorized that their rise to prominence and eventual demise was caused by changes in whale populations and migratory patterns.

The first giant shark on the evolutionary line to megalodon was a brute known as *Carcharocles auriculatus*, which lived during the Eocene epoch, or about 38 million to 42 million years ago. *Auriculatus* evolved into a beast known as *Carcharocles angustidens*, which lived during the early Miocene, or about 15 million to 30 million years ago. *Angustidens* finally evolved into megalodon. A fourth giant, the extinct mako *Isurus hastalis*, was the probable ancestor of the modern great white shark and lived during the Pliocence and late Miocene epochs, between 3 million and 7 million years ago.

The southeastern coast of the United States is one of the most fertile grounds in the world for finding the fossilized teeth of these prehistoric monsters, and one of the richest areas is a fossil bed known as the Hawthorne Formation in South Carolina. As luck would have it, a river cuts right through it. That river is the Cooper River near Charleston, South Carolina, and huge fossilized teeth from all four of the giant sharks can be found in its dark waters.

The Cooper River is black-water diving. Depths range from 20 feet to over 50 feet, and you must use a powerful dive light to illuminate the bottom only inches from your face. The river is also affected by tides and can only be dived during slack tide. Cooper River divers typically carry screwdrivers that they stab into the bottom marl to anchor themselves against the current as they crawl around in search of monstrous teeth. It is black, spooky diving that is not suited to those who may be disturbed by things that go bump in the dark. Buddy diving can only be accomplished by tethering two people together, which is a practice that involves its own risks.

There is something magical about being in the dark and pegged to the bottom of such a river, and the experience is magnified by the thoughts of those giant demons from the past. Due to the limited visibility, you cannot see a tooth until it is very close.

The author (hey, you'd look funny smiling with a mask on, too) surfaces in the Cooper River near Charleston, South Carolina, with a fine tooth from an extinct mako shark. The impressive dentition of these monsters from the past has an almost magical quality, and braving the murky river water to search for prehistoric shark teeth makes for a thrilling day of diving. SHARON ELKINS

Then it suddenly fills your vision, which is surprising and produces a wonderful feeling of discovery.

Prehistoric shark teeth are amazing things to contemplate. The extraordinary nature of the animals that produced them and the mind-boggling time that has elapsed since their connection to a living creature give rise to meditation. Virtually all the teeth are discolored near the tip—the result of compression fractures that occurred when the animals were alive. These teeth are not abstract objects; they bit and killed things. To be the first warm-blooded being to touch the deadly dentition of such formidable predators after so many millions of years is a very special feeling, indeed. Carrying a small tooth from one of these giants from the past in a pants pocket (the larger teeth won't fit into a pocket) tends to put the daily travails of life in perspective.

North Carolina: The Graveyard of the Atlantic

The treacherous waters off the coast of North Carolina have been the nemesis of seamen and their ships throughout maritime history. Early sailors making the trek from North America to Europe typically rode the Gulf Stream current up the eastern seaboard of the present United States until they caught the westerly trade winds (remember that winds are named by the direction from which they blow) that would push them eastward across the Atlantic. Many of them never made it past Cape Hatteras and the Outer Banks and shoals of North Carolina. The coast of North Carolina continued to snare mariners and their ships through the age of exploration, the golden age of pirates, and the age of steam, and it still poses a hazard to shipping today.

The shallow banks off North Carolina also served an important role during the early years of America's involvement in World War II. Soon after the United States entered the war in December 1941, German admiral Karl Dönitz began sending U-boats into American waters. The U-boats would sit on the bottom in the shallows during the day and surface to hunt freighters and tankers at night. They took a fearsome toll until the Allies instituted a system of protective convoys in April 1942, which forced Dönitz to move his submarines southward toward the Caribbean tanker lanes.

The North Carolina coast from Cape Hatteras to Cape Fear offers the best historical wreck diving in the United States, and the quality and historical interest of the diving rival that of any area in the world. More than a thousand ships lie on the bottom near the shore, which has earned the grim moniker Graveyard of the Atlantic, but the wrecks of most interest to many divers are the World War II tankers and freighters and the German U-boats that sank them.

Two of the most popular dives are the wrecks of the 412-foot tanker *Papoose* and the German submarine *U-352*. The *Papoose* was sunk by the German *U-124* in March of 1942 and lies in clear water at a depth of 90 to 120 feet. The *U-352* was sunk by a depth charge from the coast guard cutter *Icarus* in May of 1942 and lies in clear water at a depth of 100 to 115 feet. The precise record of how these vessels met their fates and their relevance to modern history add tremendous interest to their remains, and the wreck of the *U-352* provides a unique opportunity to see a German U-boat on the battleground where she fell.

The shipwrecks off North Carolina also host an abundance of marine life—the most notable of which are the large sand tiger sharks that have made many of the wrecks their homes. Many tropical species inhabit the wrecks, and even lionfish thought to be endemic to the Pacific Ocean have been reported in the area.

The wreck diving off North Carolina typically begins in Morehead City or Beaufort, but dive trips from various other departure ports along the coast are also available.

Treasure guarded by monsters has been a theme of good stories dating back to the mythology of ancient times, but the sand tiger sharks that cruise the wrecks off the coast of North Carolina are a modern reality. The sharks are not as fearsome as they look, but they enhance the sense of mystery of these world-class historical wrecks. CINDY BURNHAM/NAUTILUS PRODUCTIONS

WRECK DIVING

Few objects have the mystery and lure of a shipwreck on the bottom of the sea. Where did the vessel come from? Who sailed aboard her? What calamity caused her demise? And most compelling of all, what's inside? Shipwrecks have become a cultural icon of adventure and discovery.

There are two ways to explore shipwrecks. The first and easiest way is to explore the exterior. Familiar items such as stairways, ventilation pipes, and deck equipment assume a mystical quality, and wrecks attract marine life as they are embraced by the sea and become reefs. No special equipment or skills are needed to explore wreck exteriors within recreational-diving depths.

The second way to explore shipwrecks is to penetrate into their interiors. Wreck interiors are overhead environments similar to caves, and many of the techniques used by cave divers are applicable to wreck-penetration diving. As such, this type of diving requires special training and equipment.

The established certifying agencies offer specialty training in wreck diving. The courses cover basic penetration equipment such as reels and lines, techniques to deal with entan-

External exploration of shipwrecks within established recreational-diving depths is fascinating and doesn't require special equipment or skills. Here a diver ponders the massive scale of a ship's propeller.

Penetration into large shipwrecks involves many of the same dangers as cave diving, and wreck-penetration divers should be trained and equipped to mitigate those dangers. In addition to posing the hazards of entanglement and low visibility, wrecks lying on their sides like this one can be very disorienting.

The interiors of shipwrecks can be chaotic and full of entanglement hazards, but the organisms that encrust wrecks are beautifully colorful. Here a diver comes face-to-face with a trumpet fish near a jagged hole.

Shipwrecks become the substrata for reefs, and many ships are intentionally sunk to create these artificial reefs. External wreck diving presents opportunities to see a wide variety of marine life, such as these schoolmaster snappers loitering near a coral-encrusted rail.

glement, and low-visibility diving. The courses typically limit penetration dives to within 130 feet of the surface, including the penetration distance, and divers don't leave the "light zone" (areas lit by sunshine) during penetration dives. Diving on deeper wrecks or penetrating past the light zone involves technical-diving training that is similar in scope and intensity to cave-diving training.

Many ships are intentionally sunk in popular diving destinations to create artificial reefs, and diving on these well-known and prepared wrecks is a great way to start a career in wreck diving.

Rhode Island: Blue Sharks in Cold Water

Sharks are beautiful animals, and many consider the blue shark to be the most beautiful of all. They are deep-water pelagic sharks with distinctively slender bodies, winglike pectoral fins, and a sinewy swimming motion that gives them an almost serpentine appearance.

Remarkably little is known about the lives of North Atlantic blue sharks, but tagging programs have revealed that they migrate great distances. One tagged blue shark traveled nearly four thousand miles, and it is suspected that these great fish traverse the Atlantic Ocean following the Gulf Stream, migrate southward to Africa, cross the Atlantic again with the Equatorial Current to Venezuela, and return to the

The slender and graceful blue shark is almost serpentine in appearance and movement. Shark dives off the coasts of New England and San Diego, California, can bring you face-to-face with these magnificent no-mads of the sea from the safe refuge of shark cages. It's a great weekend trip. BARRY LIPMAN

New England coast each year—a distance of over ten thousand miles round-trip. Blue sharks are one of the great nomads of the sea.

It was recently discovered that these sharks congregate over the continental shelf off the coast of Rhode Island. Perhaps this is a staging area for the transatlantic cross-ing, or maybe a starting point toward Cape Hatteras to the south. Whatever the case, divers who venture out from Point Judith, Rhode Island, have a great opportunity to see these magnificent animals.

Point Judith shark diving involves the use of shark cages that float on the surface. The sharks are attracted to the boat through the use of chum, but they are not fed. This serves to keep the sharks in the area for a while. Divers usually have the freedom to interact with the sharks outside of the cage at their own discretion and risk. It is a perfect opportunity for New England and New York divers of every level to get out of town for a weekend of exciting diving.

New Jersey and New York: Wreck Valley

The waters of the New York Bight, more descriptively called Wreck Valley, off the coast of New Jersey and the south coast of Long Island have been a hub of maritime activity for three hundred years. Not surprisingly, the area is littered with shipwrecks, many of which are accessible to recreational scuba divers.

Wreck Valley diving conditions are diverse and range from benign, to very challenging with cold water and limited visibility. Local divers should research areas of interest and plan trips to sites compatible with their capabilities. The wrecks offer unique and tangible links to history, and many divers search for artifacts.

Many of the wrecks of Wreck Valley can be dived from shore, particularly off Monmouth County, New Jersey. An interesting site near Long Branch contains two ships that ran aground and sank on the same spot eighteen years apart. The German-built *Adonis* sank in 1859, and the steamship *Rusland* sank atop her in 1877. Known as the Dual Wrecks, the two wrecks lie in 25 feet of water, within reach of shore divers.

Monmouth County contains diving opportunities other than shipwrecks. The Allenhurst Jetties near Allenhurst, Manasquan Jetties near Manasquan, and Manasquan River Railroad Bridge near Manasquan are popular sites that offer consistently good conditions for diving and underwater hunting.

Wrecks of every description, depth, and diver accessibility litter the bottom of the ocean near the south coast of Long Island. The wreck of the luxurious *Andrea Doria*, the Italian liner that sank in 1956 as a result of her famous collision with the Swedish freighter *Stockholm*, is the pinnacle of Wreck Valley wrecks and is a benchmark dive for technical divers with her starboard side at a depth of 240 feet. However, while some of the wrecks are reserved for technical divers, many can be visited by more casual divers and many can be enjoyed without dangerous penetration into the wrecks.

Metropolitan New York divers have a virtually unlimited number of local dive sites, and the dive possibilities grow as divers attain the technical training and experience necessary to reach and explore the more difficult wrecks. Those who continue their technical training and experience to the point that they can safely dive the more challenging sites of Wreck Valley are among the most accomplished and versatile divers in the world.

Of all the stories of the lost ships of Wreck Valley, perhaps the most fascinating is the saga of the American freighter *Black Point* and the German U-boat *U-853*. The date was May 5, 1945, and World War II was finally at an end. Hitler was dead, and Admiral Dönitz had issued a personal order for all U-boats to cease hostilities. However, the crew of the *U-853* either did not get the word or decided not to heed it. They spied *Black Point* steaming from New York and sank her with a single torpedo.

The *U-853* was under attack from an American task force within an hour of the sinking of the *Black Point*. The cat-and-mouse battle went on until the following morning, when the *U-853* joined the *Black Point* in a watery grave.

The *Black Point*, the last victim of German U-boats in American waters, can now be visited by divers in 85 feet of water. The *U-853* is also accessible to adventurous recreational divers at a depth of 130 feet. Rumor has it that the *U-853* contains a treasure of jewels and mercury. Penetration into the submarine is possible for well-trained technical wreck divers, but the treasure has not been found. Do you feel lucky?

The Great Lakes

Shipwrecks Preserved in a Freshwater Sea

The Great Lakes form the "North Coast" of the continental United States. The lakes are connected to form a single drainage system, with Lake Superior, the westernmost lake, as its head. Lake Superior sits at an altitude of 600 feet above sea level, and water cascades from that starting point through the progressively lower elevations of Lake Michigan, Lake Huron, Lake Erie, and Lake Ontario. Drainage is completed as water flows from Lake Ontario down the St. Lawrence River and into the North Atlantic Ocean. These five enormous freshwater lakes have a combined shoreline of almost eight thousand miles, enclose a water area of over ninety-five thousand square miles, and form the largest group of lakes in the world.

The Great Lakes have historically been used for the transport of heavy commodities such as iron ore, lumber, coal, and grain, and extensive shipping in the fickle weather and waters of these lakes has produced thousands of shipwrecks. This fact alone should pique the interest of divers, but the shipwrecks of the Great Lakes have a twist: the cold, fresh, and relatively oxygen-poor waters have held wrecks throughout the ages in a remarkable state of preservation. Wooden ships that would deteriorate beyond recognition in just a few years in warm salt water may remain intact for well over a century in the Great Lakes, and wreck diving in this archaeological refrigerator is the call of Great Lakes diving.

How cold is the water? At depths of 100 feet or more, the water remains a fairly constant 39°F year-round. That's cold, brave hearts, but manageable with a good dry suit and proper underclothes.

Although exploring some of the lost ships in the Great Lakes requires deep and technical dives, many wrecks are in shallow water near shore. Great Lakes diving is readily available to large numbers of divers throughout the United States, as the states of New York, Pennsylvania, Ohio, Michigan, Indiana, Illinois, Wisconsin, and Minnesota have coastlines along the lakes. The Great Lakes offer an excellent weekend opportunity for divers of every skill and experience level from New England to the heartland to get out for some fascinating diving.

Because many excellent Great Lakes dive sites are most easily accessed from Canadian shores, drivers and divers from the United States might want to cross the border into Canada. It's important to remember to bring proof of citizenship, plus either receipts that establish the country of purchase for all the dive gear you bring or a customs form that itemizes all the gear you carry across the border. Of course,

The Great Lakes are a fabulous destination for divers of all levels, and the shipwrecks in the cold fresh water are remarkably preserved. The wooden side-wheel paddleboat Comet sank in 1861 near Kingston in Lake Ontario. The huge paddle wheels are still intact and rise dramatically from the bottom. TOM WILSON

no weapons can be transported across the border, and this includes spearguns and knives.

Like their fellow wreck divers in Wreck Valley, Great Lakes divers have a virtually unlimited number of dive sites. Plus, even more sites become accessible as divers gain the technical training and experience necessary to visit the deeper or more challenging wrecks. The preservation of ships in the cold Great Lakes waters offers unique opportunities to see wooden ships from the days of sail and paddle wheel. Visibility can be very good, and freshwater diving means less wear and tear on dive gear.

The stately Katie Eccles in Lake Ontario fulfills the romanticized vision of what a sunken ship should look like. Although she sank in 1922, the bowsprit and rigging on this wooden schooner remain intact and in place. TOM WILSON

Diving in the United States

Imagine diving in 90 feet of water with good visibility and coming across the remains of a wooden steamer that sank about a hundred and fifty years ago. If you're a saltwater diver, you might be satisfied to simply know that you have reached the spot where the ship sank, even if no recognizable remains could be seen. But in the Great Lakes, you would see the awe-inspiring spectacle of the giant side-wheels from this paddle wheeler, still intact and rising 25 feet from the bottom.

All you need is an appropriate exposure suit, a full tank of gas, and a dose of the adventurous spirit that got you involved with diving in the first place.

THE WEST COAST

Southern California: The Genesis of Popular American Recreational Scuba

The epicenter of recreational scuba in the United States sits squarely on the sunny shores of So Cal, and southern Californians have been making forays beneath the surface of the sea since the formation of the first recreational dive club, the Bottom Scratchers, in 1933. It was a fine place for the sport of diving to start, and the diving off the coast of southern California continues to be some of the best in the country.

Kelp beds are the signature dive environment of California diving. Kelp is a seaweed type of brown algae that grows to incredible lengths and lushness. These plants anchor themselves to the bottom through the use of rootlike holdfasts and float their stipes (stalks) and leaves with gas-filled sacs called pneumatocysts. They are the fastest-growing plants in the world and form kelp forest ecosystems of incredible beauty and fertility. Diving in the kelp forests is the Californian underwater equivalent of strolling through the redwoods.

San Diego County offers a variety of diving that includes kelp forests, rocky bottoms, and deep canyons. Diving from shore in the La Jolla Underwater Park is popular and consistently good, and the Del Mar area also offers good diving. Sea Cliff Park, known in the surfing community as Swamis, is another good shore-diving area, as is the San Elijo State Park. However, caution and local expertise are required to negotiate through the surf when entering and exiting the ocean at popular surfing areas.

San Diego also has the distinction of being one of the first areas to offer offshore shark diving from cages for recreational divers. Day trips to see magnificent blue and mako sharks are still available from the pioneers of this type of diving. More-adventurous shark divers from San Diego may also experience the ultimate in shark encounters. Trips to the Mexican island of Isla Guadalupe, which lies about two hundred miles southwest of San Diego, give divers an excellent chance to see large great white sharks from the protection of shark cages.

The Channel Islands off the coast of southern California offer some of the best

Spectacular forests of kelp and the animals that live within them are the signature diving environment for California divers. The fish are garibaldi, brilliant orange fish that are common kelp forest residents. BONNIE CARDONE

diving in the country. Catalina Island, situated only nineteen miles from San Pedro, is a popular destination that provides a diversity of excellent diving. San Clemente and San Nicolas are also popular choices.

The Channel Islands of Anacapa, Santa Cruz, Santa Rosa, and San Miguel west of Ventura, plus Santa Barbara to the south closer to Long Beach, were included in the Channel Islands National Marine Sanctuary in 1980 and collectively offer a variety of kelp beds, shipwrecks, caves and caverns, and even sea lions and harbor seals as diving companions for visiting divers. Twenty-seven different species of whales and dolphins visit or inhabit the waters around these islands each year, including humpback whales, sei whales, and the largest animal ever to inhabit the earth—the magnificent blue whale.

Northern California: America's Wild Coast

The nutrient-rich waters and wild shores of northern California have long been popular with adventurous divers, but improvements in wet-suit technology and the advent of affordable dry suits have opened this chilly area to more-casual divers. Like many of their counterparts to the south, northern California divers have the opportunity to dive from shore in several areas. Remember to arrive early to avoid the crowds, and bring plenty of quarters for parking when driving and diving from shore.

The rugged Big Sur coast offers some of the best visibility and diving in California. However, access to the water from the imposing shore is difficult. The California Department of Fish and Game has designated Yankee Point, a site about two miles south of Point Lobos, as the official delineation between southern California and northern California shores. The designation was made primarily in reference to laws regulating the taking of abalones, but it's as good a place to start as any. Most of the diving around Yankee Point and Point Lobos is accessible only by boat, but it features schools of fish, rocky pinnacles, the omnipresent kelp beds, and beautiful nudibranchs.

The Monterey Peninsula is the most popular northern California dive area. Extending from Del Monte Beach in Monterey Bay southward to Point Lobos at the southern end of Carmel Bay, the area is a cold-water shore diver's paradise, with colorful rocky reefs, hordes of fish, sea lions and harbor seals for company, and majestic kelp forests for scenery. Shore divers from areas with surf should use caution and local expertise for their entries and exits.

The Gulf of the Farallones, which includes the fascinating Farallon Islands, sits thirty miles west of the Golden Gate Bridge in San Francisco. The Gulf of the Farallones was designated as a national marine sanctuary in 1981, and the Farallon Islands (a group of seven islands) are a national wildlife refuge. The area is a resting and breeding ground for a wide variety of marine mammals and birds, and the Farallon Islands support the largest concentration of breeding seabirds in the continental United States. Adventurous divers will encounter large schools of fish, colorful urchins, wolf eels, and a great diversity of marine life. Great white sharks are known to cruise the area, and it may be possible to encounter them from the safety of a shark cage.

The Farallons form the westernmost corner of the so-called Red Triangle of great white shark activity that stretches from the Farallons in the west to Bodega Bay (seventy miles north of San Francisco on the mainland) in the north to Año Nuevo near Santa Cruz in the south. While great white sharks are normally cautious creatures that must be baited in to be observed, all California divers should be aware of their possible presence and be prepared to take appropriate action in the rare event that one of these great fish is unexpectedly sighted.

Much of the diving north of San Francisco along the Sonoma coast involves free diving for the red abalones that are common to the area. The coast is not easily accessible to divers in most places, but small coves such as Timber Cove and Stillwater Cove north of the Fort Ross State Historic Park can be dived from shore or small boats.

The Mendocino coast north of Sonoma likewise attracts many free-diving abalone hunters (abalone cannot be taken with the use of scuba). However, the northern section of the coast from Point Arena to Fort Bragg offers exceptional scuba-diving opportunities. Heavy seas, surf, and currents are common conditions best left to advanced divers with local experience, but well-protected diving can be enjoyed by divers of all levels at several sites near Mendocino—an area that includes the Van Damme State Park and Russian Gulch State Park.

The Pacific Northwest: The Domain of Soft Giants

Excellent U.S. Pacific Coast diving does not end with California. The cold, nutrient-rich waters off the coasts of Oregon and Washington State offer adventurous divers many great dive opportunities. Of course, nature pays no heed to state lines or other arbitrary delineations, and the diving conditions of the Pacific Northwest states are often similar to the conditions of northern California. However, as divers move northward, the water gets colder, the tides become stronger, and the kelp beds become seasonal (the beds shrink or may even disappear in the chill of winter, only to return each summer).

While much of the wildlife that can seen off these northern coasts is also present to some degree in California, the northern coast hosts an abundance of marine mammals such as dolphins, including the largest dolphin—the orca, or killer whale. Cold-water anemones such as the metridium anemone and the plumose anemone grow in great numbers and sizes. Wolf eels, with their Muppet-like faces, are common residents. But perhaps the most intriguing animal of the Pacific Northwest is *Octopus dofleini*—the giant Pacific octopus.

Octopuses are fundamentally different from us. They are mollusks—related to clams and snails. They have a complex brain and are capable of learning and solving problems. They use their wonderful ability to change color and shape for purposes ranging from camouflage to apparent expressions of emotion. Instead of the red, iron-based blood with which we are familiar, octopuses have copper-based blood that is a pale blue-green in color. They are truly alien creatures. Most species of octopus live for only two years and reach a maximum size of 2 or 3 feet.

The giant Pacific octopus typically grows to a maximum size of over 15 feet from arm tip to arm tip and may weigh in excess of 100 pounds. It typically lives somewhat longer than other species—four years for males and a slightly shorter time for females. It is certainly worth a plunge into cold Pacific Northwest waters to meet an alien being of these dimensions.

With the large metropolitan areas of Tacoma and Seattle bordering its twenty-seven hundred miles of shoreline, Puget Sound is the center of most Pacific Northwest diving. This inland sea is protected from the heavy seas of the Pacific Ocean and offers divers of every level of training and experience a great variety of dive sites.

One of the most popular Puget Sound dive sites is the Edmonds Wreck, located in the Edmonds Underwater Park north of Seattle. The wrecks (there are several) are divable from shore and host large fish, beautiful plumose anemones, and colorful nudibranchs.

The San Juan Islands lie seaward of the northern boundary of Puget Sound. This cluster of islands ranges from small rocks that are awash at high tide to the 57-square-mile Orcas Island—the largest in the chain. Friday Harbor on San Juan Island is the largest town and is an attraction for travelers and tourists. James Island, Davidson Rock near Lopez Island, Kellet Bluff on Henry Island, and Clements Reef near Sucia Island are popular choices for cold-water divers.

INLAND USA: A PLACE NEAR YOU

Wherever you live, there is some kind of diving within a day's drive. It could be a quarry or flooded mine; it could be a river or lake. It could be the Belmont Hot Springs in Utah or Lake Champlain in Vermont. It may be a celebrated destination like the flooded Bonne Terre mine in Missouri—an hour's drive from St. Louis. It could be the unique opportunity to explore a flooded missile silo near Midland, Texas, or maybe just a secret "honey" fishing hole in a nearby lake.

Your local dive shop is a good place to begin your inquiries about diving near you. The Internet is a wonderful tool to browse dive sites and operators in areas near and far. In fact, no matter what your secret dive fantasy might be, you will probably find a suitable operator on the Internet to fulfill that fantasy. And you know what? You should. You really should.

CHAPTER 14

INTERNATIONAL DIVE TRAVEL

NO MATTER HOW GOOD or convenient the local diving may be, sooner or later wanderlust sets in. Sometimes it happens at the very beginning of a diving career, with divers traveling to exotic destinations for their open-water training (checkout) dives, and other times it does not happen until a veteran diver finally feels that a change of scenery would be nice or that the time has come to travel to a celebrated destination just to see what all the fuss is about.

Visions of paradise fill the heads of divers smitten with the travel bug. Sugar-white beaches, transparent water teeming with life, the adventure of a lifetime—it's all out there waiting to be enjoyed.

And so it is. Exotic locations once accessible only to research vessels and die-hard adventurers are now open to more-casual travelers. However, just as mothers like the idea of their children growing up to be president but balk at the idea of them growing up to be politicians, many traveling divers focus entirely on the bliss of being at a fantastic dive site or live-aboard boat without adequately considering the practical travails of getting there.

Dive resorts are typically comfortable, casual places that often have good diving right at your doorstep. Some divers balk at diving a site more than once, but I enjoy staying in resorts with a shore dive that I can dive every day. It's a good way to observe the residents of the reef over a period of time.

Getting There

Based on personal experiences and the suggestions of veteran travelers and industry professionals, here are some tips to make your dive travel planning more productive.

Get Firsthand Information

Realistic expectations are of primary importance to the enjoyment of any dive trip. After you've narrowed your destination choices to a few places that seem to fit your budget and interests, gather as much objective, firsthand information about them as you can. Talk to members of your dive club or local diving community who have recently visited your planned destinations.

Once you select a location, learn as much about it as you can. There is more to a dive destination than what lies beneath the water's surface. Each island or area has its own unique culture, history, and ambience. The more you know, the more you will be able to enjoy.

Use a Dive Travel Specialist

Once you've become as familiar as you can with your destination, it's time to call the person who is your best friend when it comes to traveling to international dive destinations—your dive travel specialist.

Dive travel specialists are travel wholesalers dedicated to international dive travel. While you may be able to book your own trip, including airfare, from your home PC, most casual travelers do not have the expertise to avoid the subtle pitfalls of international travel to remote destinations. In addition to knowing the ins and outs of such trips, a good dive travel specialist will be able to provide up-to-date information about wherever you want to go. Chances are good that your agent has been to the destination you have in mind and will be glad to tell you all about it. There may be many dive operators available at your chosen destination, but only a few may be reliable or able to meet your specific needs.

Ask about every detail that is important to you regarding your chosen destination when you talk to your dive travel specialist. Quantity and quality of diving? Nightlife? Peace and quiet? Food and accommodations? Dive-boat and shop operations? Shore diving available? Nitrox available? Rental gear available? Follow the leader required? Seasonality of wildlife? Regularly scheduled night dives? Film processing available?

Take nothing for granted. Resort or live-aboard advertisements may pique your interest, but they will not provide you with enough information to plan a trip properly. Your dive travel specialist represents an entire area rather than a single resort. Let him or her help you. Your dive travel specialist knows the best routes and airfares and can also offer a wide selection of dive and accommodation packages from reputable operators. He or she can tailor a trip to meet your specific budget and dive preferences.

In addition to arranging your dive travel, your agent can also actually improve the service you receive once you have arrived at your destination. Dive travel specialists carry significant clout with operators, and you can benefit from that clout not only by receiving courteous service but also by gaining leverage in dealing with any problems that may arise.

Understand Trade-Offs

We all want to experience the best diving possible. However, it's important to realize that the best diving is seldom located next to the airport or resort. It may be inconvenient to reach, and it may be far away.

If a convenient and carefree getaway is what you're after, be prepared to make a trade-off in diving quality. This doesn't mean that the diving will be bad, just that it may not be the "best." Only you can decide what is most important to you.

Live-aboard boats often have the advantage in providing the ultimate in diving. While land-based operations may offer amenities that live-aboards cannot rival, land-

Live-aboard dive boats can cover large areas and reach remote sites that are inaccessible to land-based operators. While accommodations might not be as plush as some dive resorts, conditions are not exactly primitive.

based dive operators have a certain time and distance radius within which they must operate. Live-aboards offer the luxury of moving hundreds of miles to reach a prime diving location.

Get a Passport

Some international destinations advertise that U.S. citizens do not need passports to enter their countries. Although combinations of various documents such as birth certificates, driver's licenses, or voter's registration cards may be accepted, these documents always seem to cause problems. A passport is easy and inexpensive to get, is easy to carry, and will raise no questions when presented. Get one.

In addition to carrying a passport, you should check with your dive travel specialist about additional documentation such as a visa that may be required. Unless you plan to stay for an extended time or earn money during your stay, a passport is usually all you'll need.

Consider Travel Insurance

If the cost of a trip approaches twice the cost of a mortgage payment, you should consider travel insurance. Policies vary, but most cover medical problems or acts of God that cancel or interrupt travel. However, some policies do not cover weather that ruins the diving or medical conditions that keep you out of the water while not prohibiting travel.

Talking about insurance is not nearly as much fun as talking about diving, but it's important that you fully understand any policy before you buy. Have your dive travel specialist explain every detail of the available policies, including cancellation or interruption scenarios, baggage insurance in excess of airline policies, and purchase of tickets at airline counters in order to catch up with your itinerary in the event of missed or canceled flights.

Try to Avoid the Major U.S. Gateways

Miami and Houston are the two largest gateways to most Caribbean travel, as is Los Angeles for most Pacific departures. These are large, confusing airports, and going through customs at any of them can be hectic, as there are travelers arriving from all over the world. While you cannot avoid these gateways in many cases, check into the possibility of alternative routes with your dive travel specialist.

For example, Cayman Airways has a gate in Tampa as well as in Miami and Houston. Traveling to Cayman via Tampa is a breeze compared to getting there through Miami or Houston. Likewise, flights departing and returning to San Francisco or Seattle may offer a more relaxed alternative than Los Angeles.

If you must go through a major gateway when leaving or returning to the United States, make sure to schedule plenty of time for connections.

Know Your Air Provider

Some small and locally or government-owned airlines are notorious for late or canceled service. "Island time" may be quaint if you are sitting on a picturesque beach waiting for a boat, but there's nothing quaint about missing days of a dive vacation due to airline problems. Dive travel specialists can be a tremendous help with this problem, as they are up to date on trouble trends among the air providers.

If a suspect air provider is the only available transportation to your chosen destination, plan carefully for the contingency of late service or lost luggage. As a rule, reliability decreases in proportion to the remoteness of the destination.

Get Your Gear in Order

Even if you have been diving recently, thoroughly check out the equipment you plan to take on your trip. Replace any straps that are the least bit questionable. Replace computer batteries. Repetitive diving over an extended period of time is an extraordinary strain on gear, and your computer will probably remain on for your entire stay.

If you haven't been diving in a while, make a few dives in a pool or local dive site or schedule a refresher class at your local dive shop. Make sure your gear as well as your diving skills and general fitness are ready before you leave home. A remote destination or live-aboard boat is no place to discover that any item of gear needs repair or replacement.

Pack Smart

Dedicated dive resorts are generally warm, casual places. Shorts and T-shirts are de rigueur at most. A few bathing suits, shorts, and T-shirts will usually be sufficient for a week.

Winter travelers should check with their dive travel specialists about the possible need for a sweater or jacket. Pack as few clothes as possible—the luggage space you save will come in handy when packing dive gear.

U.S. airports underwent a fundamental change at the beginning of 2003. The recently created Transportation Security Agency (TSA) took control of security, which put federal employees in charge. Despite the misgivings of the traveling public, the transition has been a smooth one. In fact, TSA security agents have actually made life a bit easier in some airports. They're well paid, well trained, motivated, and courteous. They're also very thorough.

TSA personnel have the right to open any checked bag and examine it as they deem necessary, and this inspection may occur out of the presence of the owner. Any locks on checked luggage may be cut off in this process. Dive gear is likely to arouse the suspicions of TSA agents, resulting in the inspection of your checked dive gear. This presents a minor dilemma: If you can't lock your luggage, how can you protect your valuable dive gear from possible theft once the TSA people have completed their inspection? As an independent diver, you should carry a large supply of plastic ties when you fly. They must be cut to be removed, so they discourage pilfering, but they can be easily removed by TSA inspectors. If your checked luggage is inspected by TSA agents, they will put a notice in the bag that will include a customer service number you can call in the unlikely event that anything is amiss when you retrieve your bag, and they will also place a seal over the luggage that should remain unbroken during transit.

Pack personal items such as toiletries, hairbrushes, and toothbrushes in a clear plastic bag so the agents can inspect them without handling them.

If you, like many traveling divers, like to photograph your trip, be aware that the powerful X-rays used by the TSA will damage all film packed in checked bags.

Check excess-baggage requirements and charges before you pack. Many airlines charge for extra baggage based on the number of bags rather than their weight. Others charge based on the number and physical dimensions of bags. Knowing all the requirements for the different carriers will help you decide what luggage to take. Dive travel specialists have the latest information on extra baggage for all carriers they use. Remember that many small airlines that service more-remote destinations may have rigid baggage limits and may not allow carry-on luggage due to the limited space in the cabin.

Maximize Carry-On Items

The only way to guarantee that personal or delicate items will arrive at your final destination on time and intact is to carry them with you on the plane. If possible, you should carry on your camera equipment, masks, regulators, and computers.

A good way to maximize your carry-on capability is to invest in a photographer's vest with as many pockets as possible. These vests have large pockets on the inside as well as on the outside, and many also have a knapsack compartment in the back that can carry an amazing amount of stuff. The clothes you wear do not count as carry-on items. Although you can carry anything you want in your vest, remember that it will be X-rayed, and inspectors unfamiliar with dive gear may be suspicious of any dive gear in your pockets. You can carry your personal scuba gear and camera equipment in a normal carry-on bag. This equipment will alert TSA personnel when it is X-rayed at the passenger security gate, and they will search the carry-on bag. This is usually a quick and painless procedure and is nothing to fret about.

Since many traveling divers carry photographic film to document their trips, it is important to know that TSA regulations require a hand inspection of film (in place of an X-ray inspection) upon a passenger's request. While the X-ray machine used at the passenger security gate is not nearly as powerful or as damaging to film as the one used for checked luggage, the cumulative effect of several X-rays may still damage film. Remove all rolls of film from their boxes and plastic canisters and carry them in a clear plastic bag to expedite the hand inspection. If a TSA agent is reluctant to hand inspect the film or says that only high-speed films require a hand inspection, cite TSA regulation 1544.211e4. This regulation clearly states that a hand inspection of any photographic film shall be provided upon request.

The use of a photographer's vest in addition to your carry-on luggage may not look altogether fashionable, and you may sacrifice a bit of comfort, but you will stay in control of the things that are most important to your enjoyment of your trip. Unless your flight is completely booked, you will be able to stow your vest in an overhead compartment once you are aboard the plane.

Arrive Early

When leaving the United States, arrive at the airport two and a half hours before boarding time. Go immediately to the appropriate airline counter inside the airport and check your luggage. Expert opinion varies as to whether you should check your luggage through to your final destination if your flight plans call for a change of airlines at a connection stop. Some advise claiming and rechecking luggage at international connection stops involving a change of airlines to reduce the chances of it being lost or stolen. However, I personally check all bags through to the final destination.

When leaving your dive destination to return to the United States, arrive at the airport at least three hours before boarding time. If the check-in counter is not yet open, wait there until it does. Often only one or two flights leave these places daily, and the combination of a crowd of travelers and the lack of technical sophistication at the airport can create quite a mess. Get your bags checked before the mob arrives. If you get bored waiting in the lounge afterward, spending a short time watching an endless line of irritable people kicking their luggage an inch at a time toward a chaotic counter will make you feel better.

It is also important to reconfirm your departure flight two days before you are scheduled to leave. This will give you some time to make alternate arrangements if problems arise.

If you're staying on a live-aboard dive boat, generally the staff will collect your tickets when you arrive and confirm outgoing flights during the cruise. However, since land-based dive operators have visitors arriving and departing every day, they are not often able to offer this service, and it will be up to you to confirm your departure flight. Confirmation of your departure will make for a smoother and more pleasant transition back to "reality."

Schedule Plenty of Time for Connections

Do not attempt to hurry your journey to your final destination by shortchanging connection stops. In addition to allowing for late arrivals, the stops are a good time for you to stretch and relax.

Outside of comfort considerations, each airline requires a certain minimum time frame for international connections, which ranges from an hour and a half to two hours. Airlines cannot be held responsible for connection snafus unless the minimum time frame has been met.

Even if you have checked your luggage through to your final destination, take the time to go to the baggage claim at every stop. If your luggage is mistakenly loaded into the baggage claim, you can rescue and recheck it. By locating your lost luggage at stops, you can accomplish in ten minutes what may take days for the airlines to do.

Survive Customs

Going through customs, especially in a foreign country, is the one time that you want to be "one of the crowd." Prepare all necessary immigration papers before you leave the plane, and get in the middle of the group heading for customs. The object here is to be casually invisible in order to avoid the inconvenience of a close inspection.

Customs in some small countries can seem pointlessly tedious. Customs buildings are often not air-conditioned and are consequently hot and stuffy. Some customs officers can seem overly officious, with stern looks and rubber stamps that they pound emphatically on cryptic forms for every contingency. Be patient. Be respectful. Be happy. Smell the salt air.

Some customs operations select travelers for close inspection by a lottery system. A light flashes from green to red at random intervals, and whoever is next in line is welcomed "up close and personal."

In the event you or your bags are singled out for a close inspection, maintain your good cheer. Expect to open anything and everything in your luggage that can be opened. All medications you are carrying must be in their original prescription bottles in your name, and even nonprescription items such as aspirin must be in the original bottles. With your cooperation, even a close inspection is usually performed quickly and is no cause for undue alarm.

Dedicate Travel Days to Traveling

Most of us are like starving people at a gourmet buffet when we finalize plans for a long-anticipated dive vacation. The time seems short, and there is so much to see and do. The temptation to overschedule yourself is hard to resist.

Rising early, driving to the airport, unloading luggage and parking the car, standing in lines with dive gear and luggage, watching soap operas in airport waiting areas, breathing stale airplane air, enduring two-hour layovers and luggage inspections, eating airport hot dogs, inhaling more stale airplane air while cramped in that tiny seat, claiming luggage and dive gear, going through customs in a non-air-conditioned building, recollecting luggage and dive gear and carrying it out into the blazing heat, hailing a cab or bus, driving in a non-air-conditioned vehicle to the hotel, lugging the luggage and dive gear into the hotel, checking in and carrying the stuff to the room — it all makes for a pretty full day.

Did you really mean to schedule yourself for the boat that leaves in ten minutes? Do you really want to skip supper to make the night dive on the other side of the island?

Reserve a full day for getting there. If you feel like making a shore dive or catching a boat after your arrival, go ahead, by all means. But if you don't, be comfortable in the knowledge that you still have an excellent chance of being blissfully dived-out by midweek.

Stay Healthy

In addition to checking with your dive travel specialist about health hazards or the need for unusual precautions at your chosen destination, be aware of the health hazards of traveling. The close quarters, stale air, and ultralow humidity on airplanes make them a perfect place to catch a cold, which could seriously impair your diving.

Keep your resistance as high as possible. Being overtired and indulging in alcoholic beverages can dramatically increase your chance of succumbing to illness.

Be cautious with your health as long as you are away from home. In addition to carrying dive insurance in case of an accident or injury, be aware of everything that you do and eat. Some traveling divers take a dose of Pepto-Bismol or its equivalent daily to ward off gastrointestinal problems caused by unusual foods. Drink bottled water, and plenty of it. Get your rest and refrain from overindulging.

Some tropical beaches are famous for their serenity and notorious for their sand flies, gnats, and no-see-ums, which can truly be a bother. Pack and use a good insect repellent on your feet, ankles, and legs.

Travel with a Spirit of Adventure

So now your plans for the perfect international dive vacation have been finalized. You are confident that you have chosen a destination that will fulfill your every diving fantasy, and with the help of your dive travel specialist, you can predict where you will be and what you will be doing every moment you will be away from home.

Now is a good time to sit back, relax, and wonder exactly what part of your trip will go wrong.

Dive travel to remote or exotic locations is a grand adventure, and true adventure cannot be precisely predicted. Should your journey through small countries and different cultures go a bit awry, keep your eyes and mind open and your sense of humor intact. Accept every detour as an opportunity for discovery.

In addition to problems that may arise during travel, no activity as dependent on weather and equipment as scuba diving can be taken for granted. Weather happens. Equipment fails. Dives are compromised. Of course, no one wants these things to happen, but it helps to know that they do and that sooner or later they will.

If you find yourself beached for a day due to weather or equipment problems, take the time to explore your surroundings. Talk to the locals. Visit their museums. Learn about their history and culture. Your imagination will be inflamed by the stories they tell.

WHERE TO GO

The world is one vast ocean interspersed with land-based diving opportunities, and traveling divers can find diving almost anywhere they go. However, several areas of the world that are blessed with great diving have realized that dive tourism is an industry that works to the benefit of all. Local economies receive substantial income from traveling recreational divers, the divers enjoy a solid diving infrastructure of accommodations and dive operators, and the ocean itself benefits because dive tourism is a way to make conservation of natural resources pay. Of course, it would be impossible to review every great dive location in the world, but we can take a very brief look at some of the most established and celebrated areas in the world for traveling recreational divers.

Grab a globe and follow along; we're going around the world in the rest of this chapter. The Internet is full of information about all of the dive sites reviewed below, and you can find more details about any of these sites by searching online.

The Bahamas

The closest international diving to the eastern United States is in the Bahamas. Comprising some seven hundred low-lying islands and cays (pronounced *keys*), the Bahamas cover more than a hundred thousand square miles of the Atlantic Ocean between the southeastern tip of Florida and the southeastern tip of Cuba. The Bahamas are an independent country and a member of the British Commonwealth of Nations.

Diving in the Bahamas begins very near the eastern coast of Florida. The Bahama Banks is a shallow area that attracts pods of spotted dolphins, and dolphin dives on the Banks are available from Florida operators. The most-visited islands are Grand Bahama and New Providence—the island with the capital city of Nassau. The island of

Bimini is the closest to the United States and can be reached in thirty minutes by small planes from Florida. All three of these islands offer extensive recreational-diving infrastructures.

Other Bahamas islands that offer substantial recreational-diving infrastructures are Abaco (Walker's Cay), Andros, Cat Island, and San Salvador—the island generally believed to be Columbus's first landfall on his first voyage to the New World. The islands that are not populated or developed also have good diving, and all are accessible by live-aboard dive boats that depart from Florida or the developed Bahamas islands.

Sharpnose puffers are small beauties commonly found on Bahamian reefs. Look for them close to the bottom near large stands of coral.

As you might imagine based on the large area, diving in the Bahamas is varied. The Bahamas are known for shark-feeding dives, dolphin dives on the shallow banks, deep and shallow wrecks, reef diving, and wall diving.

The Bahamas also contain many geologic aberrations called blue holes, which are remnants of large caves from the Ice Age. As the sea level rose at the end of the last Ice Age, about ten thousand years ago, these caves filled with water, which caused their ceilings to collapse. The results are round, deep holes in the otherwise shallow seabed. They are an unusual and popular attraction for visiting divers.

The Caribbean

International dive travel means travel to the Caribbean Sea for many U.S. residents—the result of the close proximity of the islands to the U.S. mainland, the excellence of the diving, and the extensive advertising done by many Caribbean dive operators in U.S. dive magazines. The islands of the Caribbean are truly a diver's paradise, with warm, clear water and a mind-boggling display of undersea life. However, the Caribbean islands are not a homogeneous group, and each area offers its own particular brand of delights, diving, and culture.

The British Crown Colony of the Turks and Caicos Islands lies slightly east of the southernmost Bahamas. The largest and most developed island is Providenciales, commonly referred to as Provo. Dive operators, dive sites, and beautiful beaches abound, but the best diving from Provo is an hour's boat ride to the more remote sites off South and West Caicos.

Another island in the Turks and Caicos that is popular with visiting divers is Grand Turk, which features a funky, laid-back atmosphere and a great wall right offshore.

The Mexican island of Cozumel near the Yucatán Peninsula is one of the most popular and cost-effective Caribbean destinations. Travel time from Houston is short, and dive operators to match every level of diver experience abound. Cozumel means drift diving on the powerful Yucatán Current, and the water is some of the clearest in the Caribbean. Visitors will find spectacular walls teeming with life, wild currents, wild nightlife, and Mayan culture on this diver's island.

The British Crown Colony of the Cayman Islands was one of the first Caribbean destinations to recognize its beautiful underwater walls and reefs as a tourist attraction. The Caymans comprise three islands between Jamaica and the Yucatán Peninsula: Grand Cayman, Cayman Brac, and Little Cayman.

The island of Grand Cayman has been a diver magnet for more than twenty years, and it offers a combination of Caribbean diving and cosmopolitan sophistication that continues to draw traveling divers from around the world. The flight from Miami, Florida, is less than one hour.

Little Cayman and Cayman Brac offer a more laid-back dive trip to some of the best and most pristine diving in the Caribbean. They are more difficult to reach, which is possibly why the diving is so consistently good.

Cayman Islands diving includes shallow reefs and imposing walls that plunge thousands of feet into one of the deepest trenches in the Caribbean. Diving with stingrays at "Stingray City" on Grand Cayman and exploring a variety of wrecks round out the diving experience, and all sites are full of life.

Belize is an independent country and a member of the British Commonwealth of Nations. Its offshore cays are popular dive destinations, because the second-largest barrier reef in the world is a short boat ride away.

The largest and most developed Belize cay, Ambergris Cay, offers cost-effective Caribbean diving in a spectacular

The colorful tesselated blenny typically lives in empty barnacle shells in shallow water and may be found throughout the Caribbean. This one looks like a tank commander peering out from its barnacle shell house.

area. However, the cays farther offshore, such as Glover's Atoll, Lighthouse Reef, and Turneffe Island, are more remote and feature even more spectacular diving for the especially adventurous traveler.

The Honduras Bay Islands south of Belize are another popular and economical destination for Caribbean diving. The best diving infrastructure exists on the islands of Roatán, Utila, and Cayos Cochinos. Hurricane Mitch destroyed much of the development on the island of Guanaja, but repairs are being made. Honduras Bay Islands diving features a wide variety of small critters off Cayos Cochinos and great wall diving off the other islands. Utila is gaining a reputation for spectacular whale shark encounters. Good shore diving that includes a shipwreck and a sunken airplane in a protected cove is available from two resorts on Roatán, and dolphin diving with trained bottlenosed dolphins in open water is also available.

The Netherlands Antilles in the southern Caribbean near Venezuela include the islands of Bonaire and Curaçao. The islands are often combined with their independent sister, Aruba, and are collectively called the ABC islands. All three islands are autonomous parts of the Netherlands.

While the tourist industry is important to all three of the ABCs, the islands of Bonaire and Curaçao have the best diving. They are mountainous, arid islands with little freshwater runoff, and cacti replace palm trees for scenery. The reef lies very close to shore on both islands, and the islands are famous for the excellence of their diving from shore. Although the islands are not as close to the U.S. mainland as many other destinations, the availability of shore diving twenty-four hours a day gives Bonaire and Curaçao great value for visiting divers. The small, uninhabited island of Klein Bonaire offers many more convenient and excellent dive sites for boat divers from Bonaire. The small island of Klein Curaçao is privately owned, but some Curaçao operators have permission to dive there.

The reefs of Bonaire have been protected by the Bonaire Marine Park since 1979, and Curaçao reefs are also protected by the Curaçao Underwater Park. Automobile license plates on Bonaire contain the slogan Diver's Paradise—a difficult claim to refute. Even a sleepwalker will eventually stumble into the sea and find a good dive site on Bonaire or Curaçao.

The independent country of St. Vincent in the Grenadines (Windward Islands) is a part of the British Commonwealth of Nations. St. Vincent is not promoted as heavily as many other Caribbean destinations, but the diving is excellent and offers a wide variety of unusual undersea life. Another independent island country in the Windward Islands is Dominica, which is known for good diving and ecotourism in its lush rain forest.

Moving northward through the Leeward Islands, Caribbean travelers will find good diving and beaches in the British and U.S. Virgin Islands, Puerto Rico, and the Dominican Republic, although these destinations are not as dedicated to scuba diving as the other Caribbean islands mentioned.

The Northern Pacific Ocean

The Pacific Ocean hosts a wider diversity of marine life than does the Atlantic or Caribbean, and northern Pacific destinations include some of the most celebrated diving in the world. Pacific destinations might actually be easier to reach than the Caribbean for divers departing from the West Coast of the United States.

The international North Pacific Ocean diving most convenient to the mainland United States is found off the western shores of Mexico. Cabo San Lucas on the tip of the Baja peninsula is a popular choice, and live-aboard boats that ply the Sea of Cortés or the waters off the island of Socorro offer adrenaline-pumping encounters with large animals such as manta rays and sharks.

Costa Rica lies farther south, on the Pacific coast of Central America. Costa Rica is another popular and easily accessible destination for the traveling Pacific diver, and good diving as well as fascinating ecotourism are available from the mainland. Bat Island is a day trip from shore and offers challenging and big-animal experiences. But for the ultimate in encounters with awe-inspiring creatures of the Pacific deep, Cocos Island is the place to go. The island is three hundred miles south of the Costa Rican coast and is accessible only by live-aboard boat. It offers some of the most thrilling diving in the world.

Farther south still lies the country of Ecuador and its crown-jewel ecosystem—the Galápagos Islands. The Galápagos Islands lie very close to the equator and are accessible only by live-aboard boat. Few students of natural history are unaware of this unique ecosystem. Traveling Pacific divers can walk in the footsteps of Darwin and enjoy fabulous diving with a wide diversity of life near these fabled islands.

Of course, the fiftieth state of the United States sits right in the middle of the Pacific Ocean. Most visitors to the Hawaiian Islands go for more than the scuba diving, but there is interesting diving in Hawaiian waters. The islands of Hawaii are volcanic mountains, and lava flows and tubes are a common bottom composition. Several interesting species of fish are endemic only to the Hawaiian Islands, and sea turtles are common sights.

Unfortunately, the best Hawaiian diving is not off the island of Oahu (Honolulu), due to the heavy development there. Better destinations for the traveling diver are the islands of Kauai and the Big Island of Hawaii, and good diving is also off Maui and Molokai.

The Marshall Islands lie south of Hawaii near the equator. The island of most interest is Bikini Atoll—the site of nuclear tests in the 1940s and 1950s. Many World War II ships were sunk during those tests, including the valiant U.S. aircraft carrier *Saratoga* and Japanese admiral Isoroku Yamamoto's flagship, *Nagato*. The island was off-limits to visitors for many years, and food grown on the island is still unfit for consumption due to radiation from the nuclear tests, but divers can now travel to this unique site and visit the many ships that were sunk during the tests. These are the only

Hawksbill turtles are welcome sights to tropical divers throughout the world. While all marine turtles are endangered and protected, the spectacular shell of the hawksbill has put additional pressure on this handsome animal.

ships ever sunk by nuclear blast, and it is a somber but thrilling adventure to see them. Divers can enter the bridge of the *Nagato* and almost hear the fateful "Tora, Tora, Tora" message that informed Yamamoto that the attack on Pearl Harbor had been successful.

The Federated States of Micronesia are part of the Caroline Islands, lie west of the Marshall Islands, have a Compact of Free Association with the United States, and include the island states of Yap, Chuuk (formerly called Truk), Pohnpei, and Kosrae. All of the states of Micronesia offer world-class diving, but the lagoons of Chuuk and Yap have achieved special status.

The lagoon at Chuuk, still usually referred to as Truk Lagoon, was the site of the Japanese fleet that was bombed during the American Operation Hailstorm in February 1944. More than fifty Japanese ships went to the bottom, and there they remain to this day. The wreck diving in Chuuk Lagoon is considered to be the benchmark for historical wreck diving in the world.

The lagoon at Yap has achieved fame for an entirely different reason. Large manta rays regularly converge in the lagoon, and Yap is considered to have the most consistent close-up sightings of these huge and magnificent creatures in the world. You may remember Yap from your high school world geography class—it's the place where limestone money weighing over a ton was once used. They don't use it anymore, but it wouldn't hurt to bring exact change if you go (just kidding).

Palau is the westernmost cluster of islands of the Caroline Islands, and it is an independent nation with a Compact of Free Association with the United States. The mushroom-shaped "rock islands" of Palau are a natural wonder, and the diversity of marine life is as dramatic as anywhere on earth. The abundance of life due to the convergence of currents at a site called Blue Corner is considered to be one of the most thrilling underwater sights in the world.

The South Pacific Ocean

The islands of the South Pacific include some of the most romantic and fabled names in modern history and literature. There's some dynamite diving down there, too.

French Polynesia in the Society Islands is the romantic prototype for the South Pacific and includes the islands of Tahiti, Bora-Bora, Moorea, and Rangiroa. These French-speaking islands are attractions for tourists from all over the world and include pricey resort hotels. The diving in the area is very good despite the vigorous tourist trade, with lots of reef shark activity and undisturbed reefs.

Equally steeped in romantic history but with, perhaps, better diving is the independent island nation of Fiji. Some of the most celebrated diving in the world is south of the main Fijian island of Viti Levu in a lagoon formed by the crater of an extinct volcano at the island of Beqa. The diving off Taveuni to the north is world-class as well. The people are friendly, the soft corals are legendary, the kava (local drink) is delicious, and even male visitors can return home in a skirt (the sulu is a sarong-type skirt worn by men and women in Fiji).

Reef sharks, such as the blacktip reef shark, are commonly seen residents of South Pacific reefs.

The island continent of Australia lies westward from Fiji in the South Pacific, and all divers are aware that the northeastern corner of Australia is protected by the Great Barrier Reef—commonly referred to as GBR by traveling divers. It is the largest barrier reef in the world and one of the few structures made by living creatures on earth that is visible from space.

The city of Cairns is the starting point for most GBR diving, and overnight boats visit established sites such as Cod Hole—the home of huge but friendly groupers known as "potato cods." Townsville, a city south of Cairns, is the launching point for trips to the wreck of the *Yongala*, considered by some to be the most fish-covered and beautiful shipwreck in the world.

Australia offers more than the pretty reef diving in the northern part of the country. Divers traveling to the town of Adelaide in South Australia may embark on one of the ultimate underwater adventures—diving with the fearsome great white shark from the protection of cages at North Neptune Islands, South Neptune Islands, and the famous Dangerous Reef. Travelers to Exmouth in Western Australia have a great opportunity to see whale sharks during the coral spawning season around Ningaloo Reef.

Great diving also exists north of the Great Barrier Reef in the Coral Sea. Live-aboard boats departing from Cairns can get you there.

Some of the finest diving in the world exists north of the Coral Sea in the independent country of Papua New Guinea, commonly referred to as PNG. Located on the eastern half of the island of New Guinea, this is a country steeped in legends of cannibals and headhunters, and it retains a fascinating diversity of culture. Much of the diving done in PNG waters is by live-aboard boat, and the diving is considered by all who have experienced it to be some of the world's best for its diversity and consistent quality.

The Indian Ocean and Red Sea

The world's largest island archipelago, Indonesia, lies to the northwest of Australia in the Indian Ocean. Indonesia as a whole achieved independence from the Netherlands in 1949, but some islands have recently become independent states. Sections of Indonesia are recognized as world-class adventure-diving destinations.

The most eastern part of Indonesia starts at the western half of the island of New Guinea in West Papua, more commonly called Irian Jaya. Irian Jaya has been in a struggle for independence from Indonesia, but this struggle does not affect the quality of the diving from its shores. Irian Jaya diving off the city of Sorong in the Raja Empat islands is considered to be some of the wildest and least explored world-class diving on earth—a true diving frontier for adventurous travelers.

The island of Bali offers excellent diving and is a gateway to the more remote Indonesian islands.

Sulawesi (formerly known as Celebes) also offers some of the best diving on the planet. Sulawesi is an island in the northern part of the Indonesian archipelago east of Borneo, and the resort of Wakatobi in South Sulawesi makes a strong argument for having the world's best beach dive. The site is famous for the color and diversity of its undersea life and offers the opportunity to see the rare and tiny pygmy sea horse right off the beach. Northern Sulawesi sites include the Lembeh Straits—the dive area considered to be the best "muck diving" in the world, where weird and wondrous animals such as the mimic octopus may be encountered.

Malaysia, to the north of Indonesia, hosts several fabulous diving areas that include the island of Sipadan—the home of some of the best beach diving in the world and an astounding population of sea turtles.

Farther north up the Malay Peninsula sits the resort town of Phuket, Thailand. Phuket offers traveling divers a posh base and the seasonal (March through May) opportunity to see magnificent whale sharks.

In the middle of the Indian Ocean southwest of the southern tip of India lies the island republic of the Maldives—twelve hundred low-lying coral islands grouped into twenty-six major atolls. About two hundred of the islands are inhabited, and many provide dive infrastructures, but diving in the Maldives is also often done by live-aboard dive boats. Big fish and large concentrations of fish are the calling cards of the Maldives.

The independent country of Seychelles, which comprises about a hundred and

Mantas may reach sizes of 20 feet from "wing tip" to "wing tip" (the "wings" are actually enlarged pectoral fins). These magnificent fish may be encountered throughout the world's tropical oceans.

fifteen separate islands, lies off the eastern coast of Africa. Three large islands of the archipelago are granite, but most of the outer islands are coral atolls. The islands of Aldabra and Assumption in the Aldabra group of islands near the southwestern tip of the archipelago garnered special mention in Jacques Cousteau's 1963 adventure-diving masterpiece, *The Living Sea*. He called them the Isles of Return. That's good enough for me.

Adventure diving exists throughout South Africa, but the diving that is the current rage is the great white shark diving from Gansbaai—a fishing town about two hours down the road to the southeast of Cape Town. From there, divers go to "Shark Alley" (Dyer Channel), which is a shallow channel between Dyer Island and Geyser Island. These islands are pinniped rookeries, which provide the attraction for the great white sharks that cruise the channel. Adventurous divers enter cages to come face-to-face with these magnificent predators.

Great white sharks in the deeper water around Dyer Channel have been observed to feed by launching their huge bodies into the air to attack seals or sea lions on the surface. This awesome spectacle has earned the moniker Air Jaws. Spurred by the discovery of this feeding behavior, researchers have since witnessed similar behavior in great white sharks off Australia and California.

The Red Sea is a finger of the Indian Ocean that separates the northeastern corner of the African continent from Yemen and Saudi Arabia and is separated from the Mediterranean Sea by the Suez Canal. Red Sea diving first came into prominence in the early 1960s, when Cousteau chronicled his adventures there aboard the legendary *Calypso*. Most Red Sea diving today is done in the northernmost area near the Sinai (Egypt) Peninsula off Sharm El-Sheikh or the Ras Mohammed National Park. The Egyptian city of Hurghada is another popular northern Red Sea starting point. Excellent diving exists throughout the Red Sea, but many well-known sites to the south have been closed in recent years for political reasons. Red Sea diving is varied and diverse and includes sharks, shipwrecks, and reefs covered by colorful anthias (little fish).

Once we cross the continent of Africa, we're back into the Atlantic Ocean. The Portuguese Azores Islands offer opportunities to see sperm whales.

The lagoon called Scapa Flow formed by Scotland's Orkney Islands offers some of the best historical wreck diving in the world. Scapa Flow was used as an anchorage for the British Royal Navy during World War I, and the defeated German navy scuttled most of its High Seas Fleet in the lagoon in 1919. Many of the wrecks remain and are accessible to recreational divers.

Are you excited yet? Do you get the idea? Anywhere there's water, there's diving. We've touched on some of the most popular places in the world that offer recreational-diving infrastructures and excellent diving. Whatever your interests, it's out there. Go see for yourself.

UNDERWATER PHOTOGRAPHY

Basic Photography

Photography is the most popular underwater activity of recreational divers worldwide. The following is a primer to help make your photos better.

Light

The word *photography* means "light drawing." Therefore, any discussion of photography must begin with an understanding of light, specifically how light makes images in a camera. Some of the subjects we'll cover may seem to be self-apparent, but as you begin to think more like a photographer, you'll understand why they're so important.

Light is energy. As light moves from its source, many things can happen to it that will affect the way a photo will look:

- Refraction: A change in the direction (and velocity) of light caused by the light passing through mediums of different density.
- Reflection: The process by which light "bounces" off an object and continues on its path according to the angle at which it first encountered the object. Unless you are looking at a light source, such as a lightbulb or the sun, everything you (or your camera) see is reflected light.
- Absorption: The process by which the energy of light is absorbed by an object and not reflected.
- Diffusion: The process by which light is scattered by the reflection or absorption by many small objects or particles. All light underwater is diffused due to the density of the medium and the material suspended within it.

Ambient light: Ambient light is light whose source is not controlled by the photographer. In outdoor photography, ambient light is sunlight; in indoor photography, ambient light is whatever light is in the room.

Artificial light: Any light whose source is completely controlled by the photographer, such as a strobe or flash, is called artificial light.

The temperature of light affects its color. The temperature of light is determined by its source. While our brains adjust to temperature changes in light, films cannot automatically make this adjustment. For example, as we walk from sunlight into a room well lit by lightbulbs, we perceive both kinds of light the same way—as white light. However, if we are making photographs with a film that records sunlight as white, the film will record light from a regular lightbulb as red and light from a "white" fluorescent bulb as green. Sunlight is generally at a temperature of 5,500 degrees Kelvin, or 5,500 K. Tungsten light is generally at a temperature of 3,200 K. Therefore, "daylight" films are designed to register light at 5,500 K as white, while "tungsten" films are designed to register light at 3,200 K as white. Underwater photographers use daylight film combined with a strobe balanced for daylight for the vast majority of their work.

The temperature of light affects digital cameras as well. Digital cameras adjust for the temperature of light by the "white balance" control. Some cameras adjust white balance automatically, but others must be adjusted manually. The manual adjustment consists of simply pointing the camera at a white object and pressing the white balance button, as if to say to the camera, "This is white."

White light is composed of the spectrum of colors. As you might recall from your grade school science class, light is composed of different colors, or different frequencies of energy. The old mnemonic "Roy G. Biv" is helpful in remembering the colors (see chapter 7). Most important to underwater photographers is the way these colors are filtered by water. The low-energy frequencies (reds) are filtered first, and the absorption continues in sequence as depth increases. Most reds from sunlight will not be apparent to film at a depth of more than 20 feet.

Light "accumulates" on film and digital sensors. Unlike your eyes, film and digital sensors accumulate light as long as they are exposed to it. If the retinas of your eyes were like a piece of film or digital sensor, objects would get brighter the longer you looked at them. This "buildup" of light is central to understanding how to expose photographs.

The Camera

The camera is nothing more than a light-tight box with a mechanism to expose film or a digital sensor to light in a controlled manner. No matter how many buttons or levers your camera may contain, its basic function remains the same. The following characteristics are shared by all modern cameras:

1. A light-tight box.
2. A film plane that holds the film flat or that holds the digital sensor.
3. A means by which the film or digital sensor can be exposed to light for a controlled amount of time. This is done by allowing the light to enter through a curtain, called the shutter (some shutters are contained within the lens, but they are beyond the scope of this primer). Shutter speeds on modern cameras generally go something like $\frac{1}{8}$, $\frac{1}{15}$, $\frac{1}{30}$, $\frac{1}{60}$, $\frac{1}{125}$, $\frac{1}{250}$, $\frac{1}{500}$, and $\frac{1}{1,000}$ of a second. Remember, since light accumulates on film, the longer the shutter is opened, the more the film is exposed. Each progressive shutter speed allows exactly half as much light to strike the

film. For example, an exposure at 1/30 allows twice the amount of light as an exposure at 1/60.

4. A means by which to advance the film through the camera or to store digital images within the camera.
5. A means by which a lens can be attached (unless the camera has a permanent lens, as with point-and-shoot cameras) in order to focus an image onto the film plane.

Although there are myriad film formats available, the 35 mm camera is virtually the only film format currently used for underwater photography. Of the 35 mm cameras, the viewfinder camera and the single-lens reflex (SLR) camera are the types used for the vast majority of underwater photography.

Digital Cameras

Digital cameras are cameras that record images digitally rather than mechanically on film. The means of capture does not affect other aspects of photography, and photographic technique for digital cameras is not fundamentally different from traditional film camera technique. Digital cameras typically allow the shooter to see the actual image being recorded on a screen rather than through a viewfinder.

Digital photography is a burgeoning technology, and most photographers agree that the future of photography is in digital imaging. While the best digital cameras produce images of a quality equal to the best film cameras, most digital cameras currently available produce images that cannot be enlarged as well as images from traditional film cameras. However, the instant feedback of digital photography is a great help to beginning photographers, as they can experiment while underwater until they get the images they want.

Most digital cameras require a housing before they can be taken underwater, with the notable exception of the Sea & Sea DX-3100—the first truly amphibious digital camera to hit the market.

Viewfinder Cameras

Viewfinder cameras are cameras that contain a window for seeing the subject to be photographed, but the view through the window is not an actual representation of what is being photographed through the lens. Because of this, you cannot focus by looking through the viewfinder, and a parallax error can occur since the viewfinder and the lens are on separate planes. The most popular underwater cameras in use today—the Nikon Nikonos and the Sea & Sea Motormarine—are amphibious viewfinder cameras.

SLR Cameras

The single-lens reflex camera also contains a viewfinder (of course), but the image you see in the viewfinder originates from the lens of the camera. You see the image by way of a mirror that reflects the image into a prism within the viewfinder. Because of this, photographers using this type of camera can see what will appear on the film and can see the focus of the image in the viewfinder.

The Lens

Camera lenses are complex instruments composed of elements that allow a specific amount of light entering the lens to be refracted into a focused image on the focal plane of the camera. A discussion of lenses is difficult without first learning a bit of terminology.

Focal Length

The focal length of a lens is the distance from the optical center of the lens to the focal plane of the camera when the lens is focused at infinity. This distance is expressed in millimeters. Lenses with short focal lengths are called wide-angle lenses, lenses with medium focal lengths are called normal or standard lenses, and lenses with long focal lengths are called telephoto lenses. As you may deduce from these definitions, the shorter the focal length, the wider the angle of view of the lens.

For underwater applications, the 35 mm lens is considered "normal." Lenses with a focal length of 20 mm or shorter, including the popular 15 mm lens, are considered wide-angle. Telephoto lenses in underwater photography are generally used only for macro photography (photography of very small subjects) on SLR cameras, and the 60 mm and 105 mm lenses are popular choices.

Aperture

The aperture of the lens is a hole that allows a certain amount of light to reach the focal plane of the camera. It works very much like the iris of your eye. Although some specialized lenses have a fixed aperture (as do many point-and-shoot cameras), we will consider only lenses that have an adjustable aperture. The purpose of the adjustment is to control the amount of light hitting the film. The size of the aperture is adjusted by a series of f-stops. F-stops are a source of some confusion among beginning photographers, but the principle is simple: An f-stop is simply a ratio—a fraction—of the focal length of the lens to the diameter of the aperture. The range of f-stops typically include f/22, f/16, f/11, f/8, f/5.6, f/4, f/2.8, and f/2. What does it mean? It means several things, the most important of which is that *a given f-stop on any lens permits the same amount of light to strike the film as the same f-stop on any other lens*. Remember, the f-stop is the focal length of the lens divided by the diameter of the aperture, so the higher the f-stop number, the smaller the diameter of the aperture. So, f/22 is a much smaller hole than f/2. *Each progressive f-stop allows exactly half as much light to strike the film*. For example, f/16 allows half as much light to hit the film as f/11. Conversely, f/4 allows twice as much light to hit the film as f/5.6. Don't panic! There is no need to memorize the f-stops on your lens (although eventually you will just from looking at them). Just remember that if you want to allow more light to reach the film, or "open up a stop," you need to go to the next-lowest f-stop number, which represents a larger aperture. Or, if you want to allow less light to hit the film, or "close by a stop," you need to go to the next-highest f-stop number.

Lens Speed

The speed of any given lens is simply the largest aperture, or lowest f-stop, that the lens can attain. For example, a lens with a lowest f-stop of f/2 is "faster" than a lens with a lowest f-stop of f/3.5.

Depth of Field

Depth of field, sometimes abbreviated as DOF, can be thought of as "depth of focus." It refers to the depth of the area in front of the lens that will be in sharp focus. Depth of field is affected both by the focal length of the lens and by the aperture. The shorter the focal length of the lens (wide-angle), the greater the depth of field. Also, for a lens of any focal length, the smaller the aperture (higher f-stop number), the greater the depth of field. An understanding of depth of field is critical to using the most popular viewfinder cameras underwater, since you achieve focus by estimating distances. The greater the depth of field, the more room for error the photographer has in estimating distances for focusing. It is so important that Nikonos lenses show depth of field on their face so the photographer will be aware of the range of distances that will be in focus for any aperture (f-stop) setting.

The Film

The film is the medium that actually records the image. Simply speaking, it is composed of a backing that is coated with a light-sensitive emulsion. There are two basic kinds of films: negative and reversal.

Negative Film

Sometimes called print films, negative films are covered in emulsions that become dark (after development) when struck by light. The more light that hits any area of the film, the darker it gets. Therefore, once developed, the film contains a negative image of what the photographer saw—the areas that reflected the most light onto the film are registered as dark, and the areas that reflected the least amount of light onto the film are registered as light. This, of course is backward. Once developed, negative films must be printed to be viewed. You can think of this process as taking a picture of the negative again on negative film, which will turn things right. Negative films are developed by a process called C-41.

Reversal Film

Most often called slide films, reversal films are coated with emulsions that become darker (after development) when not struck by light. As a result, images can be correctly viewed directly on the film after development. The film itself is cut and mounted into plastic or cardboard mounts to make slides that can be projected or printed. Most slide films are developed by a process called E-6, with the notable exception of Kodak Kodachrome, which uses a specialized development process.

Film Speed

The speed of a film is determined by how sensitive its emulsion is to light and is expressed as its ISO number. The higher the ISO, the more sensitive (or "faster") the film is. The most commonly used film speeds for underwater photography are 50, 100, and 200. Each time the ISO number is doubled, the film is exactly twice as sensitive to light. Therefore, a film with an ISO of 100 is twice as sensitive as a film with an ISO of 50.

Film Grain

The grain of a film is actually the crystals of metal that make up the image. The slower the film, the smaller the grain. The smaller the grain, the sharper and smoother the image appears.

Film Latitude

The latitude of a film, sometimes referred to as its exposure latitude, refers to the range of light the film can handle before it goes completely black or completely white. For example, a film with a high latitude that is overexposed by one stop (exposed to twice as much light as the film was calibrated for) will still contain enough visual information to be printed. Print films have far more exposure latitude than slide films.

Film Temperature

Remember, light has temperature, so film must be calibrated to a certain temperature of the light. Films marked as "daylight" or "D" are calibrated to register light at a temperature near 5,500 K as white light. Films marked "tungsten" or "T" are calibrated to register light at a temperature of 3,200 K as white light. If a tungsten film is used in daylight, or with a strobe that fires at or near daylight temperature, the resulting image on the tungsten film will be a deep blue. Daylight film should be used in underwater photography.

Film Contrast

Contrast refers to the diversity or range of tones a film can record. Films with high contrast record fewer midrange tones. Slide film generally has more contrast than print film, and faster (higher ISO) films have more contrast than slower films.

So which film is best to use? As you might expect, there are advantages and disadvantages to each type of film. For photographers who are interested in getting photos to show to friends or having photos enlarged to hang on the wall, and who also want to have the most leeway for avoiding exposure mistakes, the choice is probably print film. For photographers who are interested in seeing exactly how their film was exposed, who want the best digital scans possible, or who are shooting for publication, slide film is the best choice. Most underwater photographers use ISO 100-speed film for general use and ISO 50-speed film for macro work. However, many prominent shooters use 50-speed film for all work in blue water. It is also important to know that many dive resorts and live-aboards offer E-6 (slide film) processing, while very few offer C-41 (print film) processing. Additionally, the cost of processing slide film is less than that of processing and printing print film.

Digital Sensors

Of course, digital cameras do not use film at all, as their images are recorded digitally. However, digital cameras record images at different ISO speeds just like film cameras.

Making the Exposure

So now we know all we need to know about light, cameras, lenses, and film. All that remains is for us to use the camera and lens to expose the film to make the perfect photograph, right? We're almost there, but there are a few more things to learn.

Exposure Meters

Exposure meters are instruments that measure the intensity of light in order to properly expose the film. There are two basic types: incident and reflective. Incident meters measure the intensity of light coming from the source of the light. Reflective meters measure the intensity of light reflecting off the subject. Reflective meters are used most in underwater photography simply because until recently no incident meters existed for underwater use. Most modern cameras contain a built-in reflective exposure meter, and many determine the intensity of light right where it counts—through the lens and on the focal plane of the camera where the film or digital sensor is. This type of light meter is referred to as through-the-lens, or TTL. Once the film speed is set in the light meter, the meter will give appropriate settings in combinations of shutter speed and f-stop to properly expose the film. The most popular amphibious underwater camera in use today features a TTL aperture-preferred light meter, which means that the photographer sets the film speed and sets the aperture, and the camera automatically sets the shutter speed for the exposure.

How Light Meters Decide What Exposure Is "Appropriate"

I am presenting this subject by itself because it is so important. Of course, your light meter does not know what your photo is supposed to look like, so it uses an average. All reflective light meters expose for a tone called 18 percent gray, which is a medium gray tone. This works for most subjects. However, if you take a photo of some newly fallen snow and you rely entirely on your light meter, the snow will register as a dirty-looking medium gray. Conversely, if you take a picture of your coal-black cat, the photo will make the cat medium gray. Light meters live in a strange world where everything is medium gray.

Bracketing Exposures

Due to the less-than-perfect way that a light meter decides how to set a camera for exposures, many photographers bracket their exposures. This simply means adjusting the shutter speed or aperture setting to expose the image in more than one way. A common example is to shoot one photo at the recommended setting, another photo one stop under the recommended setting, and another photo one stop over the recommended setting. Now the obvious question is how to bracket an automatic or TTL exposure, since the light meter will go to the same 18 percent gray exposure no matter what aperture or shutter speed you use. There are two ways to bracket with TTL: 1) note the recommended setting, switch the camera to manual, and bracket manually; and 2) change the ISO setting on the exposure meter. If you set your ISO dial on the exposure meter to an ISO number twice as high as the film actually in the camera, the TTL function of the meter will register an exposure that will allow half the light (underexpose) as the recommended setting. Likewise, if you set the ISO to a number that is half of the ISO number of the film in the camera, the TTL meter will allow twice (overexpose) the recommended exposure.

The Photographer's Dilemma

To this point we have covered a wide range of topics about how photography works. Now it's time to try to put it all together, and, incidentally, to explain why photographers get into so many arguments with one another. Almost every subject we've covered creates trade-offs for the photographer, and the manipulation of these trade-offs is the crux of the photographic decision-making process. Here are some of the dilemmas I'm talking about:

1. Film speed: The faster the film, the more contrast and grain. If you use slower film, you must use slower shutter speeds and/or larger apertures (smaller f-stop numbers).
2. Shutter speed: The faster the shutter speed, the more you will be able to "freeze" the action. Slow shutter speeds may cause blurring. However, the faster the shutter speed, the larger (smaller f-stop number) the aperture.
3. Aperture: The larger the aperture, the less the depth of field.

I hope you've noticed that film speed, shutter speeds, and aperture settings are set up to either double the light or halve the light. Because of this, a setting of ⅟₆₀ shutter speed and f/8 with 100-speed (ISO) film will yield the same exposure as a setting of ⅟₆₀ shutter speed and f/5.6 with 50-speed film. F/8 will give more depth of field than f/5.6. Also, with the same film in the camera, a setting of ⅟₃₀ shutter speed at f/8 will give the same exposure as a setting of ⅟₆₀ at f/5.6. The ⅟₃₀ shutter speed may cause blurring, but the f/5.6 may decrease the depth of field to the point that the image is not in focus. The photographer's dilemma is a sort of "pick your poison" proposition.

Strobes

The last thing we need to consider for making exposures is the addition of artificial light, or a strobe. For most applications other than photography in water shallower than 5 feet or for silhouette shots, a strobe is absolutely necessary to take acceptable underwater photographs. Strobes create vast amounts of light for a very short duration of time. The power of a strobe is measured in watt-seconds, and the output of a strobe is measured by its guide number, often abbreviated as GN.

Guide numbers are exposure indicators. Dividing a strobe's guide number by the distance in feet from the strobe (not necessarily the camera) to the subject will give an aperture setting for use with ISO 100 film. For example, a strobe with a guide number of 32 that is 4 feet away from the subject would give an aperture setting of f/8 ($32 \div 4$) with ISO 100 film. Of course, once you know that, you can extrapolate the information for a variety of factors. For example, if f/8 is appropriate for ISO 100 film, f/11 is correct for ISO 200 film.

Many modern strobes also offer "automatic" TTL exposure with cameras equipped to handle such strobes, such as the Nikonos V and the Motormarine II-EX. The system works by quenching (turning off) the strobe once the flash has registered 18 percent gray. So, the TTL circuitry does not affect the intensity of the light, but it does affect the duration of the flash. *The exposure system for flash TTL exposure on a Nikonos V is a separate system from the TTL system for ambient light.* Flash TTL will only work if the main subject covers at least 50 percent of the entire image and if the subject is centered within the frame. If not, the TTL system will try to "light the ocean" until it achieves its goal of an 18 percent gray world. Of course, this will only make the strobe fire at its maximum capacity, which will very likely grossly overexpose the subject. Automatic TTL flash exposures are also limited by the power of the strobe and cannot work if the subject is too far away or if the aperture is set at an f-stop that is too high for the strobe to sufficiently light.

But wait a minute—what about the shutter speed? Won't the shutter speed also affect the strobe exposure? The answer, for all practical purposes, is no. This is because the strobe light is of such high intensity that it will overpower the ambient light regardless of the shutter speed. However, like most things in photography, there is a catch. Since the strobe light is of such short duration, the light must be timed perfectly to flash while the shutter of the camera is wide open. This limits the shutter speeds that can be used with a strobe. For the Nikonos V camera, only shutter-speed settings of $\frac{1}{90}$ or slower can be used. The maximum shutter speed that can be used with a strobe is called the synch speed, and the synch speed is determined by the camera. Generally speaking for Nikonos photography, shutter speeds of $\frac{1}{90}$, $\frac{1}{60}$, and $\frac{1}{30}$ are used for flash photography. The good news is that the flash is so intense and so fast that it will "freeze" fast-moving subjects, although an ambient light blur, or "ghost," might also be recorded with a very slow shutter speed.

Virtually all modern strobes offer choices as to how to use the strobe to make the exposure. Most are dedicated to the most popular underwater cameras and offer automatic TTL exposure as well as a variety of manual power settings. *Automatic TTL flash photography is perhaps the least understood and is the reason for more bad photos than any other setting on your camera or strobe.* We cover the proper use of TTL flash in the underwater macro photography section later in this appendix, but it's never too early to get rid of the idea that the camera and strobe will take consistent photos in all conditions underwater in auto/TTL mode.

Like lenses, strobes also have an angle of coverage when they flash. It is important to match your strobe to whatever lens you are using to make sure that the strobe will cover the entire angle the lens "sees." This angle is measured in degrees from the strobe. For example, the popular 15 mm lens for Nikonos covers an angle of 94 degrees. Therefore, the strobe used to illuminate a photo from this lens must also cover at least 94 degrees. If not, only a section of the photo will be lit by the strobe.

POPULAR UNDERWATER PHOTOGRAPHIC EQUIPMENT

Cameras

These are exciting times for photography, as digital technology is poised to become the standard for all imaging. However, because the technology is developing, it is impossible to assess every new "latest and greatest thing" in this discussion of cameras.

Suffice it to say that digital cameras are clearly the future of photography. Most consumer digital cameras offered today cannot produce images of the quality of film, but professional-level digital cameras can. It is important to remember that the means by which an image is captured is only a small part of what makes a camera good or bad. Optics, smooth operation, and reliability will always be the most important benchmarks of quality regardless of how images are recorded and stored.

The most popular underwater equipment in use today is the Nikon Nikonos system. The camera is a 35 mm viewfinder camera, and there are myriad aftermarket accessories for it. Whether you own a Nikonos or not, it is important to understand this system due to the fact that virtually every photo shop at dive destinations around the world rents Nikonos equipment if it rents equipment at all.

The history of the Nikonos camera is of interest not only for its own sake but because many of the older versions are still available today and offer an opportunity for photographers to obtain high-quality equipment at a very reasonable cost.

The first design was by Jacques Cousteau and Jean De Wouters and was called the Calypso. This camera was first marketed in France in 1958. Calypso cameras are collector's items today, but few are actually used for practical application underwater.

Nikon began to market the camera, designated the Nikonos, in 1962, and in 1968 Nikon offered an improved version called the Nikonos II. The original Nikonos became known as the Nikonos I after the Nikonos II model came out (there is no "I" designation on the camera, but the Nikonos II has a "II" designation). The Nikonos II camera is quite a rugged piece of equipment, and many are still in use today.

In 1975 the camera was dramatically improved as the Nikonos III, which today is still considered to be the benchmark manual 35 mm viewfinder underwater camera.

Nikon introduced a crude automatic exposure system in 1980 with the Nikonos IV-A, a camera with a few devotees but generally considered to be a failure.

Finally, in 1984 Nikon introduced the Nikonos V, which is the most recent version and the most widely used underwater camera in the world today. Sadly, Nikon discontinued the Nikonos V in 2001, and no Nikonos cameras are currently being manufactured. The following is a brief evaluation of what I consider to be the three Nikonos models that you should consider buying:

Nikonos II
Advantages:
- Capable of taking excellent photos underwater
- Cheapest to buy ($100–$200 on eBay)
- Extraordinarily rugged

Disadvantages:
- Must replace the strobe socket to use modern strobes (which pretty much offsets the cheap original cost)
- Inconsistent framing on the film
- No tripod socket on the bottom to mount to a tray
- Must remove lens to change film
- No light meter incorporated for exposure control

Nikonos III
Advantages:
- Relatively cheap ($250–$300 on eBay)
- Extraordinarily rugged
- Can use modern strobes in manual exposure mode
- Has a tripod socket to mount to universal trays
- Consistent film framing

- Capable of taking excellent pictures underwater

Disadvantages:
- Must remove the lens to change film
- No light meter incorporated for exposure control

Nikonos V

Advantages:
- Capable of taking excellent underwater photos
- Sophisticated exposure control for both ambient light and strobe light
- Film accessible through the back
- Tremendous amount of aftermarket equipment available
- Synch speed to $\frac{1}{90}$ of a second

Disadvantages:
- Cost ($500 range on eBay)
- Electronics sensitive to abuse

A relative newcomer to the field of underwater 35 mm viewfinder cameras, the Sea & Sea Motormarine II, was introduced in 1989. A point-and-shoot version, the Motormarine MX-10, followed in 1992, and the Motormarine II-EX hit the market in 1995. While the MX-10 does not offer much photographic control, the MMII-EX does offer some interesting options. Note that Tabata USA is now responsible for the sales and service of all Sea & Sea products in the United States.

The MMII-EX has a fixed 35 mm lens to which a variety of diopters (secondary lenses that are attached to a primary lens) can be attached. Because of this setup, photographers using this system can shoot a wide range of subjects without having to surface to reconfigure their cameras.

The disadvantage of the system is in the sharpness of the optics. The MMII-EX is a clear attempt to garner some of the Nikonos market with a simpler camera. However, this very simplicity robs the educated photographer of options. For example, the MMII-EX features DX coding, which is a means by which the ISO of the exposure system within the camera is automatically set to the suggested ISO of the film. This precludes any chance of the photographer forgetting to set the ISO "correctly," but it gives the photographer no opportunity to bracket TTL exposures by changing the ISO setting intentionally.

Almost any land camera can be housed and taken underwater. The 35 mm single-lens reflex (SLR) camera currently in vogue for housing is the Nikon F100, although older models like the Nikon N90s are still very popular. The Nikon D1 and D100 digital SLR cameras are rapidly becoming the cameras of choice for professionals who have switched to the digital format. These digital SLR cameras will accept the spectrum of excellent Nikon lenses developed for Nikon film cameras. Housed SLR cameras offer greater versatility than viewfinder models like the Nikonos or Motormarine, especially in photographing macro subjects.

Lenses

The four most commonly used underwater lenses are the Nikonos 35 mm, 28 mm, 20 mm, and 15 mm. An 80 mm lens is also available for the Nikonos, but it is seldom used due to the difficulty of parallax and focusing. The 35 mm and 28 mm lenses are considered "normal" lenses, while the 20 mm and 15 mm are considered wide-angle lenses in underwater applications.

The Nikkor 35 mm lens: This is the lens that will probably come with your Nikonos camera, and it is an excellent lens to start with. The Nikonos 35 mm is somewhat unusual in that it can be used in air as well as underwater. This lens is good for fish pictures and head shots of divers. Many extension tubes for macro photography (which we'll cover a bit later) are available for this lens, and it can also produce great images with the Nikonos close-up kit (also covered later).

The Nikkor 28 mm lens: The 28 mm lens covers a bit more angle of view than the 35 mm and is considered to be a little sharper underwater, with slightly better color. It also has a bit more depth of field, which helps in focusing. The lens uses the water as a focusing element and consequently cannot be used in air. As with the 35 mm, extension tubes and the Nikonos close-up kit make good use of this lens.

The Nikkor 20 mm lens: This lens is the most cost-effective way to get into the exciting world of wide-angle underwater photography. Sea & Sea also offers a 20 mm lens for use with the Nikonos at a reasonable cost. All 20 mm lenses for Nikonos are dedicated to underwater use.

The Nikkor 15 mm lens: This is the benchmark lens for underwater wide-angle photography, and many of the magazine covers you see today were taken with this lens. These lenses are tack sharp and can capture a diver full figure from just a few feet away. Also, depth of field is so great that sharp focus is virtually guaranteed. Sea & Sea also offers an excellent 15 mm lens for use with the Nikonos camera. All 15 mm lenses for Nikonos are dedicated to underwater use.

The Motormarine cameras have a single fixed lens, which is 35 mm and can be used in air or underwater. Several diopters can be attached to simulate a 16 mm wide-angle lens or a 20 mm lens. Also, macro subjects can be photographed with the macro attachment.

Strobes

There are three major manufacturers of underwater strobes for use with the Nikonos system: Nikon, Ikelite, and Sea & Sea.

Nikon: Nikon offers two strobes commonly used for underwater photography. The Nikon SB104 is a top-of-the-line strobe. However, it is prohibitively expensive for beginner underwater photographers. The Nikon SB105 is, perhaps, the most commonly seen strobe attached to the Nikonos V camera, probably because they are often bought together as a package. This is a usable strobe, but it has some rather severe disadvantages. The SB105 requires a diffuser for wide-angle coverage and is slow to cycle. More importantly, for some reason it does not offer ½-power manual exposure control.

Ikelite: Ikelite underwater equipment, in my opinion, is the most thoughtful, most reliable, and best-serviced equipment in the business. While Ikelite offers many strobes, we will consider only two—the Ikelite SS100A and the Ikelite SS200. Either of these strobes can be used for both wide-angle and macro photography.

The Ikelite SS100A is the perfect strobe for the serious beginning photographer. It is cost-effective and offers some features that cannot be found on any other strobe, such as a dial that alters the angle of coverage of the strobe from 80 degrees to 95 degrees. It offers exposure controls of TTL, full power, and ½ power. In my opinion, the Ikelite SS100A is the best strobe available today in terms of price, reliability, and features. Look for used models marketed under the designation Ikelite Ai.

The Ikelite SS200 is perhaps the most capable strobe on the market today. It features 100-degree coverage and TTL, full power, ½-power, ¼-power, and ⅛-power exposure controls and is by far the fastest-cycling strobe ever made. This is top-of-the-line gear at a reasonable cost.

All Ikelite strobes are designed so that the battery compartment (most likely to flood) is completely separated from the electronics of the strobe. Because of this, a common flood will not ruin the unit.

Sea & Sea: Sea & Sea also offers fine strobes for the underwater photographer. The Sea & Sea YS120 and Sea & Sea YS300 are comparable in quality to the Ikelite SS100A and SS200, respectively. However, the Sea & Sea products are a bit more expensive and the electronics are not separate from the battery compartment. Also, service on these strobes is not nearly as quick or friendly as for Ikelite strobes. However, many serious and professional photographers swear by the quality of these strobes.

For a comprehensive comparison of strobes made by these three manufacturers, look at the Internet page www.ikelite.com/web_pages/compare_strobes.html. This page was prepared by Ikelite, but it is an objective comparison.

It should be noted that these underwater strobes cannot be used in TTL mode with the current crop of digital cameras. Special "digital" strobes that offer a wide range of manual power settings can be used with the digital cameras. The instant feedback of digital photography makes manually setting strobe powers easy.

What Else You'll Need

The camera, lens, and strobe are the main elements of any camera system. Unfortunately, you'll need more stuff to make it work.

Trays and Arms

The camera tray holds the camera, and the arm holds the strobe. In most cases, the strobe you buy or rent will come with its appropriate arm and camera tray. Nikon trays and arms are small and simple. The tray has a mount screw for the tripod socket of the camera. The arm is a solid bent rod that attaches to the tray with a large hand screw, and the strobe is clamped to the arm with a cam device. By unscrewing the mount, you can remove the arm from the tray for hand-holding the strobe. You can position the strobe for macro photography by reversing the arm and sliding the strobe down the arm.

Ikelite offers a universal tray and also a very compact tray for the Nikonos V. The arms are connected with a large hand screw, and they feature ball joints that can be positioned in infinite ways. The quick-release arms allow instant removal of the strobe with the push of a button for hand-holding the strobe.

Aftermarket companies such as TLC and Ultralite offer versions of trays and arms that are easy to use and lightweight.

Sync Cords

The sync cord is the wire that connects the camera to the strobe. The use of TTL flash exposure control requires a TTL sync cord. As each strobe manufacturer has its own connection system, the sync cord must be matched to the correct camera and strobe. For example, a cord linking a Nikonos camera to an Ikelite strobe cannot be used for a Nikonos camera and a Nikon or Sea & Sea strobe. Likewise, a sync cord for an Ikelite SLR housing cannot be used with a Nikonos camera.

It's time to mention here that the Motormarine II-EX comes with its own tray and arm. It is a simple and convenient arrangement. However, like many features of the Motormarine, the price of this simplicity is a lack of flexibility.

Viewfinders

For wide-angle photography, you must use an optical viewfinder to see the angle of view that will appear in the photograph. While the small viewfinder in the camera can be used for normal lens photography, the window is difficult to see while wearing a mask underwater, so you normally use a viewfinder for these lenses as well. The viewfinder attaches to the shoe on the top of the camera.

Separate Light Meter

While it is not absolutely necessary when you are using a camera with a built-in light meter, like the Nikonos V or Motormarine II-EX, it is convenient to have a separate light meter. For many years, the only worthwhile meter available was the Sekonic Marine Meter. This meter was discontinued years ago and recently reintroduced by Mamiya. The old meters required mercury batteries, which are no longer available. However, you can buy adapters to use standard silver MS76 batteries (the same ones used in the Nikonos V). Ikelite introduced a digital underwater light meter in 1999 that features both reflected and incident modes.

Taking Photos Underwater

Now, finally, it's time to start thinking about actually taking a picture underwater. If you understand the basics of photography and your equipment, most of these photographic techniques will seem obvious. But before we press the shutter release, let me mention perhaps the most important function of your success as an underwater photographer—your diving skills.

The most important skill relevant to underwater photography is buoyancy control. Also, most photographers have a tendency to hold their breath as they concentrate on a photograph—with the obvious attendant danger. Before you can photograph a subject, you must be able to approach it closely without hitting it and then remain still in the water while the photograph is taken.

The secret to getting brilliantly colored, tack-sharp photos underwater is to get rid of the water. That being impossible, try for the next best thing: *Get close.*

Setting Up the Nikonos Camera

Here is as good a time as any to discuss setting up the camera for underwater use. We will consider the Nikonos V for this discussion, but many of these guidelines can be applied to other cameras.

1. **Prepare the O-rings:** There are six O-rings that typically require attention each time you set up the camera—the main body O-ring, the lens O-ring, the battery cap O-ring, the main strobe O-ring, and the O-rings on each end of the sync cord. Carefully remove each O-ring from its groove (don't use any metal object to do this; toothpicks work). Make sure the O-ring and groove are free from debris like sand. *Lightly* apply O-ring grease to the O-ring and smooth the grease until it is evenly applied by running the O-ring through your fingers. The purpose of the grease is to keep the O-ring moist and supple. Too much O-ring grease will jeopardize the seal. The general rule is that the ring should have a sheen of grease, but no globs.
2. **Insert the batteries:** Use two silver 1.5-volt MS76 batteries. Carefully remove the battery cap with a nickel coin. Insert the batteries and carefully replace the battery cap. The battery cap is made of soft metal and the threads are easily damaged.
3. **Attach the strobe:** Attach the strobe to the camera with the sync cord.
4. **Test the TTL function of the camera, strobe, and sync cord:** Now is the time to test the TTL function of your rig if your rig has such a capability. Set the ISO dial on the camera to match the film you will use, set the camera shutter at "A," and

turn on the strobe and set it to TTL. Remove the lens cap from the camera and point the strobe at the cavity. Cock the shutter of the camera and press the shutter release until the strobe fires. The strobe should quench very quickly and recycle almost immediately. Now, replace the lens cap and fire the strobe again. The strobe should fully discharge. If these things don't happen, reconnect the sync cord and try again.

5. **Mount the lens:** Select and mount a lens for the camera. The lens can be oriented either way, but I prefer to mount the lens so that the aperture knob is accessible to my right hand and I can focus with my left.

6. **Load the film:** Load the film, close the back, and advance the film until the film counter reads "1." Remember that the film must pass between the shutter and the pressure plate on the back of the camera. Check the film spool on the left top of the camera to make sure that the film is advancing. Many photographers put the back of the camera to their ear and listen while advancing the film. If you hear the film jumping on the sprockets, the film is not advancing and must be reloaded. *Nonadvancing film is a common problem.* Obviously, if the film doesn't advance, you'll have no photos from your dive.

7. **Mount the camera to the tray and the strobe to the arm:** Mount the camera and pre-aim the strobe for the type of photography you will be doing. Make a last check to make sure that all connections are tight.

Underwater Macro Photography

The easiest way to get started in underwater photography is to start small. Macro photography is the photography of very small subjects. To do this, the photographer must get within inches of the subject. To do *this*, the lens of the Nikonos camera must be altered so as to focus closely enough. This is usually done with the use of extension tubes, which are hollow barrels that are inserted between the camera and the lens. The longer they are, the closer they will focus. The most common extension tubes for macro photography are 1:3 (records subjects one-third actual size on 35 mm film), 1:2 (records subjects one-half actual size on 35 mm film, and 1:1 (records subjects actual size on 35 mm film). As should be obvious, 1:1 macro photography covers a smaller area than 1:3. Extension tubes come with their own framers in order to focus, as depth of field with the use of extension tubes is only a small fraction of an inch.

Many manufacturers make extension tubes for use with the Nikonos 35 mm and 28 mm lenses, and the cost is very reasonable. My personal favorites are the Sea & Sea extension tubes and framers due to their rugged construction and to the fact that the framing posts can be removed for tight fits or for removing shadows from side lighting.

How to Shoot and Expose for Extension-Tube TTL Macro Photography
Shooting macro subjects with extension tubes is simplicity itself, and this is where

your TTL flash system shines (pun intended). To shoot macro with the Nikonos V, load ISO 50- or 100-speed film, insert the tube between the camera and lens, attach the framer, set the camera on "A" for automatic, set the strobe on TTL, position the strobe on top of the camera to cover the framer, set the lens aperture at f/22 (for any of the strobes discussed in this outline), set your focus to infinity, and shoot away. Some tube instructions call for focusing at the minimum of the lens, but I have found that focusing at infinity with all tubes is just as sharp and allows you to get sharp photos without actually touching the subject with the framer.

The obvious deficiency of this setup is the use of the framer to get subjects in focus, as no right-thinking fish will allow such an intrusion. It is true that many subjects cannot be photographed with a framer, but you'll be surprised how closely you can approach subjects with patience and practice. One of the negative comments commonly made about extension tube/framer photography is that you can't photograph anything with eyes (or it will swim away). However, it is great fun to try to get Christmas tree worms, arrow crabs, or anemone shrimp with this setup. Beautiful views of feeding corals are a snap, and your exposures will be close to dead-on every time.

If you want to bracket exposures for subjects that are either black or white, adjust the ISO dial on the camera. For example, if you want your subject to appear dark on the photo (because it is dark in real life), set your ISO higher than the film in the camera. If you want to brighten the exposure, set the ISO to a lower setting.

Warning! The extension tube and its attached framer add weight to the lens and put a bit of pressure on the seal between the tube and the camera. The leverage of the unit can break this seal and cause a flood if the framer is bumped against a subject or the bottom. This is a prime instance of how a buoyancy control mistake can ruin more than your photograph!

How to Manually Expose for Extension-Tube Macro Photography

So far, so good. But what if your camera equipment does not have automatic TTL exposure capability? This would apply for an older camera, such as a Nikonos III, or for situations where TTL capabilities are lost. If the batteries in your Nikonos V go dead, the camera will still operate on the manual 1/90 shutter speed but the exposure electronics will not work. Also, a faulty sync cord may cause the loss of TTL.

Determining manual exposures for macro photography is a matter of trial and error. Guide numbers on strobes do not apply at such close distances, and the f-stop you set on your camera is not the actual f-stop being used. This is because the extension tube has increased the focal length of the lens, and the lens is not calibrated for this. The actual f-stop when shooting 1:2 macro with a setting of f/22 showing on the lens is more like f/45. Fortunately, you will not have to start from scratch. The following is a "secret exposure chart" developed by the late renowned teacher and photographer Jim Church (used with his permission) from his excellent book *Jim Church's Essential Guide to Nikonos Systems.*

STROBE DISTANCE FROM FRAMER

Underwater Strobe Guide Number

Extension Tube	10–13	15–19	21–27	30–38
	Distance			
1:1 (f/22)	2–4"	3–6"	4–8"	6–12"
1:2 (f/22)	3–6"	4–8"	6–12"	8–12"
1:3 (f/22)	4–7"	5–9"	7–13"	10–12"

The exposure guide is set for ISO 100 film; to use the guide for ISO 50 film, you must divide your strobe's guide number by two. To use the chart, locate your strobe's guide number (for the film speed you're using) within the range of guide numbers at the top. Look down for the type of extension tube you are using (1:1, 1:2, or 1:3) and you will find a range of distances in inches. This is the distance your strobe bulb should be from the center of your framer at f/22 set on the lens. The range of distances corresponds to the brightness of your subject. For average subjects, use the middle of the distance range.

The Nikonos Close-Up System

Nikon makes a convenient close-up system for use with its 35 mm and 28 mm lenses. The system is composed of a diopter that clamps over the primary lens and a framer for each lens. This setup can be removed or added underwater, but it is fairly bulky to carry around and few divers do so. The frames are perfect sizes for subjects such as eels, octopuses, or sleeping fish. As with the extension-tube framers, it is difficult to get these framers around fast-moving and aware subjects.

How to Use the Nikonos Close-Up System
To use the system, select the appropriate framer for the lens you are using. The smaller framer is for the 35 mm lens; the larger framer is for the 28 mm lens. Clamp the diopter to the lens and anchor it to the rod that connects to the shoe on the top of the camera. Connect the framer and focus the lens to infinity. For powerful strobes, set the aperture at f/22 with ISO 50 film. For less powerful strobes, set the aperture at f/22 with ISO 100 film or f/16 with ISO 50 film. Set the camera to "A," set the strobe to TTL, position the strobe above the camera to aim at the center of the framer, and fire away. This is another example of where automatic TTL flash exposure works virtually every time.

Manual Settings for the Nikonos Close-Up System
Once again, your strobe's guide number cannot be used in the traditional way with

the Nikonos close-up system. If your camera or strobe does not have automatic TTL flash capability, the following is Jim Church's "secret exposure chart" for use with this system:

STROBE DISTANCE FROM FRAMER

Underwater Strobe Guide Number

	10–13	15–19	21–27	30–38
Distance	*F-Stop*			
8"	f/11–16	f/16–22	f/22–32	—
12"	f/11	f/16	f/22	f/32
16"	f/8–11	f/11–16	f/16–22	f/22–32

This chart is based on a film speed of ISO 100. To use ISO 50-speed film, divide your strobe's underwater guide number by two. To use the chart, find the guide number range that contains your strobe's guide number, look down to select the desired aperture (f-stop), then look left to find the distance your strobe bulb should be from the center of the framer in inches.

Macro and close-up photography are the easiest kinds of underwater photography to technically master, and many photographers dedicate themselves solely to these types of photography. It is an excellent way to start, since almost every shot on your first roll will be properly exposed. The only difficult aspect of it is finding suitable subjects and controlling your buoyancy carefully enough to photograph them. I personally enjoy this type of photography most at night, when the corals are feeding, the fish are sleeping, and the octopuses and eels are out. One of my favorite ways to locate suitable subjects at night is to shine my light around the reef and look for the reflection of eyes, as the eyes of various shrimp and critters always mark a promising photo opportunity.

Normal-Lens (35 mm and 28 mm) Photography

As the photographer moves away from the subject in order to photograph a more conventional view of the underwater world, photographs become technically more difficult—especially for flash photography. Here are some of the problems we will discuss:

Balancing strobe light with ambient light: For macro and close-up photography, the light from your strobe accounts for virtually all of the light used to expose the film. As you place the subject more in context, you must use ambient light to expose a larger area of the photo. In effect, the photograph is composed of two separate exposures—one for the primary subject, which is lit by the strobe, and the other for the background, which is lit by ambient light. The seamless combination of the two light sources results in the best photos. We will discuss exposure techniques to achieve this.

Backscatter: Backscatter is a problem that arises when the strobe light reflects off suspended particles in the water to create white spots in the photograph. This "underwater snow" is the bane of underwater photography. We will discuss ways to minimize this problem.

Parallax error: I have mentioned that the viewfinder of your Nikonos camera is on a separate plane from the lens. The addition of a viewfinder on top of the camera creates even more of a disparity. In addition to being much higher than the lens, the viewfinder is also not in line with the vertical axis of the lens. Although this problem is mostly overcome with practice, we will discuss ways to help.

Balancing Strobe Light with Ambient Light

Before we address the specific problem of balancing light sources, let me mention a common mistake beginning photographers make when starting to shoot normal-lens photos. Although the normal lens can "see" a wide variety of subjects, its use in flash photography with a strobe should be limited to a distance of no more than 5 feet from the subject. This is because the strobe is not able to sufficiently light subjects farther than 5 feet away with good color. The underlying rule of *get close* becomes more and more important as the focal length of your lens decreases.

Backscatter also becomes more of a problem as the volume of water between the camera and the subject increases. Conversely, many photographers will try to shoot subjects too small for the normal lens. The Nikkor 35 mm lens can focus to a minimum distance of 2.75 feet; the 28 mm can focus as close as 2 feet. Get used to photographing subjects from a standard distance of 3 feet. Not only will practicing at this standard distance result in optimal color from the strobe, it will also help you estimate the distance for sharp focus.

Determining the ambient (background) exposure: As I mentioned before, the balanced flash photograph is actually two separate exposures: one for the strobe-lit subject and the other for the background or ambient light exposure. We will discuss two ways to determine the background exposure—the "textbook" way and my own "f/8–3 feet" method.

The textbook method: To determine the ambient exposure with the built-in exposure meter, look through the viewfinder toward the background (usually toward the surface) and move the aperture knob until the shutter speed indicator in the viewfinder is either 60, both 60 and 125, or 125, depending on how you want your background to look. A reading of 60 will create a light background; a reading of 125 will create a more saturated, darker background when you use a shutter speed of $\frac{1}{90}$ (the "A" shutter speed). Note the aperture that gives this reading. You will find that most ambient readings for 100 ISO film (100 ISO set on the camera's ISO dial) in blue water will result in ambient settings of around f/8 at $\frac{1}{60}$ or $\frac{1}{90}$ of a second. Your aperture and shutter speed are now set for your ambient exposure.

The f/8–3 feet method: Set the aperture of the camera at f/8 for ISO 100-speed film or f/5.6 with ISO 50 film. Point the Nikonos V camera with the shutter speed set on "A" toward the background and note the shutter speed recommended. Manually set the shutter speed to that number or the next-highest number (for a darker background). For example, if a shutter speed of $\frac{1}{60}$ is shown in the viewfinder, set the shutter speed for M90 on the camera. Remember that the $\frac{1}{90}$ setting is the fastest shutter speed that will sync with your strobe on a Nikonos V; a shutter speed of $\frac{1}{60}$ is the fastest that will sync on a Nikonos II or III. Your aperture and shutter speed are now set for your ambient or background exposure.

Note: If you have a separate exposure meter, this is the place to use it. Point the meter toward the background and note the reading. This is easier to do than looking through the tiny viewfinder of your camera.

Achieving a background exposure is important, but the exposure is not as critical as the exposure for the main subject. An acceptable background can be a fairly wide range of tones, from light blue to a deep indigo, depending on your taste.

Determining the strobe exposure: Here's the part that many beginners find difficult—balancing the strobe exposure so the main subject is correctly exposed without upsetting the ambient settings we've just determined. Remember, the "automatic" exposure system within your Nikonos V camera for ambient light is completely separate from the TTL flash exposure system.

Once your shutter speed and aperture are set, your TTL system will work with normal-lens photography only in certain circumstances, that is, when the main subject covers 50 percent of the frame and is centered within the frame. If these conditions are not met, your photograph will most likely be overexposed. There are all sorts of "tricks" you can play by readjusting your film speed or making other adjustments to your camera controls to use TTL for normal-lens photography, but I find these tricks to be difficult to remember. There is a much easier way.

Do you remember the guide number for your strobe? Using the camera and strobe in manual mode is nearly as easy as setting up for automatic exposure. The following is my f/8–3 feet method:

There are three factors that will determine the strobe exposure for your photo: The power of the strobe, the distance between the strobe and the subject, and the aperture of the lens. The aperture of the lens has already been determined for the ambient exposure. So by adjusting the strobe's power and distance from the subject, we can control the amount of strobe light that will expose the subject. As you may recall from above, we have selected an aperture of f/8 for ISO 100 film.

Next, you must know the proper manual power setting of your strobe for ISO 100 film at f/8 from a distance of 3 apparent (4 measured) feet. Use your strobe's underwater guide number to determine this and test it in the water. For example, an Ikelite SS100A strobe should be set to full power (maximum angle of flash) for ISO 100 film, f/8, and a distance of 3 to 4 feet. An Ikelite SS200 strobe should be set at $\frac{1}{2}$ power.

Once your strobe is set to the proper power, you are ready to make properly exposed photos from a distance of 3 feet. *Ninety percent of the photos you shoot should be from a distance of 3 to 4 feet.* Once you prefocus for a distance of 3 feet, your camera is in a "point-and-shoot" mode. To make adjustments to alter the background, adjust the shutter speed. With a Nikonos V camera, you can choose from ⅓₀, ⅟₆₀, and ⅟₉₀. This system works with non-TTL cameras such as the cost-effective Nikonos III.

The f/8–3 feet method is based on the convenient fact that strobe and camera controls are set up to either double or halve the exposure. So, once a "standard" exposure is determined (f/8 at 3 feet in our case), it is easy to alter either of the two (ambient and strobe) exposures while maintaining control of the other. Here are the basic rules:

1. Changing the shutter speed will alter the ambient exposure but not the strobe exposure.
2. Changing the strobe power will alter the strobe exposure but not the ambient exposure.
3. Changing the aperture will alter both exposures. To reestablish either of the exposures, you must make an adjustment. To reestablish the ambient exposure, change the shutter speed. To reestablish the strobe exposure, change the strobe power. Each increment of one will negate the other, since all functions either double or halve the exposure.

Note: Nikon strobes do not have a ½-power setting. For this reason alone, I do not use them. Nikon's reasoning for this omission is presumably the fact that the addition of a diffuser will reduce the strobe's output by half. However, once the diffuser is attached, as it must be for wide-angle lenses, there is no ½-power adjustment. The diffuser must be removed and the strobe set to ¼ power. If this seems confusing now, you can imagine how inconvenient it is underwater.

Once you have determined the proper exposure of your strobe for manual use from a distance of 3 to 4 feet, you have essentially mastered both normal-lens and wide-angle exposures. Of course, you must be able to modify the exposure for some situations, but the modifications will make sense and are easy to remember. The following are some common modifications:

Using a different-speed film: Many photographers prefer to use ISO 50 film, like Fuji Velvia, for all of their underwater photos. Modifying the manual exposure system to accommodate this couldn't be simpler—open your aperture one stop. So, if you have mastered ISO 100 film at f/8, everything will stay the same if you open your aperture to f/5.6 to accommodate the slower film. Shutter speeds and strobe power settings will stay the same.

Shooting from a distance other than 3 feet: I do not recommend trying to shoot flash photos from a distance greater than 4 or 5 feet, as no strobe can adequately capture the colors of the underwater world when forced to flash through that much water and the resultant backscatter will be prohibitive. To take a picture from more than 5 feet, turn off the strobe and expose entirely for ambient light. Your photo will look pretty much the same as if you had used the strobe except for the lack of backscatter. However, to shoot from a distance of 4 feet, double the power setting on your strobe. More likely, you may want to shoot from a distance closer than 3 feet. For normal-lens photography, this is only possible with a 28 mm lens, which can focus down to 2 feet. To shoot from 2 feet, reduce your strobe output by half.

Shooting when the ambient light is inappropriate for the shutter speed at f/8: In the vast majority of situations, ambient light can be controlled at f/8 by adjusting the shutter speed from $\frac{1}{30}$ through $\frac{1}{90}$. For cases where the ambient light is too bright, such as when shooting in very shallow water over sand in bright sunlight, the only solution is to close the aperture one stop. However, since aperture will also affect the strobe exposure, you must double the strobe output. The more likely situation is when the ambient light is not intense enough to register a blue background, as when shooting in late afternoon or early morning. To compensate for this, open the aperture one stop and reduce the strobe output by half. Of course, there are limits to what can be done, and if the ambient light gets too low, the background will go dark.

Controlling Backscatter

Backscatter is predominately a strobe effect, caused by light reflecting off particles suspended in the water between the lens and the subject. Controlling backscatter with a single strobe is difficult or impossible in some situations. However, there are some things you can do to minimize this problem.

The first thing to remember is to not be the problem. Stay off the bottom. If you are swimming near the bottom, make sure that the wash from your fins is not stirring up sand.

Your strobe must be properly aimed to minimize backscatter. Remember that when you are underwater things look 25 percent closer than they actually are. This is not a problem when you focus your camera because the camera "sees" distances just like you do. However, if you pre-aim your strobe on land to hit objects 3 feet away, and then you get what seems to be 3 feet away from a subject underwater, your strobe will actually be aimed in front of the subject. This is the worst possible scenario for backscatter because the strobe is concentrated on the water between the camera and the subject, and it will light up every bit of suspended debris and create maximum backscatter. If you pre-aim your strobe on land (and I recommend that you do), aim it for a distance of 4 feet. Using your strobe's modeling light (if it has one) or a flashlight clamped to the strobe is a good way to properly aim the strobe.

The object of aiming your strobe to minimize backscatter is to minimize the light the strobe produces between the subject and the camera. This is impossible to do if your strobe arm is too short and too close to the lens of the camera. Otherwise, the angle of the strobe is too close to the angle of the lens, and the subject cannot be lit without lighting all of the water in between.

A second strobe is very useful in minimizing backscatter. Aim each strobe straight ahead or even angled slightly outward, and the subject will be illuminated where the angles of the output of the strobes intersect. In this way, lighting the water between the strobe and the camera is minimized, thus minimizing backscatter.

Another way to minimize visible backscatter is to minimize the strobe light used to light the photo. Slowing the shutter speed to brighten the background will tend to make the backscatter less visible.

Lastly, resort to the prime objective of underwater photography: Get closer. Obviously, the less water between the lens and the subject, the less of a problem backscatter will be.

Dealing with Parallax Error

As I've mentioned, using a viewfinder mounted on top of the Nikonos camera is the most convenient way to shoot normal-lens photos. However, it is easy to see that the viewfinder does not line up either horizontally or vertically with the lens. The only practical advice I can give you here is to be aware of the problem. Obviously, objects in front of the lens will appear in the lower right corner of the viewfinder, and the closer the subject is to the lens, the more pronounced parallax error will be. Composing photographs with a viewfinder camera, especially one with the viewfinder mounted so far from the plane of the lens, is not a precise exercise. You will become more proficient with practice, but the only way to precisely compose a photo is with an SLR camera. Some Nikonos photographers use the camera's viewfinder for composition; others simply "shoot from the hip" after much practice.

Wide-Angle Lens (20 mm and 15 mm) Photography

Wide-angle lenses bring out the best in Nikonos-type photography. Because of the very short focal length, depth of field is so great that sharp focus is easily achieved. The use of wide-angle lenses results in a very compact, thoroughly professional-quality system.

Perhaps the most difficult aspect of wide-angle photography is getting used to the angle of view, which is 94 degrees with the popular 15 mm lens. To get an idea of the field of view, take two yardsticks and hold them together at a 90-degree angle. As you'll notice, this wide view is very encompassing.

The exposure method for wide-angle photography is exactly the same as the method discussed for normal-lens photography. The only difference is that TTL rarely works with wide-angle, so you must get used to the idea of making manual exposures. As I've covered above, this is not difficult to do. To review, for ISO 100 film, set your aperture to f/8, set your shutter speed to make an appropriate background exposure, manually set your strobe power for an appropriate exposure from 3 to 4 feet at f/8, and start making photographs from a distance of 3 feet. With the 15 mm lens, this 3-foot distance will encompass a whole diver. The following are some considerations that are unique to wide-angle photography:

The optical viewfinder: Due to the coverage of these lenses, you need an optical viewfinder to get an idea of what will be in the photo. Nikon and Ikelite both make versions, and the Ikelite is far less expensive and quite serviceable. It features a parallax compensator that can be set for 3 feet, which helps in framing when using the f/8–3 feet method.

Wide-angle distortion and perspective: Since the angle of view is so broad, images become a bit distorted (they become somewhat circular). As there are no straight lines underwater, this distortion is not a big issue. However, perspectives on these lenses are still apparent underwater. Since the angle of view is so large, objects must diminish quickly as they approach their vanishing point. In other words, if you focus one of these lenses on the hand of a model who is extending the hand toward the camera, the model's arm will appear to be abnormally long. Similarly, objects photographed close to the lens appear very large while objects a bit behind them diminish in size dramatically.

Close-focus wide-angle: Continuing with the optical characteristics explained above, a whole genre of photography called close-focus wide-angle, or CFWA, has developed. Wide-angle lenses typically focus to a minimum distance of 1 foot, and the depth of field is so great that distant objects are also in focus. In CFWA, a trumpet fish can appear to be as large as a diver in the background. As a review, remember to decrease strobe power by half for subjects 2 feet away, and reduce that power by half again for subjects 1 foot away. If your strobe cannot reduce power that much, you can close the aperture by one stop and reduce the shutter speed by half to keep your proper ambient exposure.

As the focal length of the lens decreases, backscatter becomes increasingly difficult to control because wide-angle photos typically contain more "negative space" (water) in them. Be extra careful aiming your strobe when shooting with these lenses.

Photographic Composition

Photography is a creative expression of the photographer's view of the world. For this reason, I hesitate to offer too many "rules" for how that vision should be presented. It's your photo, and your expression, after all. If it looks good to you, then you have succeeded. However, I will mention a few pointers that I hope will help you attain photos that please you.

Separate the subject from the background: The underwater world is a chaotic explosion of shapes, colors, and forms. It is usually important for you to center your photograph around a specific subject. The easiest way to separate a subject from its surroundings is to shoot at an upward angle. In this way, the confusion of the reef will not hide or detract from the beauty of its inhabitants.

Avoid "tail shots": Many beginning photographers have a tendency to chase subjects. This virtually always results in photos of subjects swimming away from the camera, or "tail shots." Views of fleeing fish are generally not pleasant to look at. Be patient; get the head.

Make the eye the focal center: Attractive photos of living things require the eye to be seen in sharp focus. Generally speaking, the eye will be the center of interest of the photo.

Give moving subjects somewhere to go: Portraits of swimming fish are popular subjects. When photographing a fish, leave space in the frame in front of the fish. Otherwise, your photo will give the impression that the fish is "running out of room" in the picture.

Follow the rule of thirds: Like many composition rules, this one must be taken with a large degree of subjectivity. This "rule" calls for viewing your scene as if it has a tic-tack-toe diagram on it. The central point of interest in the photo should be near where the tic-tack-toe lines intersect—at the top right, top left, bottom right, and bottom left of the scene. This rule works in many cases, and it at least encourages the photographer to resist the idea that every photo must be perfectly centered in the frame.

Don't forget to frame vertically: Many photographers get into the habit of shooting every photo horizontally, which is the way they generally hold the camera. However, many subjects are framed more attractively vertically. Make a conscious decision as to how to best frame the subject before you shoot, or shoot both ways and decide later. When using one strobe, it is generally accepted that the camera should be tilted so that the strobe always lights from above.

Look again: One of the main differences between a roll of film taken by a beginner and one taken by an experienced enthusiast is the range of subjects photographed. The beginner will tend to have a single photo of every critter that swam by; the experienced photographer might have an entire roll of a single subject. Once you've found a suitable subject, take your time and try to see it in different ways. Your composition skills will improve with practice, and I would rather return from a dive with one excellent shot than with thirty-six ho-hum shots.

RESOURCES

BOOKS AND MAGAZINES

Belanger, Joe. *Catalina Island: All You Need To Know*. Mesa AZ: Roundtable Pub., 2000.

Berg, Daniel. *Wreck Valley Vol II: A Record of Shipwrecks Off Long Island's South Shore and New Jersey*. East Rockaway NY: Aqua Explorers, 1990.

Berg, Daniel, and Denise Berg. *New Jersey Beach Diver: The Diver's Guide to New Jersey Beach Diving Sites*. East Rockaway NY: Aqua Explorers, 1993.

Bookspan, Jolie, John Heine, and Peter Oliver. *NAUI Master Scuba Diver*. NAUI, 2000.

Cousteau, Jacques-Yves, and Philippe Diolé. *Octopus and Squid: The Soft Intelligence*. Garden City NY: Doubleday, 1973.

Davidson, Ben. *The 2002 Travelin' Diver's Chapbook*. DSDL, 2001.

Douglass, Darren. *Diving and Snorkeling Guide to Southern California: Including Los Angeles County, Orange County, San Diego County*. 2nd ed. Houston: Pisces Books, 1994.

Humann, Paul, and Ned DeLoach. *Reef Coral Identification: Florida, Caribbean, Bahamas*. Enlarged 2nd ed. Jacksonville FL: New World, 2002.

Humann, Paul, and Ned DeLoach. *Reef Creature Identification: Florida, Caribbean, Bahamas*. Enlarged 2nd ed. Jacksonville FL: New World, 2002.

Kohl, Cris. *The Great Lakes Diving Guide*. West Chicago: Seawolf Communications, 2001.

Rosenberg, Steve. *Diving and Snorkeling: Monterey Peninsula and Northern California*. 3rd ed. Melbourne Australia; Oakland CA: Lonely Planet, 2000.

Volume Library, vol. 1. Nashville TN: Southwestern Company, 2001.

Weber, Edward. *Diving and Snorkeling Guide to the Pacific Northwest: Includes Puget Sound, San Juan Islands, and Vancouver Islands*. Houston: Pisces Books, 1993.

Wuest, Patricia. "Look Deeply into My Eyes." Rodale's *Scuba Diving*. July 2002.

WEB SITES AND CD-ROMS

Aloha.com
www.aloha.com/~lifeguards/alsting2.html
"Excerpts from Thomas, Craig, M.D., and Susan Scott. *All Stings Considered: First Aid and Medical Treatment of Hawai`i's Marine Injuries*."

Center for Coastal Physical Oceanography
www.ccpo.odu.edu/~arnoldo/ocean405/ocean
_405_classnotes/western.pdf
"Western Boundary Currents."

College of DuPage Next Generation Weather Lab
http://weather.cod.edu/sirvatka/ts.html
"Thunderstorms."

Divers Alert Network
www.diversalertnetwork.org
"About DAN."

Geological and Mining Engineering and
Sciences at Michigan Tech
www.geo.mtu.edu/department/classes/ge406/
jmedward/tstorms/
"Information regarding thunderstorms and
the hidden dangers involved in them."

Global Underwater Explorers
www.gue.com/dplan/docs/Deco/Understand
ing%20M-values.pdf
"Understanding M-Values."

The Merck Manual
www.merck.com/mrkshared/mmanual/
section23/chapter308/308h.jsp
"Marine Animals."

MSN Encarta online
http://encarta.msn.com/encnet/refpages/SR
Page.aspx?search=coral+reef&x=11&y=8
"Coral Reef."

National Marine Sanctuaries
www.sanctuaries.nos.noaa.gov/
"Information about our nation's marine
sanctuaries—their history and current management, their scientific and educational
programs, and their continuing efforts to
conserve our nation's ocean and coastal
treasures."

National Park Conservation Association
http://npca.org/marine_and_coastal/marine_
wildlife/octopus.asp
"Marine and Coastal: Marine Wildlife: Giant
Pacific Octopus."

Professional Association of Diving Instructors
http://www.padi.com/english/common/
products/catalog/encyclopedia.asp
"The [PADI] Encyclopedia of Recreational
Diving Multimedia CD-ROM."

Proofofconcepts
www.proofofconcepts.com/webtextbook/
weather/flstom.htm
"Movie about Florida Thunderstorm
Development."

Steve's Fossil Shark Teeth
www.megalodonteeth.com.
"Web site dedicated to the sale of fossil shark
teeth."

The World Factbook
www.cia.gov/cia/publications/factbook/geos/
ps.html
"Reference for Palau."

GENERAL SCUBA CERTIFICATION AGENCIES

National Association of Underwater Instructors
(NAUI) Worldwide
P.O. Box 89789
Tampa FL 33689-0413
800-553-6284; 813-628-6284
Fax: 813-628-8253
E-mail: nauihq@nauiww.org
www.naui.org

Professional Association of Diving Instructors
(PADI)
30151 Tomas St.
Rancho Santa Margarita CA 92688-2125
800-729-7234; 949-858-7234
Fax: 949-858-7264
E-mail: webmaster@padi.com
www.padi.com

Scuba Diving International (SDI) World
Headquarters
18 Elm St.
Topsham ME 04086

888-778-9073; 207-729-4201
Fax: 207-729-4453
E-mail: worldhq@tdisdi.com
www.tdisdi.com/sdi/sdihome.html

Scuba Schools International (SSI)
2619 Canton Court
Ft. Collins CO 80525-4498
970-482-0883
Fax: 970-482-6157
E-mail: admin@ssiusa.com
www.ssiusa.com

YMCA Scuba
101 N. Wacker Dr.
Chicago IL 60606
800-872-9622
Fax: 312-977-0894
E-mail: scuba@ymca.net
www.ymcascuba.org

TECHNICAL DIVING CERTIFICATION AGENCIES

These agencies cover diving beyond accepted recreational limits, such as depths below 130 fsw, planned decompression diving, exotic gas mixtures beyond EANx32 or EANx36, diving within overhead environments, and using technical equipment like rebreathers.

International Association of Nitrox and Technical Divers (IANTD) World Headquarters
9628 NE 2nd Ave., Suite D
Miami Shores FL 33138-2767
305-751-4873
Fax: 305-751-3958
E-mail: iantd@iantd.com
www.iantd.com

National Speleological Society, Cave-Diving Section (NSS-CDS)
2109 W. U.S. Hwy. 90, Suite 170-317
Lake City FL 32055
Phone/Fax: 352-333-9640
E-mail: CDSManager@NSSCDS.org
www.nsscds.org

National Association for Cave Diving (NACD)
P.O. Box 14492
Gainesville FL 32604
Phone/Fax: 888-565-NACD (800-565-6223)
E-mail: manager@safecavediving.org
www.safecavediving.org

Technical Diving International (TDI) World Headquarters
18 Elm St.
Topsham ME 04086
888-778-9073; 207-729-4201
Fax: 207-729-4453
E-mail: worldhq@tdisdi.com
www.tdisdi.com/tdi/tdihome.html

INDEX

Numbers in **bold** refer to pages with illustrations.

marine life, types of. *See also* fish; sharks, types of
anemones, 162, **180**, **181**, **287**
brittle stars, **221**
brown fan worm, **178**
Christmas tree worms, 177, **178**
corals, 174–75
crabs, 162, **169**, **177**
elkhorn coral, **167**
feather-duster worms, 177, **178**
fire coral, **175**, 178
fireworms, 185–86, **225**
golden crinoid, **171**
hawksbill turtles, **328**
hydroids, 179, 181, **183**, **287**
jellyfish, **181**–82
lobster, **169**
loggerhead turtle, **284**
manta rays, **285**, 328, **331**
moray eels, 171, **173**, 186–88, **187**
octopuses, 171, **228**, 229, 311–12
orange ball corallimorph, **229**
sea fans, 167, **168**
seahorses, **170**
sea urchins, 182–84, **183**, 225
sharptail eels, **188**
shrimp, 162, 172, **173**
sponges, 162, **165**, 168, **169**, **179**–80, **287**
spotted moray eel, **173**
star coral, **166**
stingrays, **184**–85
tube worms, 177, **178**
marker strobes, 223–25, **224**
Martini's Law, 276
mask rinse buckets, 205
masks, **44**
boxes, 72
buying used, 111
cleaning, 72, 73
cost, 18
fogging, 71–72, 73
function and selection, 18–20, 133, 136
Master Diver certification, 125

mediastinal emphysema, **273**
medical dive insurance, 105–6
medical problems and injuries. *See also* first aid
arterial gas embolism, **272**–73
carbon dioxide toxicity, 275–76
carotid sinus reflex, 61–62
cramps, 258, **262**–63
decompression sickness, 46, 266–71, **269**
health hazards when traveling, 322
hyperthermia, 278–79
hypothermia, 277–78
lung overpressure injuries, 271–74
mediastinal emphysema, **273**
nitrogen narcosis, 276–77
oxygen toxicity, 274–75
pneumothorax, 273–**74**
seasickness, 202–4
subcutaneous emphysema, 273
unconscious diver, 264–65, 266
megalodon sharks, 293, 294, 298–99
moldable mouthpieces, 100–**101**
moon
coral spawning and, 164
effects on tides, 149–50
moray eels
characteristics, 171, 186–88
golden-tail moray, **187**
green moray eel, **187**
photographing, 188
spotted moray eel, **173**, **187**
Motormarine II-EX camera, 342, 345, 348
mouthpieces, moldable, 100–**101**
muscle cramps, 258, **262**–63
M-values (decompression), 47–48, 52

National Association for Cave Diving (NACD), 290
National Association of Under-

water Instructors (NAUI), 123, 124, 209
National Diving Accident Network, 105–6
National Oceanic and Atmospheric Administration (NOAA), 145
National Speleological Society, Cave Diving Section (NSS-CDS), 290
navigation, underwater, 231–32
advanced, 242
anchor as fixed point, **232**–33
charter dive boat briefing information, 234
compasses, 236–**39**, 241–42
in currents, 240–41, **246**
depth gauges, 235
distance estimating, 239–40
natural aids, 235–36
point-to-point navigation, 241
reefs, 234–35
sight navigation, 233–34
three-point navigation, 235–36
walls, 234–35
neoprene
buoyancy of, 39, 56–57
compression compensation, 39, 57
dry suits, 60–61
hoods and vests, 59
mask straps, **18**–19
pocket belts, 68
wet suits, 39, 56–58, 114
neutral buoyancy, 132
New Jersey and New York diving, 304–6
night diving. *See also* dive lights
marine life observation, 220–**21**, **228**–29
photography, 228, 353
predatory fish, 229
safety tips, 225–28
weather conditions and, 7
Nikon photography products
Nikkor lenses, 346, 352, 354
Nikonos close-up system, 352–53
Nikonos II camera, 344